DOCTOR DEALER

MARK BOWDEN

GROVE PRESS

New York

ALSO BY THE AUTHOR

Bringing the Heat

Black Hawk Down

Killing Pablo

Originally published in 1987 by Warner Books, Inc., a Warner Communications Company, New York, New York

The article beginning on page xiv is reprinted with permission from *The Philadelphia Inquirer*, May 16, 1986.

Published simultaneously in Canada
Printed in the United States of America

The events in this story are true. Names and physical characteristics of many individuals have been changed in order to protect their privacy.

Library of Congress Cataloging-in-Publication Data

Bowden, Mark
    Doctor dealer / Mark Bowden.
        p. cm.
    Originally published: New York, NY : Warner Books, c1987.
    ISBN 0-8021-3757-1
    1. Lavin, Lawrence W. 2. Narcotics dealers—United States—Biography.
3. Dentists—United States—Biography. 4. Cocaine habit—United States—
Case studies. 5. Narcotics, Control of—United States—Case studies. I. Title.
HV6248.L325 B69 2000
364.1'77'092—dc21
    [B]   00-032146

Design by H. Roberts

Grove Press
841 Broadway
New York, NY 10003

03 04   10 9 8 7 6 5 4 3 2

For Tom Scheye

Acknowledgments

First among those I would like to thank for helping me write this book are Larry and Marcia Lavin, who answered my innumerable questions with patience, thoughtfulness, and candor—even when the subject matter concerned things they would prefer to forget. Thanks are also due to Chuck Reed, Sid Perry, Mike White, Peter Scuderi, Agnes Osborn, Nancy Payne and her family, Jess and Babette Miller, Steve La Cheen, Henry S. Ruth, Jr., Willie Harcourt, Ricky Baratt, Glen Fuller, Brian Riley, John Sidoli (pianist and mathematician), Suzanne Taylor, Christine Pietrucha, Tom Bergstrom and Lynn, Chris, and Anita Furlan, Ron Noble and Tina Williams Gabbrielli, Pauline and Justin Lavin, Sr., and others who will appreciate not being named.

I would also like to thank Gene Roberts for giving me time off to work on this book, Jamie Raab, Ed Sedarbaum, Rhoda Weyr, David Hirshey, Hank Klibanoff, Donald Kimelman, Avery Rome, Katherine Hatton, Elizabeth Coady (because I owe her one), and Rosie Patterson (for watching Danny). A special thanks to Gail, to my mother and father, and to each and every member of my family for their continuing love and encouragement.

Contents

DOCTOR
DEALER

Prologue

Virginia Beach

There was no reason to suspect anything unusual when Larry saw Pat O'Donnell on the dock in a business suit. Pat was a semiretired FBI agent who kept his boat berthed at the Lynnhaven Dry Storage marina. He often came by after putting in a morning at the office, and spent the afternoon talking to his friends as they came in off the water. Sometimes he carried a walkie-talkie in case the office needed to get in touch.

Larry had been out all day with his friend Roy Mason. It had been a lazy fishing trip on a calm sea under a sky so bright it hurt the eyes. Larry looked tousled and tired, the picture of a man of leisure back from a day at sea, his thick black hair windblown, his long narrow nose and cheeks sunburned. He was dressed in a maroon rugby shirt with wide chest stripes of yellow and blue, worn baggy jeans, and leather deck shoes with no socks. He smelled of fish, and was eager to get home and clean up. Larry didn't enjoy fishing as much as Roy; he had gone along mostly to keep his friend company. They hadn't caught much, just a few cove fish that were a nuisance because they snapped at your fingers when you tried to take them off the hook.

As the vessel swung alongside the pier, O'Donnell strode out to meet them. Larry figured Pat wanted to ask, as dedicated fishermen always did, what they had caught and where. Docked across the narrow slip of water, facing seaward, Larry was surprised to see a high-performance Wellcraft, a sleek speedboat called a Scarab. Pat had been talking to two men in that boat. They were also in business suits . . . that was odd.

When the boat got close, Larry jumped up to the wharf and, with Roy feeding him the lines, quickly secured them and skipped back aboard to begin retrieving his gear.

"How's the fishin'?" asked Pat.

Larry smiled and turned and stooped to open the cooler. He knew the sight of three or four cove fish would make Pat laugh. But before he could turn and display the largest of their catch he was grabbed under both arms by men he had not even seen approaching.

"Larry, it's all over," said Pat.

"You're under arrest," one of the men said.

Larry looked at Pat, who was no longer smiling.

"You are Larry Lavin, aren't you?" asked one of the men holding his arms.

"Yes. I am," said Larry quietly. The man clapped handcuffs on his wrists in one quick motion.

"Wait just a minute . . . there must be some mistake!" shouted Roy. "Pat, what's going on here?"

Larry was already being rushed forward along the pier, now with a group of five or six men around him. Behind him he overheard Pat O'Donnell hushing Roy's protests, trying to explain.

(The *Philadelphia Inquirer;* May 16, 1986)

FBI ARRESTS ALLEGED HEAD
OF 'YUPPIE' COCAINE RING

Lawrence W. Lavin, the former Northeast Philadelphia dentist who allegedly masterminded a major cocaine-distribution ring, was arrested without incident yesterday as he disembarked from a fishing boat in Virginia Beach, Va., the FBI said.

Lavin, 31, had been a fugitive since November 1984, a few months after he was charged with heading a $5-million-a-month cocaine ring involving many other young professionals. He was free on $150,000 bail when he and his then-pregnant wife fled their Devon home.

An FBI spokesman in Philadelphia said agents arrested Lavin about 5:20 p.m. as he and another dentist—who did not know Lavin's true identity—were docking the other man's 25-foot sport fishing boat at a marina. He was wearing blue jeans and a rugby shirt. He had been using an alias but had made no effort to disguise his appearance, the FBI said.

At the same time agents were arresting Lavin, other agents were arresting his wife, Marcia, at the couple's home in an exclusive Virginia Beach development known as Middle Plantation, the FBI said. She was charged with harboring a fugitive.

Both were being held in Virginia last night pending an arraignment before a federal magistrate. The couple's two children, including a baby, had been living with them, according to the FBI.

Lavin faces drug charges in U.S. District Court here that could bring him a life sentence if he is convicted. In addition to a 40-count indictment on drug offenses, he is also charged with evading $545,000 in federal income taxes.

Federal authorities said the cocaine ring—which they dubbed the "Yuppie Conspiracy"—was one of the largest ever uncovered here, handling up to 175 pounds of cocaine a month. The drug in turn was distributed to others in Pennsylvania, New Jersey, New England and the Southwest, according to federal prosecutors.

More than 50 people, including three graduates of the University of Pennsylvania dental school, two lawyers and two stockbrokers, along with many other professionals, have been charged with being part of the drug conspiracy that Lavin allegedly headed.

At the courthouse in Norfolk the clerks gossiped about television. Just another ordinary night shift. As he waited to be fingerprinted, Larry was told to sit on a bench in a corner of the room. With his hands cuffed behind his back, he was forced to lean forward awkwardly. He stared down at the manacles clasped tightly over his jeans around his lower legs, inches above his bare ankles. They were connected by a heavy chain about two feet long. Under the leg irons were his deck shoes, worn and familiar. Just an hour ago he had been standing on the deck of his friend's boat, at sea. . . .

And the clerks made small talk about soap opera. One of the arresting agents phoned Chuck Reed, the FBI man who had haunted Larry's dreams for the last three years, to report that Lavin was finally in custody. At first Larry figured Reed would want to talk to him. He thought about what he might say—"Hi, Chuck. Long time no see"—but the conversation went on between agents as though he weren't even there: "How's the family?" "Give Sid my regards." "Now you can get to work on other things." They had just destroyed his life and they were congratulating themselves like salesmen who had just closed a big deal.

As he waited, dejected, Larry mostly worried about Marcia. What had they done with Marcia?

Just minutes after they had picked him up at the marina, as he sat in the backseat of the gray government sedan, the agent had turned and asked, "Are there any neighbors you could leave the kids with?"

Larry had gasped, "You don't have to arrest my wife!" and realized at once that the curt instructions being radioed from the front seat had directed agents to close in on his house. It was . . . what? Five-thirty. Marcia would be cooking dinner. Chris would be watching cartoons. Tara, who was only a year old, would be in Marcia's arms or in her wheeled walker.

Hours later, after the fingerprinting and phone call to Reed, husband and wife faced each other. Down a long tile corridor on an upper floor of the Norfolk courthouse, Marcia had heard his voice and had asked to see him. They were left alone for a moment, a small act of kindness, in an office with a broad desk of polished oak and plush leather chairs. Lawbooks lined the shelves. Outside wide windows, dusk bathed in soft rose and orange the rooftops and streets of the city below. Marcia seemed calm and sad.

"I don't blame you," she told Larry, placing her hands on his. Tears had welled in Larry's eyes and he could not speak. Marcia's hands were cuffed. There were no tears in her almond eyes. She said, "I still love you."

After that they rode together in the backseat of a government sedan to the prison in Virginia Beach. Larry kept seeing the handcuffs on Marcia's hands, folded in her lap. He tried to put the picture out of his mind.

Now for hour upon hour there was nothing to do but dwell on these things. Larry's cell was a windowless cube. He had paced the length and width, two and a half strides each way. The walls were cinderblock coated thickly with beige paint, cold and smooth to the touch. The floor was concrete. Through the bars to the right was a bare wall and hallway. Larry sat on a thin, clean gray mattress on a steel platform, his knees drawn up under his chin and his long arms wrapped around his legs. There was no pillow, sheet, or blanket. Across the cell was a toilet and sink. No towels. A Gideon's Bible was on the edge of the sink—*No, thanks*, says Larry. Overhead burned a light bulb in a wire cage. It had burned on through the night and into the day—a dawning he could detect only by observing subtle changes in the color of light down the dimly lit corridor. It was noisy. Drunks in other cells raved and sang, vomited and snored. The air was moist and warm and smelled of soap.

On his way in, waddling in those needless leg irons, Larry had passed under a sign that read, "Security and Professionalism." It was a fair description of how he was being handled. Once inside, his manacles had been removed and he was ordered to strip. Guards took his watch and wedding ring. They they searched his mouth and his hair and told him to turn around and bend over and pull his buttocks apart so they could shine a light up his ass. All the while Larry was eagerly obliging, smiling, trying to be helpful. He was handed a crisply folded zippered jumpsuit of bright orange and a pair of worn black cloth slippers—"Get dressed." There had been nothing threatening or abusive in the guards' manner. In fact, everyone had been polite. But it was all nightmare. Larry moved in numb obedience as uniformed men processed him, poked at him and probed him, ordered him to sit or stand or step forward, to turn and bend, touched him with scrubbed, hard hands, managed him with bored efficiency. It was as though his life had slipped, like the life of some character in one of the cheap sci-fi novels he liked to read, into a maddening mirror dimension where nothing about him mattered except physical entity— Lawrence W. Lavin, D.M.D., Phillips Exeter Academy, University of Pennsylvania, businessman, investor, former member of the Philadelphia Stock Exchange, husband, father, sportsman, and, yes, multimillion-dollar drug dealer, none of this mattered. He was an object, six feet three inches tall, 185 pounds, eyes green, hair black, something to be inspected, cataloged, numbered, transported, stored. All of it filled him not with despair or anger or even sadness, but with a paralyzing sense of futility. All of it, the walls, the bars, the light bulb in its own small cage, the clerks chatting about their favorite TV shows. It was upon him so suddenly, as though yesterday's blue ocean and blue sky and all the days and years before it had all been one dream and now he had awakened abruptly to another . . . *and this is now to be my life!*

"Do you think it's possible to kill yourself by jumping off the bed and ramming your head into the bars?"

Larry had dozed; the voice startled him.

It came from the next cell, the voice of a boy, distressed. There had been a drunk in the next cell who had made incoherent noise for hours before falling asleep. Now the drunk had evidently been released, and this kid had been brought in. Larry could tell by the light in the hallway that it must be midmorning. He had been sitting there about fourteen hours.

"No," said Larry, chuckling sympathetically. "I've already figured out there's no way to commit suicide in this cell." He meant this to sound like a wisecrack but the kid in the next cell didn't laugh.

"I read about you in the paper this morning," said the kid. "You're that yuppie coke dealer. The fugitive."

There was awe in his voice. It didn't surprise Larry that his story was big news. He had been through that once before.

The kid had been busted for possession. Larry did his best to sound avuncular. It was a familiar role. At home when he stepped out into the front yard to water his flower beds or trim the lawn, the neighborhood children, especially the teenagers, were drawn to him, Marcia used to say, like iron filings to a magnet. He had time for them, treated them like equals, took their teenage problems seriously. He was teaching this one to scuba dive and this one how to program his home computer and this one about the stock market. It was a role he had played only in the eighteen months they had lived in Virginia Beach as fugitives. He was Brian O'Neil, the computer whiz who had made a bundle quickly, sold off his company, and was now taking a few years off—thirty-one years old, rich, and temporarily retired. He was someone the kids could look up to who lacked the distance and authority of their parents, someone who could give them advice that didn't sound patronizing . . . and they would listen. The Miller boy across the street had given up his new chewing-tobacco habit after Larry's talk about cancer of the mouth. The Payne boy next door had decided on a career in the stock market after Larry had come to his school and talked to the class about investing. What would they think of him now? What would his new friends, their parents, think? Their Brian O'Neil, volunteer treasurer of their civic association, was Dr. Lawrence W. Lavin, notorious criminal kingpin, in hiding. Their role model was a secret corrupter of youth, evil genius of the Yuppie Cocaine Conspiracy, largest drug ring ever discovered in Philadelphia, the city he had fled. That was how the newspapers would be playing it right now. He didn't have to see the papers to imagine. He remembered vividly the day of his first arrest nearly two years ago, at the Philadelphia courthouse, when he was amazed to find a courtroom filled with reporters to witness his arraignment. Every time he looked up the artists would start scribbling frantically. And the prosecutor went on about a "major criminal conspiracy," "the most elaborate cocaine organization ever uncovered in this region," and about him as a "criminal mastermind." Larry had always gotten a kick out of the legend he had built among his friends, but hearing incriminating bits and pieces of his past spoken by these humorless, literal detectives and lawyers somehow rang so false, and yet, what could he argue? What parts of the story could he deny? He had first felt the futility that night when the sketches of him by the courtroom artists and the cold mug-shot image of his face were the lead items on the TV news. The first story! At home in his den with the shades of his big Main Line home tightly drawn, seated in his leather armchair with a remote control flipping channels, half stunned and half amused, he had watched them all until Marcia had pleaded angrily from the kitchen, "Larry, why in the world would you want to listen to that?" But he had wanted to listen because he wanted to formulate answers. If he could only explain . . . yes, *that's true, but . . . but . . .* where would he start? How could anyone understand? The FBI and federal prosecutors had built such a labyrinth of solid evidence, hostile interpretation, and ugly innuendo that Larry felt lost and hopeless. Now it was all happening again, only this time there would be no bail, no escape. These walls, these bars, the light bulb in its own cage burning, burning, accusing. There was no escape . . . *and this is now to be my life!*

It seemed so absurd. Larry felt no more like a criminal kingpin than the kid the next cell over. For selling pot and cocaine? Come on! But there was no use even trying to explain. What judge or jury would ever see it his way, would ever understand that his drug sales weren't like a heroin pusher's, that it was just between friends, that he had meant no harm?

Footsteps echoed down the corridor. Keys rattled and a door creaked. The kid in the next cell was taken out. The cell door shut with a clang that stayed in Larry's ears for minutes after the voices and footsteps were gone.

He caught his head nodding between his knees and jerked it back upright. Larry had not showered since yesterday morning. He felt crusty and worn and longed to escape his own odor. Even if he wanted to sleep he knew he could not with the light bulb boring through his eyelids. This must be some kind of game they play with your mind. They had given him papers to sign, and it was only a matter of time before they would want him to start talking. He figured this waiting alone was meant to soften him up. He had eaten a starchy meal off a tray and was now feeling gas pains that doubled him over. Marcia had said the children were with neighbors and would be okay. Had they let Marcia go home? Tara had never gone to sleep without being rocked by her mother. And Chris. What answers did they have for that restless four-year-old mind? Where is Daddy? Where is Mommy?

What was Pat O'Donnell doing on the dock yesterday afternoon? Was that how they had found him? Or was it the phone calls? Larry had known he was making the single biggest mistake a fugitive can make when he called home. But in eighteen months there had only been a handful of calls. Most from pay phone to pay phone at pre-arranged times, and only to Rusty, his brother, or to Ken Weidler, his best friend and former dental partner. Marcia had talked only to her mother and sister. Surely none of them would have betrayed him! Even if they had, Larry had never told anyone where he and Marcia were living. He poked and probed at the problem like a sore tooth. Had his brother betrayed him? His best friend? Larry could accept neither possibility, so the conundrum returned to Pat O'Donnell. Could Pat have had something to do with it? Marcia had thought Larry was crazy when he came home one day from the marina and said that he had been out fishing with an FBI agent. "Larry, let's move. We can't stay," she said. She had been in a panic. But Larry hadn't felt threatened at all.

"He's retired," said Larry. Besides, Pat was such a nice guy. They had really hit it off. Larry had felt sure that even if the ex-agent did stumble over his real identity, he would be more inclined to tip Larry off than turn him in. He knew what kind of husband and father Larry was. He knew the kind of guy Larry was. What good would it do society to take him away from his wife and children? But if it wasn't Pat, then who? How? There had been the article in *Philadelphia* magazine last month, entitled "Dr. Snow." His brother had read it to him over the phone. There were pictures of him and of Marcia. Could someone have seen it who recognized him? It might be as simple as that. But, then, why had Pat been waiting for him on the dock?

And arrest Marcia? Marcia who hated the business, who had tried every way she knew to pull him away, everything short of leaving him? If he had only listened to Marcia.

What returned again and again was the image of her hands, folded on her lap in the backseat of the car, in handcuffs.

Marcia in handcuffs?

Strike One . . . Strike Two . . .

Fall 1972, on the campus of Phillips Exeter Academy in Exeter, New Hampshire. Upperclassman John Sidoli was studying in his third-floor room in Langdell Hall when in jumped his friend Jeff Giancola with a plastic bag full of white powder. Jeff looked around frantically, his eyes coming to rest on Sidoli's closet. He blurted, "John, let me stash this in there. Just for a little while. If Larry finds it he'll kill me!" Before Sidoli had a chance to sacrifice good judgment to fellowship, Giancola stashed the bag in his closet and fled.

Sidoli listened to the footsteps retreat down the corridor. Setting aside his book, he stood and walked to his window in time to see Giancola fly out the front door and sprint into the Commons. Behind the girls' dorm across the way the sky had the warm glow of dusk. Shadow covered half of the green between the tall redbrick Georgian dormitories. Two broad white elms in full autumn display were enclosed in this space. Sidoli had lived in the same corner of Langdell for more than a year, across the hall from Giancola and Larry Lavin. Sidoli was closer to Giancola, who had confided several weeks ago that he was involved in a drug deal with Lavin, which came as no surprise. Even though Sidoli had known and liked Lavin since the middle of their year as "Lowers," as sophomores at Exeter are called, he had never really felt close to him. There was something outrageous about Larry, something that made Sidoli believe Giancola's story. Of all the hundreds of students he knew at Exeter, Larry Lavin was the one most likely to get involved in something like that.

Giancola had said that Larry was working a heroin deal with the Boston Mafia. He said that whenever the drug connection called at Langdell Hall, a message was left for Larry to call his mother. Sidoli knew there were messages on the board nearly every day for Lavin

1

to call his mother. Ever since, whenever he saw the note on the board, "Lavin, call Mom," it lent credence to the tale.

Looking down now through the magnificent elms, he saw Giancola stop midway across the Commons. Just inside the shadow stood a tall, thin figure Sidoli recognized as Lavin and some big guy with a hat and overcoat. The two strode up to Giancola, who appeared to be pleading. They knocked him down. Giancola jumped up swinging, and was knocked down again. He was kicked by the man in the overcoat. Then he was pulled to his feet and dragged toward the front door.

Sidoli panicked. He ran from his room and down the hall to the lavatory, where he opened one of the toilet stalls and closed the door behind him.

All was silent for long minutes. Then he heard Giancola call for him in the hall. He didn't answer. The calls got closer until Giancola burst into the bathroom and discovered him hiding in the stall. Jeff looked desperate. He begged Sidoli to cover for him. Somehow, he said, Lavin suspected that the bag of white powder was stashed in Sidoli's room. Jeff needed his friend to swear that it wasn't.

Reluctantly, Sidoli agreed, but as they entered the room, Lavin was already holding the plastic bag in his hand.

"You were holding out on us," he sneered. "You stole an ounce. We'll show you what we do to people who steal from us."

And the big man lunged at Giancola with a Coke bottle, shattering it against the side of the door. Sidoli leapt back horrified as Lavin and the other man wrestled Giancola to the floor. Straddling Jeff, Lavin opened the baggie and held the white powder over Giancola's face.

"Kill him," said the big man. "Shove the whole ounce down his throat."

Just then, Sidoli's voice interrupted, quavering, shouting a plea he would be embarrassed about for the next twenty years. "No, don't! Don't kill him here! Please, kill him somewhere else!"

Then Lavin and Giancola and the other fellow were on the floor, laughing. Sidoli suddenly recognized the big man as a football player who lived two floors down. It was a joke! It was all a joke! Larry, laughing so hard he could barely speak, showed Sidoli the baggie, and sputtered, "Confectioners' sugar!"

Larry laughed and laughed, and, after a while, Sidoli laughed, too.

Larry Lavin had entered Phillips Exeter Academy in January of 1971 as an awkward "townie," a tall, skinny fifteen-year-old with a ludicrous retainer on his teeth. He had an especially hard time pronouncing the letter *L*, which was unfortunate, because every time he introduced himself it came out, "Hi, I'm 'arry 'avin," with the *L*s coming out as slippery Ws. But Larry didn't seem to mind. He talked and talked and talked. Even without the retainer his Haverhill accent was so bad that his classmates found him hard to understand. Still, people liked Lavin. He had charm. He was black Irish and full of the devil. His pale green eyes would fix you with a gaze like a dare. His black hair was thick and long, framing his head like a helmet and falling down across his forehead to the eyebrows—which was a thing that preppies didn't do. He affected gaudy plaid pants and pastel polo shirts and had a closet full of three-piece suits. Larry's mom had worried about her son fitting in with his upper-class schoolmates, so she had spent months shopping in secondhand stores to find bargains on conservative suits and altering them to fit her youngest son's gangly, uneven frame. Like his father, everything about Larry was long—a long thin face and nose, long torso, long arms and legs. His left leg was longer than his right, which set his left shoulder slightly higher, which made him always seem off-balance, thrown together loosely, an impression enhanced by the way his thick mop of black hair made his head seem to teeter atop such a pole of a neck.

His mother's efforts to help her son fit in with his wealthy class-mates had precisely the opposite effect. At Exeter the despised coat-and-tie rule was mocked. Students wore the rattiest sport coats and most ridiculous ties they could find to top their rumpled, faded jeans. Tennis shoes were not permitted, so students wore battered penny loafers held together with electrical tape. These were the Vietnam years, when the normal conflict between administration and students bordered on war. On most college campuses students had plenty of avenues to vent their outrage against the war and act out their fash-ionable disdain for social convention, but Exeter was just a high school, with curfews, a dress code, and other strict regulations against non-conformity. The same generation gap that troubled so many American homes during the sixties and early seventies was magnified a hundred times on a campus like Exeter's. There were dozens of expulsions every year. Hardly a weekend went by that someone was not caught in violation of one or more of the school's cardinal rules. This tension had left many in the student body with open contempt for the prep school's proud 190-year-old traditions.

Enter Larry, a full year and a half behind the rest of the students in his class of '73, wearing his tacky suburban wardrobe, talking nonstop through his braces in a Massachusetts accent few could readily understand. His politics, such as they were, were just a reflection of those of his father, who felt America had lost its last best hope when it rejected Barry Goldwater. It isn't enough to simply say that this gangly local boy didn't fit in with the tight teenage dormitory society of Langdell Hall—he stood flamboyantly apart.

But he seemed oblivious to this. If anything, the young eccentric seemed more sure of himself than any of his classmates. He reveled in being different, but not with the underlying anger of many singular adolescents. He liked people and wanted to be liked back. Moreover, Larry seemed to like himself. He enjoyed nothing more than telling people all about himself.

His mother, Pauline, and his father, Justin, had grown up in Haverhill, a nearby Massachusetts town that was one of the oldest in America and which billed itself as "The Shoe Capital of the World." Both were from Irish Catholic families who had settled in Haverhill to work in the town's famous four-story brick shoe factories, and who had gone on to better themselves. Pauline, a short bosomy woman with artistic leanings, had been raised as an only child, a rare up-bringing among the big-familied Irish. Although her parents sent her to college, Pauline's chief ambition was to build the family she had missed as a child. She had a daughter and three sons, of whom Larry was the youngest.

Larry's father, Justin, was a lanky, dark-haired, contentious man who enjoyed commanding center stage. His father, William S. Lavin, was a successful real estate speculator who had laid the foundations for great wealth by borrowing to buy up acres of land in Bradford, a growing residential community across the Merrimack River south of Haverhill proper, and around Chadwick Pond and Kenoza Lake, where the expanding town's most successful citizens were beginning to build summer cottages. The twenties were a boom time for the shoe and leather industries along the river. Justin was raised as one of Haverhill's elite. He excelled at high school sports, winning a scholarship to the University of Notre Dame to play football. When his athletic career was stalled by a broken leg in freshman year, he transferred to M.I.T., where he was graduated with a degree in chemical engineering in 1939.

But during the Depression, while Justin was away at school, his father was forced to sell most of his real estate holdings at a loss. The Lavin family retained a measure of social prominence in Bradford, but lost most of its wealth. When World War II started, Justin enlisted as a naval aviation cadet. For more than three years he flew dangerous combat missions in Wildcat and Hellcat fighter-bombers in the Pacific. Twice he was shot down and survived, once after drifting for four hours in the ocean aboard a rubber raft. He returned from the war a local hero, decorated with two Navy Cross medals, the Air Medal, a Presidential unit citation, and the Purple Heart, but a man whose life had been permanently changed by the war. Larry remembers that many years later his father could be startled out of his chair by a fork accidently falling to the kitchen floor. His experience as an officer in a navy ruled by a tight coterie of predominantly WASP Naval Academy graduates left him with bitter feelings toward the U.S. government. Despite his acknowledged heroism and skill, Justin felt shut out of paths toward more power and responsibility. Long after the war had begun to fade in people's memories, Justin could invest his harrowing war stories, stories of life and death, danger and triumph, with enough detail and enthusiasm to make them seem as though they had happened only yesterday. He seemed to pine for those days of daring and adventure.

Back in Haverhill, Justin found a different life from the one he had known as a child. During the fifties he became president and treasurer of the Keeler-Cochran Heel Co., Inc., one of the town's oldest and most durable manufacturers. His executive position for a time afforded Justin the income and social status he was raised to expect. He and Pauline joined the Bradford Country Club, and Justin sat on the board of trustees for Bradford Junior College. In 1960 they bought a handsome two-story house on Highland Street with gray shingles and a brick front walk and a detached two-car garage in back. Justin added black shutters cut with the silhouette of a sailboat on the top, and would build on a redbrick patio with a small pool decorated with porcelain dolphins at either end that spouted water from their blowholes. Then came decline. Competition from foreign shoemakers, whose postwar economies had been subsidized by the United States, crushed Haverhill's three-hundred-year-old shoe industry. Justin's heel factory closed. He found work at an employment office in Boston, an hour's commute south, and spent the next decade trying to find work for other displaced executives, earning commissions only when he was successful. Pauline found work as a medical secretary, and the Lavins often lived for months on her salary alone.

Larry, who had been born March 14, 1955, had no memory of the heel factory. He grew up in a family determined to live beyond its means, maintaining an active social schedule, planning ski trips all the while fending off creditors. He remembers being told to stand beside his desk at Sacred Heart School with the other children whose parents had fallen behind in tuition payments, or being turned away at the Bradford Swim Club because dues were unpaid, or taking an excited trip with his father to the department store to buy a color TV, only to be disappointed when Justin's credit card was rejected. Justin would explode with anger. His children would feel ashamed for him, and somehow betrayed. Larry was a teenager when the family moved from its Bradford home into a small townhouse in a new development called Colonial Village across the river in Methuen. His mother supplemented family earnings by selling floral arrangements to local restaurants and eventually by teaching this skill to other women.

An outspoken conservative Republican, Justin Lavin blamed U.S. policy under the Kennedy and Johnson administrations for these hardships. He could go on and on, working himself into a fine Irish froth, about "The jerks went to work for the government. Have you ever dealt with some of the government boys in Washington? Some of the stupidest sons of bitches I have ever met in my life. . . ." Justin became the kind of man with whom people avoided serious conversation. A friendly chat would often explode into argument or serve as an excuse to launch a red-faced diatribe against the ineptitude and corruption of authority. Larry grew up absorbing his father's bitterness for the system that had rewarded his wartime heroism with financial failure.

Still, despite his setbacks, Justin remained a talented and hardworking man. He took up cabinetmaking as a hobby, and over the years developed such skill that he furnished their home with handsome, inexpensive reproductions of delicate antiques. Larry remembers his parents' tireless ingenuity in keeping up with bills and maintaining their ambitious living standard. When the back patio was under construction, there were late-night drives to demolition sites where Larry and his brothers would help his father scavenge valuable red bricks. If his father drove past a pile of mulch dumped for road crews gardening along the interstate, he would pull off the road, open the trunk, and hurriedly fill several plastic bags. *If they're stupid enough to leave this lying by the side of the road* . . . that was how his father saw it. Larry loved and admired his parents, but at the same time, as he grew older, he felt sorry for them. If there was one lesson in their experience, it was that in the pursuit of wealth, talent and hard work weren't enough.

Larry's oldest brother, Justin, Jr. (the family called him Paul), and his sister, Mary (who was known as Jill), were quiet, hardworking, accomplished students. His other brother, Rusty, with his pink face and red hair and fearless personality, had a wild streak. Rusty ended more than a decade of feuding with teachers and school officials by dropping out of high school, the first member of his family who did not attend college. In a family fiercely intent on bettering itself, Rusty seemed defiantly downwardly mobile. He found work off and on as a trucker and moved into an apartment in Haverhill, spending most of what he earned on the ski slopes, where he became expert. Paul and Jill, for all their success in school, were sensitive, withdrawn, and sometimes troubled children. Jill fought with her father so much over politics and style—she was against the Vietnam War, he favored it; he wanted her to wear a dress, Jill preferred blue jeans—that she moved into an apartment with a girlfriend when she was only sixteen.

Paul, who was more diplomatic than Jill, nevertheless found himself frequently at odds with his father. He would come home from college with liberal ideas that gave his father apoplexy. In the midst of all these battles with teenage children, young Larry, who looked so much like his father, was a blessing. He seemed to have acquired the best traits of all his older siblings with none of the worst. He was a straight-A student whose grades seemed to come even easier than Paul's or Jill's. If it was true that Larry possessed a touch of Rusty's rambunctious style, he was blessed with a unique counterbalancing charm.

Once, after a teacher took exception when Larry threw a pencil out a classroom window in the middle of a lesson, he assigned the boy a punishment essay. Larry invented a story entitled "My Life as a Pencil," envisioning the plunge through the open classroom window through the pencil's eyes. As it fell earthward its life passed before its eyes, giving Larry a chance to invent a satire of the teacher and classroom as seen through the eyes of a pencil at rest on the sill under the chalkboard. As a final indignity, the pencil crashed to its death on the roof of the teacher's car. The teacher, who had a sense of humor, thought the work so clever that he read it out loud to his advanced composition classes.

This and other incidents like it imbued Larry with a cocky individuality beyond his years. He was someone whom other children admired and imitated. When he violated the dress code at Sacred Heart School one spring morning by showing up for classes wearing bright yellow pants, which were a fad with Haverhill children that spring, he was taken to the principal's office and sent home. The next day the school hallway blossomed from the waist down in bright colors.

Justin and Pauline learned early to accept warm compliments about their youngest son. Larry shoveled driveways and sidewalks for people in the neighborhood, raked leaves, cut lawns, delivered newspapers. When Justin drove the paper route one week while Larry was away at a summer camp, customers lavished praise on his youngest son. Along the way he discovered cards and notes left out by customers for "Dear Larry," asking him to please deliver a loaf of bread or gallon of milk the next day, or reminding him to take out the garbage cans. Larry earned Boy Scout merit badges, served as an altar boy at funerals and weddings in Sacred Heart Church, and was twice elected president of his class at Cardinal Cushing Academy. When he was only fourteen, Larry talked himself into a job at a local restaurant. When the employment board found out and he lost that position, Larry hitchhiked out to a newly opened Friendly's restaurant on Main Street and got hired there. Larry filled in extra hours helping his friend Glen Fuller's father roast and package peanuts for sale to local bars, and often contributed his earnings to help pay late electric or gas bills at home. Larry's parents were used to leaving their youngest son alone. He seemed gifted with some prodigious sense of inner direction. Unlike Paul and Jill and Rusty, Larry was not a child to cause them concern. To the contrary, Larry's parents were continually amazed by their youngest son's accomplishments.

He saved up enough money from his paper route to help pay for his own braces, which corrected a pair of incisors so misdirected that Larry had long suffered the nickname Fang. He helped to offset the cost by doing odd jobs for the neighborhood dentist, who took such a liking to the boy that he would spend hours talking to Larry, explaining his procedures and detailing the advantages dentistry offered over other kinds of work—comparable pay with general medicine and more regular hours, and a profession that was immune to the shifting economic fortunes that had ruined his father's business and so undermined the whole town. Before his sophomore year of high school Larry announced his choice of career. When Cardinal Cushing Academy was forced to close after Larry's freshman year because of dwindling enrollments, Larry, on his own, signed up to take a competitive examination that admitted one or two local boys each year to the nearby prestigious Phillips Exeter Academy. After less than one semester at Haverhill High School, Larry won the scholarship, which paid more than half of the $3,800 yearly tuition. His parents were reluctant to send him to the public school, which was rougher and less academically challenging than the private Catholic schools his brothers and sister had attended. But they knew they couldn't afford anything better. Suddenly, on his own, Larry had found his way into one of the oldest, best preparatory schools in the country!

Exeter was a big challenge for Larry. He had to work hard to catch up to classmates who had more than a year of the school's demanding curriculum behind them already. In French class—Larry had always earned A's in French at Cardinal Cushing—he found himself competing with students who had spent summers, even years, living in Europe. He took a heavy load of math and science courses, which were considered the hardest. Larry learned quickly that, unlike at the schools he had attended before, doing well at Exeter meant spending hours preparing for classes, and days preparing for tests. Many classes had fewer than ten students, who sat around a big table in a room heated by a crackling fire. It was impossible to escape notice and censure if you came unprepared. Likewise, the intimacy of life at boarding school made all failures and successes public. He felt a steady strong pressure to succeed.

Larry found an outlet for his interest in writing by contributing accounts of sporting events to the *Plain Dealer*, a campus newspaper that had been founded by an embattled minority of Nixonites to counter the fuzzy-headed liberalism that then prevailed on the *Exonian*, Exeter's official, better-funded, and more polished student newspaper. Larry himself soon abandoned his conservative political convictions, but he did enjoy the *Plain Dealer*'s freewheeling rebel posture. He was named sports editor in his second year, but lost interest in the paper; his name dropped on and off the masthead from week to week. His colleagues remember that even after losing interest Larry had a talent for recruiting others to turn in stories. His scholarship job in the school library gave him a chance to get acquainted with just about everyone at the school. When Exeter's dramatic new Louis Kahn Library opened across the street from the main campus, Larry helped to organize the student chain that moved more than sixty thousand volumes from the old building to the new. He played water polo and joined one of the school's club lacrosse teams, and was considered fairly good with a stick. His grades soon recovered from the initial shock of dealing with Exeter's demanding course load. All this would have been enough for a normal student, but as those who came to know him soon realized, it was all just the surface Larry Lavin.

This exceptional scholarship student was usually as engrossed in some illicit caper as he was in his schoolwork. On the surface Larry displayed such innocent charm that the faculty at Exeter counseled him to avoid the more rebellious of his classmates, fearing they would lead him into trouble. The truth was, Larry was into things even these students wouldn't dare. He snuck a TV into his room, against dorm regulations, and then crawled with a wire out on the ledge and up onto the sharply angled roof, a good fifty feet up, and attached it to the housemaster's big antenna. Somehow Larry had obtained a master key to the dining hall, so he could lead his friends on midnight raids to the commissary storehouse in the basement. Even more impressively, he was the only one who dared sneak a girl into his room and have sex with her, a chubby, unattractive girl from Haverhill named Sherry whom Larry had a crush on in his senior year. It was funny how Larry seemed to get as excited about the logistics of sneaking Sherry into his room as he was about the sex. To Larry, risk was like foreplay.

As it was in high schools all over the country, marijuana smoking was common at Exeter in the early seventies, despite the prep school's rigidly enforced expulsion policy. Easily half of the students at Exeter smoked dope. It wasn't just infatuation with the drug; it was a form of cultural expression, a clear litmus test of cool—an intoxicant with fewer harmful side effects than alcohol, a magical substance that only adults and the uncool condemned. Larry couldn't afford to buy dope, something that was no problem for his wealthy classmates, so he held up his end by shouldering the risk. He moved his clothes to a room next to his in Langdell Hall and rigged his own walk-in closet as a smoking den, with a bong at stage center, with layers of screens and wall hangings shielding the inner sanctum from the outer room, and three fans, including one area fan that stood eight feet high, to blow away the smoke. Larry had devised an alarm system, an intercom wired to the room of a friend downstairs who alerted him whenever David Walker, the housemaster, left his first-floor quarters to come upstairs. It was the safest place on campus to get high.

Larry thrilled to these things—the master key and the TV and the girl, the hot plate he had smuggled to his room against regulations. He would host postcurfew pot parties, serving warm hot dogs filched from the commissary fridge. These were his delicious secrets, little illicit triumphs. If you were his friend he would let you in on them, give you a glimpse of the real Larry.

But he wouldn't tell you everything.

Only Larry's best friends knew just how wide was his larcenous streak. To adults and to those who knew him only casually, Larry was a bright, pleasant, promising kid. This wasn't just a facade, either. Larry really was all those things: hardworking, ambitious, sensitive, caring. He took pleasure in treating other people well, in keeping his word and doing favors. Yet, despite this, he already believed that beneath even the most spotless reputation, most people were dishonest. Everyone was hiding something about themselves, pretending to be more than they really were. Authority figures in particular tended to be hypocrites. This gut-level cynicism excused all manner of moral quibbles from Larry Lavin's conscience. Even though he did dishonest things, Larry felt he was, in fact, more honest than most people because he did not deny the truth about himself. If he saw a chance to improve his own lot at someone else's expense, well, why not? Wouldn't they? Once you got to know him well, Larry wasn't hiding anything. What the hell! Larry was positively cheerful about his bad streak. If you're going to work a caper on the side, why be bashful? Why, he'd even cut you in on it, for fellowship's sake. And Larry always had something cooking. . . .

One of those who saw this side of Larry Lavin was his childhood friend from Haverhill, Ricky Baratt. At home, on vacation from Lawrenceville School, Ricky was Larry's constant companion. They would drive aimlessly for hours in Ricky's father's car. In the wooded hills outside Haverhill they would get high and drink beer and take whatever drugs they could find. One night they swallowed horse tranquilizers at Ricky's house while his parents were away. They wound up crawling down the hallway from Ricky's bedroom to the living room. Larry didn't want to drive, so Ricky volunteered. Larry and Ricky and their friends have vague memories of riding on top of the car with Ricky driving, and waking up the next morning sleeping on a cliff called Big Rock, an outcropping that was the highest spot in the area. Normally Ricky was afraid of this spot. He couldn't remember how they got there. Last thing he remembered was crawling down the hallway of his house.

Blackouts were not new to Ricky. Ever since the eighth grade it seemed he stayed stoned or drunk most of the time. He was a nervous, chubby boy with pale blue eyes, curly brown hair, and a skin problem. Ricky's father was a successful Haverhill obstetrician/gynecologist. Ricky had grown up in the house next door to Larry until the Lavins moved. Both boys had older brothers who excelled in school and in sports—Paul Lavin had been a high school and college track star and was on his way to a distinguished career in medicine at the University of Pennsylvania, and Ricky's older brother, Bobby, was a champion wrestler and skilled equestrian who planned to pursue a career in veterinary medicine. Ricky and Larry had always been an unlikely pair: Ricky short and chubby, nervous and shy; Larry tall and skinny, bold and outgoing. Larry's grandmother had a house by Sunset Lake close to the Baratts' summer home, and during the summer Ricky and Larry had learned to water-ski and ride horses. Some of those summers Larry had seemed to belong more to the Baratt family than his own. He openly admired the Baratts, with their big suburban home, their lakefront second home, and their boat. "This is the kind of life I want to have someday," he told Ricky.

For his part, Ricky knew his parents would like him to exhibit some of Larry Lavin's levelheaded, hardworking gumption.

But Ricky knew things about Larry that his parents didn't. He knew that despite appearances, Larry was as much of a drinker and doper as he was, only these things didn't seem to have the same debilitating effect on Larry that they had on Ricky. He had introduced Larry to pot, hiding in the Lavins' garage with Jill and Rusty and Larry passing around a joint awkwardly, enjoying the nervous titillation of *doing something illegal!* After that, Larry and Ricky smoked just about every chance they got. Yet, while Ricky floundered, Larry continued to breeze through school. With Ricky, the drugs and alcohol seemed to crowd everything else out of his life. His first blackout came when he was in the eighth grade. One day in the same year, he dropped acid before going to school. His father had to come and bring him home. It was a terrifying experience. A week later Ricky tried mescaline and barely made it through the day. His grades were terrible. His parents, who were heroically understanding, grew increasingly frustrated. When Ricky nearly overdosed on pills at home one afternoon, his father saved his life, forcing him to vomit and pulling him into a cold shower to keep him awake. Despite such catastrophes, despite declining performance in school, despite all his parents' loving patience and pleadings, nothing seemed to help. Ricky would feel so overwhelmed that the only thing to make him feel better was to get high. So he would call Larry. During summers and vacation breaks he partied night after night with Larry, and marveled at him.

On one of those lazy, stoned days, in the spring of 1972, Larry had an idea. He showed Ricky a key.

"Not just any old key," he explained. "I borrowed a master key to my dorm at Exeter from a senior proctor, and copied it. You should see some of the stuff these guys have in their rooms."

Ricky and Larry drove together the twenty miles to the redbrick Colonial campus. Larry opened the front door of the dorm adjacent to Langdell Hall with his key, and then took his friend from home on a tour. He led him down the hall, using the key to open doors to his classmates' rooms. Ricky felt queasy about it, so at first he resisted taking anything for himself, but he helped Larry carry two big, expensive Advent speakers from one kid's room. They hauled the speakers out the front door in broad daylight, with Larry grinning, and loaded them gently into the trunk. On one of the last trips Ricky picked up a typewriter. Larry gathered additional stereo components, a shag rug, and helped himself to a tapestry he had admired on another classmate's wall. He paused to flip through record collections, and picked out albums by groups that he liked: Yes, Pink Floyd, Crosby, Stills and Nash, Cat Stevens. Larry felt no qualms about doing this. These were things that the privileged people at school had that he did not. To Larry, there was something wrong about *that*.

In the car on the way back he told Ricky, "These people are all so rich it's like nothing to them."

Some people blamed Larry's bad streak on Glen Fuller. Larry was at Cardinal Cushing Academy when he started running with Glen, a thickset rebel with light brown hair and wild pale blue eyes. As a student in elementary school Glen had been the butt of his classmates' humor; there was something indefinably cockeyed about him. By the time he met Larry in high school, Glen had learned to fight back. First it was just to defend himself against the bullies who had poked fun at him for years. Then it became something else. Glen learned that the secret to being tough was to be unafraid of getting hurt. All of a sudden, he was a student whom others feared—and respected. There was hardly a day at school when Glen wasn't in a brawl, his long, tangled brown hair flying and a wicked grin on his broad, round face. School didn't interest Glen half as much as the ski slope, where he could compete on the downhill slopes of Vermont and New Hampshire with young Olympic hopefuls. His parents, who wanted to encourage Glen's talent for skiing, began allowing him to stay away on weekends in ski resorts at a time when most children still had strict curfews.

At the ski resorts Glen learned about a lot more than skiing. Most Academy students lived on campus and came from well-to-do Catholic families. They had been raised in genteel suburbs, where breaking the rules meant raiding Dad's refrigerator Friday nights after basketball for a six-pack of beer. Glen came from a working-class Haverhill family. If the Lavin family was determined to avoid being mistaken for middle class, the Fullers seemed to rejoice in it. His father, Kenneth Fuller, had known Justin Lavin when they were both in school, and they hadn't gotten along then either. Justin had grown up believing that success was due to hard work and dedication over many years. Ken Fuller had a different approach. He was more of a free-form entrepreneur, someone who believed that success was not so much earned as *snared*, by taking chances, by making a sudden daring move in the right direction at the right time. Glen's father had done well, but until Glen and his siblings had grown up and moved away, the family stayed in its modest corner home on Fifth Street in downtown Haverhill. They kept an assortment of Cadillacs parked in front, a new model for Glen's parents and an old one for him.

Because Glen helped out with his father's peanut business, he had learned to drive a few years before the legal age. With his car, his relative freedom from parental supervision, his experiences with alcohol, drugs, and women, by age sixteen Glen seemed remarkably free of the fears and inhibitions that torment a normal teenage boy. At the resorts he had met people who could get him marijuana cheap, so Glen made extra money by dealing to his more sheltered classmates at Cardinal Cushing. He wore a jeans jacket with extra pockets sewed on the inside. On Fridays he would fill them with dope and exchange it for the money he needed to go skiing that weekend. He had friends a few years older who lived in their own apartments, friends like Larry's older brother Rusty, so he was used to staying out all night. He knew girls who did more than kiss you good night at the front door. In different ways, Glen and Larry were two of the most extraordinary students in the school. Predictably, they were drawn together.

To Glen, Larry was a smart kid from a rich neighborhood who didn't look down his nose at him and who wasn't afraid to break the rules. Glen would stop by Friendly's while Larry worked the cash register and buy an ice cream cone. He would pay with a one-dollar bill, and then Larry would casually hand him back change for a ten. A half gallon of ice cream cost $1.19. It was easy in the course of a four-hour shift to ring up ten half-gallon transactions, nineteen cents each. If anyone noticed, Larry would smile and thank them and say he'd correct the mistake on the next purchase. Most nights Larry and Glen could siphon out at least twenty bucks, which was enough to buy an ounce of pot and a six-pack of beer.

To Larry, Glen's life came close to fulfilling every adolescent want. Larry went to work for Ken Fuller on weekends, helping to deliver roasted peanuts to local bars. Glen had, in addition to his old Cadillac, a deep green 1957 International Metro van, which looked like an old laundry truck. Larry would outfit the van with the stolen stereo speakers, albums, and the shag rug he had stolen from a classmate's rooms. They called the van Fuller's Fuck Truck. Out on deliveries with Larry, Glen had friends who would get them beer or whiskey. Then they would pick up girls. The girls Glen knew were chubby and unattractive, but they were willing to have sex. He introduced Larry to Sherry, who had a pornographic manual showing 1,001 ways of having intercourse. No matter that Sherry was no beauty queen; Larry fell in love. He and Sherry went to work on the book, page by page, in the back of Glen's van.

Glen broadened Larry's experience in other ways. There was nothing Glen wouldn't do. If Larry had an idea, Glen was at once ready to act on it, no matter at what difficulty or risk. Once, when Larry mentioned that his father needed lumber for a construction project at home, Larry and Glen took the Fuck Truck on a night trip to a nearby home construction site. The next day Larry told his father, "We found some lumber that somebody dumped out in the woods," and directed him to it. Justin was delighted. Larry would always remember how happy his father was . . . and that he hadn't asked any questions about the windfall.

It was in December 1971, shortly before Larry was to start at Exeter, that he got his first taste of serious crime. Larry had talked his folks into letting him go off with Glen Fuller for a three-day ski trip, but when the friends got together they realized that their cash was short. Over a bottle of syrupy sweet Boone's Farm Strawberry wine, Glen proposed a quick way of fixing that.

"I know this guy in Salem who'll give us a hundred bucks for a hot Ski-Doo, no questions asked," he said.

The Ski-Doo, a compact little skimobile, was the newest snow toy in rural New England.

Glen added, "And I know where we can get a Ski-Doo."

That night, he and Glen visited two local dealerships, loading the Fuck Truck with two Ski-Doos, an engine, and a set of tools. At the first location, Mears Trust in nearby Plaistow, New Hampshire, Larry rigged an ingenious sequence of overturned barrels and a ramp to ease the heavy snowmobile up and into the back of the truck.

With the truck loaded with booty, Glen and Larry drove out to the snowy New Hampshire hills and roared around on their new toys until dawn.

They got caught the next day. Glen had sold the Ski-Doos to a fence in Salem, New Hampshire, but not before insisting on one last joyride. He threw a tread on that ride, and as he worked to fix it, stranded on the back lot of a local high school, a man had stopped his truck and walked across the field to help him.

Hung over and strung out from the excitement and lack of sleep, Larry and Glen drove back into Haverhill later that morning. As they passed by Fifth Street, Larry noticed a police car parked in front of Glen's house. They drove by without stopping. Larry was convinced they had been discovered already.

"You're paranoid," said Glen. "How could they know?"

Glen stopped the truck around the corner and dropped Larry off. Filled with nervous energy, Larry ran the four miles through a heavy snowfall back to his own house. When Larry got home, his father sent him out to help his brother, Paul, shovel the walks. As they worked, Larry explained to Paul what had happened. Paul was dumbfounded. Home from the University of Pennsylvania, he was completing his premed studies at the top of his class. He hadn't been around his little brother that much over the last few years, but he had thought he knew him better than this! Larry would always remember the look on Paul's face.

"Oh, my God, Larry! Why in the world would you do that?"

The police phoned while Larry was outside shoveling. Glen had been arrested when he got home, and he had given Larry's name to the police.

Justin fumed as he drove his son to the police station.

"How could you do this?" he kept asking. "Why?"

"I did it for you," said Larry, and he tried to explain that he was going to use the money to help buy something for the house.

This just angered his father further.

"How can you say you did this for me! I would never condone stealing!"

Larry thought of the lumber, but his father was so angry that Larry didn't dare bring it up. To Larry, the only difference between this and the bricks, the mulch, and the lumber was that he had gotten caught.

And that wouldn't have happened if it weren't for Glen. At police headquarters Larry learned that the man who had stopped to help them align the tread in Salem had recognized the skimobile as one that he had recently returned to the dealer—it had been his machine! He had jotted down the license number on the truck and called the police, who had just taken the robbery report from the dealer. The license number led police directly to Glen Fuller's door.

Because of Glen's previous troubles it was assumed that he had planned and instigated the theft, and that Larry was just an innocent kid who had been drawn along. Larry, of course, knew there was more to it than that, but he kept his mouth shut. The case was handled by a judge who used to live across the street from the Lavins' old home in Bradford. Larry got a lecture, and the charges against him were dropped. Glen was convicted and received two years' probation. It soured their friendship for a time. Larry was angry at Glen for being stupid enough to insist upon joyriding all over the place, and for giving his name to the police. Glen was angry because Larry had let him take the whole rap.

But the most memorable consequence of the incident for Larry was the write-up the crime got in his local newspaper. His name wasn't in the article because he was a minor, but a local policeman was quoted as saying he doubted that two kids could have pulled off such a professional job by themselves, that someone else must have been behind it.

Larry liked that—"such a professional job."

Larry wrote an account of the skimobile incident for a creative writing class at Exeter. It was the first writing assignment since "My Life as a Pencil" that excited him. He tried to re-create every little detail: cutting through the padlock to break in; Glen starting up a forklift motor all of a sudden as they fumbled through the garage; the ironic way they had gotten caught. He was proud of the story. So he was surprised at the critical reception it got from his teacher. The writing teacher, perhaps alarmed by the evident pleasure his student took in the caper, said something was missing.

"Haven't you learned anything from the experience?" he asked Larry when they discussed the paper. "This does nothing more than tell the story, blow by blow. What does it mean to you? What's the point?"

Larry didn't have answers to those questions. He was disappointed by the paper's reception, but decided against trying to rewrite it. He just accepted a C, and concluded creative writing just wasn't his thing. He was no good at putting things between the lines.

*   *   *

Few of Larry Lavin's classmates were surprised when he got kicked out of Exeter in his senior year. With his aptitude for pranks and disregard for school rules, it was bound to happen. Housemaster Walker had checked Larry's room one evening when he wasn't there, and had spotted the smoking den with its three big fans and waterpipe. The room was chock-full with contraband. Larry had a box of munchies that had been taken from a storage shelter under the cafeteria, and a cassette tape player that belonged to the library, where he worked part-time as one of the terms of his scholarship. Evidence of dope smoking alone meant expulsion.

Larry's trouble with the administration was, in its own way, a victory. Dope smoking was so universal on campus that getting caught elicited an underground outpouring of sympathy and respect. More than thirty students had been thrown out that year alone. The awkward townie with the scholarship job in the library became an overnight campus hero. His skimobile story got passed around and repeated until the long, loose guy with the thick mop of black hair was seen as a romantic rebel, a cheerful eccentric who thumbed his nose at uptight administrators. Girls who would never talk to him before stopped by his room to wish him well. Larry basked in his newfound status.

Six weeks before graduation, Larry was summoned before Dean Donald C. Dunbar and the seven-member discipline committee. He was formally charged with committing two of the seven offenses at Phillips Exeter for which a student can be dismissed.

Larry had to be escorted to the disciplinary hearing by Mr. Walker. He showed up at the housemaster's quarters downstairs without wearing a tie, which was required at Exeter.

"Is this the kind of impression you want to make?" asked Walker. Despite the trouble Larry was in, Walker liked him. Larry was such a cheerful, friendly kid. Walker had mixed feelings about sending him up on charges, but rules were rules.

"It's no use anyway," said Larry.

"You've got to at least give it the old college try," said the housemaster.

In a grand room with a high ceiling, wide fireplace, rich wood-paneled walls, and an oriental rug, around a great oblong table watched over by the glass-eyed stares of wide-horned trophy heads, Dean Donald Dunbar's disciplinary committee met in solemn session to consider the charges against scholarship student Lawrence W. Lavin. Wearing a tie borrowed from Walker, Larry pleaded his case. He had tears in his eyes. He really had only borrowed the cassette player.

Library workers often didn't bother signing things out. The cereal from the basement had been left there by some underclassmen. The fans in his closet, well, sometimes things got real stuffy up there. . . .

A faculty member on the committee grinned. "One fan, Larry. Two fans. But three fans, Larry? *Three fans?*" Larry could see that he wasn't helping himself.

"How could you let down your friends on the lacrosse team this way?" asked Dunbar.

Larry didn't know what to say. Dunbar was the lacrosse coach, and although Larry wasn't on the team, most of his friends were (including the dean's son), and Larry was considered a good enough player to practice and scrimmage with them. How could he tell the coach that few team members had not visited Larry's closet, usually bringing their own supply of marijuana and hashish?

In the previous semester, the same committee had expelled Larry's friend Jeff Giancola for a different offense. Larry had made a joke of it when he wrote the lines that would go beneath his photograph in the 1973 Exeter yearbook. His words about his friend had added meaning when the book came out and Larry Lavin, too, was gone. They read, "This year the seven mortal sins became but venial. Woe were the Giancolas who were forced to confess them to Father Dunbar and his committee of angels." Larry's attitude was: *Can't these people take a joke?*

Larry called his father when the verdict was in.

"Are you sitting down?" he said.

"What?"

"Are you sitting down? I have some news and I want you to sit down before I tell you." His father erupted with anger when Larry told him he had just been thrown out of school. Larry interrupted his father's outburst.

"Okay, forget it, Dad. Don't bother to pick me up. I'll just hitch out to California."

Justin Lavin picked up his son the next morning. He had cooled off overnight. As he sat and listened to Housemaster Walker's explanation he felt more and more like his son was getting "fed the wrench," as he put it. On the way home he told Larry that Walker had seemed to him like a "typical WASP wimp." Larry defended Walker, but his father was convinced they had had it in for him because he was Irish Catholic. Larry's mistake had been in giving them an excuse to come down on him that hard.

Larry never did get his high school diploma. Methuen High School refused to accept him for just a few weeks of classes. Larry signed up to take a high school equivalency exam that summer, but before the date he got word that the University of Pennsylvania, where he had applied before getting thrown out of Exeter, had accepted him in their freshman class. A sympathetic administrator at Penn agreed to overlook the lack of a diploma in Larry's case. So with no further need to take the high school equivalency exam himself, he signed his brother Rusty's name at the top, and aced it nonetheless.

Just before Larry left for Philadelphia to begin his freshman year in the fall of 1973, Justin Lavin warned his son, "The skimobiles, that was strike one. Getting thrown out of Exeter, that was strike two. Three strikes, Larry, and you're out."

T W O

From Nothing to Zoom

Marcia Clare Osborn met Larry Lavin on her first day at the University of Pennsylvania. A day-long series of freshman orientation sessions was done. There was a loud party on the Quad lawn. It was too warm even in early evening to be indoors. A local band was playing country rock, and Marcia had positioned herself on the edge of a third-floor balcony overlooking the scene.

Marcia was from a small, insular Catholic family. Her father had been an elevator repairman at the RCA Building in Rockefeller Center until severe heart and circulation problems forced the amputation of his right leg in 1962. Her mother had worked as a cardiac intensive care nurse for nearly as long as Marcia could remember—she had gone back to work full-time when Marcia was four years old. Marcia was the baby of the family—she had an older brother and sister—so she grew up resenting her mother's long workdays, as though she had been cheated out of the childhood her brother and sister had enjoyed. Her father became increasingly reclusive and despondent after the loss of his leg, rarely leaving the house. At night he was in the habit of wedging a two-by-four between the bottom stair and the door of their suburban home in Dumont, New Jersey. It was added insurance against break-ins, but the door shut, locked, and tightly wedged was a fair image of the Osborns' relationship with the rest of the world.

Marcia had never been away from home. She had excelled in the Catholic schools she attended in Dumont and Englewood, and had decided, after years of witnessing her father's struggle with disability, to become a physical therapist. In 1973 it was a growing field, offering ample employment opportunities. So Marcia had applied to and was accepted at the University of Pennsylvania's School of Allied Health.

At seventeen she looked like a young hippie, still childlike, with a figure too short and wide to be flattered by the wide-belted, low-slung bell-bottom jeans and tight blouses with no bra. Marcia wore those clothes, but she preferred to wear a dress. She had a wide face with full cheeks and long full eyebrows over big brown eyes. Marcia shunned makeup, and wore her brown hair long, parted in the middle on top and hanging down below her shoulders. There was nothing arresting about her, but she had the quiet wit and inner calm of someone who was comfortable with herself and who knew what she wanted in life. Unlike most incoming freshmen, her choice of career was set. It was based on hard personal experience. But, beyond that, unlike most young women in Ivy League universities in the mid-seventies, Marcia Osborn knew that physical therapy was going to be secondary to bearing and raising children. She wanted a family, and she intended to stay home with her children.

So it was like Marcia to be taking in the party from a cautious distance, alone on a balcony overlooking the Quad lawn. Then this bean pole of a boy with thick, straight black hair, wearing plaid pants loud enough to stop a bus, stepped up from behind and grabbed her shoulders as if to push her off the balcony. He gave Marcia a playful push, just to startle her, and then pulled her back and grinned. Marcia didn't know whether to giggle or get angry. She giggled.

As she turned, she recognized him.

"You look like the guy I saw passed out on the lawn earlier," she said.

"Yeah, that was me!" said Larry happily. "My name is Larry Lavin . . ." and just kept on talking. Marcia could hardly understand him, his Massachusetts accent was so thick and the music was so loud. But she stayed and listened and smiled. It felt good to be singled out, even by someone slightly goofy like this, on the first day. As a recent high school graduate on her first day away from home at a new school in a strange city, she was pleased by Larry's eager attention. Marcia had a boyfriend she had met the year before working at the Shop-Rite in Dumont. He had gone off to Penn State out in State College, Pennsylvania, and the romance was still warm. So she wasn't shopping for a boyfriend, but she had not been approached by boys often enough in her life to cease being flattered by it. Marcia told her roommate later, "This guy talked to me for almost two hours and I have no idea what the hell he said to me. I know his name is Larry. He must have been interested; he talked a lot."

Larry was interested. In fact, he had gone out that morning with the express purpose of finding a girlfriend. His roommate, who unpacked two ounces of pot before Larry had even introduced himself, passed along a warning with his first joint.

"By the end of this week all the freshman girls will have upperclassman boyfriends. So if you plan on getting any this year, make friends fast."

Marcia saw Larry again the next evening. He was passed out on the lawn.

"Are you all right?" she asked, stooping over him and shaking him by the shoulder.

"It's this heat," said Larry. Along with many of his new class-mates, most of them away from home for the first time, Larry was testing the limits of his tolerance for beer and marijuana.

That same week he recruited Marcia to accompany him on a search for a parachute. One of the freshmen had decorated his room in the Quad by draping a silk parachute from the ceiling. Larry thought it looked cool; it gave the room a soft, cavelike quality. With that and a black light, some posters, a stereo, and some candles, it would make a perfect doper's lair. He found the address of an army-surplus store in the phone book and set off with Marcia to find it. It was their first date.

In North Philly they exited a subway stop that smelled of piss. Up and down the street were boarded-up storefronts covered with extravagant graffiti. Sidewalks were littered with broken glass, aban-doned appliances, fast-food wrappers, empty plastic milk crates, and brown paper bags with bottles protruding from the open end, the detritus of civilization in full retreat. Parked along curbs were hulking wrecks of automobiles, some resting on cinder blocks like pagan of-ferings with hoods up over gaping holes and with windshield glass shattered over interiors reduced to corroded metal shells. The corners in this neighborhood were occupied by idle, confident black men who made no effort to hide their amazement on seeing this short, wide-eyed, chubby coed in bell-bottom jeans and white blouse, and her tall, skinny, dark-haired companion, who was sporting red-and-white checked bell-bottom pants and a white cowboy shirt complete with a lacy trim. Larry approached with his best brazen "Hey, bro!" grin, inquiring in this flat-out *Bahston* accent, "Is there an army-surplus store around here somewhere? I'm looking for a place to buy a parachute."

The men on the corner didn't seem to know, so Larry and Marcia set off looking. Around a corner a tall man with a bottle in one hand, wearing a long overcoat (in sweltering heat), stepped in their way and pushed Larry against a wall. The man's black face was covered with gray stubble and dried spit, and his eyes from pupils to lower rims were bloodred. He mumbled something that Larry didn't understand, except in a general way, and Larry reached in his pocket for a quarter.

As he handed it over, another man shoved the first one aside and they began to shout and push one another. Larry and Marcia eased away and retreated back down the sidewalk at a fast walk.

A cop on the next block took one look at Larry and Marcia, marched across the street, and asked sternly, "What are you kids doing in this neighborhood?"

"We're leaving," Larry said.

The cop pointed them toward the nearest Broad Street subway stop. There were more derelicts down the stairs, lounging on benches and against the cool, damp concrete walls.

A bored woman behind a thick plate of milky glass scowled at Larry's dollar bill.

"I don't make change," she said.

Larry was stumped. Then one of the drunks piped up, "Here, give me the dollar; I'll go get change for you!" and the walls echoed with hilarity.

The woman in the milky glass booth softened.

"I'm not supposed to make change, but you really look lost, honey." She slipped two tokens and change through the slot to Marcia.

Back on campus Marcia's roommate, Patty, who knew better, said, "He took you to North Philly? To North Philly!"

"Oh, I don't know," said Marcia. "He didn't know it was like that. He was just looking for a parachute."

Heat records were challenged that first week of September 1973. Into the Quad, fraternity houses, the two high-rise dorms, and throughout the surrounding neighborhood moved trunks and suitcases, rugs and stereos, boxes of books and albums, lamps and chairs, all of them hoisted by students soaked with sweat. Larry and Marcia had both moved into the Freshman Quad, a four-walled Gothic structure enclosing several city blocks that looks more like a medieval cathedral than a college dorm. Its gray stone walls have long, narrow leaded glass windows; its roof is topped by ornate spires. More than a hundred different bat-faced gray gargoyles peer down from under its ivied eaves.

Despite this and other flourishes of antiquity, the university founded by Benjamin Franklin is the least formal of the Ivy League Schools. Across busy Fortieth Street to the west, Penn upperclassmen live in West Philly tenement housing, where the shabby gentility of undergraduate rental units rapidly gives way a few blocks west to ghetto. To the east the campus is bounded by a muddy, slick bend in the Schuylkill River. Beyond the river is the low, aging skyline of Philadelphia's Center City.

Nineteen seventy-three was not a boom year for Philadelphia; the city seemed crippled by economic forces outside its control: rising oil prices that drove its manufacturing base to the Sunbelt, rising unemployment, a permanent black/Hispanic underclass. Ham-handed Frank Rizzo, the colorful former police chief who spouted cheap racist slogans and who once offered to invade Cuba with his black-leather-jacketed force, was a newly elected mayor, guaranteeing years of dangerous racial polarization and reactionary municipal government. Set near the urban core of this troubled city, Penn was a liberal academic island, a world removed from the harder reality of its surrounding city streets. Penn students, few of whom were native Philadelphians, tended to be more interested in national politics anyway. The Vietnam War had turned the campus into a recruiting center for radical student groups. There wasn't a street corner or campus walk that was not lined with folding tables proffering militant socialist literature, manned by earnest upperclassmen or a breed of drifting veteran activists still intent on student revolution. But by 1973 these hippie revolutionaries were already losing their grip on campuses like Penn. The Vietnam War was hastening to its ignoble end, and Richard Nixon was embattled by near-daily revelations concerning Watergate. On campus there were "Impeachment Rallies" featuring crowds of long-haired, flannel-shirted, blue-jeaned students celebrating what seemed a lot like victory.

It was a heady time for students. There was a widespread feeling that youth had triumphed over calcified establishment wisdom. All tradition was suspect. On college campuses authority was viewed not just skeptically, but with open contempt. With no impassioned political battles to fight, this contempt found quieter, less profound ways of expression—1973 would be the year of "streaking"; sex was casual and commonplace; and pot rivaled alcohol as the intoxicant of choice at most campus events.

Very few Americans under thirty bought the establishment line that recreational drugs, including acid, mescaline, and speed, were harmful. A favorite campus film was *Reefer Madness*, the ridiculous antimarijuana propaganda film that depicts dope smokers being turned into murderous lunatics. Even the most thoughtful, cautious students scorned the illogic of harsh penalties for pot possession. Surely toking weed was no worse than guzzling six-packs until your higher brain functions signed off—which was still considered good all-American fun.

Through the seventies, as conventional wisdom has it, campus political anger gave way to personal ambition. The new college student was caricatured as an accounting major more interested in his résumé than social reform. But this was a different kind of ambition from the

Horatio Alger variety. It was as if you had crossed Calvin Coolidge with Abbie Hoffman, coupling vigorously rationalized greed with utter scorn for social norms. Drugs were a big part of this attitude; they remained—marijuana, LSD, mescaline, peyote, speed, cocaine —a symbol of the unalloyed coolness of youth. Teen dopers of the seventies had a fantasy about their future. Their lives would be like their parents', only better. They would cut their hair, clean up their acts, and not so much join the establishment as *infiltrate* it, play along just enough to master the system without getting co-opted. Pulling it off meant you could have it all, you could dabble at a profession, hobnob with the rich and powerful, marry and have kids, drive a fancy foreign car; you could be respected by your elders, admired by your peers, honored by your children; you could have all these things without taking a goddamn one of them seriously, without dropping a decibel of adolescent anger, *without growing up!*

In Larry Lavin's case, he had decided to become a dentist. Dentists made good money like doctors, but they had regular office hours. That was how Larry saw it.

From inside, the Quad was just a set of hallways that never stopped. They wrapped around and around, one on each of three floors, with rooms off to both sides filled with freshmen taking their first plunge into the total freedom of adulthood. Many were swiftly in over their heads. Anytime, any day, there were parties going on in the Quad, quiet downer parties with Jethro Tull piping on the turntable, intimate wine parties that evolved into sex, acid tests for the serious druggies, boisterous beer and whiskey and uppers parties that could lead to anything—party mingling with party, mind with mind, body with body—the Quad was a place where all the rules that had bound their teenage lives at home were gone . . . Valium or Quaaludes to help you cool out, and, to pick you right back up, speed or even—*now for something rare and expensive!*—cocaine. For many of the students freshman year meant total immersion in forbidden pleasures.

Larry lived in Monk's Row, the one corridor of the Quad that was all-male. It was considered a bad break. His three years at Phillips Exeter had given him a number of distinct advantages in his new freshman society at Penn. His authentic "preppie" credentials gave him precisely the aura of wealth and class that he had lacked at Exeter. His three years in Langdell Hall had prepared him better than most of his classmates for dorm life. And the academic rigors of Exeter made the freshman course load at Penn seem laughably easy. His roommate, Max, a native of the Main Line, Philadelphia's most exclusive suburban region, had enrolled at Penn less out of any academic ambition than with plans to perform as coxswain on the Schuylkill for the school's crew, for which he had been awarded a scholarship. But in the summer before starting, Max had gone through such a growth spurt that he was no longer suited for the job. Both roommates had a lot of free time, and Max, as Larry learned, had access to a steady supply of Mexican pot and LSD.

So Larry spent month after month ingesting drugs, staying high on pot virtually all the time, sometimes overindulging in beer, often experimenting with acid. Heavy users like Larry were like Quad jesters, a source of amusement to the less intrepid. One night Larry got so lost in an acid experience that he was unable to speak. Max led him around campus like a stoned puppy, a disheveled, long-haired goof in faded flannel shirt and unwashed bell-bottom blue jeans, stopping to show him off, just for the fun of it:

"This is Larry. He's tripping. You've just got to forgive him; he can't talk."

And people thought it was hilarious. Scenes like these made Larry one of the most popular members of his class. He was called "insane," "totally whacked-out," "weird," and other terms of warm tribute.

Larry had a scholarship at Penn that required him to work in Penn's Government Studies Library, a little-used repository where he spent most of his time playing chess and Ping-Pong with the elderly staff. More and more often Larry hung out in his friend Marcia's room, which was the largest in the Quad. Marcia's roommate, Patty Simon, was one of the prettiest, most popular girls in the new class. And Marcia, attractive in a quieter way, soon became the center of her own social circle. She played the guitar and gave sweet performances of Simon and Garfunkel songs. Both young women had considerably more domestic skills than most of their classmates; their room, which was called MOPS, after the girls' initials, was an oasis of vaguely maternal calm in the tumultuous Quad. And though Marcia still had her boyfriend at Penn State, she was always glad to see Larry. He was always cheerful and fun to have around. He had a childlike wholesomeness that seemed to belong to some earlier era— Larry was the only person Marcia knew who exclaimed, "Oh, my gosh!" or who actually used the expression "Okeydokey." She invited him to swim with her after classes and often sat with him in the dining room. Larry had no success at first in trying to move their relationship beyond friendship. Marcia was a one-man woman. But she enjoyed having male friends. Besides Larry, she had been befriended by a bear of a freshman named Paul Mikuta, another Main Line native, who kept much of the Quad supplied with marijuana from his local sources. If Larry was Marcia's hapless suitor, she had adopted Paul as a kind of big brother.

Larry's first stoned, carefree months at Penn came to an abrupt end in late October.

Max got hold of a BB gun from his older brother, and one afternoon he and Larry invented a game. Max would sprint across the lawn while Larry took aim from the dorm window and tried to shoot him in the back. It was chilly fall weather by now, and with a shirt and jacket on it didn't hurt too much to get hit, but you felt it. After perfecting their aim on each other, Larry and Max began taking aim at unsuspecting students. Hapless students crossing the Quad would jump and turn their heads angrily and reach for the pinch in their back. Stoned Larry and Max would giggle and giggle off in their room, out of sight.

For a week, word spread and the mystery grew. Who was the Quad's mysterious mad BB gunner? Everyone thought it was funny except the students who had been hit. Then, one afternoon, Larry got careless. He shot at a girl as she crossed the Quad facing the window. The BB stung her right breast, and as she looked up quickly she caught a glimpse of the gun barrel in the window. She screamed.

"I've been shot! The mad BB gunner!" she screamed.

Larry threw the gun in the closet and fled. He and Max drove off campus to Max's brother's apartment, where they settled in to smoke opiated hash wrapped in a layer of Virginia tobacco. They were lost in the lush effects of this mix, listening to Yes's *Fragile* album, when the phone rang.

Max answered the phone. When he hung up, he was in tears. It had been the dorm counselor. The girl had reported being shot and she had led campus security guards to their room. They had found the gun in the closet. The counselor was angry. Everyone was looking for Larry and Max.

In the same week, as Larry and Max sweated out a scheduled disciplinary hearing, Larry got even more distressing news. His girlfriend from Haverhill, Sherry of the 1,001 positions, was pregnant! She had waited three months before telling anyone. Her parents didn't know, and she desperately needed three hundred dollars for an abortion. Larry said he would get the money, one way or the other.

But he had no idea where he was going to find three hundred dollars. He figured there was a chance that after the disciplinary hearing next week he would be out of school. What was he going to tell his father? He kept hearing that angry warning, "Three strikes, Larry, and you're out." Sitting alone in a friend's room, ten floors up in one of the high-rise dorms, Larry had glanced at an open window and considered jumping. But the thought, which seemed disembodied somehow, just made him laugh at himself. He figured if all else failed he could always just hitch a ride out to California and be a beach bum.

Larry turned to Marcia for help. She listened patiently as he explained his plight. The BBs really didn't hurt anybody, he said; it was just a prank. She told him she thought that was pretty stupid, and, in retrospect, he agreed, but, you had to admit, picturing the look of surprise on the face of a student just stung from nowhere in the ass . . . it could make you laugh. This and the pregnant girlfriend, all in the same week! This kind of thing seemed to happen to no one but Larry. Trouble seemed to be staged for him on a grander scale than for other people. Yet his good cheer was infectious and seemed indestructible. He was goofy but he was sincere; he was wild but he could also be vulnerable and tender.

Marcia got her friend Paul Mikuta to buy Larry's prized Advent speakers (the ones he had stolen from a classmate at Exeter) for three hundred dollars. That paid for Sherry's abortion. Marcia asked her dorm counselor, a law student, to help defend Larry at the disciplinary hearing. Her counselor knew Larry.

"The guy is a jackass," he told Marcia, "but if you want me to help him, I will."

There was not much of a defense he could offer before the twelve-man disciplinary panel of upperclassmen. Larry said that the BB had ricocheted off the wall and out the window to hit the girl. The panel saw through the obvious lie. Larry and Max were asked to leave the room while the panel decided their punishment.

While waiting, an administrative dean, who had observed the hearing, waved Larry into his office for a chat.

"We're very liberal here at Penn," he said, peering across a cluttered desk at Larry. "We tolerate most things: the marijuana, the acid and other drugs, most horseplay, except for fires, but we really can't have people shooting other people!"

As it turned out, Larry's and Max's fears of being expelled were overblown. The board called them back in and gave them a choice: They could either move off campus or work for the rest of the school year picking up dog shit from the Quad lawn. After some initial indecision, Larry and Max swallowed their pride and became temporary "Pet Inspectors."

There was one more run-in with campus authorities that year. Larry got a supply of "Sunshine" acid from a Haverhill friend, and sold some of it in the Quad. He wasn't trying to make money; it was viewed as a public service.

One evening a freshman who had gotten acid from Larry freaked out. He went solo-streaking across campus pulling fire alarms, and ran campus security guards on a chase that led up to the peaked rooftop of the Quad. There the fleeing tripster took some frightening leaps before his roommate was able to coax him through a window back into his room. There, he doused a Russian textbook with lighter fluid and set it on fire before guards wrestled him, screaming, into custody. When the effects of the drug wore off, the student told campus officials that Larry had sold him the acid.

But Larry had made friends with young staff workers in the dean's office. One of them paid Larry a visit, and warned him that the dean had a list of ten campus dealers whose rooms were going to be searched. So Larry and Max cleared out their inventory, filling two laundry bags with pot and acid and drug paraphernalia. The searches came several days later. There were drugs in most of the targeted rooms, but the penalties were not harsh. The worst was meted out to a girl who lived in the Quad who had stashed a pound of Colombian marijuana in her closet. Even then, her six-month suspension from the university was prompted less by the dope than by the fact that she was discovered to be living with a nonstudent friend, a teenager who had recently run away from home.

Years later, Larry Lavin would see his first year at Penn as his introduction to a subculture dominated by drug use. He lived on a roller coaster of stimulants, depressants, and alcohol. He nevertheless earned high grades. He found that many of the freshman classes at Penn were far behind the course work he had completed at Exeter. So he scored well on tests in classes in which he put forth only minimal effort. His success, under these circumstances, fed Larry's natural cockiness. It reinforced a growing perception of himself as someone especially gifted, as someone who could break the rules and get away with it. He knew students who did as well or better than he did in class, and he had classmates who partied just as hard or harder than he did, but he knew of no one who excelled at both. His natural cynicism kicked in. If a college diploma, even from an Ivy League university like Penn, was this easy, then academic accomplishment itself was a farce—it depended more on going to the right school than on brains and hard work. Larry still planned on taking premed courses and going to dental school, so he suspected that his science courses would eventually be more demanding and competitive, but as a freshman and sophomore the emphasis was on partying. And in 1973–74, partying on a college campus meant drugs.

As freshman year progressed, Larry found himself more and more in the company of Penn's fraternities. After his years of living in dormitories full of boys, Larry felt more at home with the idea of joining a fraternity than with finding his own off-campus housing for sophomore year. So, toward the end of his first year, he began to cultivate the friendships he would need to join one. The fraternity that most appealed to him was Phi Delta Theta, which occupied a dilapidated mansion on the corner of Thirty-seventh Street and Locust Walk, on the western edge of campus.

Most of the Phi Delta Theta brothers were from western Pennsylvania and shared a small-town perspective that Larry could appreciate. They tended to see academics as a necessary evil, hurdles on the path to a financially successful career. They exhibited a rugged, macho, independent style that resisted the vestiges of liberal idealism still present on campus, scorning political activism and, more important, the growing impact of women's liberation. Young women at Penn tended to be feminists, looking more toward careers than husbands and families. Many treated sex casually, feeling that they were as entitled to "score" as the young men on campus. And their approach to serious relationships tended to be confrontational—few female Penn students wanted anything to do with conventional sexual roles. Midway through freshman year, apart from his deepening friendship with Marcia, Larry had casual sexual relationships with several young women. The new sexual freedom suited Larry and his friends perfectly; they postponed serious relationships and competed with each other in hedonistic pursuits.

There were other things that set Larry and the Phi Delta Theta brothers apart from the mainstream at Penn. Most of the students came from large cities, many from Philadelphia and New York, and had grown up attending multiracial and ethnically diverse schools. Larry, like many of the western Pennsylvanian brothers of Phi Delta Theta, had been raised in smugly racist, subtly anti-Semitic communities. Their fraternity was an ark of "normalcy" in the swirling currents of Penn's complex community. Like all of Penn's frats, it was by definition all-male, and by long-standing tradition virtually all-white and all-Christian (or, rather, non-Jewish). Few of these attitudes and practices were overt, but they formed a homogeneous underpinning to fraternity life that made the "Greek system" in the seventies a haven for more conventionally minded young men.

Larry's first friend at Phi Delta Theta was Dan Dill, a tall, gregarious, long-haired life of the party who rolled joints the size of cigars and who brought an old-fashioned beer-drinker's approach to drug use—he prided himself on being able to ingest more of everything than anyone else. Larry admired that. There was a party in the spring of 1974 when fraternity brothers had to count off Dill's pulse as he lay unconscious on their front lawn to be sure that he was still alive. Dill was responsible for keeping the house supplied with marijuana, but by the standards of the times, he was strictly a social drug dealer.

He would purchase only a pound or two at a time, split it into ounces, and sell it in the house. This trade made Dill the fraternity's informal social director. A bong was usually burning in his room, and there was often a crowd around it. It was precisely the way Larry wanted to live.

So he pledged with the fraternity that spring, and set about to fulfill its initiatory tasks with a gusto that took the house by surprise. There was a point system for scavenging; more points were awarded for more daring and unique prizes. High on the list were parking tickets, so Larry and his friends set about collecting from windshields not only tickets issued by the campus police, which was the tradition, but also by the city of Philadelphia. Taking swings through Center City at midday, Larry and other pledges collected over several weeks a total of two hundred parking tickets. No one had ever collected that many before. Once Larry's points were credited, he packed the tickets in a shoe box and mailed them to City Hall.

But by far the most prized items in the scavenger hunt were trophies from other fraternities. In this, of course, Larry had experience. He set his sights first on one of the most unique and dramatic targets on campus: a moose head that hung in the hallway at rival ZBT, the predominately Jewish fraternity on campus. Larry recruited his friend Paul Mikuta to help—Paul was not pledging with a fraternity but enjoyed pranking as much as the next guy. In the middle of the night, Paul watched while Larry climbed up a rear wall of ZBT's house, using window ledges and gutters for hand- and footholds. Easing out along a utility pipe three stories up, Larry worked himself over to a window. With a penknife, he chipped away at the putty around a small pane that had recently been replaced, and removed it. He reached inside and unlocked the window, and stepped inside.

Larry found himself standing in darkness in an empty bathtub. When his eyes adjusted to the darkness, he crept over to a pile of clothes draped over the back of a chair and rooted through the pockets. He found a bundle of keys. Then he climbed out the window and back down to Paul.

One of the keys opened the front door. They went directly to the moose head and lifted it off the wall. After carrying it across campus, thrilling in their daring and good fortune, they deposited it in Phi Delta Theta's foyer. It had all gone so smoothly, Larry and Paul didn't want to stop. They went back for more. This time they wrestled a heavy, prized poker table out the front door, delivering it to Phi Delta Theta shortly before dawn. More items were collected over the next few weeks, much to the surprise and delight of Larry's prospective fraternity brothers. Eventually ZBT was summoned to recover its belongings amidst catcalls and jeers. Larry stole another fraternity's official flag, and when a group from that house tracked him down and came to retrieve it, Larry displayed a machete that he had bought at an army-surplus store in Boston—its blade was heavy and had a sinister bend. The group backed off. When a complaint was filed with the frat council about his machete, Larry was contrite. He agreed to return the flag. So he and Paul Mikuta climbed up in the Quad rafters and captured two pigeons. They wrapped them in the flag, put it in a box, and left it on ZBT's front porch. The fraternity recovered a soiled flag and had a hell of a time catching the frightened pigeons.

Larry ran up more scavenging points than any pledge before or since. In the process he became one of the house's most popular characters before he was officially even a brother.

By the end of freshman year, Larry's relationship with Marcia Osborn had moved beyond friendship. Though Marcia was still writing to her high school boyfriend at Penn State, Larry's persistence and charm had gradually worn away her resolve. They were in bed together often in her room at the Quad during spring semester, where Larry would often return with ridiculous stories about things he had taken, things he had done. Larry brought out maternal tendencies in Marcia; he was someone who needed to be loved in spite of himself. Larry was wild, but his drug use was really no more extreme than that of many freshmen in the Quad, and his grades were considerably better than most. Their personalities complemented each other, Larry affording Marcia a bit more joy and excitement than she had known, and Marcia offering Larry a reliable base of affection. Larry was reckless, loud, and impulsive, while Marcia was cautious, quiet, and analytical. Larry trusted and liked people instantly, while Marcia could spend months and years with a person before developing trust and affection. She committed her heart more cautiously than Larry did, but once committed, Marcia was like a rock. She figured that time would wear out Larry's wildness, and that her own good sense would ultimately prevail.

Larry didn't tell Marcia about the other girls. His relationship with her was to be the most important, but not the only one.

At the beginning of sophomore year Larry moved into Phi Delta Theta. He chose a room on the second floor of the thirty-room mansion, overlooking the front door, and began an ambitious paint job. Larry wanted to paint a fluorescent spectrum across his walls against a black backdrop in imitation of the cover of *Dark Side of the Moon*, an album by Pink Floyd, as though the colors were spilling on the wall from a giant prism. He got as far as painting his room pitch black and the ceiling white. Then things got busy.

Over the summer after freshman year, Larry had worked in the giant Converse factory in Haverhill. When he was not working at the factory, Larry had a second job as a lifeguard at the swimming pool of his parents' townhouse complex. He had scholarships and a government loan to help pay his tuition and board at Penn, but he needed every dollar he could scrape up to pay the rest. He especially liked the Converse job. At the factory, workers had fashioned a cave out of the pallets in the warehouse. It couldn't be seen from the floor, and was entered by climbing up and across the top layer of boxes and then climbing down inside. Out of sight, he and his co-workers, including his friend Ricky Baratt, spent many idle hours smoking dope.

But unlike many of his co-workers, Larry actually enjoyed his work at Converse and found himself growing more and more reluctant to spend so much time getting high. His job in the warehouse was to make up orders for shipments to shoe stores around the country. He would fill pallets with different-sized boxes and cartons of tennis shoes, a time-consuming but important procedure. Converse took pains to package each order exactly to the specifications of each customer, each of which had ordered different combinations of sneakers. Some of the orders were just for a few boxes, some for whole pallets. It fascinated Larry. He had dated the daughter of the man who supervised him, so his boss took a special interest in Larry, who, as a college kid attending an Ivy League school, was regarded as only temporarily suited for such labor. So Larry found himself infected with a new, managerial perspective. He watched his friends and co-workers sneaking off to get high—and continued to join them now and then—but it bugged him that they were working at only 50 percent of their potential. He could hear old echoes of his father's lament: *Unions have spoiled American workers; it's no wonder the fuckin' Japs are kicking our ass!*

Larry was surprised to feel such conservative instincts in himself. He had never thought of himself as ambitious, but those stirrings were there, too. Looking back over the way he had spent his first year at Penn, he realized that he couldn't expect to continue pulling high grades if he lived that way. He resolved to work harder during sophomore year, and to find a way to make more money during the school year so he wouldn't have to work fifty hours a week again next summer.

It was during this summer that Larry had the first seeds of a notion. He knew that Dan Dill, who was his big brother at Phi Delta Theta, had contacts who sold him two or three pounds of pot at a time, enough to supply the house with ounces and maintain a free supply for Dill's bong. Dill didn't see it as a business. But Larry did. It was a business! It worked on the same principle as the Converse factory: The key to higher profits was higher volume, and the key to higher volume was having a steady supply of product on hand, neatly packaged to suit the customer. If Dill multiplied the number of buyers—nearly everyone Larry knew smoked dope—and maintained a larger supply, profits would quickly grow beyond what it took just to keep himself high.

Immediately on his return to Penn in the fall of 1974, Larry apprenticed himself to his big brother. Dill introduced Larry to the two main sources of marijuana at Penn, Bob Chance and Ed Mott, two upperclassmen who lived in off-campus apartments and drove cars and lived a life that, while not lavish, was far beyond the financial reach of most underclassmen. Chance was a studious personality who kept careful track of business dealings. Mott was a freewheeler who spent his money as fast as he made it. Larry noted that every time he stopped by Mott's apartment there was a different girl with him —each of them a knockout. Chance and Mott had started dealing together as freshmen and after four years had connections that could deliver hundred-pound bales of pot, thirty-pound lumps of hashish, and large quantities of the other drugs—notably speed and Quaaludes—in demand on campus.

Dill was not as eager as Larry to expand the operation. But shortly after the semester began, he left on a week-long hunting trip to western Pennsylvania. In his absence, Larry paid a routine visit to Chance and Mott to replenish the house dope supply, handing over the standard two hundred dollars. Only this time Larry said he wanted to buy more. He asked them to front him ten pounds—or eleven hundred dollars' worth of pot.

"Give me one week," he said.

Chance and Mott agreed. Back in his black fraternity room, Larry used his machete and Dill's scale to cut the dope into pieces. He sold it for ten dollars per ounce. Before the week was up he drove out to pay Chance and Mott their eleven hundred dollars—a whole brown bag full of bills, mostly tens and twenties. The sequence went Washington, Lincoln, Hamilton, Jackson. It felt good to go to the branch bank and exchange the smaller bills for hundreds, crisp pale green Ben Franklins. After all, Franklin had founded Penn! When Dill returned from his trip that weekend, Larry handed him five bills. It was hard to believe something so slight as these five slips of green paper could be worth so much—five hundred dollars!

"That's what I made off your connections this week," Larry said.

After that, Dill conceded the pot business to his little brother.

L.A. was stuck. While he was away over an October weekend, Ed Mott had dropped off forty pounds of pot. Forty pounds! Who was he trying to kid? The most L.A. had ever ordered at one time was ten pounds. And he had just moved that much over the last two weeks. All of his customers were well stocked. But there it was, filling a large blue American Tourister suitcase on the floor of his living room.

"Are you kidding me?" he asked Mott, who laughed on the other end of the phone.

"Don't worry about it," said Mott. "Take it on credit. Pay me when you move it. No hurry."

"But you're nuts," said L.A. "I'm not going to be able to sell it."

"Really?"

"Ed, it's going to grow mold where it is."

"Well, just hang on to it for a while, sell any of it you can."

L.A. was annoyed. He knew Mott's methods. By dropping off that amount he was urging L.A., daring him, to expand his business. There was nearly two thousand dollars in profits there if he could sell it. But he didn't know where to begin. L.A. was a hulking junior with a broad face and big glasses perched on a wide, crooked nose. His thin, untended brown hair sprayed out like an aura. He was a bit of a loner, an awkward, extremely intelligent young man who liked to stay high—a habit he had started and perfected in high school in California. L.A. had connections in Florida dating back to high school days who were willing to sell him as much or more as Mott could deliver, but he had kept his dealing strictly to a small circle of friends, selling little more than it took to keep him in spending money and to maintain his own steady, free supply. The supply end was L.A.'s strength. How was he going to retail 640 ounces? Yet he knew that if he didn't sell it, then Mott was just using him to store it, parceling out the risk to his minions. It troubled L.A., but not enough to do anything. His laid-back nickname had stuck for more than one reason. With the exception of a few minor sales, the suitcase was still nearly full when Mott checked back toward the end of November. L.A. told him it was hopeless, and he wasn't thrilled with having the stuff lying around his apartment.

"Okay. I'm going to send over this guy named Larry."

And within an hour this cheerful, skinny guy with black hair was at the door. L.A. smoked a joint with him. He thought Larry looked awfully clean-cut and wholesome to be dealing with Mott—most of the pot dealers he knew, including himself, were holdovers from the sixties, long-haired goofs who cultivated their own spaced-out brand of cool. Larry wore his hair shorter and had actually combed it. He looked to L.A. more like some kind of ROTC freak. But there was something almost inspiring in the cheerful gleam that came to Larry's eyes when L.A. showed him the forty-pound bundle.

"Thanks," Larry said.

Larry took the whole suitcase. He sold the contents in three days.

When Mott came by L.A.'s apartment to collect the money from Larry, he said, "You and L.A. ought to start working together."

People were still coming to Dan Dill at Phi Delta Theta to buy dope, and when word got out that there was always good and plenty to be had at the corner of Thirty-seventh and Spruce, the crowds grew. L.A. introduced Larry to friends in New York City who were willing to loan him money at 10 percent interest, and soon he was buying up to hundred-pound bales at a time. Larry would recruit one of his fraternity brothers to help him break down the bale with his trusty machete into smaller portions.

Word got out fast when a shipment was in. Soon after Larry started selling seriously he met Andy Mainardi, a freshman living in the Quad who had attended Lawrenceville School. Andy was short and chubby, with thin brown hair, a round face that made the lower part of his head seem larger than the upper, and glasses. He had been friends with Ricky Baratt at Lawrenceville and had done some dealing there, so Andy sought out Larry at Penn. He was a cheerful, energetic, and ambitious fellow, always ready with a story or a joke. He came from a well-to-do, prominent New Jersey family—his father was a judge—and planned eventually to go into business for himself. Andy, like L.A., loved pot. Larry viewed it primarily as merchandise. When Larry suggested cutting it with oregano to increase profits, L.A. and Andy reacted like outraged purists—it wasn't just dishonest, it was *heresy!* Andy's approach in particular was more that of a connoisseur than a retail merchant. If Larry was always looking for the most favorable profit margin, Andy was always looking for the best dope. One of the biggest attractions of dealing was that it gave him a chance to pick out for himself the choicest portions of each load as it came through. Andy preserved small samples of the best shipments the way a collector preserved bottles of rare vintage wine.

Dan Dill had connections throughout his senior class, L.A. had his buyers among the juniors, Larry seemed to know everyone in the sophomore class, and Andy, being nearly as gregarious as Larry, was plugged into the ongoing party in the Quad. Dill's bong would be fired up downstairs on the second floor, where he entertained customers by getting them high and playing music and making them laugh, and then, one by one, customers would go upstairs and collect their orders—anything from a few ounces to ten-pound bags. Within two or three hours the hundred-pound bale would be gone. There would be as much as five thousand dollars' profit on a deal, an untidy mound of small bills that Larry enjoyed separating and stacking into piles. L.A.'s instinct was to bank the money and lay low for a while, but Larry would hear none of it.

"If you want to make money, you have to keep it rolling," he said.

So Larry would get right back on the phone to place another order with Chance or Mott or one of L.A.'s connections in Florida. Soon Larry had sources of his own. Through a fellow sophomore named Tom Finchley, Larry met a big dealer at Virginia Tech named Ralph, who worked with smugglers who flew the stuff in themselves. Larry spent a weekend in Blacksburg, Virginia, partying with Ralph, who took him out in the woods and showed him a barn that was a marijuana warehouse, with bales stacked and shelved awaiting delivery just like in the Converse factory in Haverhill. Larry opened another pipeline.

Packaging was Larry's specialty. When Larry and Marcia went on their weekly trip to the supermarket, Marcia would fill a cart with groceries while Larry filled one with an assortment of different-sized boxes of Ziploc plastic bags. While dealers like Chance and Mott had avoided selling in quantities smaller than pounds, and handed over the stuff carelessly wrapped in newspaper or whatever else it had come in, Larry would sell to anyone and package to specifications. If Andy Mainardi wanted ten pounds, which he would be selling by the ounce, Larry would break down the ten pounds into ounces himself, delivering a box filled with neat baggies—just like an order from the Converse plant! With Larry it was almost a fetish. When a messy order of hash oil came in, he put on a lab coat and visited a scientific supply house off campus to order boxes of tiny glass vials. His customers were delighted. Larry even started delivering. Across campus and through the surrounding West Philly neighborhoods, Larry would carry green plastic sacks filled with Ziploc bags of grass and fling the orders up to dorm windows into the waiting arms of his customers, like a newsboy on his rounds.

The business operated on one simple principle: Whatever Larry could buy, he could sell.

Where in the past campus dealers had adhered to a kind of unspoken hippie tradition that it was unseemly to make too much money dealing marijuana, Larry was guided by something more basic, that emerging yuppie precept: greed. He was on the phone constantly, taking orders, scouting out new sources, comparing prices to keep his own competitive. His net worth was plotted carefully after each deal, and detailed records of purchases, sales, and debts were kept in tiny handwriting on sheets of paper hidden inside selected album covers —Larry's collection of albums had grown considerably since the ones he had stolen from classmates at Exeter. Unlike traditional campus dope dealers, who sold only when they happened to have a large supply, Larry maintained a constant supply so that customers would know they could always buy from him. He even varied his inventory, dealing the basic user's Mexican pot he got from Ed Mott or Bob Chance or Tom Finchley, typically in 100-pound bundles packed in boxes he bought for $90 to $100 per pound and sold for $165 per pound, while for more expensive tastes Larry stocked Colombian or Jamaican pot from Ralph in Virginia or from new sources at Penn State from whom he bought shipments of anywhere from 5 pounds to 220 pounds at about $320 per pound and sold at $425 per pound. For those who preferred a quick, powerful high, Larry sold blond hash that he could get from L.A.'s sources in Florida for $800 per pound and sell for $1,200 per pound; for those exploring more exotic highs Larry had rare black opiated hash that he bought for $1,600 per pound and sold at $2,000 per pound; and for those who liked their dope to hit them over the head hard he had messy hash oil, which Larry bottled to order, gently warming the tarlike stuff by the potful until he could pour it into his tiny glass vials. The hash oil, supplied by a student at Swarthmore College who delivered the sticky black drug in jars for $75 an ounce, Larry sold sometimes for as much as $150 per ounce. For retail sales he kept his pricing in line with the current prices listed in *High Times* magazine—that way he could point to proof that he was not gouging his customers. But perhaps the single most important feature of Larry's booming trade was his almost kamikaze willingness to front the drugs and wait for payment. You didn't even have to have money to buy dope from Larry.

He had good business instincts. Toward the end of his sophomore year, he and L.A. and two other partners pooled funds to buy 100,000 Black Beauties, black capsules of amphetamine. It was a sure thing —Larry was really excited about it. Each capsule cost only two cents wholesale. Larry knew they could sell them at Penn for fifty cents each—a $48,000 profit! Before buying the capsules, Larry and L.A. found a couple of students willing to try them.

"If the deal goes through, we'll give you each two hundred dollars," said Larry.

But the effects of drugs are sometimes tricky. So much depends on your state of mind. Evidently, Larry's guinea pigs wanted the two hundred dollars so much that it warped their judgment, because despite their insistence that the capsules had given them a powerful rush, it was evident within days after the purchase and delivery that the Black Beauties were duds—little better than placebos. Inside the frat house it was a joke. Larry faced facts quickly and slashed the price of his capsules to five cents. He sold off his portion of the buy within a few days, recovering his investment and turning a small profit. L.A. and the other investors hung tough—and graduated more than a year later with boxes of black capsules in their closets.

Matched against the traditional campus dope dealer, who sold only when a shipment came in and even then only to keep himself well stocked, Larry had little trouble cornering Penn's market. He learned (and liked) the feel of neat stacks of hundred-dollar bills, the preferred unit of currency for underground transactions, crisp pale green Ben Franklins about a half-inch thick. There was something indescribably macho about a bundle of hundreds. Larry got in the habit—which Marcia deplored—of carrying a thick wad of cash around with him at all times.

Larry was always willing to front dope to people, even those he hardly knew. It just was not in him to distrust others. Larry worked on a principle that most of his friends considered painfully naive: He figured if he treated people well, they would treat him well in return. For most people that was true, but as the months went by the list of tardy debtors grew. In the first months there were only a handful who owed Larry a few hundred dollars total. But the list of names steadily grew. By the end of sophomore year there were more than thirty people on the list, and the total owed was in the thousands. Larry just didn't worry about it. It bothered L.A. and Ed Mott and other dealers, but not Larry. The amounts he was making far outstripped such losses.

It all happened so fast that Larry never even had time for second thoughts. By spring of 1975 the business had made him one of the most popular students on campus. He was making what seemed like a lot of money, even though, after paying off interest and splitting the profits with L.A., he was earning only a few thousand dollars on a hundred-pound deal. Toward the end of sophomore year he moved into more spacious quarters in the fraternity, a two-room suite that was painted a shade of green close to the color of money. He bought himself a '66 Chevy Nova for three hundred dollars and also a leather coat. But most profits were poured back into the next deal.

Dope dealing swept Larry up as surely as addiction sweeps up its victims. It played just the right chords in his personality. It allowed him to capitalize at once on his cynicism, his playfulness, his hypersociability, his ambition. It challenged his mind and satisfied his appetite for risk.

The business went, as Larry would put it later, "from nothing to *zoom!*"

T H R E E

Less Risk, More Exposure

Larry moved in with Marcia in the spring semester of his junior year, 1976. They had been sleeping together most nights for more than a year, and Larry had kept clothes in her closet and books in her place all that time. But Marcia knew they were really living together when Larry carried in his stereo. He set up the big Advent speakers he had bought back from Paul Mikuta in two corners of the bedroom.

Marcia only recently had moved out of an apartment she had shared with two friends for more than a year. There had been trouble between her and her roommates for some time, mostly over Larry. Marcia had moved with them from the Quad into an apartment at 4002 Spruce Street during junior year. It was over a barbershop and two doors away from University Pinball, a favorite off-campus hangout. Her roommates had started off liking Larry, but as his dealing grew more and more notorious, they viewed him with a mixture of awe and revulsion. Having money in his pockets intensified his cockiness. They found him insufferable. Every time Larry came over they would ignore him, even though he had tried to make peace by helping to furnish their place. He had separate telephones installed for them in their rooms and purchased shelves, a couch, shower curtains, and wall hangings. When he stopped over he always stocked their refrigerator with goodies. But when he wasn't around they told Marcia how surprised they were that she kept seeing him. They told her that he was running around with other girls behind her back. Marcia chalked their warnings up to spite. Marcia had fallen in love with Larry.

As she saw it, complaints about Larry were indirect complaints about her. Both roommates led more active social lives than Marcia.

They were Jewish, which had never mattered before, but now, along with their other differences, it made Marcia feel outnumbered. She noted that hers was the smallest of the apartment's three bedrooms and began to keep score of a multitude of minor inequities. Finally, after a particularly bitter argument, Marcia moved out. She took the couch and other furnishings that Larry had given them, and before leaving she stalked angrily through the apartment removing all the gifts he had given her roommates—she took down the shower curtains, pulled the phones from the wall, etc.—and tossed them in a trash can on the sidewalk in front of the barbershop downstairs. She found a small apartment for herself at the corner of Fortieth Street and Baltimore Avenue, in a building called Calvert Hall, which overlooked the big green-and-silver trolley cars that shuttled back and forth down the center of the old avenue all hours of the day and night.

It wasn't that Marcia disagreed with her old roommates about Larry's drug dealing. While she had nothing against people getting high—Marcia was in a minority of nonusers—and it was generally known that you couldn't get in much trouble for keeping a private stash of an ounce or so, selling was another matter. Marcia thought it was stupid—he was sure to get in trouble.

"Don't worry so much," Larry would say. "The worst they're going to do is make me take a semester off, or something like that. If I got caught by the city I might be in more trouble, but it would be pretty hard to get caught because I'm in a fraternity house. There are rules. I read about it in *High Times*. They can't search the whole fraternity house. If they want to come into my room, they'll never find anything because I'm paying people to hide things in their rooms. There are thirty rooms! They actually searched a whole frat house once, and the case got thrown out of court because . . ."

Larry had it all figured out, as if *High Times* magazine were the last word. Marcia would just nod and grimace. She didn't believe Larry's reassurances, but what could she do? Who was she to give Larry advice? She was the one who struggled in science courses that Larry mastered with ease. Besides, as Marcia fell harder and harder for Larry, the balance of their relationship shifted. At first, when Marcia had another boyfriend, Larry had pursued her. Now things were the other way around; Marcia was the eager one. He was so wrapped up in the business, and was such a big hit with all his friends, that sometimes it seemed as though Larry had no time for Marcia. Even when he was with her in the apartment he was on the phone all the time. Larry thought he loved Marcia, but at times it was hard for him to be with her. She was so different from his other friends. She didn't like to go out drinking and partying. She thought most of the fraternity brothers were juvenile slobs and their attitudes toward women were demeaning. But deep down she knew that if the issue were forced with Larry, he would leave before he would give up dealing. It was like some necessary extension of his personality. But it was crazy! He did not know the meaning of discretion. It seemed like everybody on campus knew Larry Lavin was selling marijuana.

Even Phi Delta Theta was worried. The fraternity had held a meeting to try and rein Larry in. A panel of senior brothers told him that they were getting worried about the amoun'.; of dope he was handling, about the steady stream of customers in and out of Thirty-seventh and Spruce.

"People are stopping us as we walk across campus, asking us what Larry has this week," said one.

"It's just gotten too obvious," said another. "Larry, if they search the house they may not find your stash, but almost everybody in the house has some personal dope in their rooms. Any one of us could get in trouble. You've just gotten too big. You're attracting too much attention."

At first Larry was wounded, but when he cooled down he could see their point. He compromised with them. He would continue selling but he would no longer stash the product in the frat house. Still, there were grumblings. Even Dan Dill wished out loud that the dealing would go back to what it was before, more of an ongoing party than a business. Larry began looking for someplace else to live.

Marcia kept waiting for something to happen, for Larry to get busted or beat up or suspended for a semester. Maybe it wouldn't come to that. Maybe the premed courses, which were getting more demanding—even for Larry—would eventually crowd dealing out of the picture. He still wanted to get into dental school more than anything. And just when Marcia seemed ready to give up on him he would come around for a while, or say something really sweet.

In the middle of spring semester, Larry leased an entire four-story row house at 3939 Chestnut Street for eight hundred dollars a month. He figured if he moved in L.A. and Andy Mainardi and other friends, he could carry on his dealing without worrying about people across the hall or upstairs getting suspicious, and besides, Larry liked living in a big house with all the boys. If Phi Delta Theta wouldn't have him, then he would set up on his own. He slept in the house one night. There were so many cockroaches that to defend himself he kept a sneaker in his hand all night. The next day he called an exterminator and paid cash to have the whole house bombed with roach killer.

That night he moved in with Marcia.

* * *

Even L.A. thought Larry was crazy. Every time the son-of-a-bitch made a few bucks he would pump it right back into the next deal.

"Why don't you just take fifty percent, or even twenty, and put it away somewhere, in a safe-deposit box or something?" L.A. would ask. He had been saving from his drug earnings for several years and had almost thirty thousand dollars. "It does add up," said L.A.

Larry would just laugh.

"And let inflation eat me alive?" he said. Larry's philosophy was: The only way to make money dealing is to keep increasing the margin—the bigger the buy, the lower the cost and the greater the profit. He said, "If you want to make progress you got to keep letting the money roll!"

"When do you stop?" asked L.A.

"When do *you* stop?"

"When I've got fifty grand together, that's when I'm getting out," said L.A.

Larry laughed. "Fifty thousand dollars! You're nuts! I'll be happy if I can put together twenty."

"Don't you want a boat?" said L.A. "I'd like to have some financial security, to be able to buy a boat, a nice car, a big house. Don't you want those things?"

In fact, Larry had never really imagined such goals. Dealing was a way to get by, it was fun, and it earned spending money and helped pay his bills. Even with his loans and scholarship job, money remained tight. Through most of his freshman and sophomore years he had periodically made trips to a clinic near Drexel University, which was just a block east of Penn's campus, where he and his friends would donate a pint of blood for twenty-five dollars.

Yet L.A. remembers Larry seemed intrigued by the fifty-thousand-dollar mark, and within months he had adopted it as his own.

Larry told Marcia that after fifty thousand dollars he was getting out. It was a lot of money, but it was the first time Marcia had known him to contemplate stopping. Larry even had himself half convinced.

Marcia was hopeful, but L.A. was suspicious. He guessed it would be harder for Larry to quit than that. His younger partner enjoyed it too much. You could see it in the way his eyes lit up when he was putting together a deal, or in how much he enjoyed presiding over the "breaks," as the packing sessions were called. Larry enjoyed being the king of his own little circle. As time passed, the two dealers' roles reversed. L.A. came to consider dealing a short-term risky business, a way to make a few fast bucks and stay high. He enjoyed the constant partying and the drugs, but scrambling to put together deals and to sell more and more dope was not his idea of a good time. But as the deals and profits continued to grow, Larry's goals grew with them.

To Larry, it was obvious that his partner's strength was not marketing. L.A. had better contacts—by now there were four or five Florida pot dealers eager to do business with them—but Larry felt he was doing 90 percent of the work. So toward the middle of his junior year Larry enforced a new division of labor. From then on, L.A. would be responsible for running back and forth to Florida every two weeks or so. Larry would handle packaging, marketing, and sales. It made sense. Larry worked his magic at Penn, while L.A. fed the inventory.

Of course, as L.A. knew, the unspoken agenda in this arrangement was that he took the bulk of the risk. Dealing pot on a college campus was not terribly risky. By 1976, national surveys of high school students indicated that more than 60 percent had smoked marijuana. On college campuses, where so many students lived away from home and without any supervision, those numbers were higher—one study found more than 80 percent were casual marijuana users. In most cities, campuses were free zones for recreational drug use. Fifty-three percent of the nation's students believed that laws against marijuana ought to be repealed. But venture off campus—and not just with an ounce or two in your backpack but with a hundred pounds or more packed into suitcases—and travel across state lines, and you were flirting with a prison sentence. Not all college students fully comprehended this. They tended to believe that the rest of society was as flexible as campus cops and administrators, or as for- giving as their parents. L.A. knew his trips to Florida were risky, but they were also fun. They were adventures that enhanced his repu- tation among friends, and they earned him 50 percent of the profits from Larry's remarkable sales network—which by the end of junior year reached off campus and even out of state (for instance, Paul Mikuta had left Penn and was attending college in Rochester, New York, but he still frequently bought wholesale from Larry. Larry had made other friends at Penn State, and at other college campuses). L.A. figured the risks he took for the business were worth it, but he tried to be careful.

Because most pot was distributed on college campuses, the busi- ness tended to dry up at the end of May and stay dormant until September. Off-season dealing was potentially more lucrative. De- mand fell off sharply, while supply held steady—the Puerto Ricans, Cubans, and Colombians getting rich off pot in Florida weren't in college. So a dealer looking to make a big buy could get incredible summer bargains. Larry was eager to take advantage of the opportunity, but L.A. balked. Off-season was also the most dangerous time to make buys in Florida because the various federal, state, and local agencies busting dealers didn't take off for the summer either. So there were fewer dealers and more cops—too many cops.

But Larry was insistent. He had parlayed the first few hundred dollars he made early in his sophomore year into about forty thousand dollars, and he saw a chance of closing in on his fifty-thousand-dollar goal before the summer off-season. He went to work on L.A., ragging him about being such a doper that he had gotten lazy and unmotivated, threatening to cut him out of the business next year—which was okay with L.A. because he was due to graduate in a few weeks anyway— and otherwise needling him. When Larry was able to put together thirty thousand dollars for the buy, L.A. gave in.

So Larry's reluctant partner flew to Fort Lauderdale. He called his main contact, a would-be pro golfer named Sammy whom he had known in high school in California. Sammy hooked him up with a dealer who was selling Hawaiian, which was the current favored brand of potent weed—$280 per pound. L.A. liked to buy Hawaiian dope because it meant dealing with Americans, usually Californians like himself. He was always frightened by the Hispanics. L.A. spoke very little Spanish and never quite felt in control of the situation. But with his own crowd he felt he could relax. So he met with the Hawaiian dealers and right away they all got blitzed. The next morning he woke up in his hotel room with more than a hundred pounds of ragweed. He had been had.

"Larry, I can barely get high off this stuff," he said, in a mournful long-distance phone call.

"Then why did you buy it?"

"I didn't know. I was wrecked . . . what can I say?"

Disgusted, he said, "Maybe we can still sell it."

But L.A. said no. "I think I can trade out of it down here," he said.

So L.A. spent several more days, all the while exposing himself to greater and greater risk, calling around to all of his contacts trying to dump the lousy weed. He got rid of about nine thousand dollars' worth of it, and recovered a lump of cash, but the bulk of the so-called Hawaiian just sat in his hotel room like a bad joke. So L.A. called Sammy and threatened him every way he knew how. The golfer was unsympathetic—"Don't you try it before you buy it?"—but he agreed to help. He called L.A. later to say he had set up a meet with somebody who would take the rest of the load off his hands.

L.A. drove out to an apartment building outside of Fort Lauderdale, the same place where he had picked up the dope two days earlier. He parked his car outside the building and walked upstairs, leaving three plastic garbage bags full of pot—seventy-five pounds in all—in the trunk of his car. As he crossed the lobby the crowd made him nervous, but he knew that he had to dump this stuff or he and Larry were going to take a beating. It was even more alarming when, inside his friend's apartment, there were three other people L.A. had never met before. Sammy introduced everyone, which calmed L.A. somewhat, and then they sat down and counted out the money. It was all there. So Sammy and L.A. walked out to the parking lot. Sammy went to his car; L.A. went to his. They drove to a prearranged spot off to the side of the apartment building, where L.A. was to get out of the car and move the bags to Sammy's trunk.

But just as L.A. got his trunk open and reached in for a bag, he heard, "Hold it right there!"

He stood up, startled, and there were cars pulling up all around him, and two young men pointing shotguns at his head.

L.A. thought, *Oh, shit, we're being ripped off!* But after a closer look at the men with guns, a worse thought occurred. *Oh, shit, we're busted.*

Poor L.A. He was back in Philadelphia to graduate in June, but beyond that his whole life was on hold. He was afraid to see his parents for fear they would see how down he was and work the truth out of him. So even though his mother fell seriously ill in Los Angeles, he spent the summer of 1976 laying low in Philly. His conscience bothered him about that. He didn't dare start looking for a job because then he would have to disclose his arrest, and besides, who knew where he would be in six months? Prison terrified him. He was afraid to think more than a few days ahead. Larry let him have a room at 3939 Chestnut, even though having him around was depressing. L.A. tended to be an introspective, moody guy anyway. His arrest sent him into a six-month-long funk. When he was well stoned—which was most of the time—sometimes he would weep.

"You'll look good in stripes," Larry would joke. "I'll send you a jar of Vaseline every month."

Andy Mainardi, who was around 3939 Chestnut a lot that summer, told Larry to lay off.

"I'm just kidding," said Larry. "Somebody's got to try and cheer him up."

"Give the guy a break," said Andy.

"Come on," Larry said. "What's gonna happen to him? He's a college kid dealing pot."

There was a measure of unspoken hostility between Larry and L.A. that summer. L.A. had always believed that Larry was passing most of the risk off on him, but he had never adequately assessed how much risk that was. L.A.'s lawyer in Florida had told him that this was a case with "exposure." He wasn't sure exactly what that meant, but assumed it had something to do with the case's notoriety. Back in Philadelphia Larry had gotten a big kick out of the word. Around 3939 Chestnut the fun word for that summer was "exposure."

Everybody laughed except L.A. Larry's little jokes infuriated him, and when Larry got off on one of his tangents about risk taking, about the importance of taking risks and about what a risk-taker he, Larry, was . . . well, it made L.A. want to throw up in his partner's lap. He should have had the good sense to stop taking Larry's risks a long time ago.

But Larry felt entitled to rag his partner a bit. The bust had cost him. He had been hoping to turn his money over once more before the semester ended and end up close to his goal of fifty thousand dollars. But he had lost his complete stake in the deal, which was nearly twenty thousand, and he had kicked in almost fifteen thousand to help with his partner's legal defense. He still had a few thousand dollars left, but on Larry's private net-worth sheet he was nearly wiped out. And though he never directly confronted L.A. with his feelings (that was not Larry's style), down deep he blamed his partner for the loss. L.A. should have known better than to get blitzed before making such an important buy—how did he know what he was getting? It was clear the dealers in Florida had suckered him with some terrific weed and then slipped him the garbage. Larry felt his own mistake had been hazarding his cash with such a hopeless pothead.

By the end of his junior year there was very little of the old marathon doper left in Larry Lavin. He was 90 percent business. Larry still enjoyed partying, and when his studies were done and his money was counted and tucked away he enjoyed getting high as much as anyone. But business was business. Larry's thick black hair no longer hung down to his shoulders. He still combed it across his forehead, but it was carefully barbered around the ears and in back. In keeping with his more conservative image, he had traded in the '66 Nova for a big white '73 Impala—paying nearly four thousand dollars in cash. Marcia was domesticating Larry. Her parakeets filled their apartment with soft chirping all day. Larry had a soft blue carpet installed. Marcia draped an easy chair and sofa with paisley covers and scattered throw pillows and blankets she had crocheted herself. She painted the kitchen yellow and kept it immaculate, with flowered curtains over the sink and neat racks and shelves for spices. Larry bought a brand–new Sony TV and two aquariums, one for keeping hermit crabs and the other for tropical fish. Marcia had a black cat named Spooky. Corners and surfaces and windows and even the tops of Larry's precious Advent speakers sprouted like tropical forests. It was the first real home Larry had known since leaving his parents' house on Highland Street in Haverhill five years ago.

But although Larry's living habits had quieted considerably, his dealing had not slowed. To the contrary, the time that Larry had formerly spent out carousing was now spent wheeling and dealing. Marcia more or less staked out the bedroom as private turf. Whenever people stopped by to visit Larry—and they came and went at all hours of the day and night—Marcia would do her best to make them feel unwelcome, often retreating to the bedroom with a defiant slam of the door. She grew to hate the telephone—Larry had five of them, five different lines, and it was not at all unusual for him to spend all night talking on them, sometimes two or three calls at the same time. For her the phones embodied the business and were an ever-present rival for Larry's attention and heart. His premed classes took most of his time during the day, and studying and talking on the phone kept him awake most of the night.

One evening, when Marcia had contrived to get Larry away from the phones by taking him out to dinner, he fell asleep at the table!

Now that she was living with him, Marcia fought harder against the dealing. She wanted it to stop; it was foolhardy and it frightened her. But having spoken her mind, and having been reassured by Larry that he was about ready to stop, Marcia was not inclined to be a nag. Larry had such a winning way about him. He would start off arguing, then he would just listen or walk away. He would come back an hour later, smiling, contrite, acknowledging the truth of Marcia's complaint, promising some sort of compromise. For a few weeks he might even strive to do his dealings out of Marcia's sight. But the all-day, all-night routine would eventually return, and there would be another row over it. Marcia knew that if it came right down to it, she could either put up or shut up. As a junior in college, Marcia was willing to put up with it a while longer. Larry had, after all, begun to settle down.

But there was no use trying to stop him during the summer of 1976. Larry was a man possessed. He *had* to make back the money he had lost. It had taken almost two years of dealing to reach that thirty-thousand-dollar level, and now he was almost back to zero. Larry had the necessary connections. He knew where to buy mari-juana, and, even in the campus off-season, he had enough customers to sell it. All he needed was one more big deal to get back on his feet.

His determination took some of the fun out of dealing. This was the first summer he had devoted full-time to it. He felt restless staying in West Philly all summer. The year before, in the summer after his sophomore year, Larry had managed the frat house's rental program, and he had worked with Paul Mikuta. He and Paul had worked for the Mikuta family's roofing company, until Larry got fired for goofing off. Then he had driven a taxi for another small company owned by Paul's father. Larry had gotten to know the back roads and beautiful estates of Philadelphia's Main Line suburbs. He and a friend one afternoon broke into several big houses and stole odd items from mantelpieces and bookshelves, then left little notes behind. In one house they had sat at the dining room table, sipped whiskey, and taken a golf club; in another Larry had unplugged a telephone and carried that home—Larry had this thing about telephones. "Can you imagine coming home to discover that someone has broken into your house and stolen . . . *your telephone?*" Larry would say. He thought that was *so* funny.

But this summer there was little time for fun and games. He worked a few small deals with friends in western Pennsylvania, and for the big deal he needed in order to get back on his feet, he contrived a plan. He would wait until Phi Delta Theta's rental account was fat at midsummer, use it to make a big buy in Florida, sell as much as he could by the end of summer, and be in good shape for an even bigger deal by the time senior year began.

Larry was so desperate that, for the first and last time, he planned to make the run to Florida himself.

First Larry had promised Marcia a vacation. He still had a few thousand dollars left after L.A.'s debacle. He and Marcia took off first for New Orleans, where they stayed with the family of a wealthy classmate Larry had known at Phillips Exeter.

It was a style of life that wowed Larry and Marcia. His friend belonged to a fabulously wealthy social circle, people who lived on estates surrounded by high fences, where you had to show an I.D. card just to get in. At a party one evening, cocaine was set out on tables around the swimming pool. Larry went off on a friend's motorcycle, and when he came back the crowd was all naked—all except Marcia, who sat clothed and very uncomfortable, awaiting Larry's return.

Next they flew to Florida. Larry grabbed a pile of brochures at the airport. Snapping away with Marcia's little Instamatic, he and Marcia hit every theme park and tourist trap they could squeeze into the week. At Sea World, Larry snapped a fuzzy sequence of pictures of leaping whales, performing porpoises, and a barking walrus. Marcia took Larry's picture feeding three tame deer. He wore a bright yellow sportshirt and blue-and-maroon checked pants. At the wax museum in Orlando, with Marcia mildly protesting, Larry snapped pictures of all the wax figure displays—Captain Kirk and Spock, Butch Cassidy and the Sundance Kid, Burt Reynolds in his role from the movie *Deliverance*, the Beverly Hillbillies in their jalopy, Hoss, Ben Cartwright, and Little Joe. They went to Disney World one day, Cypress Gardens the next. Larry snapped Marcia's picture before a beautiful botanical display. Marcia wore a white sundress and sandals. At Gatorland, Larry took pictures of writhing alligators, and at the Kennedy Space Center he took pictures of rockets.

Suntanned Marcia was pictured wearing a red dress sitting on Larry's lap, smiling, at Rosie O'Grady's. Larry looked sunburned and weary. Marcia looked radiantly happy. At nineteen she was slimmer and prettier than she had been two years before. Her face had outgrown some of its baby fat, and her high cheekbones framed big brown eyes. She had reason to be delighted—she had kept Larry to herself, away from telephones and nights out with the fraternity boys, for almost two weeks!

Back in Philadelphia, Marcia bought a big brown scrapbook with a cutesy painting of a kitten on the front, a binder with sticky pages of thick cardboard and clear plastic sheets that lifted to cover and protect her photographs. Snapshots from their trip filled the first ten pages. Marcia lovingly labeled and dated the pictures of their first vacation together.

When they returned home from their vacation, Marcia went to northern New Jersey to visit her folks.

Larry talked Paul Mikuta, who was home from Rochester for the summer, into going down to Florida with him. It would be like another week-long vacation, only this one with the boys! Paul Mikuta was a big, brassy guy who swaggered through life, courting risk with bravado. Having Paul along had turned a nerve-wracking trip—with memories of L.A.'s bust so fresh in mind—into a joyride. Larry figured he could complete the trip and package and sell the shipment before Marcia returned in two weeks.

So Larry and Paul flew to Miami together, and after a night on the town, they met with two of L.A.'s contacts and bought the marijuana. They had planned to just drive back to Philadelphia together, but at the last minute something came up in Paul's family and he had to rush home. Paul carried some of the pot with him in his suitcase on the plane, but Larry refused to get on the airplane with such a large amount of contraband.

He felt deflated when Paul left. He was left alone in a hotel room with nearly a hundred pounds of pot.

First he bought three big suitcases, the kind with wheels at the bottom. Then he bought a one-way ticket to Philadelphia from Trailways, checked the bags, and settled in a seat far back in the bus for a long, long drive home.

It seemed to take a whole day just to get out of Florida. July in the Sunshine State was sweltering. He couldn't get comfortable on the bus. When he tried to read, it upset his stomach, so he watched the scenery for hour after hour.

About five hours into the drive, somewhere in northern Florida, a tough-looking young woman got on the bus, walked down the aisle, smiled at Larry, and sat down next to him. She had pale blue eyes and straight blond hair and was wearing a faded pair of jeans over a pudgy figure. She said her name was Heidi. Considering that there were many empty seats in the back of the bus, and considering the way she kept smiling at him, Larry figured she had more in mind to pass the time than conversation. Somewhere near the border of North Carolina, Larry slipped his arm around her shoulder and she reached down to unzip his pants. And there, three rows behind the nearest passenger, in broad daylight, Heidi sucked and stroked him to orgasm, and then loudly—in case anyone on the bus hadn't noticed what was going on back there already—spit his semen into the aisle.

Larry began to consider that this had not been a good idea. He had always lectured L.A. about staying inconspicuous.

Heidi then started talking about herself to him, loudly—too loudly. She said her parents had sent her to a mental hospital because she liked to have sex too much—it was hard to imagine that anyone on the bus was not listening to her—but that she had gotten back at them by having sex with everyone in the place, patients, orderlies, doctors . . . maybe they could get off at the next stop and go to a motel. . . . Toward late afternoon, a few hours away from Washington, D.C., she stood up and walked to the front of the bus, shouting for the driver to pull over. He did, and she bounded down the front steps and threw up by the side of the road. All eyes on the bus turned to Larry, who smiled sheepishly and looked away, willing himself someplace else. Then Heidi got back aboard, sat back down next to him, and fell asleep.

At the next stop, Larry told Heidi that he had to take a leak. He phoned his friend Stu Thomas from the station and begged him to drive down and meet him in Washington.

"It's a nightmare," said Larry. "You got to save me."

Several hours later, as the bus pulled into the terminal in Washington, Larry again told Heidi he was going to the men's room. Outside the bus he grabbed the driver and explained that he wanted to get off the bus, now. So the driver removed Larry's bags from the compartment underneath, and Larry pulled them into the men's room with him, where he waited until well after the bus was scheduled to leave. Then he let another ten minutes go by just for good measure. He eased from the men's room warily, and felt enormously relieved to find the bus, and Heidi, gone.

But as he waited for Stu arrive, Larry noticed that his bags smelled funny, and that small pools formed under them when he left them sitting in the same spot for a few minutes. He opened one of the suitcases after loading them in the trunk of Stu's car, and was nearly knocked over by the odor. Locked in the hot compartment under the bus for nearly two days, the pot had gone bad. It smelled as potent as ammonia.

Back at Marcia's apartment Larry dumped out the sodden, foul-smelling weed. Fistful by fistful, Larry attacked it with a hair dryer and packaged it. But the stuff never sold well. Larry was able to replenish the fraternity's bank account, but he ended in debt to the friends who had put up money for the trip.

He made the best of it, telling his friends at 3939 about the sex maniac who gave him blowjobs all the way from Orlando to Washington, and everyone agreed that things like that only happened to Larry Lavin. But inwardly it hurt. Larry felt that all his hard work over two years had been for naught.

Word of Larry's disaster spread unhappily through the small dealing community at Penn. He had become a cottage industry, and his fall was sure to swamp a few lesser entrepreneurs. Larry was performing service much valued by his fellow students. Use of marijuana and hashish was so prevalent on college campuses in 1976 that dealers were like precious resources—they were the ones taking criminal risks so that students could maintain their relatively "safe" one- or two-ounce stashes. At Penn, Larry was trading in such large amounts that he had become dealer to the dealers. He made the most money, but he also took the greatest share of risk.

To repay his debts and get back on his feet in time to profit during his senior year, Larry knew he would have to take even more chances than before. Few student dealers dared branch their drug sales off campus; in addition to the greater risks involved in getting caught by municipal authorities instead of campus cops, there was a greater chance of getting ripped off, beaten up, or even killed. But Larry was in a hurry. It was through another dealer that Larry was introduced early in his senior year to Tyrone, an uneducated hustler from Southwest Philly who sold marijuana on the streets of his neighborhood. Tyrone was a slight, short, light-skinned heroin addict, who had a hulking bodyguard named Gene who accompanied him at all times. Larry's new partner, Andy Mainardi, wanted nothing to do with Tyrone and his people. L.A., who was still waiting to face charges in Broward County, Florida, when school began again in September, told Larry he was crazy to risk dealing with Philly blacks. "Think about Marcia," he said. But Larry felt he could trust Tyrone so long as he treated him honestly. Besides, Larry needed him. Tyrone was the only dealer who seemed able to sell Larry's spoiled Florida pot. He bought it in small amounts, just five to ten pounds at a time, and always came back for more.

It was also during this period of desperation that Larry was introduced to an ambitious young South Philly street vendor named Billy Motto.

Billy was a few years younger than Larry. He was short and fit, a smart, cocky self-made kid from South Philly who always seemed as though he were ready to pounce on something. When he stood he stood straight, balanced like a fighter on the balls of his feet. When he was sitting he would sit straight, leaning slightly forward, with his hands poised to gesture freely while he talked. There were traces of old trouble with acne on Billy's face, but it just made his good looks more rugged. Billy had dark blond hair and perfect white teeth and piercing green eyes. He liked to wear expensive jogging outfits and jewelry.

Contrasted with Larry's easy suburban, prep school, Ivy League background, Billy's background was rough and remarkable.

He had grown up on the rough sidewalks and streets of Passyunk Avenue, at the industrial bottom of South Philly. He was smoking dope by the first years of grade school, and by the time he was in the sixth grade he was hooked on heroin.

Billy would joke sardonically about the hall monitor who banged on the closed bathroom stall door, shouting, "Open up, Motto, I know you're smoking cigarettes in there!" as Billy had emptied a syringe into a vein of his forearm.

He was then thirteen years old and he was killing himself. His liver was shot and his skin was pocked and riddled by rampant acne. He weighed only ninety-eight pounds the night his friends drove up to Saint Agnes Hospital on Broad Street, opened a door, rolled him unconscious to the sidewalk, and sped away. Billy had overdosed, and they were afraid to be caught with him.

Billy recovered from the overdose, and was sent to The Bridge, a drug treatment center, where for the first time in his young life he faced down his self-destructive tendencies. He stayed for fourteen months, gaining weight, having tattoos and needle tracks removed from his arms by plastic surgery, learning the joys of living drug free and forming, for the first time, a measure of self-respect.

He would later say, "It got me back in touch with life. I started living again and I rediscovered all the things that were beautiful in life, like a pretty girl, like a kiss."

He spent the rest of his teenage years in a halfway house away from his old neighborhood. Billy never went back to school. He worked as an assistant in a funeral parlor, and in his off hours he discovered girls. He spent his money going to dances and discos, and discovered that without drugs he was considered handsome and charming. Billy was fastidious to excess about his appearance—he had his teeth cleaned regularly by a dental hygienist, his nails tended by a manicurist, his hair barbered weekly. He worked out at a South Philadelphia gym like a professional athlete, ate healthy foods, and ordered Perrier water at bars. Although drugs and alcohol were a big part of the social scene in South Philly during his teens, Billy never backed off his new, strict regimen.

Eventually, Billy's father gave him a '65 Chevy and made him a partner in the family's small produce business, which sold wares from four milk crates on the corner of Juniper and Sansom streets in Center City. Billy's self-assurance and charm came to life on the street corner. He would flirt with the pretty girls who walked by and entertain the customers with his cheerful salesmanship—"Three pounds for a dollar, a quarter will put you in order!" Billy loved being on the streets, and with the low overhead, he and his father made good money. When the cops came by and told them to get moving, Billy would see his Dad slip them a few bucks to let them be. On the side he collected numbers for the illegal lottery and began keeping book on sporting events—something that was common and accepted in his neighborhood.

Billy loved the produce business. On his own he began to build it into something more. He used his earnings from running numbers to expand, buying additional crates of lettuce and tomatoes and getting up at dawn to hustle them in hoagie shops and restaurants, pushing his business farther and farther west from Center City along Walnut Street. Restaurant owners would look at the cocky kid the first time he came in with a crate of lettuce and tell him to get lost.

"We have a regular supplier," they would say.

"I'll beat their price," Billy would say.

They would tell him again to get lost.

But that afternoon Billy would come back in, nicely dressed, with a group of his friends. They would order a big meal and leave a big tip. He would keep coming back that way until people took him seriously, and he picked up their business. By the fall of 1976 Billy's produce route stretched from Center City all the way out to the popular student eateries around Penn.

It was through friends Billy made around the campus that he started selling pot. A dealer named Hank Katz, whose father owned a popular hoagie shop off campus, fronted Billy five pounds of pot, which Billy quickly sold to friends in South Philly and paid for with a brown bag full of rumpled bills. Then he took ten pounds and sold that. It was so easy! When Billy asked for twenty pounds, Katz said his supplier wouldn't sell him that much without meeting him first.

So Billy was introduced to the supplier.

He met Larry at Andy Mainardi's apartment on Forty-third Street. The South Philly produce vendor said he wanted to buy twenty pounds, and instead Larry laid out forty pounds of Colombian.

Larry was clearly the better person to be dealing with.

"I'm impressed, but I can't afford that much," said Billy.

"I'll front you," said Larry.

"How much?"

"Three hundred and sixty-five." That would put Billy in debt to Larry for $14,600.

"I'll give you three hundred," said Billy. "And I only want twenty pounds."

Larry grinned. They spoke each other's language. They eventually compromised at $325 per pound. Billy took thirty pounds.

He was back within the week with messy bundles of small bills, ones, fives, tens, and twenties all thrown in together in a big brown grocery bag. No one ever paid up that fast.

"Couldn't you bring me money a little neater than this?" Larry groaned, but Billy could see that he was impressed.

"Hey, don't push your luck," said Billy.

After that, Billy continued dealing through Hank at the hoagie shop, but he began selling larger and larger amounts. Larry would have liked to deal with Billy directly, but protocol demanded that the middleman, who had brought Billy into the business, continue to profit.

But there was instant rapport between the preppie Irish kid and the charming Italian street vendor. In time they dealt with each other directly, on an almost weekly basis. Billy found Larry's Massachusetts accent as comical as Larry found his thick South Philly patois. Billy could see that this tall, black-haired college kid was as serious a businessman as he was—he had expected some longhair, stoned wifty-eyed. Larry found Billy's style impressive and was amazed by his trustworthiness and ability to sell. From that first meeting on, whenever Larry sold something directly to Billy, they would begin the same way: Larry would name a price, Billy would make a lower bid, and then they would haggle and laugh until they found a comfortable middle ground. Billy, who felt insecure about his lack of formal education, was flattered to be treated as an equal by a college kid. Larry, who like most suburban youths felt somewhat deprived of hard knocks, got a charge out of dealing with authentic street characters like Tyrone and Billy, but with Billy it was more than that. He liked Billy.

There were rumors that Billy Motto was "connected," that he had ties with the city's legendary organized-crime family. After all, he had an Italian surname, he was from South Philly, and he ran numbers on the street. Billy didn't go out of his way to dispel this impression. It was good for business. He was feared as someone too dangerous to cross, which helps a business survive on city streets. Billy subtly cultivated this image by employing friends and relatives to accompany him wherever he went. There was menace implied by the quiet, dark, muscular men who stood in the background and took orders from Billy. If you were with Billy and he wanted to order out for pizza, one of his men would promptly run out and get pizza. This was a source of constant amusement to the Penn crowd. He never personally handled the pot. He believed that if he never touched it, it would be a lot harder to get caught dealing it. So Billy would deliver money, haggle over prices and purchase orders, and then he would shake hands and leave. He had this superstition about leaving. After making a deal with Larry, he would always turn back before he left and say, "Tell me it's going to be okay, Larry."

Larry would grin and say, "It's going to be okay, Billy."

Then one of Billy's boys would come by an hour or two later and pick up the order.

In his business records, Larry penciled in "Billy South Philly," which soon became just "B.S.P." It was to be a fruitful collaboration.

With the added efforts of Tyrone and Billy South Philly, Larry was back on his feet shortly after his senior year began. He was soon swinging hundred-pound pot deals again on a regular basis. Tyrone had begun supplying Quaaludes—which were obtained by his neighborhood friends on Medicaid who knew physicians in Southwest Philly who sold them scripts—illegal prescriptions. Larry had one friend who could obtain jars of pharmaceutical cocaine, which was a sort of novelty item in late 1976; Larry began using it on occasion to help him stay awake during class. Sometimes when he was working a pot deal he would be offered an ounce or two of cocaine on the side, which he accepted for his own use and as something to pass out to his friends—like a little bonus for paying up on time. It was fun, but too expensive for most students. Besides, his customers still wanted more pot than he could buy.

With many of his earlier suppliers now graduated from college, Larry found he was buying most of his pot from Florida. Having personally resolved never to make a Florida run again, Larry needed someone to step in for L.A. For this he offered Andy Mainardi a chance to become a full partner in the growing business.

It was risky, but Andy trusted and admired Larry. He liked associating with him. Most of the people involved in drug dealing were spacey holdovers from hippie days, but not Larry. Larry was smart and reliable. If he said he was going to meet you someplace, he was there on the dot. Larry was the first person Andy knew to attach an answering machine to his phone, which made it easy to get ahold of him night or day. And Larry was so personable and charming. Andy thought he was a natural salesman, someone whom people instantly liked and trusted. Once, when Andy was still a freshman, he had attended a party at Phi Delta Theta. There must have been a hundred people in the frat house. Larry was out somewhere, and didn't show up until the party was in full swing. But as soon as Larry came in the door it was like . . . *the king had arrived!* People just mobbed him. Larry's personal magnetism was stronger than that of anyone Andy had ever met.

Andy had profited by his dealings with Larry. During his freshman year he had bought two or three pounds twice a month from Larry. By sophomore year he was buying up to ten pounds every two weeks. And some of Larry's magnetism rubbed off. When Andy threw parties at his house off campus on Forty-first Street, sometimes two to three hundred people showed up. Andy always footed the bill and paid the lion's share of expenses for renting the house. Dealing Larry's pot had given Andy a lot of good times—and he even had a few thousand dollars of his own in the bank! So when Larry asked him to start running to Florida, Andy found it hard to say no. He figured he was smarter than L.A. No one was going to bust Andy Mainardi.

Andy liked the idea of running to Florida. He disliked living in the city so much that he had planned on leaving Penn that year anyway. Larry had talked him into staying, so now he was making money and looking forward to spending his winter in a warm place. He drove down by himself in a rented car for his first trip, but it was such a long drive that he resolved to take the train thereafter. Planes were too risky for all but the recklessly ballsy—guys like Mikuta. So on the second trip Andy rented a sleeper car. He passed the time getting high, reading, and listening to music. When he got to his hotel room in Florida, it seemed as if Larry was on the phone every couple of hours, fussing over his money and pot like a mother hen.

He took his second train trip south in November, and made his connections without incident in Fort Lauderdale. On the morning after making the buy he boarded a train north with about sixty-five pounds of pot stuffed in two large suitcases. He worried a little about the suitcases—after three loads the luggage smelled strong enough to give someone a contact high. Andy had taken the precaution of reserving a sleeping berth on the train and getting his ticket in advance so that he wouldn't have to go to the ticket counter, but at the station Amtrak's computers were down and everyone had to reconfirm their tickets at the counter. He felt conspicuous, a college kid with two huge, reeking suitcases, but everything had gone smoothly. Andy tended to be jumpy. In Jacksonville it made him nervous when, early in the afternoon, a man in a suit and tie got on and took the sleeper directly across the aisle. Out on the platform he had heard a barking dog. *Now, why would someone be taking a dog on the train?* Andy told himself to calm down and lit a joint. It was probably just a blind person with a seeing-eye dog.

It was almost two hours to Savannah. Shortly before they were due to arrive there, the door to his compartment crashed open, a gun was pointed at his face.

A voice screamed, "Freeze!"

Andy was allowed one phone call at the Chatham County Jail in Savannah. Marcia answered the phone. It was November 11, 1976, Marcia's twenty-first birthday. She had some people over for a party in the apartment, so she had a hard time hearing Andy at first. He asked to speak to Larry.

Larry's voice came on with its usual cheer: "Andy, what's up?"

"Larry, I'm in jail. In Savannah. I was arrested."

"Oh, my gosh."

There was silence on the Philadelphia end.

Then Larry asked, "Does that mean they got it all?"

L.A. was sentenced in early 1977. After all that worrying, it turned out that Larry had been right. The judge gave L.A. ninety days at a work-release center. Too inexperienced to realize he had just been cut a huge break, L.A. shot his lawyer a look of shock and panic.

"I thought I was supposed to get probation!" he said.

"I told you there was exposure in this case," said L.A.'s lawyer.

So *that's* what he had meant by exposure! It meant jail time!

"Appeal it," said L.A.

Over the next few hours the lawyer was able to convince L.A. of his good fortune—an appellate judge could always remand the case with instructions for a *sterner* sentence. Larry's former partner was given a job at a bait-and-tackle shop outside of Fort Lauderdale. It turned out his co-workers there were small-time pot dealers themselves, so L.A. spent his ninety days fishing and getting high. On the phone he was able to help Larry steer Andy to his old connections in Florida.

In legal battles over the next few months, Andy's Savannah lawyer managed to get the charges against him dropped. It was a big story in *High Times* magazine. Police in Florida and Georgia were cracking down on marijuana smuggling by train, bringing specially trained dogs on board to sniff out contraband. On the same train with Andy they had busted two other college students, en route to other campuses. At first the police had thought the three were working together, but it turned out that each came from a different school. So there were deficiencies in the search warrants that led to the charges being dropped.

Andy had learned his lesson. He told Larry that he had been convicted of the charge and placed on probation. He remained partners with Larry, but he had a good excuse for not taking road trips anymore.

Larry recovered more quickly from the losses and legal expenses of Andy's bust. He recruited Paul Mikuta and two other younger students to make runs for him, and from then on the trips were made strictly by car. His business was spread throughout the area around Penn's campus, in South and in Southwest Philly. Limited only by how much marijuana, hash, and Quaaludes he could find to buy, Larry's net-worth sheet soon passed the thirty-thousand-dollar mark again and kept on climbing.

He did most of his banking at two Girard Bank branches, one on Thirty-sixth Street and the other at the corner of Thirty-ninth and Market streets. It wasn't sophisticated. Larry just walked in regularly with his pockets stuffed with cash. He would bring in as much as twenty-five hundred dollars at a time, changing fives, tens, and twenties into hundreds. On one visit, a bank executive told Larry that it was generally known that there was a large drain on hundreds in the Penn area. So Larry began to use busier bank branches in Center City to make his exchanges.

At home one afternoon, Larry got a call from one of the banks.

"We just wanted to know if everything went all right with your transaction earlier today," the man said.

Larry felt sweat forming on his palms.

"What do you mean?"

"We think you might have been shortchanged."

"Oh. Wait a minute. Let me check," said Larry. He set the phone down. There was nothing for him to check; he had already sent the stacks of hundreds on their way back down to Florida with Paul. He stood confused in the center of the living room for a few moments, then returned to the phone.

"I think you're right. There seems to be some missing."

"Oh, we're so relieved to hear that," said the man from Girard. "We came up with five thousand extra today, and we thought it might be yours."

Larry stopped by the branch the next morning to collect a neat stack of fifty one-hundred-dollar bills . . . no questions asked.

"Why do you want to go to dental school? Why not medical school?" asked the interviewer from Penn's School of Dentistry.

Larry was ready for the question. He knew that dental schools were wary of applicants who had chosen dentistry because they couldn't get into medical school. They preferred students with a singular interest in dentistry.

"That's not a problem for me," said Larry. And he told the interviewer how he had wanted to be a dentist ever since he was a kid, about the work that had been done on his own teeth and how the dentist had befriended him.

"And besides, there are doctors and there are dentists, and I want to be a dentist."

"What do you see as the crucial difference?"

"Being a dentist is not the same as being a doctor," Larry explained. "When you're a doctor you're dealing with life and death every day. As a dentist, the worst that can happen is, well . . . if you mess up, it's only a tooth!"

"You could not be more wrong," said the interviewer, who seemed offended by the remark. He proceeded to put Larry in his place.

"I'm an oral surgeon," he said, "and I do deal with life and death every day. . . ." As the doctor of dentistry lectured, Larry grew increasingly dismayed. But then the questions moved into an area where Larry felt more comfortable.

"How are you going to pay for it?" the interviewer asked.

"I have some money saved, and I plan on applying for financial aid," said Larry.

The interviewer grinned. "Do you know how much it costs to set up an operatory when you graduate?"

"I think the investment is currently about seventy-five thousand," said Larry.

"How are you going to get that much money?"

"I intend to work, and borrow if I have to," said Larry.

The interviewer seemed impressed with Larry's confidence. He said the school was tired of students who came expecting a free ride —and he could tell from Larry's application (which revealed nothing of his substantial drug earnings) that he would need help. The interviewer looked over Larry's grades; they had slipped somewhat as he approached graduation day, but he was still near the top of his class. He had done extremely well on his dental boards. Overall, Larry left the interview feeling that he had been impressive talking about finances, but he had probably blown it with his answer to the first question.

So when he got an acceptance letter from the dental school at Tufts, Larry assumed he would be moving at the end of the school year. Marcia agreed to go with him. She was secretly thrilled. At last Larry would be out of his drug-dealing circle at Penn! Tufts had other advantages. It offered a three-year dental program instead of four, it would take Larry back up near his home in Massachusetts, and Marcia's first physical therapy clinical assignment was in Boston (she had to successfully complete six months of clinical work after graduation in order to be licensed). Late in the spring of 1977 they had traveled to Boston and looked for an apartment. Larry began thinking about turning over his whole business to Andy Mainardi and wondered what he ought to charge him for it.

But shortly before graduation, Larry got his letter of acceptance to Penn. He was surprised, and delighted.

"So what?" said Marcia. "I thought you had decided on Tufts already."

Larry explained that Penn was his school. His older brother had gone through medical school at Penn. He didn't mention the dealing, but there was a tug-of-war going on under the surface. Marcia knew that the chances of Larry's getting out of dealing were slim if he stayed on the same campus. Larry agreed to keep his appointment in Boston at Tufts to discuss his application for financial aid.

But at the Tufts interview, Larry learned that he could expect no financial aid. Marcia thought they could still swing it in Boston, living on a tight budget with Larry finding a part-time job, but Larry had made up his mind. They were going to stay.

At the end of May 1977, Larry and Marcia got engaged. They were both graduating; they had been living together for more than a year; it seemed like the appropriate thing to do. There was no dramatic proposal; there wasn't even one particular romantic moment when the decision was made. Marcia wanted a ring, so Larry bought her a diamond mounted on a gold band. Larry said he wanted to wait until he was finished with dental school before getting married, but that was just a way of postponing the day. Marcia knew that marriage and children were what she wanted, but Larry wasn't that sure. He preferred to let things stay the way they were for a while longer. Besides, if they waited a few years he figured he'd be able to afford to help with a much nicer wedding and reception.

Shortly before graduation, they moved to an apartment at 4300 Osage Avenue that would be their home for the next three years. It was a great gray-and-tan battleship of a house, three stories high, that commanded a high hill overlooking a quiet intersection just five blocks west of Penn's main campus and only three blocks from the dental school. Set one block north of busy Baltimore Avenue, the house was the most impressive structure in a neighborhood of ornate row homes that some forty years ago was a relatively affluent residential enclave. It had long since become home to hordes of transient student renters, against whom landlords fought unceasingly to maintain the bare essentials of legal habitability. Any little patch of yard was littered and untended. Trash cans, often overturned, lined the broad uneven sidewalks with contents half in and half out. Rising above it all was 4300 Osage, reached by ascending a concrete staircase forty feet through trees and sparse but stubborn ground cover to the wide front porch, which wrapped around the west and north corner of the house. There were eight windows across the front on the second floor. A simple concrete addition had recently been added to the south end of the house, just a gray cinderblock cube built without regard to the Victorian style of the rest of the house, but it added a sunny extra room to Larry and Marcia's spacious first-floor apartment.

Larry liked the basement, which was not broken up into separate storage areas in the manner of many of the rental houses around Penn. A common basement meant it would be hard to hold him liable for anything seized down there. He put a few old dressers down there, the kind with lots of drawers that locked with skeleton keys. He stored merchandise and cash in the drawers.

On the day they moved in, Marcia opened the door to the apartment to discover that rugs were already down, furniture had been set up in the proper rooms, boxes had been unpacked and books were already on shelves, lamps were in place. . . . She turned to thank Larry, but found that he was also surprised. Larry and his friends had been moving furniture and boxes over for a week or two, but he had left it all piled in the center of the front room. He and Marcia had planned on spending most of the day unpacking boxes and arranging things. Now 80 percent of the work was already done! A note on a living room windowsill explained: Two of Larry's co-investors,

Stu Thomas and Paul Mikuta, had arrived with a bale of marijuana and needed Larry's scale and baggies. Thinking Larry and Marcia had already moved into the new place, and there being no answer at the door, they had let themselves in a window to discover the furniture and boxes. To find the things they needed they had to open the boxes, so, to make amends, they had taken an hour or two to arrange the furniture and unpack everything. Marcia didn't know whether to be furious or delighted.

She decorated the apartment cozily, painting the rooms with soothing colors, a pale blue for the living room, pale green for Larry's office and study. There was a lot more room to work with in this apartment than there had been on Baltimore Avenue. Larry bought a much larger aquarium and filled it with tropical fish: nervous silver danios that hid in the rocks at the bottom, flat square tetras and brown-and-white clown loaches, half-inch-long rasporans of neon red and blue, and a sinister black knight fish that despite its size and martial name was soon eaten by its tank companions. Illuminated against the pale yellow kitchen wall, the blue tank water assumed a glowing aqua hue. Marcia bought a white-plumed cockatoo she named Max, and twin parrots she named Chip and Dale. The plush blue rug fit on the living room floor. They picked out and framed a piece of stretched cotton fabric that was dyed in such a way that it looked like clouds against a blue sky. That was hung behind the couch in the blue living room. On other walls she hung framed needlework of her own and art prints from art shops that she and Larry liked. To make a coffee table, Larry bought an oversized baccarat board with a glass top and set it on top of a heavy wood lobster trap he had picked up one summer in Boston for five dollars. He brought home a mirror overlaid with a reprint of an old Coca-Cola poster—from the days when Coke really had a touch of cocaine in it—that read "Relieves Fatigue, Most Refreshing Drink In The World!" Just beyond the living room was a small kitchen, and then off the kitchen a hallway led back to their bedroom and a sunny back room where Larry put a big wooden desk his older brother Paul had given him, and where Marcia put her sewing machine.

Larry thought graduation was really neat—he had never attended one before. His parents and the Osborns came down. Larry and Marcia wore gowns and walked in the seemingly endless processional in the Philadelphia Civic Center to get their diplomas. Hubert H. Humphrey, battling the cancer that would kill him within the year, gave a moving oration. Afterward there was a polite party at Phi Delta Theta. Larry posed in the front door wearing his white-and-blue plaid pants and a white polo shirt with a blue collar.

* * *

While they were furnishing the new apartment, Larry and Marcia made weekly trips out to the Sears store in Upper Darby. Marcia would go off in search of a variety of things they needed—linens, silverware, furniture, shower curtains, whatever—and Larry would usually head for the tropical fish or the TVs and stereo equipment or the tools—he wasn't particularly good at using them but he loved to buy them.

On one of their trips in May, shortly before graduation, Larry ran into Tom Finchley. Tom, the son of a wealthy Pennsylvania family, had been buying and selling dope on a somewhat smaller scale than Larry all through his undergraduate years. A slender, athletic young man with fair hair and a moustache, Tom dressed in expensive clothes and liked jewelry; he wore gold rings, a gold watch, and a gold necklace. Larry and his friends distrusted Tom; he was just as avaricious as Larry but lacked Larry's boyish charm. Larry's friends, Paul Mikuta, L.A., and Andy, tried to avoid Tom, but Larry respected his resources and connections. They had done some business together, but Tom had his own connections in Florida through a Cuban named Miguel. Whenever he and Larry met they compared notes about busts, prices, and dealers.

They stood off to one side of an aisle by the tropical fish displays and briefly talked business. Lately, every time Tom saw Larry he was pushing Penn's biggest pot dealer to begin investing more in cocaine. They had been over this ground before. Tom would argue that the profit potential with coke was so much better than grass; you could mark it up more and cut it before reselling it.

"Why don't you do more with Miguel?"

"Well, you know, my guys are doing pretty good, Tom."

"Come on, Larry, you know the profits are there. What are you waiting for?"

Larry shrugged. He wasn't buying it. He knew Tom was just trying to expand his business, grab a portion of Larry's customers. If Larry agreed to start buying coke, with Tom as the middleman, Tom's volume could double or triple overnight. Miguel would charge him less, so he could make more off his own sales and he could earn a commission by acting as a broker for Larry.

"If you look at the overall percentage, you're gonna make a lot more," said Tom. "And there's less work involved."

"Yeah, but think about the risk, Tom. If someone gets caught, what's going to happen?"

"You don't have to deal with the bulk," Tom argued.

That was true. The single most risky thing about dealing pot was its bulk. It was difficult to traffic in amounts large enough for profits without handling shipments as conspicuous as hay bales.

"My customers want pot, not coke," said Larry. "If I had more than a few ounces of coke I wouldn't know where to sell it."

"You know how it works, Larry. If you start selling it, they'll start buying it. The market is there right now."

Larry wasn't so sure.

"Maybe, but my business is just starting to really pay off for me," he said. "Why should I change it now? Especially with the extra risk?"

"Look what's happened already," said Tom. "How many busts have you had this year?"

"Yeah, but not much happened to them."

Tom reminded Larry of a shipment one of Tom's people had brought back by plane; when they opened the suitcase they found that someone from baggage handling had opened it and ripped off about forty pounds of pot. Something very similar had happened on a shipment from Virginia for Larry.

But Larry knew Tom had a point. They were both increasingly aware of federal efforts to crack down on marijuana in Florida. Until recently, the big pot boats—dealers called them the "motherloads"—just anchored in the ocean outside of U.S. territorial waters, and smaller, faster boats shuttled freely back and forth from ports up and down the southeastern coastline. Now that traffic was being interrupted regularly, sometimes violently. Bales of pot tossed overboard by fleeing smugglers had begun washing up on beaches in Florida and South Carolina. The world was changing.

"They're looking for pot, not coke," said Tom. "You can slip a kilo bag inside your carry-on luggage. . . . There's *less risk*."

"Yeah," said Larry. "Less risk, but more exposure."

F O U R

Why Carry an Elephant?

Ken Weidler was a broad-backed, fresh-faced boy from central Pennsylvania when he showed up at Penn to begin dental school in the fall of 1977. He had fair hair, blue eyes, a square jaw, and perfect teeth. Despite his good looks, Ken was hesitant and awkward. He figured dental school was going to be a grind. College had been fun, but now it was time to knuckle down. His father was a dentist, so Ken expected his classmates would be like his father. Dental school would be populated by mature, serious, hardworking students preparing for a normal, responsible life. This is how he saw it. There would be no more drinking bouts, no more all-night parties, and, even more likely, no more pot. It wasn't going to be easy, but he had thought it through and he was ready for it.

That perception lasted only a few weeks. Ken found that although most of his classmates in dental school were more serious students than those he had known at Muhlenberg State College, and did tend to be more reserved socially, there was nevertheless a sizable proportion of potheads to keep him company. Ken had done some petty dealing at Muhlenberg and still had his small-time dealing connections. So, soon after moving to Philadelphia, he renewed his practice of buying marijuana a pound or two at a time and peddling enough to provide for his free personal stash.

After Christmas break, at a party thrown by Chris Furlan, a popular first-year dental student, Ken was getting high with his friends in the basement, away from the main body of the party, when they were joined by this lanky, smiling, talkative classmate with a thick mop of black hair named Larry Lavin. Ken knew Lavin as one of the more studious members of his class, or at least it seemed that way, because it was rare to see him at a party. He was surprised when Larry showed up in the basement and accepted the joint. When they started talking, Ken found Larry to be altogether different from the perception he had gathered from classes and the dental lab.

Both students lived in the West Philly neighborhood of the dental school, which is housed in a dignified stone building at Fortieth and Chestnut streets, a busy corner west of the main Penn campus. As they walked home from the party together that night, Larry invited Ken to stop in his place for a drink. Ken was impressed by how nicely Larry's apartment was furnished. They smoked a joint together in the living room—Ken admired Larry's aquarium—and talked about first impressions of dental school. Ken told Larry a little about himself, and then he said something that made Larry laugh.

"If you're ever looking for some weed, I can get you an ounce of Colombian for forty bucks."

"I can do better than that," said Larry. He got up and crossed the room. From under the sofa he pulled a box. Lifting the lid, Larry showed Ken four one-pound bags of pot.

"That's a lot of dope!" said Ken.

This made Larry laugh. "You're kidding!"

"No I'm not," said Ken. "I've never seen that much pot before."

"Look," said Larry. "This is nothing. I'll call you later this week and really show you something."

Ken left that night very stoned, and amazed that someone he had met only hours ago would reveal that much about himself. He chalked up Larry's boast about calling to show him even more pot to the effects of the wine and the dope, if he remembered it at all. But Larry did call two days later.

"We just got some in," he said.

"You're kidding."

"Can you come over right now?"

Ken walked over to Larry's apartment. Larry greeted him at the door, but instead of inviting him in, he told Ken to wait for him on the porch. He ran back in the house and then came back out and led Ken across Forty-third Street to a three-story row house. Larry let himself in and led Ken upstairs.

In a big front room there was what must have been two hundred pounds of marijuana spread out on the floor. It formed a pile deep enough that Ken could wade into it over his ankles. The room reeked with the musky sweet odor of weed. There were about eight people —they looked like undergrads—working away at it, breaking it down to smaller amounts, weighing it, and packing it in Ziploc bags. They hardly even looked up when Larry and Ken came in. Larry bent over and pinched some of the new shipment into a rolling paper, deftly rolled a joint, and passed it to his friend.

All that afternoon, Larry held court. People came and went from the apartment handing him stacks of money, tens and twenties and even hundred-dollar bills. Larry accumulated a pile of the money beside his chair—there must have been thousands! His customers would leave with shopping bags filled with pot. All of the people who came in knew Larry, and they seemed to get such a kick out of him. They sat around the front room sipping beer and passing joints while Larry laughed and talked and talked and talked.

Ken was dazzled. What an amazing guy this Larry Lavin was! He had only known him for two days, yet Larry treated Ken like his best friend. He was not at all what Ken thought a big-time drug dealer would be like. Larry and his associates were college kids just like him, looking for a good time. Only *they* were making money—what looked to Ken like *a lot* of money. It was like something Ken had seen in the movies, all the money just piled up there on the floor.

Larry told Ken that they were always looking for new places to break stuff down. So Ken walked with him over to his apartment, which was situated perfectly. Next door was a supermarket parking lot that was set just a short drop from the foot of a fire escape. The fire escape gave Ken a side entrance out of sight from the street. Larry saw right away that instead of looking conspicuous walking down the street with huge suitcases or gunnysacks filled with grass, they could just drive his white Impala around to the side of Ken's place, park, hand the sacks of pot out of the trunk, and carry them up the fire escape to the apartment. When they finished breaking the pot down into orders, they could just drop the bags into the trunk and drive away. So Larry offered to pay Ken a few hundred dollars if he would let them use his place to break down the next shipment.

Without hesitation, Ken accepted. He wanted in. Before the month was up Larry was sending him to Florida for weekend trips with neat bundles of cash.

Dental school was tough. There was one exam after another. Larry found that to stay afloat he needed to cram every night. He would attend classes in the morning, spend hours in the afternoon doing lab work, then from late afternoon until late at night he would be on the phone managing his pot business. The business had grown more complex. So many of his friends had graduated and moved to different cities, different states. Larry had to coordinate orders, make payments, collect debts; he had to recruit runners to make the buys in Florida and supervise the packaging and distribution . . . it was exhausting. Then, when he got off the phone late at night, it was time to start studying. He would turn on the *Tonight* show and open his books, studying straight on through the weird *Creature Features*

that showed in the wee hours of morning. So many of his friends
in dental school were putting in the same kind of study hours that
the awful movies were a favorite in-topic of conversation at school—
"Did you catch *Invasion of the Star Creatures* last night? Was that
outrageous?"

Through freshman year of dental school Larry's pot business
continued, earning him enough to help meet tuition bills and pay the
expenses incurred by a lifestyle only slightly better than the average
graduate student's. One of his few luxuries was a skiing trip to Aspen
over Easter break with his brother Rusty, Paul Mikuta, and Andy.
Marcia performed her clinical work in Boston and then was in Princeton for two months. She finished her internship at the Veterans Administration hospital in Philadelphia and was awarded her physical
therapy license in October. She and Larry had another small graduation party for the Osborns at their apartment. Afterward, Larry
took everyone out for drinks and dinner at a fancy restaurant. Marcia
was offered a job at the VA hospital by the group with which she
had completed her internship, so she went right back to work.

Meanwhile, as her stake in their relationship grew, Marcia was
turning up the volume of her complaints. After one unscheduled visit
by Tyrone, she blew up.

"How can you bring people like that into our home!" Marcia's
anger flashed so infrequently that it always caught Larry by surprise.

"Tyrone's okay," he protested.

"He's trash right off the street! And you bring him and the rest
of these slimeballs into our home! You're going to get us both beat
up or killed or arrested!"

Larry responded to her complaints meekly. He assured Marcia
that Tyrone wasn't as bad as she thought. After that, he tried to make
sure people came by when Marcia was away at work. But even that
wasn't enough. Marcia and Larry had been engaged for nearly a year,
and living together for nearly three years, but Marcia for the first time
was considering leaving. She had had enough. She reminded Larry
of earlier goals and promises. He had explanations, apologies . . . but
he was still dealing. All Marcia wanted in life was a loving husband
and family. They didn't have to be rich. Why couldn't Larry just
concentrate on dental school? She would pay the bills until he was
ready to practice. Together they would do just fine.

But the occasional outbursts did no more than drive home to
Marcia how powerless she had become in their relationship. Larry's
string of broken promises forced the issue. Although he said he loved
her and would plead with her to stay, he had given her every justi-
fication for leaving. But she stayed. Truth was, she couldn't imagine
setting a new course for herself without him. So Marcia waited. She

would be the steady drip that wears through the stone. Larry was sure to leave behind this foolishness eventually, if she only kept up the pressure. Larry placated Marcia's anger with another promise: He would be out of the business before the school year was over in May 1978. He just needed to swing a few more deals and he would have enough money to pay his way through dental school, buy a car, and have fifty thousand dollars in the bank.

At the time Larry made the promise, he meant it. He liked dental school. He wasn't the best student in his class, but he was far from the worst. He was quite good at keeping up with the rote memorization required in his anatomy classes, and he found particularly rewarding the hands-on work in the laboratory, making false teeth, preparing the mixtures to fill and cap. With school and with his deepening relationship with Marcia, there was little time left for the carefree tomfoolery of his undergraduate days. Other than on social or business occasions, where Larry might smoke a joint or sip a drink, he no longer cared for getting stoned or drunk. His years of heavy drinking and drug use as an undergraduate had left him with no desire for the stuff. And now that he was out of the cheerful circle of his fraternity brothers, dealing pot was strictly business. More and more, Larry found irritating the people he had to deal with in Florida, the Philadelphia street dealers, and even the new undergraduate customers. He enjoyed wheeling and dealing on the telephone, playing the businessman and boss, but, in truth, no one knew better than Larry how little he had to show for all of it.

But to an extent even he had not yet realized, Larry was hooked. He was hooked not on the drugs or even the excitement (which he did still enjoy), but on the little train of figures he tallied almost weekly and slipped inside the covers of his albums. Playing with the numbers was a fetish with Larry. He bought himself green accounting pads and penciled in his figures tiny and neat—outlay, income, debts, credits, profits—and played with them until they added up. Those numbers kept mounting despite the constant growing drain of bad debts. Lacking the inclination to bully payments from deadbeats, Larry had written off more than twenty thousand dollars to them over the last few years. In his mind the numbers mounted toward a goal like a climber on the side of a sheer cliff. Every time a deal fell through, every time somebody ripped him off, the climber's foot would slip and he would lose some precious ground. But so long as he could regain his footing—and by now Larry was expert at that— the ground would be recovered, and the climb continued. Larry thought a hundred thousand would do it. With that he could pay his forty-thousand-dollar tuition in full, spend ten on a nice car, and still have fifty thousand in the bank toward a house or starting up a dental practice. It would make for a nice head start. Larry knew plenty of classmates whose parents were footing the tuition bill, and who looked forward to being subsidized when setting up practice. He figured his earnings just put him on an even competitive footing.

So Marcia believed Larry's promise. She couldn't have cared less about fifty thousand dollars and a new car, but it would be nice to have Larry's dental tuition paid up. Still, Marcia would have even been content to do without that. She never counted on it. As far as she was concerned, her paycheck from the VA hospital was their primary means of support. Rent and utility bills and food came out of her pocket—partly because Larry was worried about showing any of his illegal earnings. As a result, to Marcia, Larry's money was something illusory, a game he played with little numbers on sheets of green accounting paper. His future prospects in dentistry were good, certainly worth all the time and effort school required. Dealing was like some sort of dangerous, childish undergraduate stunt that Larry refused to quit.

At the end of his freshman year, Larry took Marcia on a two-week vacation to California. They flew to San Francisco, rented a dark blue Chevy, and toured the city, including the abandoned prison on Alcatraz Island. Larry was fascinated by Alcatraz. He snapped pictures of the guard towers and of the high walls with barbed wire on top and of the stark concrete-and-steel cells. He climbed down into the "Hole," a cell with steel walls that had been used to isolate prisoners singled out for special punishment. The guide described how prisoners in the Hole were fed a mash that was prepared by throwing all the leftovers from the dining hall into a big pot, and how they were allowed to shower only with cold water. Larry asked to be closed in the punishment cell for a few moments, just to get the feel of it.

He and Marcia drove over the Golden Gate Bridge and north to the wine country and then back down through the redwood forests to Yosemite. They drove across to Monterey and then down the coastal highway to Los Angeles. Larry posed lifting a fake pickup with one hand at Universal Studios in Hollywood. He and Marcia went to Disneyland and toured the Anheuser-Busch brewery; they took the ferry out to Catalina Island and miniature-golfed; they drove down to San Diego and saw that city's famous zoo, and visited Old World and Marineland. Then they flew east to Las Vegas, where Larry gambled with quarters, and drove out to see the Grand Canyon. Staying at relatively cheap hotels, they spent just two or three thousand dollars on the whole trip. Again, Marcia was thrilled to have Larry to herself, away from the damn telephone, for weeks at a time.

When they got back to Philadelphia, Marcia started a second photo album, filling twenty pages with snapshots of the trip. Under

the plastic sheets of those pages her relationship with Larry was as-
suming a history, a wholesome, normal history full of sunny days
and close friends and happy moments. It was as if Marcia were willing
their life to be this way.

With the onset of summer, Larry's dealing fell off again, enough
so that he was able to maintain the appearance of keeping his promise.
But he and Andy were still short of Larry's goals, and the climb
continued.

Marcia was not the only one who thought Larry was flirting with
disaster by dealing with Tyrone, and even with Billy South Philly.
Her sentiments were echoed by L.A., who had returned from serving
his time in Florida and landed a job on the Philadelphia Stock Exchange, and by Andy Mainardi, who was about to graduate from
Penn. Both Larry's partners warned repeatedly that drug dealing on
a college campus was worlds away from drug dealing on the streets
of a city like Philadelphia.

Larry believed that Marcia and his friends were too timid. Dating
back to the days when he and Glen Fuller had ripped off the skimobiles, Larry fancied himself as someone who could cross class bar-
riers more readily than most of his sheltered, suburban-bred peers.

During the summer, while Marcia was away in Boston, Paul
Mikuta had invited Larry to a bachelor party out at his parents' house
in Frazer for a friend who was getting married the next day. Larry
had called Tyrone, who had given him the names and addresses of
two women willing to entertain at the affair. So Larry had driven his
white Impala down to the housing projects in Southwest Philly and
picked them up. He drove them out to the party on the Main Line.
When he arrived at the party with these two blunt, impatient black
women, eager to finish their business and get going, the houseful of
white college students seemed intimidated, as if Larry had thrown
them a challenge. The groom was pressured into having sex with the
women, and Larry indulged himself, but nobody else wanted anything
to do with them. It became awkward. So Larry left early and took
the women home. Later, Paul called to say that he had taken the
sheets off the bed they had used and burned them.

The episode just confirmed Larry's suspicion that he was more
ballsy than most guys. They might get together at a bachelor party
and watch stag movies and boast about going out to poke a few whores,
but they faded away fast when Larry delivered the hookers to their
beds. Tyrone might be considered a tough "street nigger," and Billy
might be considered a member of the South Philly mob, but Larry
could handle it. All it took was a little more nerve and a little more
smarts. Actually, his dealings with Billy Motto were a pleasure—

Billy was charming and honorable and he looked up to Larry as an older brother. Larry knew that rumors about Billy's Mafia ties were just that, rumors—*useful* rumors, in fact, because he noticed Billy had none of the bad-debt problems Larry faced continually. And Tyrone? Tyrone was a businessman just like him. Larry knew Tyrone was making money off their relationship. Why would he want to do anything to interfere with that?

Andy Mainardi had more reason than most to doubt Larry's assurances in these matters. He was a full partner in the pot business, so he had a lot to lose if Larry did lose control of the situation. And ever since his arrest in Savannah, Andy was wary of the risks Larry took—wary because Larry's risks had a way of becoming Andy's risks. For instance, in May of 1978, in the spring of Larry's freshman year at dental school, he had been sending Andy out to deliver bales of pot to a new customer at Franklin and Marshall College in Lancaster. After some months of dealing with this character, his debt began to accumulate unreasonably. So Larry, on his own, for once decided to try and get heavy. He phoned the guy and told him that he was sending out someone to collect the money. If the debt wasn't paid now there would be trouble. Then he sent *Andy* to collect. Andy drove to Lancaster unaware of the threats Larry had made on the phone. He thought it was just a routine trip to collect some money from a customer. When he pulled up in the guy's driveway, four big men strode out of the house to meet him. Andy muttered hasty apologies when he realized what was going on and quickly drove home. He and Larry had lost about ten thousand dollars, but Andy was grateful to have escaped unharmed. Back in Philadelphia, Larry laughed as if it were nothing and insisted that he thought he had worked things out beforehand with the guy on the phone.

This business with Tyrone was exactly like that. Andy wanted nothing to do with it.

"These people carry guns and knives, Larry!" he would say.

"I know what I'm doing," Larry would say. "I can handle these people."

And, in fact, Larry did manage to keep on collecting from these guys, and the numbers on Larry's tally sheets kept growing—which meant money in Andy's pocket. So Andy put up with it. He put up with it until May of 1979.

Just before a weekend when Larry and Marcia had planned to visit her parents in northern Jersey, Larry was called by a friend of Tyrone's who wanted to buy a few pounds of pot right away. Larry said fine, anything for a friend of my man Tyrone, but said, since he was going to be out, that they would have to meet with his partner Andy. Then Larry phoned Andy.

"These people are going to show up at your door in about a half hour," Larry told Andy.

"You gave them my name and address!" Andy shouted. He had never been so angry at Larry. Andy said he didn't want anything to do with these people.

"Come on, Andy. You're the one who gives me shit about having these people over to my place with Marcia here," Larry said. "I'd do it myself, but I promised Marcia. . . ."

Andy knew how much trouble Marcia had been giving Larry about dealing, so he gave in. Before the half hour was up, Larry's contact was at the door. He made his buy, and then told Andy that he had a friend who wanted to buy more—a lot more. He asked if Andy could sell this guy forty pounds.

"But not at my house," said Andy. "You tell them to meet me at the Roy Rogers at Forty-first and Walnut."

Andy ordered a burger at the Roy Rogers but was too nervous to eat it. At the appointed time, three young men walked in and approached his table. They frightened Andy. They were younger than him, with black skin and fearless eyes. The one who spoke to him had a gold front tooth.

"You Andy?"

"Yes. Do you have the money?"

"Yeah. Let's go," said Andy. "Follow me." He walked out to his car, started it, and drove to a dark parking lot behind a fraternity house on Penn's campus. The car with the three black guys pulled up alongside.

Andy got out and walked back to the trunk. The three men got out and opened the trunk of their car. Andy hesitated just before opening his.

"Let me just see the cash," he said.

The one who had spoken to him walked up close. "Okay," he said. "Over here." He led Andy over to their open trunk. As Andy turned to look inside, the man reached in his pocket and pulled out a gun.

"Here's the cash," he said.

"Take the pot," said Andy. "Leave. Please don't hurt me."

The other men grabbed him, handcuffed him behind his back, and pushed him to the pavement. They kicked him and kicked him. Andy kept shouting, "Take the pot! Take the pot!"

When the man with the gun had thrown the contents from Andy's trunk into his own, the other two ran back to the car, got in, and drove away.

Andy got up slowly. There was nothing for him to do but

walk the few blocks back to his house with his hands cuffed behind his back. One of his roommates located a bolt cutter to remove the handcuffs.

When Larry and Marcia returned Sunday afternoon, Andy was waiting. He had cooled down, but when he explained what had happened, Larry was furious. Andy had lost not only the forty pounds, but additional dope that he had been carrying around in his trunk. They were out nearly fifteen thousand dollars.

"How could you be so stupid!" Larry said. He blamed Andy for setting up a second deal with someone they had never met.

"You don't go out and do business like that with somebody you don't even know!" said Larry. "You could get killed! And you don't take more product with you than you're gonna sell!"

Andy was upset that Larry put all the blame on him—to say nothing about the fact that he seemed more disturbed about losing the money than about Andy's close call. For his part, Andy suspected the only reason Larry had involved him in the first place was because he wanted to avoid taking the risk himself.

They parted angrily. Mulling it over the next day, Larry concluded that it was time to end his partnership with Andy. He felt he was working night and day while Andy treated the business as a hobby, staying stoned all the time and taking frequent trips out of town—Andy had recently booked himself on the Concorde and flown away to Paris for a few days. On his own, and for different reasons, Andy was reaching much the same conclusion. He felt that Larry was expanding the business off campus, which was foolhardy, as evidenced by the fifteen-thousand-dollar loss they had just sustained (not to mention the beating).

When Larry marched across the street the next day to confront Andy with his decision, he was suprised to encounter no resistance at all.

"Andy, I think I'm doing too much work here. This is, like, the final straw."

"You're right," said Andy.

And they agreed immediately, without rancor, to part ways.

There was another reason for Andy's decision to get out. In the early months of 1979, Larry had been pushing the business more and more away from pot, and more and more into cocaine. Two years after his discussion with Tom Finchley at Sears, Larry bowed to the inevitable. Cocaine was fast becoming the major drug of choice even in Larry's own crowd. Pot use was still strong, but waning. It was getting harder to buy in Florida and it was taking longer and longer to move.

Cocaine had been just a novelty at Penn when Larry was an undergrad. Larry sometimes bought a few grams to use himself or share with his dealer friends. It was too expensive for most students and it was not the kind of high most students wanted. Marijuana is a passive drug. It offers the illusion of escape. It eases boredom and insecurity by making the commonplace seem less so and by temporarily suspending the pressures of daily life. Most college undergraduates manage to succeed with minimal effort, so they have a lot of free time and they are often bored. Couple boredom with the usual trials of adolescence—sexual anxiety, worries about choosing and starting a career, doubts about self-worth, etc.—and you have a large potential market for marijuana. Cocaine is an active drug. It offers the illusion of power. It is the preferred drug of a person in a hurry. Cocaine replaces insecurity with a feeling of omnipotence, imparting a fleeting visceral courage and sense of competence.

By 1979, Larry was finishing his second year of dental school, and his friends were pursuing other professional degrees, majoring in business administration or already holding down good jobs. Getting high had been fine for a boring lecture in cultural anthropology, or for cutting classes to goof off for an afternoon, but it was unthinkable for someone trying to maintain that competitive edge in the white-collar workplace or master a profession. How much more appropriate was a drug that imparted a feeling described as a "rush," that made you feel smarter, stronger, sexier, and more successful, and that could be turned on or off within a matter of minutes? Cocaine helped you stay awake when you had more work to do. It picked you back up when you had a few drinks too many. It *intensified* everything that you did. Even the expense of cocaine had begun to work in its favor. If you could afford to lay out a few lines for friends on the coffee table after dinner, it was just another way of advertising success.

Through his sophomore year of dental school, while he was still primarily a pot dealer, Larry dabbled with cocaine, mostly by investing his money in deals arranged by his friends.

He visited the head shops around Penn looking for books about cocaine. Unlike marijuana, which you could just smoke to determine its quality, cocaine was harder to evaluate. And with the amounts of money involved—a kilo (2.2 pounds), a bag small enough to slip inside a valise, cost fifty-six thousand dollars!—the incentive to deceive was extreme. This presented Larry with the kind of challenge he loved.

His years of lab work as an undergrad and now as a dental student had given him a good grounding in basic science. From the books Larry bought, he learned that cocaine was an alkaloid, one of a group of nitrogen-containing compounds derived from plants. Alkaloids have a distinctively complex molecular structure and exhibit a wide range of powerful pharmacological effects. Morphine, codeine, emetine (a potent emetic), quinine (used in treating malaria), ephedrine (used for treating asthma), colchicine (used in treating gout), synephrine (shrinks swollen nasal passages) are all alkaloids. Cocaine was originally isolated and produced for use as a local anesthetic, for which it is quite effective, but it produces side effects that medical science considers undesirable—the very effects that were turning it into the recreational drug of choice in America. Cocaine stimulates the central nervous system, increasing heart rate, blood pressure, and body temperature and inducing a temporary euphoria—followed, one might add, by a strong craving for more.

It was that strong craving for more that distinguished cocaine from marijuana as merchandise. Larry began dealing coke by throwing in a few gram bottles with the purchase of a certain amount of pot. With pot sales slowly falling off, Larry found he could use cocaine as an incentive, not to the pot users at the end of his supply stream, but to his own customers, each of whom was a substantial pot dealer in his own right. Cocaine was considered too expensive for the average pot smoker, but as a special gift to dealers buying ten thousand dollars of pot or more at a time, it worked as a discount mechanism.

But quickly the dealers came back asking for more. They, in turn, had shared cocaine with their customers, which further multiplied the demand. Larry's coke business increased exponentially.

Larry put himself through a crash course in dealing cocaine. From a head shop on Pine Street, Larry bought a nifty melt box enclosed in a wood case that was a foot and a half long, four inches wide, and three inches high. Before buying a few ounces or a quarter pound, Larry would press a pinch of the powder between two glass slides and put it in the box. Most of the substances used to cut cocaine by wholesalers (in 1979 they were primarily using a baby sugar called Nanitol) melt at far lower temperatures than cocaine. Then Larry would fire up the box. Coke wouldn't liquify until 150 degrees (F), while cut would begin to blacken and smoke at between 75 degrees and 100 degrees. Compared to his later methods, the melt box was clumsy and crude, but it worked—and Larry loved gadgets.

In time, Larry's runners would learn from Cuban suppliers in Florida how to quickly test for quality by simply rubbing the cocaine on the web of skin between the thumb and index finger—good stuff would readily melt and be absorbed by the skin. For more accurate measures, they learned other techniques. There were tiny prepackaged capsules into which a trace amount of cocaine was placed and then mixed with chemicals when the bond at the capsule's center was broken. The cocaine would turn either blue or pink. A light blue like an azure sky meant the cocaine was pure. A bright pink indicated there was mostly cut. Later, Larry employed the Clorox test, where a trace of cocaine was dropped in a small glass of bleach. Cocaine would drift slowly to the bottom of the glass, leaving in the bleach a trail that looked like an icicle. Cut would just drop quickly to the bottom, leaving no trace in the bleach. Clorox was also excellent at revealing the presence of a cheap iodine-base cutting agent that was mildly poisonous. The iodine would leave a dark brown smear on top of the bleach. Eventually, Larry abandoned all these methods for a simple methanol test: Cocaine would dissolve in a spoonful of methanol, while most of the cutting agents employed at that time would not. It was enough to ensure that Larry got what he paid for.

From the scientific supply house where Larry had been buying cartons of glass vials for years, now he purchased an expensive electronic scale that could weigh items down to fractions of a centigram.

Larry's first significant cocaine deal was in partnership with L.A., whose friends in Florida had gotten in on the ground floor. He put up some of his cash to help buy a half kilo. L.A. drove the shipment back, and Larry went to work on it.

From Tom Finchley, Larry had learned something about the successful marketing of cocaine. The average coke user on the street had neither the time, training, or inclination to adequately test what he was buying. So the first step was to "step" on the product, to mix in some cut of your own. Larry invested in some Manitol. Eventually, he perfected the cut mixture, abandoning the baby sugar, which added too much sweetness to the cocaine, for inositol, a sugar alcohol sold in health food stores as a vitamin. Inositol was whiter than Manitol. Blending this substance with lidocaine, a mild local anesthetic, covered the sweetness of the inositol and replaced the numbing effect lost by blending the cocaine with cut. This mix went into a blender to fluff it up to a whiteness and consistency similar to the cocaine's. That got mixed in. Then it was time to make rocks.

It wasn't that pure cocaine came in rocklike chunks; rocks were an illusion in the coke business from start to finish. Customers tended to believe that a rocklike chunk of cocaine was pure cocaine, which it wasn't, though it did tend to possess a higher percentage of pure cocaine than shake because shake was so much easier to cut. Larry's first step in packaging a shipment of cocaine was to sift it, separating the rocks from the loose powder, or shake. The rocks were left alone. The shake was then mixed with the Manitol. Larry's standard formula was 9.7 grams of cut per 20.3 grams of cocaine. Then Larry would try to press the shake into what he called "man-made" rocks—although all the rocks were, in fact, man-made, the "real" ones having just been made earlier in the supply chain.

His first efforts at making rocks were crude. Larry tried pressing the shake under a pile of heavy books, which didn't work. Eventually, from dealers in Florida and his books, Larry learned that by using acetone or ether to moisten the cocaine and pressing it tightly together with his hands, then pressing even harder with the lump between his knees, he could form tight, hard lumps. He would then break that apart with a butter knife, put the chunks on a pie pan, and place them under a heat lamp. Acetone left the rocks slightly yellower than the rocks in the initial purchase, so Larry experimented with ether, and finally began regularly using methanol. Using a gardening spritzer, he would squeeze a gentle spray of methanol on the powder until it was moist enough to mold.

His first buys of cocaine were half kilos, which Larry purchased in partnership with friends. But the return on the investment was incredible. A half kilo costing $28,500 could be stretched into twenty-seven ounces by cutting it with inositol and lidocaine. At the time, Larry could sell a single ounce for $1,500, which meant a $12,000 profit. Even with the overhead and the constant trouble with bad debts, Larry could be sure of clearing $10,000 or more on the deal. The profit on a single kilo was more than $20,000, on two kilos (he got a price break of $1000 per kilo for buying two) nearly $40,200! The numbers multiplied in Larry's head like the certain clicks of a winning combination on a one-armed bandit. After only two or three buys, Larry contacted Miguel, the dealer Finchley had wanted him to use in 1977, and began buying two kilos of cocaine at a time. It was an extraordinary risk—$112,000! The money represented the joint investment of several of Larry's longtime friends, but it included just about every penny he had ever made.

He was ready for another shipment of the same amount within two weeks. Larry had never seen anything like it.

In a matter of months, over the winter of 1978–79, Larry's prodigious six-year-old pot business got shouldered aside like a crippled pensioner in the stampede for more cocaine. The net-worth total on Larry's private accounting sheet climbed so quickly past his goal of a hundred thousand dollars that it seemed stupid to consider that milestone a place to stop. Larry was filled with precisely the kind of rush he had felt four years earlier when he had started selling large amounts of marijuana. Stop now? Why, Larry was just getting started!

His new goal, which he announced to Ken Weidler, was *One Million Dollars*.

Early in 1979, Hank Katz, Billy South Philly's contact at the hoagie shop, got shot in the stomach in an argument with some Greek dealers in Center City over an unpaid loan. Billy was sick. He had lost his pot connection. He had no way of getting in touch with Larry.

Although they had met several times over the past two years, Billy didn't even know Larry's last name. He had no idea where Larry lived.

So he went to the Katz hoagie shop in West Philly and began asking employees, customers and employees behind the counter, if they knew Hank's friend Larry, tall, thick black hair, liked to talk a lot, a dental student. It didn't take long—almost everyone seemed not only to know Larry, but to know exactly where he lived.

Billy buzzed at Larry's door and got no answer, so he tacked a note on the door: "Larry, this is Billy. I would like to have an opportunity to speak with you. Let's have lunch." He wrote his phone number on the note and left.

Larry called back that same day. He said he was too busy for lunch, but that he would like to see Billy. So the next afternoon, Billy met Larry at the Osage Avenue apartment. Larry was wearing a white lab coat. He led Billy back to his study. They talked about Hank, who was making slow progress at a local hospital.

"He's crazy to get mixed up with those Greeks," said Billy, who was actually relieved to have him out of the way. Billy had been wanting to deal directly with Larry for a long time. He liked Larry more, and it would lower his costs up front. He saw new levels of profit for his pot business. But Larry had other plans.

"I've got a business proposition for you," said Larry. Larry sat down in front of his broad wood desk and from one of its many small drawers he withdrew a glass jar containing one ounce of white powder.

Billy just shook his head. "Hank was after me to start buying that. He wanted, like, sixteen to eighteen hundred dollars for a little jar like that."

"I'll sell it to you for fifteen hundred," said Larry.

"My people don't use cocaine," Billy said.

"Just try. See what happens." Larry reached over his open dental textbooks to hand Billy the jar. He explained that Billy could mark the stuff up and make an easy couple hundred dollars.

"Who are you trying to kid?" said Billy. "I don't know who your customers are, but mine are scraping to come up with forty bucks for an ounce of pot."

Billy said he could see no reason to start dealing something new anyway. Larry, who could hear echoes of his own old arguments in everything Billy said, was convincing. He offered to front the coke, and to discount a hundred dollars off each ounce bottle if Billy would take four.

"Why carry an elephant around when you can put a mouse in your pocket?" he said.

Billy took the four bottles. He didn't want to sour his relationship with Larry, because he had hopes of being introduced to Larry's pot connections in Florida. He wrung from Larry a tentative commitment to be allowed to make a Florida run. He took the cocaine home reluctantly. It took months and months to sell. Billy saw Larry several times during that period, but Larry never bugged him about the money. Slowly, Billy peddled the last of the powder, pushing it on his people, discounting it, anything to get rid of it.

Then something unexpected happened. All of the people who bought it came back asking for more.

Miguel, Larry's new connection in Florida, was so delighted to have a new buyer in Philadelphia that he flew north to discuss matters with Larry personally. Larry met him in a hotel room near the airport. Miguel was a cadaverously skinny Cuban with a sallow complexion and the dreamy-eyed look of a man who overused Quaaludes. He was about ten years older than Larry and dressed in high southern Florida fashion—designer jeans neatly laundered and pressed, brightly colored shirts worn open to midabdomen, and lots of gold, including a Rolex nearly as big as his fist. The eager dental student explained that if his two-kilo, or "two-key," gamble went well, he wanted to continue buying at that amount for a while. Miguel was eager to oblige.

Larry offered Miguel a ride back to the airport, and he walked the Cuban dealer to the gate for his flight. On the way to the gate, Miguel was waved down by an acquaintance, who happened also to be a friend of Tom Finchley's.

That night Tom phoned Larry. They chatted for a few minutes about unrelated things. Larry had not told Tom that he was dealing with Miguel directly, so Tom's question was angry and abrupt.

"What the hell are you doing with Miguel, Larry?"

"Look, Tom, it just happened."

"You son-of-a-bitch!"

"What can I say?"

"You son-of-a-bitch!" Tom drew the words out slowly.

"Come on, Tom. Miguel has been trying to use me for the last two years. It would be foolish for me to deal with him through a middleman."

Finchley was furious. He knew Larry would be dealing in much larger volume than he was. This move meant not only that he would not be getting a cut of Larry's business for introducing him to Miguel, but that he would have to start buying from Larry if he wanted to get the best price. It was humiliating. And Larry wasn't making it any better.

"It's not my fault, Tom. Miguel was tired of dealing with you. He says you're Quaaluded out all the time and you're too busy with your legitimate business. He can never get ahold of you when he wants."

"You wouldn't even know fucking Miguel if it weren't for me, Larry. Don't give me this shit."

"Don't take it personally, Tom. It's just business."

"You're fucking crazy it's just business, Larry. Are we going to have to go to war over this?"

"Don't be ridiculous."

Tom hung up the phone. Larry didn't hear from him for a day or two. When Tom called again he had calmed down. He knew there was no margin in cutting off his dealings with Larry, especially now. Larry tried to be conciliatory.

"Look, Tom. You know I've always treated you right, fronting you things, getting you things at cost." Larry had paid some of Tom's legal fees the year before when he was arrested—Philadelphia police had searched the trunk of his MG and found cocaine, but the charges were later dismissed because they didn't have a warrant for the search. Larry reminded Tom of every good turn he had done him in the last few years.

"And you know you're a preferred customer, you'll be buying from me at cost," said Larry.

After the first three two-kilo shipments, Larry had accumulated enough cash to make the buys himself. Making the flights to Florida were Matt Weder, a tall, fat member of Phi Delta Theta who had graduated a year behind Larry and had been living with Andy Main-ardi, and Ken. Ken couldn't believe that Larry just kept sending the piles of cash he made back down to Florida.

"You might lose it all!" he would say.

Larry was so used to shocking people with his dealings that he considered it a form of tribute.

"You gotta have balls, Kenny. You gotta have balls."

Dealing cocaine reversed the usual transportation problems. With pot, one had to cope with the smell and bulk coming home from Florida. With cocaine, the bigger challenge was moving so much money south. Even in 1979, when cocaine use was just beginning to join the mainstream, airport security guards would stop and ask questions when large bundles of hundred-dollar bills showed up on their X-ray machines.

At a secondhand shop as an undergraduate, Larry had bought for seventy-five cents an old gray-brown tweed overcoat that was much too big for him. Marcia had tried to throw it away once or twice, but Larry always spotted it out in the trash and saved it. It had big deep pockets on the inside and outside and hung down to his knees. It was perfect for carrying money through airports. He and Ken would accompany Matt to Philadelphia International Airport. Matt would pass his luggage through the X-ray machine and walk through the metal detector. Then Larry and Ken would go through. They then went to one of the men's rooms on the concourse, and with Larry and Ken taking stalls on either side of Matt, they would pass bundles of hundreds under the partitions to him. Matt would then stuff the cash into his carry-on bag.

"Come on . . . come on," Larry urged Matt on one of dozens of these trips. Larry was always in a hurry.

"I'm going as fast as I can," said Matt. "It won't fit."

"Just stuff it in," said Larry.

Ken started to laugh. On his way out of the men's room he said, "Can you imagine what that sounded like to someone overhearing us in there?"

When the weather turned warm, overcoats were out. On one trip Matt taped five-grand packets of hundreds three-deep all over his chest and legs. He wore an oversized shirt and baggy pants and just walked through the airport by himself. When he got to Florida, the bottom layers of money were soaked completely through with sweat. After that he doubled-wrapped the bundles in plastic and dripped all the way to Miami.

Through freshman and the first half of sophomore year in dental school, Ken Weidler was selling small amounts of the pot and Quaaludes he bought from Larry to a classmate named David Ackerman.

David was a short, slender New Yorker with thick, very fair brown hair and big green eyes. The son of divorced wealthy parents who for years had used money to vie for his affection, David was used to having and spending money. He had been a regular at expensive Center City restaurants all through his undergraduate years at Penn, and he liked to dress well at a time when most of his classmates' wardrobes were a heap of unwashed denim and flannel on the floor next to their beds. Women loved David. With his pronounced long thin nose and sensitive eyes, he was strikingly handsome in a delicate, almost pretty way. David had the personality of a pampered little boy, combining self-assurance that was at times overbearing with an underlying sweet helplessness. He was shy about his jejune appearance, and tried to counter it with a succession of sparse moustaches and beards—a different combination almost every month. David was a brilliant student, with a crisp clear intelligence that announced itself in everything he did. He was animated to the verge of being hyperkinetic. In conversation he could be captivating, with eyes that flashed with enthusiasm or delight or anger. David had won a prestigious competitive examination after his junior year at Penn that permitted him to skip his senior year and start in at Penn's dental school immediately. His father was a successful dentist, so David's passage from college through dental school and into a ready-made, lucrative practice seemed effortless and assured.

As Ken Weidler began to make money dealing the pot Larry sold him and eventually making the runs south for cocaine, he was able to keep up with David's tastes for wine, fine restaurants, and women. David had a membership at Elan, a fashionable disco club in the Warwick Hotel that was easily the best place in town to mingle with beautiful single women. Through their sophomore year in dental school, Ken and David began taking cocaine along with them on their frequent nights on the town. The cocaine was like a magnet. At Elan, David and Ken were minor celebrities. They spent a lot of money, drank a lot, shared cocaine, and often went home with women.

Larry and David knew each other from dental school, but David had no idea that Larry was the source of his friend's steady drug supply. Larry had never found time to become a part of the dental school's low-key social life. He was too busy, for one thing, and his home life with Marcia had removed most of the old incentive to go out and mingle with his classmates. Marcia herself was a confirmed homebody. Her idea of fun on a Friday night was to sip wine and knit in front of the TV with Larry. So David's impression of Larry was that he was a dull, studious fellow. When Ken finally relented to David's insistent demands to meet his supplier, Ackerman was flabbergasted—"That guy who sits next to you in the lab?"

Overnight, David's ambivalence toward Larry turned to hero worship. Larry thought it was comical. His impression of David was of an unbearably egotistical runt who made up for his youth and stature with bluster and strut, the kind of person who will just interrupt someone else in midsentence, as if to say, "What I have to say is more important." David sometimes argued with his teachers, as if he believed he already knew more dentistry than they did. It was either that or he was busy sucking up to them. Larry didn't like the guy. Ackerman was, thought Larry, "a typical New York Jew." Then, suddenly, this David Ackerman was all over him, as if they had been best friends for years.

David made it clear right away that he wanted in on Larry's business. Larry was always in the market for a runner, even one he didn't particularly like, so on the first occasion that Ken could not make the trip to Florida, Larry asked David to go. Ackerman jumped. He handled himself so well dealing with Miguel in Florida, and his whole attitude was so eager and bright, that Larry couldn't help but be impressed. He started employing David for a lot of different chores.

In addition to making runs, Larry soon had David changing money for him at local banks (a time-consuming chore with the growing amounts of cash on hand), making up orders, purchasing cutting agents, and so on. David had a quicker mind than Ken; intricacies that Larry grew frustrated explaining to Ken, David understood instantly. Because David understood more, his admiration for what Larry had accomplished was deeper and more rewarding to Larry than Ken's simple amazement. Larry began to entertain notions of handing some of the business over to David eventually—it would reduce the demands on his time, reduce the risk, and reduce the mounting pressure he was getting from Marcia.

They had been living together for three years and been engaged for two. Marcia's father had died in 1978, and one of the effects it had on her was to make more urgent her desire for a family of her own. In May of 1979, Marcia and Larry began looking for a Catholic church to be married in—they wanted one close to Penn because most of their friends lived there. Marcia wanted a traditional ceremony in June 1980. She wanted Larry completely out of the business before they were married, and he promised.

But for the time being, Larry had a new edge in his differences with Marcia over dealing. Before, with his constant losses and bad debts chipping away at his earnings, Larry arguably had been spending too much time and effort for the return—maybe thirty to forty thousand dollars to show for more than four years of work. But once the cocaine business took off, there was no question but that the business was making him rich—richer than he had ever dreamed of becoming. As the totals mounted, and the stakes grew higher and higher with each deal, Larry's excitement grew with it. Marcia might warn him about getting caught, but so far that threat remained very distant. Larry assured Marcia that he had it arranged so that other people took the risks. He had never come close to getting caught. And those of his friends who did—L.A., Andy, and Tom—got off so lightly that even to a cautious person like Marcia the rewards appeared to heavily outweigh the risks.

Moral objections to drug dealing never entered Marcia's mind, or Larry's or any of his friends'. Dealing cocaine was nothing like dealing heroin. Coke was a party drug, a harmless, quick stimulant in great demand, not by derelicts and street people intent on destroying their lives, but by some of the brightest, most promising, most successful people they knew. People didn't turn their noses up at cocaine dealing; they turned their noses toward it! Whatever social rewards Larry had gotten at Penn for dealing marijuana were multiplied tenfold by dealing cocaine. And it was making him rich!

Marcia's objections were purely personal. She knew the risk wasn't worth it, she resented the time Larry spent engrossed in the business, and she was angered by his overgrown adolescent need for time "out with the boys." But Larry was in another one of his phases where it was no use arguing with him about it. He had definite goals, a definite timetable . . . he had it all figured out.

Larry, David, Ken, and Paul Mikuta flew out to Colorado in March of 1979 to visit Larry's old friend Glen Fuller. The trip introduced a new element to Larry's life that was to become his specialty—the outrageous, expensive, decadent party.

Fuller had packed up his van in Haverhill in 1973 and headed west. He had heard about the great skiing in Aspen, and he was eager to strike out on his own. In Aspen, Glen kicked around from job to job, working as a short-order cook until a particularly good day for skiing came along, then he would walk out the door and head for the hills. Jobs were plentiful those days in Aspen, and Glen could always hustle a few more bucks on the slopes by stealing students out of the lines waiting to take lessons with the official ski instructors.

Glen eventually got into the produce business and sold marijuana and small amounts of cocaine on the side. In 1977, he took the money he had saved selling pot and opened a little seafood store in Vermont. There he met a pretty, dark-haired young woman named Rita Long and for the first time in his life considered settling down. By late 1978, Glen had a refrigerated delivery truck and a delivery route with more than a hundred restaurants as customers. He was doing well enough to lease a house in Aspen while he was living in Vermont, just so that he would have a nice place to stay whenever he felt like skiing. Through the years, Glen had kept in touch with Larry's brother Rusty, and it was Rusty who told him about Larry's sudden incredible success in Philadelphia with cocaine.

So Glen had visited Larry and expressed an interest in starting up a New England branch of the operation. His stocky, well-muscled frame filled Larry's Osage Avenue apartment with the hell-raising enthusiasm of old. Old animosities over the Ski-Doo incident were forgotten; Glen was thrilled to discover that his preppie partner in teenage crime had made good—"Let's get it on!" said Glen—reintroducing some of that old joy in deviltry that Marcia had been trying to mature out of Larry's system. Larry prepared Glen's first order himself, whipping up the cut in a blender on the living room floor at Osage Avenue while Marcia was away at work, and packing up a cardboard box with about six ounces. Within months, Glen was chartering a small plane down to Philadelphia on a regular basis to pick up orders of a kilo or more.

Larry was resisting his old friend's efforts to be let in on the business. He enjoyed Glen's company, but he considered him too wild and unpredictable to be trusted with serious matters—i.e., Larry's money. Glen didn't get the message. The more Larry tried to keep him at arm's length, the more determined Glen seemed to be. He wanted badly to be a part of Larry's inner circle.

A year earlier, when Larry had flown out for a week of skiing in Aspen with his brother Rusty, Paul Mikuta, Andy Mainardi, and Ken Weidler, Larry had avoided Glen. Rusty knew that Glen had a house nearby, but Larry knew that his old friend had a way of commandeering events and steering them out of control. This year, though, he was obviously going to be impossible to avoid. Glen was making plans for Larry's trip before Larry was. They would stay at his place and party like madmen for a week.

Larry and his friends flew out in March, over Easter break. When they arrived, after a long drive through the spectacular snowy scenery of the Rockies in winter, Glen introduced the Philadelphia boys to their companions for the week—Rita's two sisters, one for Ken and one for David, a girl named Lisa for Larry, and a girl named Stacy for Paul. There was ample cocaine, marijuana, and a supply of Quaaludes on hand, plenty of expensive wine, brandy, and hard liquor, ski lift tickets, and a whole week to enjoy it. Any reservations Larry had about partying for a week with Glen fell away with his clothes when he got into bed with Lisa. This was going to be more fun than he had imagined.

The group hit a fine restaurant in Aspen every night, and then returned to party with the drugs and each other until late. They bedded down separately, and woke for a late breakfast, a day of skiing, time to unwind, and then back out to another fine restaurant for dinner, where they would drop fifteen hundred to two thousand dollars. They reserved private rooms for the dinners, and brought out cocaine and marijuana to share with the help. Larry filled a sugar bowl with cocaine and rolled strawberries in it and fed them to the waitresses. Glen scared the wits out of David Ackerman, whom he instantly disliked, by taking him for a "hell ride" in his four-wheel-drive Bronco, at one point speeding so recklessly through an underground garage that David screamed for him to let him out. On one of the nights, Glen hosted an extravagant dinner party at his own house, inviting his friends in Aspen to meet his Philadelphia friends, serving expensive steaks and wines. Women at that party were urged, with only partial success, to perform sexual acts together, for the amusement of the men. When Larry decided things were a little too crowded at Glen's, he rented an expensive apartment nearby with a heated swimming pool, so toward the end of the week the party bounced back and forth between the house and the apartment.

There was a triumphant exhilaration to that week, the gorgeous snowy peaks, blue sky, the blinding whiteness of the snow, the fine foods and wines, the drugs, the sex. They were young and healthy and beautiful and rich . . . and this was just the beginning!

Soon after the Aspen trip, Larry gave in to Glen's persistence. Glen said he had a contact in Dayton who could sell him two kilos for $110,000, but he had to meet them at a hotel there that night.

"Okay, let's do it," said Larry.

Glen was delighted. They drove in Larry's white Impala over to David's house on Fitzwater Street to pick up more money, and while Larry barreled down Baltimore Avenue toward the Schuylkill Expressway on his way to the airport, bouncing over the beat-up pavement and trolley tracks, Glen tried to count and bundle a great heap of hundred-dollar bills on his lap. Money had spilled all over the front seat and floor. In his haste, Larry was paying little attention to a succession of traffic signals at the end of each short block, and somewhere near Forty-third Street the law caught up to him.

A cop tooted his siren and flashed his red lights. Larry pulled over, swore, and then grabbed his overcoat, which was in the back seat, and threw it over Glen's lap and the front seat, trying to cover the money. He gave the cop his license and registration, his heart pounding and his mouth dry, and explained that they were just in a hurry to catch a flight at the airport. Larry listened to the officer's lecture and thanked him for not giving him a ticket. Both he and Glen burst out laughing when the police car pulled away.

"I don't know," said Larry. "This kind of shit used to be fun, but it's not so much fun anymore."

Larry walked the money through the metal detector, and they passed the bundles into Glen's bag in the men's room.

That night, after Glen checked into the appointed hotel in Dayton, he was met in his room by two Puerto Ricans—Glen called Hispanics "Funny-talkers." They ordered a drink from room service, and Glen showed them the money. But before leaving the hotel to exchange the money for cocaine, the men convinced Glen to step downstairs for a bite to eat. Glen hadn't eaten since morning. He slid the leather case full of money under one of the beds in his hotel room, and the three went downstairs to eat. Before he finished eating, the Puerto Ricans excused themselves. They said they would make a phone call, pick up the coke, and give him a call at his hotel room to arrange for a swap.

So Glen finished eating. When he returned to his room, the money was gone.

He went berserk. Slamming the door open, Glen strode down the hotel hall screaming. When a housemaid stepped out of a room in front of him, he grabbed her, wrapping one arm around her waist from behind and grabbing the back of her neck with the other hand. The maid protested in Spanish as Glen dragged her down the hall, accusing her of taking the money from his room. He stopped before the laundry chute—they were on the sixth floor—opened it, and leaned the woman's head into the chute.

"You tell me where you put that money or you're going down," Glen shouted.

The frightened woman was screaming that she didn't know what he was talking about, she knew of no money. The two men who were with Glen earlier had come back. They had forgotten their key and asked her to let them in the room.

Hotel security guards came running down the hall, and within minutes Glen was giving a report to the Dayton police.

When the confusion died down, he phoned Larry with the bad news.

Larry was too depressed to be angry. So much for letting Glen make deals. He made it clear that he held Glen responsible, that he owed Larry the full amount. The only thing to do when Glen got back to Philly was to put him to work.

"Get yourself some nice luggage," said Larry.

Glen's life for the foreseeable future was going to be spent shuttling from Philadelphia to Florida, back to Philadelphia, to Vermont, back to Philadelphia, to Florida, etc. In addition to continuing his dealing in New England, Glen Fuller had become Larry's mule.

F I V E

Never Carry Cash

Tuesday, January 22, 1980, was a rare balmy winter day in Philadelphia. Marcia had opened the windows of the Osage Avenue apartment to air things out. With his dental clinic hours scheduled for afternoon, Larry was enjoying a quiet morning at home. David Ackerman was over. In addition to making more frequent trips to Florida for Larry, David had begun keeping the books. He and Larry were going over some of his figures when Paula Van Horn rang the bell.

Paula was older than Larry and David, who were in their midtwenties. She was an articulate, cheerful woman of thirty-three with short brown hair and brown eyes. Paula had been married and divorced before entering dental school. She shared custody of her children. In between school hours and homework, Paula had been recruited by David to take piles of cash in small bills and drive around the city to various banks, where she would, through a series of relatively small deposits and withdrawals, gradually change the money into neat stacks of hundred-dollar bills. Larry paid her fifty dollars for every thousand she changed.

It was unusual for Paula to stop by Larry's place. She usually dealt with Ackerman, who lived in the same house with her on Fitzwater Street in Center City. In fact, just that morning he had given her fifty thousand in small bills to change. When Paula asked Larry for more, David said, "What happened to the money I gave you this morning?"

Paula said that she had left it at her apartment, because she had not expected to have the afternoon free. Now she had the time, but didn't feel like going back to her place to get the cash. Larry gave her another fifty thousand to change.

The following afternoon, as he was preparing to work on a patient in the student dental clinic, Larry was distracted by a commotion on the sidewalk out the window. Peering down, he saw Paula surrounded by a small crowd on the front steps. Larry excused himself from his patient and ran downstairs. He pushed his way through the crowd and found Paula sitting on the front steps in tears. She said she had been robbed. Between sobs, Paula described her assailant. He was a black man, six feet tall, thinly built, in his mid-twenties, wearing a green knit cap, black pants, and a black leather jacket. A man in the crowd stepped forward to verify Paula's account. He had seen it all happen and had chased the mugger but couldn't catch him. The man accompanied her and David Ackerman to police headquarters, where Paula repeated the same sad story.

"How much did you have in the purse?" she was asked.

The policeman looked astonished when Paula said "ten thousand dollars."

"*Ten thousand dollars!*" said the cop. The figure that amazed him came, of course, as tremendous relief to David.

Paula explained that she had been on her way to pay her boy-friend's dental school tuition. She said her boyfriend was named David Ackerman.

When Larry had a chance to question Paula alone later, he learned the truth was a lot worse. She had been carrying the full hundred thousand. She had broken it all down and had planned on delivering the hundreds to David that afternoon.

That night Paula's story was on the television news, and the next day an item ran in *The Philadelphia Daily News* under a headline that played on the American Express commercial slogan, "Never Carry Cash."

"It was an awful thing," she told the newspaper. "I was stunned. I want to forget the whole thing."

Larry was out another hundred thousand, and he was worried about what the police really believed. Who pays their dental school tuition in cash?

But David, whose name Paula had given to the police and the press as her boyfriend, had a different worry. He was convinced that Paula was lying.

Larry would hear none of it.

"No way. Paula hurt her head and arm when she fell. How can she fake that? And why would she lie to me? I'm paying her better than she could ever make anywhere else. It doesn't make sense."

David and Ken thought Larry was too naive for belief. David offered a deal. If he could recover the missing hundred thousand from Paula, could he keep half?

Larry, who really did believe Paula, figured he couldn't lose on that deal, so he agreed. He would hear more about this promise in a few months.

One morning shortly afterward, as she prepared to leave the apartment for work, Marcia was startled by the bell. It was only 7:30 a.m. At the door was a short, slender man with dark curly hair and oversized rose-tinted glasses. He had a light beard and was finely dressed, wearing his camel's hair overcoat open over a three-piece dark wool suit that fit him too well to be off-the-rack. Marcia glimpsed gold on several of his smaller fingers. He said his name was Mark Stewart, and that he had an appointment to see "Dr." Lawrence Lavin. Larry was not yet a doctor, so it was unusual for someone to refer to him as one, which Stewart had done. He seemed especially eager to come in. Marcia stepped to one side, and he brushed by in a pungent aura of after-shave. She shouted for Larry, and, having taken an instant dislike to the person she had just let in, exited directly without explanation. Marcia was used to expressing her displeasure with Larry's business by being stubbornly, quietly rude to his associates. Now they were coming by before breakfast. Marching down the steep front steps, buttoning her coat against the morning chill, she saw Stewart's long, shiny black Cadillac parked below, looking especially out of place among all the beat-up student-owned heaps along Forty-third Street. It gave her a sinking feeling. Something about that man, that briefcase, the rings, the after-shave, that car, and being here at 7:30 a.m. . . . it spelled trouble.

She thought, *What has Larry gotten us into now?*

In fact, Marcia was one of the reasons Mark Stewart was there that morning. With their wedding only six months away, Marcia's deadline for Larry to stop dealing was growing close. She knew little of the particulars, but Larry had made his million. Although much of it was still tied up in the next deal, or in uncollected debts, Larry had accumulated quite a stash in safe-deposit boxes and in the drawers of the old dressers in the basement. While he and Marcia were students, they really had had little to spend money on, so Larry had kept rolling his back into the business and making more. But now things were going to change. In a few months they would be married. In a little more than a year he would be finished with dental school. Larry knew Marcia wanted children. So did he. They would want a nice house in the suburbs, and a car . . . no, two cars, one for him and one for her. Larry had fallen in love with the Main Line on trips out to Paul Mikuta's house and during the summer when he drove a taxi. That was definitely where he wanted to move after leaving dental school. But how could he consider spending this way without showing a sudden, inexplicable jump in income? For years he had been filling out financial aid forms at Penn that showed his earnings to be just a few thousand a year.

Larry's most recent plan was to make a million, then turn the business over to David and Ken and find a way, somehow, to legitimize his cash. He wanted to be able to spend his money without running afoul of the IRS, and he wanted to invest his cash in something that would protect it from galloping inflation.

Larry had a phobia about inflation. He was afraid his million would shrink to mere thousands if he just buried it. Other people had nightmares about falling or drowning or about losing a loved one; Larry had nightmares about double-digit inflation. He wanted the money working for him, not growing mold in the earth. What he needed was to translate his illegal wealth into sturdy, legal capital.

For help, Larry turned to a classmate named Jonathon Lax, who in addition to carrying a full course load in dental school owned a thriving appliance business. Larry admired Lax, and felt they had a lot in common. Both were managing successful businesses on the side while they attended dental school. The only difference was, Lax's appliances were legal.

Lax was hardly astonished to learn that Larry was a dealer. Nearly everyone at Penn knew that. But he was shocked to learn how much money Larry had made at it.

"I kind of want to live the lifestyle I can afford, but I don't want to show any of it," said Larry.

So Lax introduced Larry to a lawyer, who referred the rich young dealer to a managing partner of a prominent Philadelphia law firm. They had met in Center City on Tuesday, the day before Paula Van Horn's mugging. Seated on leather chairs in a stately paneled conference room, Larry had shaken hands with the lawyer, a middle-aged man in a well-cut wool suit, and begun to explain his problem. At first he had planned to keep the source of his millions out of the conversation, but it was awkward talking about it without explaining. Finally, he just admitted the money had come from dealing. How else to describe his predicament?

"My concept is that I set up a corporation, and that corporation pays me a salary so I can start putting money in the bank," said Larry. "Then I could invest in real estate."

The lawyer stared out the window for nearly a full minute before answering. Larry held his breath. Had he gone too far?

"Maybe I should call someone," the lawyer said.

"Who?" asked Larry.

As Larry would recall later, the lawyer explained that what he needed was a tax expert, someone who knew how to avoid "red flags," things like large jumps in income and other line items on tax returns that IRS accountants were likely to note.

Larry breathed a silent sigh of relief.

The lawyer said that the cash was doubly valuable just then because interest rates were high. He said he would introduce Larry to a fellow named Mark Stewart.

Larry was so relieved. *The man had not even batted an eye!* This was one moment that strongly buttressed Larry's rationale for dealing cocaine: It was a harmless party drug (like marijuana) that had society's tacit acceptance, and it was bound to be legal eventually. Here was the managing partner of an eminently respectable law firm; Larry had just confessed that he was dealing hundreds of thousands of dollars in illegal drugs; and the man was as ready to give him advice on how to manage his money as if Larry had made it selling socks!

The lawyer explained that this Mark Stewart had done a lot of real estate development deals in Philadelphia explaining that he had built a Jewish retirement home on Roosevelt Boulevard, and had a lot of wealthy friends in the Jewish community. The lawyer also said that Stewart was financial advisor to a number of professional sports figures. He represented Freddie Shero, the coach who had led the Philadelphia Flyers hockey team to two Stanley Cups in the seventies, had done some work for Larry Bowa, the Phillies' shortstop, and was into boxing promotions.

"Like I said, Mark knows everybody. He's had his ups and downs in this town, but he's always been able to pay people back."

That was something Larry, especially, could appreciate. He knew from hard experience about the ups and downs of business. He had lost quite a bit himself from time to time, but he took pride in the fact that he, too, had always been able to pay people back.

"I really think he can help you out," Larry remembered the lawyer saying.

Larry agreed to meet with Stewart, but he was wary. He knew he was getting into things he knew little about. As Larry would later recall, Stewart called the next day. Larry said his schedule was crowded.

"How early do you get up?" asked Stewart.

"I'm usually up by seven a.m.; that's when my girlfriend goes to work."

"How about seven-thirty?"

"That early? Where?"

"I'll come by your place. Where do you live?"

After Marcia left that morning, Stewart sipped fresh orange juice—Larry never drank coffee—in the living room. Larry ate a bowl of cereal. They chatted about Larry's new lawyer, then started talking business. Larry said he had a lot of cash he wanted to invest quietly. He mentioned the figure five hundred thousand dollars.

"Where did you get that kind of money?" asked Stewart. It was hard to disguise his astonishment.

"Dealing," said Larry.

Stewart was going to ask "Dealing what?" but he thought better of it. There was a hint of a smile on Larry's face, a faintly wicked smile. In that instant the thirty-nine-year-old businessman made a choice. What his business had always lacked was liquidity. Here was more cash than he would ever need. And yet . . . crime was a road he was reluctant to venture too far down.

As Larry later remembered the meeting, he began to candidly explain his predicament. Stewart listened attentively and asked good questions. Larry sensed that he was being sized up. He could see that the financial expert wanted to make sure he wasn't dealing with an amateur, someone who might drag him down in a drug bust.

Larry explained that the business was handled almost exclusively by others, and that in nearly six years of dealing (and more than a million in profits) he had never even come close to being busted.

Stewart had made his decision. He began by explaining how he might go about converting some of Larry's cash into mortgages, certificates of deposit, and other financial instruments. He said he often handled large transactions for his friends in the Jewish community, and that he knew people at the Philadelphia branch of Bank Leumi Le-Israel, an Israeli bank. He saw plenty of ways to launder Larry's cash. The easiest was to begin by selling Larry a half interest in some of his businesses and start paying him a salary. Larry said he would want to start with a somewhat modest salary, something like $15,000 annually, or $290–$300 per week, and gradually increase it over the next few years. Stewart saw no problem with that. Another option was to set up a parent corporation that would own all the businesses and that could periodically issue Larry stock in return for cash payments.

The businessman explained, according to Larry, that every dollar in cash in the current market was worth about two dollars on paper. He said Larry could convert the cash into mortgages and real estate holdings easily, because so many people would prefer to deal in cash.

"You buy the mortgage and maybe give somebody fifty grand under the table. That way you buy something worth two hundred and only a hundred and fifty shows." He made it sound easy.

He outlined his tax shelter business, his sports promotions efforts, his involvement with a local record company, other things. . . . Stewart talked fast, looked him straight in the eye, and sounded reassuring and convincing.

"Look, I don't know that much about business," said Larry.

"You don't make a million dollars without knowing something about business," said Mark.

"Oh, I know about *my* business, but all these other things . . . I think I'd like to stick with real estate."

Larry said he wanted some time to think about it and check things out. Stewart didn't seem at all put off.

"Why don't you stop up at my office in Center City tomorrow and I can show you more?" he said.

Larry was impressed. He was so relieved to have found someone to help him. What if it all really could be arranged so easily? He walked Stewart out to his car and shook hands with him happily.

"Tomorrow afternoon," he said.

"So, who is this person?" asked Marcia when she saw Larry again that evening.

Larry explained that this was the guy who had been recommended to him; the one who was going to help him legitimize his money.

"That explains why he was so eager to get in here. Couldn't wait to get his hands on the cash."

"He's all right, Marcia."

"He's just another one of your sleazeballs. I can smell 'em a mile away."

"Oh, don't worry," said Larry. "He's fine. He's fine. My lawyer wouldn't steer me wrong."

The next afternoon Larry drove over to Center City, parked, and walked to the front door of the Wellington Building, an imposing building right on Rittenhouse Square, one of Philadelphia's choicest Center City locations.

A guard asked Larry whom he wanted to see, and made a call to verify the appointment before buzzing him through glass doors into Stewart's first-floor suite. Larry was impressed. The office furnishings were plush, modern, and colorful. He was screened by two more secretaries before being led into Stewart's inner sanctum, a broad carpeted office with a giant desk, wood with fancy leather inlays. Larry was most impressed with the telephone on Stewart's desk; it had about twenty lines, including extensions in the personal bathroom off to the left! Stewart gladly spent a few minutes showing off his handsomely decorated office, unrolling a soft felt pouch that was filled with unusual, expensive pens, showing off his collection of nearly three hundred pipes, explaining that all the phone lines were WATS

lines, displaying an autographed copy of Fred Shero's biography . . .
Larry was like a kid in a candy store.

Stewart spent the next hour laying out on his desk detailed financial statements for each of his companies. It was a confusing assault
of facts and figures. Larry did his best to follow the explanations and
ask intelligent questions, but there was no way for him to evaluate
these things critically. On paper, Stewart looked like a wizard. His
long list of investors and clients included doctors and dentists, prominent attorneys, wealthy Philadelphia businessmen, and some well-
known local sports figures such as Eagles linebacker Jerry Robinson
and running back Reggie Wilkes and Fred Shero. For any questions
Larry did ask, Stewart had ready, convincing answers.

Larry noted that several times during their meeting Stewart had
picked up the phone and asked impatiently, "Are they here yet?"

Finally, a young man opened the door to the office, walked across
to Stewart's desk, and handed him a box. Stewart leaned across and
gave them to Larry.

"These are yours."

Inside were nearly a thousand business cards, still warm from
the printing press. They read, "TEC Records, Inc.," and listed, "Dr.
Lawrence W. Lavin, Vice-President," underneath. Larry grinned with
pleasure. This was the topper. The cards quite literally seemed to
place his goal in his hands.

In fact, as Larry would learn much later, at the time Stewart was
in financial straits. TEC Records and the property owned by 20th
and Penrose Corp. were losing investments, valuable only as tax shelters. Stewart was only a managing partner with no equity in the
Wellington Square Apartments, his most impressive asset, and he was
close to a hundred thousand dollars in debt to his partners—but Larry
had no way of knowing that. This entrepreneur's eagerness to sell half
his assets to a twenty-four-year-old dental student he had never met
should have been a clue, but Stewart had, after all, come highly recommended. And besides, Stewart was a bridge. Larry couldn't expect
someone wholly on the up-and-up to help legitimize his drug money.

To Mark Stewart, Larry Lavin was the Golden Goose. For a
man who made his living by handling other people's money, it was
a once-in-a-lifetime opportunity.

He named five companies: TEC Records, the Wellington Square
Apartments, 20th and Penrose Corp., Sports Management, Inc., and
Professional Talent Management, Inc. Larry later recalled that Stewart said if Larry paid five hundred thousand for a 49 percent interest
in all five companies, he could start collecting a paycheck on Friday.

"We'll even backdate a few, so you can start off with seven or
eight checks," he said.

Larry was tempted. But he recalled that he told Stewart that if they made any deal, it would have to be in writing.

"Are you sure that's a good idea?" Stewart asked.

"Well, there's a risk, Mark. But suppose I give you half a million and you, God forbid, get run over by a truck. Who is going to believe that I own half interest in these things?"

So Stewart agreed. He would have papers drawn up. Larry said he would come back in two days, on a Friday.

Larry had left the meeting with a sense of relief. The box of business cards was still on Stewart's desk. He had at least a day or two to think things over.

The following morning, before his clinic hours, Larry went to look at the tangible portion of what Stewart wanted him to buy. He had already seen the Wellington Building and was impressed with that. So he drove out to Twentieth and Penrose. There, he was surprised to find that the building supposedly owned by Stewart was a Quality Inn!

He would later remember that on Friday, when he arrived in Stewart's office, he confronted Mark with what he had discovered.

"That's a Quality Inn out there, Mark. You don't own that."

"That's true," Mark said.

"Why did you represent this to me as yours?"

"Let me explain."

Stewart's explanation was swift and convincing. He had borrowed money to build that motel in 1974, but before the project was complete his financial backers had pulled out. Stewart suspected that it had dawned on them that hotel rooms would be at a premium in 1976 when tourists were expected to crowd into Philadelphia for the Bicentennial celebrations. They foreclosed on the hotel and opened it as a Quality Inn. Feeling cheated, Stewart had challenged the foreclosure in court and had won a verdict that forced the lenders to turn over to him a property of equivalent value—which turned out to be a small hotel in Atlanta. The company was still named 20th and Penrose, but the property was in Atlanta. He had documents to back up the story.

"To be honest with you, that Georgia property is not all that valuable," Larry recalled that Stewart said, "but it makes a terrific tax shelter because it generates so much loss." Stewart explained that one of his specialties was selling tax shelters.

Larry felt foolish.

Sheepishly, he said, "You wonder what you're getting for five hundred thousand dollars."

Stewart was gracious about it. He complimented Larry on his thoroughness.

The papers were simple, just a single sheet with three paragraphs, labeled "Assignment," and an attachment called "Schedule A." The Assignment declared that in return for "Five Hundred Thousand, $500,000"—Stewart wrote in the amount thickly with a black felt-tip pen—he was transferring to "Lawrence Lavin . . . forty-nine percent of my right, title, ownership and interest in the companies listed on Schedule A." Schedule A, which was attached, listed twelve separate companies, including one "Larmark, Inc.," a parent corporation that he had just invented. After Larry signed, with grand sweeping *L*s and a tiny elevated *W*, Stewart handed him his first seven paychecks, each, after taxes, worth about $230.

Larry had fifty thousand in cash in his black briefcase. There was another hundred ten thousand in transit to Miami Beach, in the hands of a new runner named Willie Harcourt who had been recruited by David and Ken. They worked out a payment schedule, and Larry left with his box of new business cards.

Larry had converted the first installment of his fortune into "legitimate" earnings. It was one of the happiest moments of his life. That weekend he went out with Marcia and made a down payment on a brand-new black Volvo and an assortment of lenses, big and small, for his 35-mm camera.

Billy Motto hung on to his pot business, despite the growing demand for cocaine. He had pot people with no interest in cocaine, and cocaine people with no interest in pot. But either way he was making more money than he had ever dreamed would be his.

So much money that he was able to convince his mother to retire early from her longtime job as a seamstress at the Quartermaster "sweatshop," as she called it, and to give his father enough money to retire from his street-corner produce vending. Billy sponsored a neighborhood softball team. He hung out on the same street corner down off South Street, where people who used to laugh at him now came to ask for a loan, or for advice.

Larry had big plans for Billy South Philly. He had begun to think of Billy as someone who could eventually run the business for him. He liked Billy even more than David, although Ackerman was clearly better educated. As David had made more money and taken on more responsibility, he had lost some of his initial respect for Larry. Once David had mastered the details of the breaks, of keeping the books and changing the money, recruiting runners, etc., much of Larry's mysterious aura of power and success evaporated. At times, there were signs that David felt he knew how to run things better than Larry himself. There were times when Larry could see David eventually becoming a rival—and a dangerous one at that. Billy, on the other hand, had proved himself to be eminently capable—his payment for goods delivered was always punctual and accurate to the penny—and admired Larry so openly that he was a joy to have around.

He knew he could trust Billy because of something that had happened six months earlier, in the early fall of 1979. Even after Billy had begun dealing cocaine, he had kept after Larry, month after month, about his desire to be introduced to marijuana contacts in Florida. Finally, by summer of 1979, about the time cocaine had reduced Larry's interest in pot dealing to a minimum anyway, Larry agreed to let him make a run to Florida. Billy had never even been on a plane.

Larry gave him sixty thousand dollars. Billy showed the money to a few of his friends down in South Philly.

"Take it," they said. "Rob him. He's just some college kid; what's he going to do about it?"

But Billy said, "No. I'll stay with him and make more money than this."

Billy flew to Miami, barely taking his eyes off the window the whole trip. Larry had coached him on every detail. At the airport he would have to take a cab to the hotel, where he would be contacted by a supplier. Billy flagged a cab, checked nervously into the hotel, and waited, pacing his hotel room.

And it all happened just as Larry said it would. Within an hour this short, mugsy guy showed up with a big bodyguard. They walked out to the hotel parking lot. The mugsy guy showed Billy two to three hundred pounds of pot in the trunk of a new model Chevy. Billy handed over the cash.

"So you're Billy," said the supplier. "I've heard a lot about you from Larry. Why you doing business through him? You and me, we should do business directly."

Again, Billy resisted. Larry had been good to him. He knew Larry was bringing him along, letting him get bigger. Something told Billy that he would do better by sticking with Larry.

"No thanks," he said. "I don't do business that way."

The two men left Billy with the car, which he then drove directly back to Philadelphia.

In time, the story about Billy's response to the offer in Florida got back to Larry. It said something about Billy that really impressed him. Larry had to ask himself: *What would David Ackerman have done?*

Stewart started sending Flyers tickets over to Osage Avenue regularly, great tickets just two rows up behind the players' bench at center ice. Larry took Marcia to one game and she was hooked. So they started going out to dinner and then to the Spectrum every two weeks. Larry took along his new camera and huge telephoto lens for closeup shots of the action.

After one such outing in late March, Larry and Marcia and L.A. returned late to the Osage Avenue apartment. Larry invited L.A. in for a drink.

They had been inside only for a moment when the doorbell rang. Marcia had gone into the kitchen to make her lunch for work the next day. Larry opened the apartment door and crossed the first-floor hallway to the front door of the apartment building. He opened the door a crack and peeked out at a face he didn't recognize.

"There's been an accident outside; can you help us?" the man asked. He was a black man about Larry's age. Judging by his accent he was not a Penn student.

Larry turned the handle to open the door, and as he did he felt a sudden impact against it, pushing him over backward, off-balance. Larry could see there were two men pushing through. In one man's hand was the blue-black metallic flash of a gun.

Larry quickly threw his full weight back against the door, partly closing it. Only two arms and hands and guns protruded through the doorway. Larry screamed for help.

"Call the police!" he shouted.

He knew he couldn't hold the door. Just as it gave way, L.A. came running out to the foyer. One of the men smacked L.A. across the face hard with the pistol, knocking him down. Larry lunged at the man's back, but got hit over the back of the head by the man behind him. He went down.

When Marcia heard the doorbell ring she had assumed it was someone coming by to do business with Larry again, which irritated her. Then she heard Larry scream. She wheeled around and looked out toward the front. She saw the arms sticking through the door with guns, and Larry and L.A. struggling. She stepped back into the kitchen confused. Should she call the police? But then she knew Larry had drawers full of money and cocaine and Quaaludes in the back room. . . .

Then one of the men was in the living room shouting, "Don't look at us! Don't look at our faces!"

He saw Marcia in the kitchen.

"Come here, bitch!" he shouted, showing his gun. Marcia stepped toward the living room and he grabbed her by the arm and pushed her down on the floor. L.A.'s face was pressed straight into the thick blue rug. He was bleeding and his glasses were shattered. Next to her Larry raised his head, and one of the standing men clobbered him again with the gun. One of the men held a gun to the back of her head.

"Just don't look at us and nobody is going to get hurt," he said. Marcia pushed her nose into the carpet.

Larry lifted his head again. "I know who you guys are and you better leave right now!" He got hit over the head again. Marcia thought, *Why doesn't he just shut up?*

One of the men had gone directly back to Larry's study. They could hear him trying the drawers to Larry's desk. He came striding back into the living room hollering, "The keys. We know you have keys to the desk back there. Where you keep the money."

Larry fished the keys from his pocket and handed them up. "Look, this man's hurt; we have to get him to the hospital," he said, and got hit on the back of the head again.

"Stop lifting your head up, you idiot," Marcia told him.

L.A. hadn't stirred.

One of the men went through the kitchen and down the hall. They could hear the keys jingle and the desk drawers being opened. The other man moved around the living room, jerking the phone cords from the wall and then trying, still holding the gun, to work Larry's stereo out from its space on a shelf by the TV. Suddenly, the gun went off.

There was a moment of stunned silence.

"Did anyone get hurt?" Larry shouted.

Both men bolted. They slammed the door shut behind them and were gone.

Larry, Marcia, and L.A. lay quietly for a few moments until they were sure the men had gone. Then Larry bounded up to check out his desk in the back room. Marcia turned to help L.A., who sat up dazed and bleeding. A neighbor from upstairs, a dental school classmate whom Larry paid to help break up cocaine shipments, banged on the door.

"Are you all right?" he shouted through the door. "Should I call the police?"

The men had taken off with Larry's keys, and in the confusion of the moment Marcia couldn't remember where she had put hers, so she couldn't open the door.

In the back room Larry inventoried his drawers. Two cash drawers had been opened. One was filled with neatly stacked ten-dollar bills. They hadn't been touched. The drawer that had been filled with twenties was empty. There had been a pound of cocaine in a Ziploc plastic bag on top of the desk. That was gone. They had evidently torn the bag open before taking it, because there was a mess of white powder on the floor.

Larry was thinking fast. Someone had surely heard the shot. The police were going to be there soon.

He ran out to the living room.

"Are you okay?" he asked Marcia.

"Yeah."

"Good. Go vacuum the back room."

Through the locked door, he told his neighbor to run around back to the window of his study. With Marcia running the vacuum, Larry hurriedly passed handfuls of bills and bags of drugs out the window to his neighbor. They had the room completely cleaned long before the police arrived.

Larry's wheels were turning fast. He found Marcia's keys and opened the front door. Then he got his neighbor to help him move the stereo. The more stuff he could remove to the basement fast, the more he could claim had been stolen. He certainly couldn't report that they had gotten away with thirty thousand in cash and a pound of cocaine.

He was carrying the stereo down the hallway to the basement steps when the police arrived.

Larry blurted an explanation. "I was afraid they'd come back, so we're moving a few things out," he said.

The cops couldn't have been nicer.

"They got the stereo, huh?" one of the cops said.

Larry caught on immediately. "The stereo? Yeah, my five-hundred-dollar stereo."

Inside the apartment the same cop glanced over at Larry's new Sony.

"They got your TV, too, did they?"

"Oh, yeah," said Larry, smiling.

"Damn shame," said the cop, adding it to his report.

When the police were gone and L.A. had bandaged his head and gone home, Marcia collapsed on the bed. She was numb, and frightened. As usual, Larry went right to the phone. He called Tyrone and Mark Stewart—lately it was as if Mark Stewart were taking over their lives. Marcia couldn't stand him. She sobbed.

Paul Mikuta stopped by to see if she and Larry were all right. He sat on the bed and wrapped his arms around Marcia to comfort her.

"I feel sorry for you," said Paul. "All the things that Larry puts you through."

"This wasn't his fault," she said.

Then Larry marched in and angrily announced that he knew why this had happened.

"It's Warren," he said.

Warren was one of the toughest characters among the West Philly dealers Larry had met through his dealings with Tyrone. Even Tyrone had warned Larry about him. That afternoon Warren had come by with some Quaaludes. Larry had a weakness for Quaaludes, and in 1980 they were becoming rare. So he had counted out a few thousand dollars to pay for them, being careful not to open the drawers where major cash was stacked. But as he was counting, one of his runners had stopped in unexpectedly and, without thinking, had cheerfully poured sixty-five thousand in cash out of a tennis bag onto a chair in the back office. Larry had half expected Warren to pull a gun right there. He was so nervous he inadvertently overpaid for the Quaaludes.

"I just talked to Tyrone, and he said Warren was telling people just this afternoon that if I wasn't more careful, I was going to be ripped off," said Larry. "Anyway, I got word out on the street about these guys. I'm going to get them."

Marcia had listened to all this as though in shock. She was no longer just frightened. Now that she knew how and why this had happened, she was furious!

"This *is* your fault!" she said, glaring at Larry.

"What?"

"How could you let that happen to us! You let those people into my home bringing money and drugs at all hours of the day and night. I can't even sit around on the couch at night and watch TV without people coming in and out of my own home! You let anyone in from off the street! I'm not surprised this happened! We could have all been killed!"

Larry was stunned. Her sudden outburst took Larry and Paul by surprise.

"This wasn't my fault," Larry protested.

"Larry, you have got to stop. You have got to stop doing this. Something worse is going to happen! Don't you see?"

"I've got word out on the street right now about these guys," Larry said. "It's not going to happen again. I'm going to get these guys."

"Oh, that's just great!" said Marcia. It was as if they were on different wavelengths.

Paul excused himself, awkwardly, leaving Marcia and Larry to fight things out. She could not get him to see that it *was* his fault, that it had grown out of his dealing, not just because one stupid runner had dumped money on the couch in front of the wrong person.

"You're like an addict," Marcia said. "You keep promising to quit, and then you don't. It's like you're crazy or something, Larry. You're addicted to this. And you can't even admit it to yourself."

"That's not true, Marcia. I know what I'm doing."

"Well, I'm leaving. I just can't take any more of this."

Larry was, for once, silent. Marcia had gotten angry before about his dealing. They had shouted at each other about it often enough. But she had never before threatened to leave.

"Please don't," he said at last. There was no cockiness in his voice now. "Don't leave," he said. "I'll stop."

Marcia was moved by his depth of feeling. In recent months she had had serious doubts about his affection for her, and as their wedding date approached the issue was coming to a head. It was more than six years since Marcia's first day at Penn, since the day she met Larry. She had matured from a pudgy, insecure teenager to a very poised and pretty young woman. She wore her straight brown hair short. Her face had lost all trace of its teenage chubbiness. It was now a wide oval with gentle contours at the high cheekbones, with large brown eyes and dark eyebrows. Gone was the round, childlike figure of freshman year. Marcia had a small, lean figure and kept herself in good shape. And just as she had physically shed baby fat, Marcia's personality had become more lean and sharply defined. Earning her own degree and making her own way as a physical therapist had given her confidence in herself. Although she remained resolutely devoted to him, she no longer hesitated to criticize Larry. She had no doubt that her judgment was sounder than his. To Marcia, Larry's obsession with dealing and making money had become pathetic. She knew she loved him, despite everything, and it relieved her deeply to see that he was not so far gone that he was ready to throw away their future. Surely Larry was too bright and too basically decent to avoid eventually being drawn into her orbit.

So Marcia stayed.

Of course, in the next few weeks Larry explained that he would have to wrap up a few loose ends, jut to shore up his million.

"After that I'll never have to do this again," he said. "We'll have money for the rest of our lives."

Larry always tried to emphasize the benefits of his dealing: They had spent a lovely week in the Bahamas the previous spring after Larry came back from Aspen, and in the fall they had traveled to Williamsburg and Virginia Beach—she and Larry both loved the area. In a month they were planning to take off again for Miami Beach. And it was true that Marcia loved the vacations. But what Larry couldn't seem to grasp was that she loved them mostly because they took him away from the damn telephone for a week. When they were on vacation they were like a normal couple! She would have been just as happy to spend a week at the Jersey shore on her own salary.

Before Marcia went to bed, Larry had also promised that they would move out of the neighborhood immediately, and that he would never again allow the world of his drug dealing to intrude on their home.

Marcia tried to sleep while Larry spent the rest of the night on the phone. She could hear his voice in the back room, sharing his anger over the lost money and conspiring to get it back.

Larry was talking to Tyrone, who said he had a friend who would get the thirty thousand back for a fee of five thousand dollars.

"How are you going to do that?" asked Larry.

In a tone that conveyed menace, Tyrone explained, "Well, Larry, Fred is just going to go in there and get it back . . . you know what I mean?"

"I don't want them killed!" said Larry. "I just want the money back!"

"Supposing they don't want to just give it to us?" said Tyrone, laughing.

"Then forget it," Larry said, exasperated.

"You don't do anything about this, word will get around and you'll get ripped off a lot, man," said Tyrone.

First thing in the morning Marcia insisted that Larry call a locksmith to have the front and back door locks changed. She called her boss at the VA hospital and explained what had happened, and got the day off.

Then Larry called Mark Stewart again.

Before noon they were driving down to look at a townhouse in Society Hill, which featured the most expensive residential real estate in the city. Society Hill originally took its name from a pre–Revolutionary War maritime commerce firm called The Society of Free Traders, but the name had long since come to signify the pinnacle of Philadelphia's neighborhoods. Larry and Marcia were shown a three-story maroon brick townhouse, 4 Willings Alley Mews, one in a row of small modern structures that blended easily with the Colonial architecture in the heart of Philadelphia's most historic district. The new houses were shoehorned in a tiny alley, just two blocks away from Independence Hall and directly opposite Saint James Church, the oldest Catholic church in America. The house had one room on each of its five levels, counting the basement kitchen and rooftop patio, and cost $150,000. Larry was worried about the IRS. If a $150,000 home out of the blue wasn't a "red flag," nothing was. But according to Larry, Mark reassured him.

"Look, Larry, you need the house," Mark said. "If worst comes to the worst, I can always say that I loaned you the money."

These were much fancier digs than those of ordinary Penn graduate students. The basement kitchen was spacious and modern, with all new appliances and a black-and-white checkered tile floor. The first level, which one ascended to up an open stairwell on curving stairs, was a completely open living room with a fireplace and with floors inlaid with beautiful parquetry. The second floor was a big bedroom and bath with a wide closet area with a new washer and dryer. The third floor was another bedroom, a good place for Larry's study and Marcia's sewing machine and, thought Larry, maybe a pool table. The rooftop patio overlooked the city's most quaint, historic sights and offered, in the distance, a panoramic vista of America's fourth largest metropolis. To the east was the Delaware River and the lights of Penn's Landing. Upriver was the blue steel Ben Franklin Bridge. Downriver the gray span of the Walt Whitman Bridge. Below, on the slate gray river, moved vessels of all shapes and sizes: tiny speed-boats, tugs, warships, barges and giant tankers. Larry loved it.

Marcia hated it.

"It's too vertical," she said. "It's like living in an elevator shaft. And there aren't any trees or grass."

But Larry wanted it. Marcia knew she couldn't go back to Osage Avenue. And she had hopes that by moving away from Penn, Larry's dealing connections would dry up.

So they took it. Mark Stewart was only too eager to make the financial arrangements. Larry gave him sixty thousand in cash and Mark wrote him a check, which Larry deposited at Bank Leumi. Larry then obtained a ninety-thousand-dollar mortgage. Larry hired two men and a truck to move their belongings, and they were living in Society Hill by evening. Larry didn't tell Tyrone and Fred that he was moving. He promised Marcia that he was leaving that kind of dealing behind for good.

Sometime in the next few weeks Larry bought a gun, a black .22-caliber short Beretta. He had been advised to get a .25-caliber, because it was small enough to fit comfortably inside a vest pocket when he wore a three-piece suit, but the gun shop didn't have any of that model so he settled on a smaller but equally suitable model. Mark had been angry when he heard about the robbery, with concern that was both paternal and proprietary. He offered Larry help in tracking down the people who had done it, and chided him for being so casual about letting people come by his house. Mark helped with arrangements for the gun, telling Larry where to buy it and directing him (with instructions to pay a hundred dollars) to Abe Schwartz, the Philadelphia police detective responsible for processing gun permits. Larry put the pistol in the top drawer of the table beside his bed.

Three months had passed since the afternoon when Paula Van Horn reported the robbery. For all of that time, David Ackerman had spied on his housemate. He hid a long-playing tape recorder in her room and steamed open all of her mail. Slowly, he accumulated evidence. Paula had bought skis for her children. David thought that was odd, because Paula never had seemed to have any extra money before.

"Oh, come on," said Larry. "She bought skis for her kids. What's the big deal?"

Next, Ackerman came up with a phone conversation where Paula, from what could be learned listening only to her end of the conversation, appeared to be discussing plans for buying and rehabbing a dilapidated row home in South Philly.

"This is nothing," said Larry. "I've been paying her well."

But when Ackerman found the key to a safe-deposit box, and a receipt that showed Paula had opened it shortly after the "robbery," Larry's faith was shaken. He still wasn't convinced, but he agreed that it was worth checking out.

Through Mark Stewart, Larry had met Slim Robinson, a big black man who trained fighters. Slim was a stylish man, favoring wide-brimmed colorful hats and matching suits. He drove a big black Delta 88 with a plush velour interior and spoked wheel covers—all of it adding an aura of mystery, power, and menace. Larry asked Slim to accompany him on a visit to Paula's apartment. When Glen Fuller showed up from one of his Florida runs, he wanted in on it, too. This was Glen's kind of action. Larry gave Glen his unloaded .22-caliber pistol.

"This'll get her thinking," he said.

Before leaving, Larry phoned Paula. He said he was coming over with two Philadelphia police detectives.

"They think they've finally got a break in the case, and they want you to come down to headquarters to pick the suspect out of a lineup," he said.

When Paula opened the door of her apartment on Fitzwater Street, she took a long look at his companions and decided they looked nothing at all like policemen.

Glen immediately reached out and stuck the gun in her belly.

"We want the money back," he said.

And Paula confessed. It happened that fast. None of it was her idea, she said. She said she met this guy—the man who had come forward on the day of the robbery and told police he had witnessed it and given chase to the thief. He had forced her to do it.

"Where's my money?" asked Larry.

"He took it," she said.

"Well, where is he?"

"I don't know."

Then Larry produced the safe-deposit-box key. Paula seemed shocked.

"Where'd you get that?" she asked.

"Never mind about that."

"The guy was nice to me. He let me keep some of the money."

"How much?"

"Half—but I spent some of that already."

"Let's go," said Larry.

Paula said she had to change her clothes first.

"What for?" Larry asked.

She scowled. "I'm wet," she said. Her bladder had failed when the pistol was pushed into her side. The men laughed.

Larry didn't want to let Paula out of their sight, so Glen volunteered to go upstairs and keep an eye on her. In the bedroom, as Paula quickly pulled off her clothes in the bathroom, Glen said, "Since you're stripped down, how 'bout a little quickie?"

Paula screamed. Larry and Slim came running. Paula said Glen was going to rape her.

"Just kidding, just kidding," said Glen, chuckling. "Boy can she scream!"

Larry had to laugh.

On the long drive out to Pottstown, Slim entertained Larry and Glen by telling Paula that Larry was really dealing drugs as a front for the "Black Mafia."

"You don't think we'd let this little white boy make all that money for himself?" said Slim.

At the bank, Glen claimed to be Paula's boyfriend and accompanied her into the small room where she opened the safe-deposit box. There was about forty thousand dollars there, and plane tickets to Europe. Paula explained that she had planned to take her children on a vacation.

Afterward they all went to Smokie Joe's, a popular tavern and restaurant just off Penn's campus, and Larry bought Paula lunch and some drinks. He said she could keep the plane tickets and the money in her bank account so she could take her kids to Europe.

The bottom line, after David Ackerman got his reward, was that Larry was out eighty thousand dollars.

Sometime in Larry's junior year of dental school, one of Larry's classmates wrote an anonymous letter to the dean. The writer explained that someone in authority ought to know, if they didn't already, that Larry Lavin was a major drug dealer. Already six of his classmates had been drawn into the business, and several had become heavy cocaine users.

The letter was forwarded to Penn's security police, who had a few scraps of similar information about Larry from his undergraduate days. They called the Philadelphia police.

On and off during junior year, city detectives began surveillance of the comings and goings at 4300 Osage Avenue—which added credence to the initial report. Then, when Larry and Marcia suddenly moved into a new three-story house in the city's most expensive neighborhood, that seemed to clinch it. After all, this was a student who annually filled out financial aid statements at Penn reporting an income of less than $10,000. How could he afford a $150,000 home?

Larry Lavin's name was added to a hit list at the Philadelphia district attorney's office.

Marcia was feeling better about things in the spring. Her last few months on Osage Avenue had been bad, the worst in her years of living with Larry.

"Why do you want to marry me?" she had pleaded with him one night after he had been out late again, and then preoccupied on the phone until past midnight.

Larry was always quick to reassure Marcia. He was good at it. Couldn't she tell how much he loved her? Wasn't he just about completely out of the dealing business, just as he had promised?

The move to Willings Alley Mews, even though Marcia hated the house, had at least ended the traffic of drug dealers in and out of her home. There were no more rent bills, and Larry's new "legitimate" income enabled her to practically bank her paycheck from the VA hospital—no more paying his ridiculous $350 monthly phone bills. For Larry's birthday in March she brought home a chestnut Labrador puppy. They gave the dog the same name as Larry's red-haired older brother, Rusty.

She and Larry had found a Catholic church to get married in, Saint Cornelius out off Route 1 in Chadds Ford—most priests refused to schedule wedding masses for couples who were not members of their parish—and set a date, Saturday, June 7 at 11:30 a.m. That kept Marcia busy. Their invitations had gone out in fancy script on pale yellow stationery embossed with flowers. Larry, of course, wanted to invite about five hundred people. Marcia wanted something small.

"I don't want any drug dealers at my wedding," she said. Trouble was, nearly all of Larry's friends were drug dealers.

Glen Fuller was definitely out, but Ken Weidler and David Ackerman and Stu Thomas and Andy Mainardi and Paul Mikuta would all get invitations. Marcia said Mark Stewart was definitely out. Larry battled hard to put him on the list, and finally Marcia gave in.

The reception was set for one o'clock at the D'Ignazio Town House in Media. Marcia bought white satin for her own dress, yards of yellow cotton with a small flower print for her bridesmaids, and went to work at her sewing machine.

In April, over spring break, Larry and Marcia flew to Miami Beach for four days. They visited Jungle Land and a serpentarium, lay in the sun, and dined out at fine restaurants. Now, with his money filtering out of the illegal business, with Ken and David handling most of the time-consuming details of dealing, recruiting runners, breaking down the coke according to the "Lavin method," changing money at local banks, etc., Marcia felt certain that marriage was the final push Larry needed to break away from the whole scene, to settle down and concentrate on dentistry, on her, and eventually on their children. She was determined to help that happen. To stress the point, at home Marcia would take the phone—all three lines—off the hook. Each time she did it Larry was furious, but Marcia stubbornly persisted.

Still, the ugly reality continued to intrude. One night Larry's old pot contact from Virginia Tech, Ralph, stopped by Willings Alley Mews with his girlfriend, uninvited. Marcia recognized Ralph, who was short and stocky with thick black hair, as one of Larry's louder, cruder drug associates. She said that Larry wasn't home. Ralph stood with his girlfriend for a moment on the front step, obviously waiting to be invited in.

"Is he coming home soon?" he asked.

"He should be. You can just wait for him out in the car," said Marcia, and she started to close the door.

Ralph put his hand on the door and forced it open.

"I'm coming in here and showing my girlfriend this house," he said angrily, pushing past Marcia into the living room. He took his girlfriend on a tour of the house while Marcia sat downstairs fuming. When they finally left, she slammed the door behind them.

Later, when she angrily told Larry what had happened, he shrugged it off.

"That's just the way he is," he said.

"I don't care how he is. He has no right to push his way into our house!"

"Marcia, you've got to be nice to these people. They owe me money."

"I don't have to be nice to them!" she said.

When intrusions like Ralph's occurred, even Larry's friends sided with Marcia. They couldn't understand why Larry persisted in trying to have things both ways, to maintain the quiet little domestic scene, with a wife opposed to his drug dealing, and yet continue trying to expand his criminal enterprise. When David Ackerman heard the story about Ralph, he said, "Larry, how can you let these people come into your home where your wife lives?"

A few nights later, it was Glen Fuller. Of all Larry's friends, Glen was Marcia's least favorite. He had a grin that struck Marcia as lewd. He stood for everything in Larry's life she hated. She had first met him when she and Larry were undergraduates, on a visit to Haverhill, and was disgusted with the way Larry seemed drawn to him. She had heard a hundred times Larry's boastful stories about stealing a snowmobile with Glen, about ripping off a stereo. . . . It was bad enough having to deal with Glen Fuller in the past. Now Glen was back on the scene, in the thick of things. Marcia didn't care to know the specifics about what Glen was doing for Larry. But she knew he was trouble. She knew that if she was pulling Larry one way, then Glen was surely pulling him the other way. Every time she saw Glen or even heard his name she could feel Larry slipping away.

Glen sensed that Marcia's hard feelings toward him seemed out of proportion, so he tried especially hard to overcome them. As the wedding approached, he got a few of Larry's friends to chip in with him to buy Marcia an antique Hamilton watch, gold framed and studded with diamonds. It had cost Glen thirty-five hundred dollars from someone he had met in Florida, but he figured it was worth closer to ten thousand. When Glen stopped by the house one evening to pick up Larry, on their way to break down his most recent two-kilo delivery, he asked if he could come in; he had a present for Marcia.

Larry stepped out into the alley and told Glen that it would be best if he didn't come in. Marcia was especially touchy about people connected with the business coming by, he explained. Glen could tell that his friend felt bad about it.

"I got something for her, a wedding present," Glen said. "Here. You give it to her. Tell her it's a peace offering."

He waited out in the alley.

Marcia was in the living room watching TV. Larry handed her the present. It was wrapped in silver paper.

"What's this?"

"A wedding present. It's from Glen."

"I don't want it," she said, handing it back.

"Come on, Marcia, just open it."

"No."

"Why? He's just trying to be nice."

"I don't like these people. I don't want them at my wedding and I'm not taking anything from them."

Larry sat down and opened the present. He could see that the watch was expensive, although it was more like one an elderly woman would wear. He was embarrassed for his friend.

"I can't believe you won't take this," said Larry. "Just to be polite. It must have cost him a fortune! It's something he wanted for you."

"He probably stole it."

"You could learn a few things about manners from Glen," he shouted.

So Larry stashed the watch in his desk drawer and left. He told Glen that Marcia was going to wait to open the presents after the wedding. He later gave the watch to his mother.

As the wedding day approached, Mark Stewart began to fret.

Over their four months of working together, the older businessman had taken Larry under his wing. He gave him fatherly advice about his wardrobe, encouraging him to have shirts and suits handmade (as Mark did) and to generally improve his lifestyle. Mark had urged Larry, before the robbery, to find himself a nicer place to live.

"Marcia really likes the apartment," Larry had said.

So Stewart had been delighted to have an excuse to move Larry and Marcia into a nicer home after they were robbed—it was almost like his way of saying "I told you so."

Quickly, Marcia began to loathe Mark Stewart with the same intensity that she loathed Glen Fuller—he was, in a sense, a rival. It seemed as if Larry wanted to *become* Mark Stewart. All of a sudden he wanted nice clothes and a nice car . . . no, not just *nice* things, *expensive* things, often the most expensive things—a handmade this, an imported that. Larry had never cared about such things before. The whole mentality clashed severely with Marcia's style, which was homespun, ordinary, and eminently practical.

For both Marcia and Larry, Mark Stewart came to symbolize—even though he wasn't dealing drugs himself—the other pole of Larry's existence. The Wellington Building became a soothing shelter for Larry. He would go in at night and sit behind Mark's broad desk and juggle the WATS lines to hold conference calls to Florida and up to Haverhill and Vermont, piecing together deals. He worked up his little personal accounting with tiny handwritten numbers on pads of green paper with one of Mark's exotic, expensive pens. Or he would count and bundle money he kept in Stewart's safe, or reread their secret written agreements. Surrounded by the trappings of success that Stewart so assiduously acquired, twenty-five-year-old Larry Lavin could feel himself amounting to something. He could see himself behind the wheel of his own corporate empire. Mark's attitude toward women offered Larry a way of coping with (if not resolving) his differences with Marcia. It was an unabashedly traditional, sexist perspective, one that wrote women off as a species only slightly more significant than the domestic servant. It was like a woman to be frightened about taking risks, right? All women nagged their men, right? Can't live with them; can't live without them. Mark understood.

Several days before the wedding, Larry got a message that Mark wanted to see him at the office.

It was late afternoon when Larry stopped by. Stewart waved him in cordially and introduced him to a man he identified as his staff lawyer.

"I've had him draw up an agreement I want you to see," said Mark, pushing a piece of paper across the desk to Larry.

It was a prenuptial agreement, essentially divesting Marcia of any claim to Larry's assets in the event she and Larry were ever divorced.

"You've got to be kidding," said Larry.

"I know it seems ridiculous now," said Mark. "Trust me."

"Marcia will never sign this."

"Maybe not. Why don't you just ask? If she says yes, it could save you a lot of trouble down the road."

Stewart's lawyer joined in the sales pitch, explaining to Larry the legal nightmares of a divorce action—especially in light of his illegal earnings.

So Larry agreed to try.

Marcia was in the basement kitchen, preparing dinner, when Larry got home. He just came down the steps, crossed the room, and handed it to her.

She read it silently.

"Whose idea was this?" she asked.

"Mark thought it would be a good idea; he said—"

"No way," said Marcia, cutting off Larry's nervous explanation and handing him the piece of paper.

Larry chuckled.

"I didn't think so," he said. "I said I'd ask."

Larry's friends threw him a bachelor party. They invited him to a corporate suite at the Sheraton Hotel by Philadelphia International Airport. It was a fabulous place for a party. In the main room was a long glass conference table covered with a sumptuous spread of meats and breads and salads and candies and desserts. There was an open bar to supplement the ample stores of Quaaludes, joints, and private stashes of white powder. There were stereo speakers and several recessed television screens in the side wall. Connecting with the main room were three bedrooms. Larry's friends had also reserved rooms down the hall.

A cheer sounded when Larry arrived. Paul Mikuta had helped arrange it, and in attendance were Stu Thomas, Andy Mainardi, Larry's brother Rusty, Ken Weidler and David Ackerman and about six others. The party was in full swing when Larry arrived. There had already been heavy drinking and drug taking, so Larry's boys were feeling no pain. Five or six whores were among the crowd. One, a plain-looking black woman, was very workmanlike. Taking the young men off to bedrooms one at a time, slipping a condom over their erections, screwing them, and then stepping out to pick up someone else, her goal was clearly to service the party efficiently and move on.

Then Larry's wedding present arrived: two stunning blond hookers. A stir of excitement went up among the assembled men.

"Don't get any ideas," one of the blonds said. "We're here just for the groom."

Amid cheering, Larry and the blonds were led by the crowd to one of the back bedrooms. To Larry, the blonds were both a perfect 10, like women clipped from the steamy pages of a men's magazine. His friends had arranged through Mark Stewart for this special treat.

In the back bedroom the women undressed Larry and fondled him. Then they stripped and took a shower together, toweled off, and entertained Larry with an exhibition of cunnilingus. Together they had intercourse with him. Then they got dressed and left. To Larry, who was feeling the effects of a Quaalude and some scotch, the whole hour he had spent with these women felt like a dream sequence from an erotic fairy tale. Years later he would keep a snapshot of the women tucked in one of his dental books at his office.

Later in the evening Larry took another hooker to bed. In the bed next to his, Stu Thomas was having sex with another. Larry was spent, just chatting with the naked woman by his side, when the other woman got up from Stu's bed and tapped Larry on the shoulder.

"He said he wants to know if you're ready to switch," she asked.

Larry just laughed.

"Okay, climb on in," he said.

He woke up in the bed alone in the early hours of morning and took a walk around the suite. At some point there had been a food fight, so there were pieces of sandwiches and globs of salad on the rug, ceiling, and walls. His friends were all passed out. Some of them had made it back to beds, others were sprawled on chairs, couches, or the floor, all in various stages of undress. Clothing was scattered everywhere. The whores had all gone home.

* * *

On Saturday morning Larry, clad in his white cutaway tuxedo, white ruffled shirt, and white bow tie, started out early for the church. He was afraid he might get stuck in traffic.

So he was the first to arrive. He parked his new black Volvo on a hill in the far corner of the church parking lot and watched from a distance as cars began to pull in. Larry felt as if he had arrived at the end of a long journey to a place where he was uncertain he wanted to be. He loved Marcia, but after living together for more than four years there was little passion or sexual thrill between them (certainly not like the bachelor party's). It was a deeper, more important connection. But in light of Marcia's feelings about his dealing, about his friends, they had actually grown further apart during the last six months than they had ever been. It seemed an odd moment to be getting married.

Larry realized that he was not going to be able to keep his promise to Marcia, at least not soon. He was making so much money so fast that he knew he couldn't bring himself to just walk away from the business. At the rate he was going, he could triple his million dollars before 1980 was up. And with Mark Stewart starting to funnel some of that cash into legitimate holdings, Larry was on the verge of success beyond his wildest dreams. Danger seemed at an all-time low. After years of dealing openly from his fraternity, from the apartments on Baltimore and Osage avenues, after all the pot busts and hassles with Penn authorities, Larry had finally set things up so that he was virtually uninvolved with the day-to-day management of the business. He was living across town from Penn, and he had learned to keep his dealings and associates away from his house. He had stopped dealing with Tyrone and the other street hustlers, so all of his customers were his best friends—even Billy South Philly, who had become one of Larry's closest confidants. It seemed like the perfect way to run an illegal business. He knew he could trust his friends. If any of them were ever busted, they would never turn on him or their other friends. It was like an unwritten pact. No one forced you to deal cocaine. You knew the benefits, you knew the risks. If you got caught, you took the punishment and called it the luck of the draw. There was no sense dragging your friends down with you. Larry knew he wouldn't.

So he felt more insulated than ever from danger precisely when profits had begun to multiply magically. Mark Stewart had plans enough for ten million dollars. Larry was looking at a lifetime of financial security. Options for his own life, where and how he wanted to live, were suddenly thrown wide open. Yet, try as he might, Larry couldn't imagine any life he would want without Marcia.

He restarted the car and drove down the hill to the church.

S I X

Batten Down
the Hatches

On their honeymoon, Larry and
Marcia toured the Hawaiian Islands, staying two days each at a series
of resorts, starting with the least populous islands and gradually working their way up to a final blast in Honolulu. On the main island they
had a suite at the Mauna Kea, a spectacular hotel with an open plaza
surrounded by interior balconies. Enclosed palm trees reached up to
the full height of the structure from gardens with cascading fountains
and pools that were illuminated at night so guests could watch the
manta rays come in to feed on plankton. The giant blue-black rays
moved with sweeping glides in a natural underwater ballet. Much to
Marcia's delight, fantastic tropical birds populated the hotel interior.
There were no TVs, just the spectacular island scenery, fine restaurants with cornucopian spreads of fish and fruit for breakfast, lunch,
and dinner. There were expensive shops for clothing and curios. When
they returned to their room at night they found the bed strewn with
a bounty of fresh blossoms.

During these weeks Larry hunted up adventures, sometimes
dragging Marcia along. They took a helicopter tour of the islands,
swooping down alongside the verdant slopes of volcanoes and out over
clear aqua bays, and then climbing up at a sharp angle over the rugged
green landscape that jutted so suddenly from midocean. Larry was
thrilled. Marcia couldn't wait for the flight to end. On Hilo they drove
up Mauna Loa through the clouds until the road was just a mud path
through a barren pockmarked landscape of lava and stone. They went
on a tour of the macadamia nut factory and a pineapple-canning
factory—Larry was always fascinated by the manufacturing process.
Larry learned to scuba dive. He begged Marcia to join him, the water
below was so clear and the sights so extraordinary, but she was content
to go out on the boats and relax in the sun on deck.

After a week of his urgings, Marcia agreed to give diving a try. Larry assured her that it was much easier than it looked. She went along reluctantly, and it turned into a disaster. All of Larry's other diving groups had been relaxed and fun. This group was led by a drill sergeant of a diving instructor who seemed more intent on scaring his students than teaching them. To reach the beach where they were to dive, the class had to make a long, hard hike across sand. Marcia slogged along uncomfortably in her diving suit and heavy tank. When they reached water, the instructor offered some last-minute instructions on how to equalize pressure within the mask, offering, as an aside, "If you fail to blow hard enough at that point the pressure can pop the eyeballs right out of your head."

Without a word, Marcia removed her mask, turned, and marched back toward the beach. Larry and the others stood knee deep in ocean water and watched her go.

That night, to make matters worse, Larry got an urgent phone call from Mark Stewart and David Ackerman.

"Couldn't this wait?" pleaded Larry.

Mark said it could not. He wanted to buy the Arena, a dilapidated indoor, six- to seven-thousand-seat sports stadium at Forty-fifth and Market streets, a poor, predominantly black West Philly neighborhood. The place was a wreck.

"Are you crazy?" said Larry.

Opened in 1920 as the Philadelphia Auditorium, it had hosted college ice hockey games, basketball games, and cultural events and eventually became one of the premier boxing and wrestling arenas in the country. During the 1950s it was called the Ice Palace, home to the Shipstad and Johnson Ice Follies, the Ice Capades, and an ill-fated professional hockey franchise called the Arrows. But the Arena had long since been supplanted as the city's premier indoor stadium by the Civic Center, and in more recent years by the large, ultramodern Spectrum. The old Arena in recent years had been home to WHYY, Philadelphia's public television station. When the TV station built new quarters in the early seventies, it sold the aging structure to a Camden lumber merchant who planned to level it and use the 1.4-acre lot as a storage yard.

But Mark Stewart had more dramatic plans. They could pick it up for a mere ten thousand dollars down, a 10 percent deposit on a hundred-thousand-dollar down payment. Then they could spend a minor amount on essential renovations and start booking rock concerts and boxing and wrestling matches. Mark said he knew someone who could, perhaps, bring a Continental Basketball Association team to Philadelphia—the CBA being a second-string professional basketball league with teams in small cities. Larry's investment wizard could scarcely contain his excitement. He had another idea. To make instant friends in the community around the Arena, out of which would come fans for the second-rate sporting events, he had made contacts with the Coretta King Foundation, seeking authorization to rechristen the aging edifice the Martin Luther King, Jr., Arena.

Larry listened while David chirped his enthusiasm on the other line. David had followed Larry to Mark Stewart and was now, perhaps, even more in Mark's thrall than Larry. But in the six months Larry had known Mark, he had learned how much air his advisor could blow into a small balloon. He understood how much Mark admired the owners and promoters of Philadelphia's most successful and glamorous sporting franchises, and who ran the Spectrum and Veterans Stadium. This was exactly the field Mark wanted to break into. The Arena was his chance to play, on a somewhat more modest scale, a sports-world power broker. So Larry knew that much of Mark's enthusiasm might have to do with his fantasies. After all, Larry had lived in Philly for seven years. He had seen the Arena. It was hard to picture it making money. But with Mark right there on the line, he could hardly explain all that to David.

"Look, Larry, the guy who owns it will agree to accept a hundred thousand for it up front, and will carry all the paper," said Mark. "It's perfect for you."

David said that if Larry wasn't interested, he was going to back the project himself.

"Can't we talk about this when I get back?"

"Got to move on it fast," said Mark.

Larry gave in.

"Go ahead," he said. "But here's the thing. I'll agree to put fifty thousand into it, and if it doesn't work after that we're walking away from it."

Everyone agreed. After all, fifty thousand was like two weeks' earnings in the coke business.

Willie Harcourt met David Ackerman and Ken Weidler because his roommate owed them ten thousand dollars.

Willie was a big man, easily four inches over six feet tall, with broad, thick shoulders and hips and not a lot of excess weight. He wore his blond hair down over his ears. Willie was from Naperville, Illinois, and although he had spent much of his childhood in southern California, he retained a Corn Belt common sense and conviviality that was especially disarming in someone of his size. He wanted to be a writer, and had always been a serious reader, so even though at age twenty-four he had never managed to stick with college long enough to graduate, he mixed comfortably with the affluent, educated crowds that drank at The Latest Dish, the club where he tended bar. The club was on Fourth Street between South and Bainbridge, in the heart of Philadelphia's trendiest nighttown district.

He had arrived in Philadelphia in late 1978 on a motorcycle he rode all the way from Pasadena. He had decided to leave the University of California and seek his fame and fortune in the real world. Without friend or acquaintance in a new city, Willie started in working fifty- to sixty-hour weeks and lived alone in a small apartment near the club.

After the first year, Willie pooled funds with Michael Linley, a regular customer at The Latest Dish, and leased a much nicer apartment on Third and Fitzwater streets, just down the street from the house rented by David Ackerman. Michael met David, and started getting cocaine from him in 1979, at a time when the drug was in short supply and tall demand among denizens of the sexy singles South Street disco scene. There were no sinister, dangerous connotations to cocaine use; it was considered glamorous, exciting, fun, stimulating, and only unlawful in an uptight, technical way. Michael proved to be better at distributing cocaine than collecting for it, and within two months he had accumulated a ten-thousand-dollar debt to David and Ken.

Willie felt bad for his roommate. He could see that Michael had a problem with cocaine, and that he had gotten himself in over his head. So the big, friendly bartender offered to help Michael collect some of his debts, police his future sales, and ease him back out of the hole. After a few weeks they had begun to make small progress.

But not enough. One night, despairing of ever seeing Michael's money, David and Kenny stopped by The Latest Dish and confronted Willie with the problem directly.

"You owe us ten grand," said David. "What are you going to do about it?"

"Hold on," said Willie. "Michael owes you that money, not me."

"Michael said you're his partner."

"Did he now?"

Willie was not really surprised or even alarmed. He had come to enjoy working at the nightclub and had ambitions of eventually opening one himself, but the owners of The Latest Dish had recently been considering splitting up. He knew the place wasn't going to survive much longer. Willie was a long way away from having the kind of money he would need to open a club of his own. He had gone looking for a job behind the bar at Elan, without success, and was feeling frustrated. His vision of the future had gone blank.

So Willie was not distressed when these obviously successful cocaine-dealing dental students tapped him for Michael's debt. He knew that despite the ten grand, David and Ken (whether they meant to or not) were dangling temptation. Willie knew enough about cocaine to know that the product they were selling, and of which they had such an apparently endless supply, was superior to most coke on the streets. For more than a year he had been steering customers to Michael and other dealers from behind the bar. The demand wasn't just steady, it was clamorous. Judging by Michael's experience, David and Kenny were not averse to fronting considerable amounts of product. They were not a couple of hoods; they were precisely the opposite: two attractive, popular, *exciting* young men. Willie liked them both immediately. He could see his own nightclub opening much sooner than he had dreamed.

So Willie promptly offered to assume Michael's total debt if they would front him enough cocaine to start earning the money back.

During the last months of 1979, working from his very visible platform behind the bar, Willie began to even the accounts of his roommate. David and Kenny were impressed. When they offered Willie a chance to pay off the debt more quickly by delivering cocaine to customers in Chicago and Los Angeles, Willie quit his bartending job. By Christmas 1979 he was a full-time runner.

He was into the business with both feet when he saw his first whole kilo of cocaine. Within a matter of days after starting, he was moving heavy bags of product and tens of thousands of dollars in cash through airports. It happened so fast that he hardly had time to reflect on the extent of the business's illegality. It was daunting. This was no group of college kids distributing contraband among themselves; this was wholesale criminal enterprise. The profits were magical. Very rapidly, Willie's dream of owning his own club seemed like a small thing, something he kept in mind to put a brake on his ambitions instead of a distant, only vaguely realistic goal.

In late January of 1980, after a few successful runs back and forth across the country, Kenny offered Willie a chance to do something even bigger. Ken said that Larry, whom Willie had still not met, had agreed to let him and David begin making their own buys in Florida. In the past, whenever a shipment came up from Florida, Larry selected the kilos he wanted and David and Kenny got whatever was left. Larry's recruits were eager to branch out on their own, and that meant making their own purchases in Florida. So they needed someone willing to take a large bundle of cash to Miami Beach.

"How much?" Willie asked.

"One hundred and sixty-five."

Willie agreed. First, though, he had to meet with Larry, who was putting up a substantial portion of the cash. Ken gave Willie the address on Osage Avenue.

Willie was excited and a little nervous about meeting Larry. He knew David and Kenny had the same kind of awe for Larry as he initially had had for them. What kind of a twenty-four-year-old man had the savvy and know-how to set up a million-dollar illegal business while attending college and dental school? Willie had found the challenge of college alone frustrating. He pictured Larry as someone like David, only more so, someone commanding, very caught up in the moment, very intense.

Instead he found himself seated across the room from this very ordinary, easygoing fellow his own age, dressed in a Lacoste sportshirt and blue jeans and white Adidas track shoes with green stripes—the boy next door! Larry was not at all like David. Where David liked people to know immediately that he was the boss, Larry was laid-back, joking, unassuming. He treated Willie as an equal. Sensing that the big bartender was nervous about the trip, Larry joked about it and tried to put him at ease. He explained exactly whom Willie would be meeting, and where, and outlined step by step what would be expected of him in Miami.

"When you get to Florida, walk out of the airport and there will be a gray Cadillac with a guy sitting in it who has a beard, with dark hair," said Larry. "His name is Lester. Just get in the car and he'll take it from there."

Willie would be taking the money down, meeting Lester and another runner, Larry's friend Dick Muldair, a tall, skinny Penn student who had met Larry a few years earlier and had begun making runs for him. Muldair would be bringing back Larry's two kilos. Willie would be bringing one kilo—David and Kenny's—home on the plane.

Back at his apartment on South Street, Willie waited for the rest of the cash. Kenny brought it in a Glad trash bag. Willie had never seen so much money before.

"Now, what do I do with this?" he asked.

"Just stick it in a bag, throw it through the X-ray machine, and get on the plane," said Kenny. "No sweat."

"Great," said Willie. "Nothing like a professional setup."

Ken said it would be wise to mix the cash bundles in with clothes and things in a bag so that it wouldn't be too obvious when it went through security. When Ken left, Willie got out a handbag he could carry on the plane and mixed the bundles in with socks and balled-up shirts and underwear, trying to blend them in as well as he could. At the airport, watching the screen of the X-ray machine as the bag went through, he felt a tug of nausea. The cash blocks were plainly visible. But the bag passed through without notice, and he boarded the plane. When they were airborne he ordered a double vodka. His hands were shaking.

In Miami, as he exited the airport, his heart sank. There was not one Cadillac waiting, but about eighteen! There was a row of Caddies, Mercedeses, and BMWs. To Willie it looked like Drug Central. He managed to find Lester, even though he had shaved his beard. Willie just went down the line of cars, stopping at Cadillacs to peer down and ask, "Are you Lester?" until one said yes and let him in. He prayed he had the right Lester.

Lester sat in the back seat with a bodyguard. Willie sat in the passenger seat in front, and the driver took them to Coconut Grove, to an apartment building right on the bay. Lester had a clothing business on the side, making jeans for the Dominican Republic, so he told Willie about his business on their way up to the apartment and asked for his size. Muldair was already there. He and Lester set Willie up in the bedroom with a drink in front of the TV and asked him to wait. A short while later, Muldair came back in and handed Willie a plastic bag of off-white cocaine.

"Here's your kilo," he said. Muldair described some of the cocaine's characteristics to Willie, pointing out that its rock content was over 50 percent and taking out a melt box to demonstrate how to test for cut. He showed Willie how to wrap the cocaine in baking soda to cloak its faint odor in case police dogs came sniffing. Lester came in and gave Willie several pairs of jeans, which would do a better job of shielding the contents in the X-ray machine than his shirts and underwear. Then Lester rode back to the airport with Willie and watched him through the security checkpoint.

Willie was back in Philadelphia that night. He delivered the kilo to David's apartment. Then they drove to another apartment where they broke down the contents into rocks and shake, pressed rocks, and packaged the amounts for David's customers. Willie was paid five hundred dollars for his efforts. David was clearly delighted with how smoothly things had gone.

"We want you to go again next week," he said.

By summer, Willie was making three trips to Florida every month, bringing back four to six kilos at a time. He got used to walking into motel rooms alone with a quarter of a million dollars in cash in his suitcase to meet total strangers, typically Cubans, who sometimes did things like point automatic weapons at him. It occurred to Willie fairly early on that he was the one taking all the risks. David and Kenny and Larry were the ones getting rich.

But then, by this time he was being paid a lot more. Where else was he going to earn almost ten grand, tax free, every month?

* * *

One of the first things Larry did on returning from the honeymoon was drive out to meet Mark and David at his newest acquisition.

It was worse than he had pictured it. One look inside and Larry knew the project was never going to work.

In one of the offices off an upper hallway that looked down into the cavernous interior, Mark laid out his financial statements and plans, detailing the cost for new plumbing, new toilets and sinks, new electrical engineering, new refrigerators for beer and food concessions, an eccentric plan to convert the giant old ice-making machine (for the hockey and ice show rinks) into an air-conditioning system. Out of curiosity, Larry said he wanted to take a look at the device. Mark took him downstairs and pointed it out.

Larry stood in front of the thing for a long time.

"Mark, there's no chance in the world that this machine will ever make ice again," he said.

Mark insisted his plan was doable. He had already begun booking fight cards, and was planning to install a screen so he could open the place on June 20 with a closed-circuit screening of the Sugar Ray Leonard–Roberto Duran championship bout. The Spectrum, the Civic Center, even the arenas in Atlantic City were completely sold out. Promoters had come to Mark begging to use the Arena.

"This place must be in violation of every fire and building code on the books!" said Larry.

But Stewart seemed unconcerned. To make Larry feel better, Mark told him that they already earned a five thousand dollar return on his initial investment. They had already begun selling tickets for the televised bout, and the place was sure to be sold out. It was the first return Larry had ever gotten on one of Mark's investments, and it did a lot to placate his doubts about the arena—he couldn't complain too hard about hazarding only forty-five thousand. And Mark did have his heart in it.

On the night of the scheduled opening there was a line of ticket holders wrapped all the way down Market Street to Forty-sixth, and down Forty-sixth to Chestnut. The gates were supposed to have opened by 8:00 p.m., but they were still closed when Larry drove up at 9:00. When he stopped his black Volvo to wait for guards to open the gate to the VIP parking area, his car was surrounded by an angry mob. Several of the security guards Mark had hired, off-duty Philadelphia cops, waded out through the crowd and cleared the way for Larry to pull in.

Inside, Mark was frantic. The satellite dish he had just installed didn't work.

Outside, the mob was shattering windows and prying hinges off the giant doors.

Larry would remember Mark protesting, "It's not my fault."

Their grand opening made the newspapers the next morning, but not as they intended. It was reported as the scene of a small riot. Ticket holders eventually got refunds.

Larry's house. A man's voice on the phone.

"Batten down the hatches. There's a storm coming."

"Who is this?" asked Larry.

"This is a warning from a friend," said the voice.

"Wait!"

But the caller had already hung up.

Larry and Marcia had been home from their honeymoon less than one week.

Larry could only assume that some kind of trouble was coming, but what? Dick Muldair had gotten busted making a deal at a shopping center on the Main Line with a guy who turned out to be a Drug Enforcement Administration (DEA) agent, but that was something Dick had done on his own, so even if he talked about Larry (which Larry was sure Dick wouldn't), they couldn't get enough to come after him. The amount involved had been fairly small, and Dick was facing only about six months. But if not Dick, then what?

There was nothing to do but clean house. Larry and Marcia spent the night combing all four levels of their house for every trace of drugs. Larry filled a small brown bag with all they had collected, a small bag of marijuana, his pipes, and a vial of Quaaludes. He walked over to Mark Stewart's office that night and locked it in the safe.

Nothing happened.

When the same voice came on the phone with a similar message two nights later, Larry begged for an explanation.

"Can't you give me a little bit more of a feeling for what's going on?" he pleaded.

The caller relented. He gave Larry a number and told him to call back from a pay phone in twenty minutes. Larry thanked him and left the house in search of a pay phone.

A woman answered. She was the wife of a Vietnam veteran with a contracting business in New Jersey who had been buying indirectly from Larry off and on for several years. Larry had met with them once, a year ago, when the vet had gotten into serious debt, and Larry had agreed to give them more time to pay him back. Anyway, she explained, her husband had gotten busted. She was grateful for the way Larry had handled their indebtedness, so she had gotten her brother to phone with a warning. She wanted Larry to know that under questioning her husband had given his name to the state police.

Not long afterward, at dental school, one of Larry's classmates drew him aside in the hall. His classmate's wife was a lawyer working as an assistant in the office of District Attorney Ed Rendell of Philadelphia. One of her co-workers had come up to her in the office and asked if her husband was at Penn dental school. She said yes. So the man asked if he knew someone named Larry Lavin.

She said yes.

"Well, tell him to stay away from the guy. He's on Ed's list of suspected major drug dealers in the city."

That afternoon, Larry had talks with David and with Ken. He wasn't worried about his house being searched; there was nothing there. But he was going to have to keep the coke business at arm's length for a while. He might be under surveillance. Larry figured his phones were tapped.

Unaware that city police had, in fact, been watching him for more than a year, Larry assumed that the New Jersey state police had given his name to city prosecutors. He was hot. But—it was funny—Larry didn't feel the least bit threatened. To him, the fact that the information about official suspicions had twice leaked to him confirmed his feeling that there was a generational conspiracy at work to protect him from the law. It was the same kind of subcultural context in which he had dealt marijuana as an undergrad. Young people used harmless recreational drugs; the authorities tried to enforce pointless laws. It was "us" against "them." Larry was too smart and had too many friends to get nailed by a force of square-headed high school graduates in cheap suits with badges.

Still, it was a good idea to lay low.

A more pressing problem continued to be bad debts. Ralph, Larry's old pot connection from Virginia Tech, had bought cocaine from Larry and worked himself fifty thousand dollars into debt.

It was an unusually large debt, even for Larry's books. He had been doing business with Ralph ever since he was a sophomore undergrad. His friend had a legitimate business now, so Larry had reason to assume his mounting debt would eventually be paid. So he had let Ralph get in deeper and deeper.

But in the summer after his wedding, when Larry had not heard from Ralph for several weeks, he tried calling. The number he phoned had been disconnected. So Larry looked up Ralph's father's number outside Philadelphia, and began telephoning and leaving messages there every day.

After a week of this, Larry got a phone call. The caller identified himself as a friend of Ralph's.

"Larry, how you doin'?" he said. "Ralph just asked me to call and convey congratulations on your marriage and your beautiful wife. And, oh yeah, he wanted me to tell you that if you ever call his house again he'll have her cut up into little pieces no bigger than an inch."

"Let me talk to Ralph, would you?" asked Larry.

"No bigger than an inch."

Larry slammed down the receiver.

On a cold Friday night in the fall, after Larry and Marcia came home from dining out, Marcia showered and put on a blue terry cloth robe and stretched out on the living room couch in time to watch *Dallas*. Marcia was an avid *Dallas* fan.

Then the doorbell rang.

Larry crossed the room and pushed the intercom button.

"Who is it?"

"Police. We had a report of a burglary in progress and we're searching the neighborhood. We want to look around."

Larry pressed the button that unlocked the door to the outside gate. The door opened on a courtyard common to all the houses on the alley, but with one glance out the window Larry could tell by the number and urgency of the men moving through the gate that they had come for him. There were uniformed and plainclothes police, most carrying flashlights.

He turned to Marcia with an apologetic look and said, "This is it."

Larry opened the door and said, "Let's get this over with."

Two of the men with flashlights grabbed him, wheeled him back into the living room, and threw him to the floor. One thrust a sheet of paper right up to his face.

"This gives me the right to search your place," he said.

"We're happy to let you search," said Larry, standing. "Let's go. If you're going to search my house, I want to be present."

Larry was worried they might plant something.

As they entered the living room, the dog Rusty ran across the room happily and jumped on them, barking. Marcia started down-stairs to get the leash, and one of the cops shouted, "You can't leave!"

"Where do you think I'm going?" Marcia said. "I'm just getting a leash for the dog."

He motioned for her to sit back down and she did. One of the uniformed men went downstairs for the leash.

As the house was searched, room by room, Marcia was joined on the couch by the cop who had gotten the leash. She gave him some background information about that night's *Dallas* episode.

Larry was feeling especially cocky. He followed the team of searchers through the house. They pulled out drawers, shined their flashlights up and under tables and chairs, pulled Larry and Marcia's nice new Scandinavian teak cabinets away from the wall and inspected the shelves front and back, bottom and top. In the bedroom they were intrigued by Marcia's hope chest, which was locked at the foot of the bed. She was summoned upstairs and readily produced a key and opened it. It was filled with neatly folded linen. Up on the third floor, where Larry had his prized new pool table, the men were about to give up when Larry announced—he couldn't help himself—"You guys, you don't know what you're doing. You missed the best place in here."

Then he stooped over to show them how panels on the pool table legs opened to hollow spaces inside.

Back downstairs, Larry and Marcia were directed to sit at the round kitchen table. There they were confronted with the evidence: two Quaaludes that had fallen behind a drawer in Larry's dresser, a tiny silver coke-snorting straw, and five thousand in cash.

"We're going to take you downtown," said one of the men.

Larry held out his hands and said, "Let's go. What can they do to you for two Quaaludes?"

"It's pretty unusual for a senior in dental school to have five grand in his house," said one of the detectives.

"I'd like to tell you something off the record," said Larry.

"You can tell it to us on the record or off the record," said one of the detectives, indicating that whatever Larry had to say they wanted to hear and would use against him. Larry went ahead anyway.

"You guys are late," he said. "I'm just a dental student now. Those days are long gone."

"Well, I think what we're going to start doing is to take this house apart brick by brick," a detective answered.

"Okay," said Larry, wearily. "If that's your job, go ahead."

"No, not now," the detective said. "Now we're going to go over to 1228 Spruce Street."

That was the address of TEC Records. In an apartment on the third floor of that building, Larry had a large stash of cocaine and the papers outlining his agreement with Mark Stewart. Often there was cash stored in that apartment. For the first time that night he felt a touch of panic.

"You're going to take us down there and show us around the offices," the detective said.

"No, I'm not," said Larry. "That's not my building, and I'm not taking you in there. If you want to search there, you're going to have to go get the owner and serve him with a search warrant."

Abruptly, the two detectives who had been questioning Larry walked up to the living room. Larry assumed they had gone to confer with the others. He and Marcia sat alone at the table. They both fully expected that Larry was going to be taken to police headquarters, so Larry whispered to Marcia to call his lawyer as soon as they left. But after a few minutes of sitting alone they realized that the house was silent. Larry got up and walked up to the living room. It was empty. The door was open wide and all of the men had gone.

"They left!" he called down to Marcia.

"Are they coming back?"

"I don't know."

Marcia looked out the window down at the street. There were cruisers and vans pulling away.

Larry closed the door.

Marcia was delighted at first. She busied herself picking up drawers and putting things away. She was filled with nervous energy.

But later on that night, when she couldn't fall asleep, she got up to look out the window. There was still a blue police van parked down at the end of the alley. She got back in bed, turned her head away from Larry, and quietly cried.

Glen Fuller made thirty runs to Florida for Larry from the spring of 1979 until the fall of 1980. His deliveries had grown from the standard two-kilo orders to routine deliveries of ten or more at one time. He was a stocky, moustachioed dervish during that year and a half, living life on a circuit of flights and marathon drives from Philly to New England to Philly to Florida, back to Philly and back north. . . . There was always a rush, either sellers in Florida who would only have cocaine for sale that day, or customers in New England or Philadelphia who wanted a delivery before Friday in time for the big weekend sales. Glen was tireless and fearless. He did everything on impulse. At a time when most dealers wouldn't dare carry cocaine through airports, Glen would wake up late in Miami from a drunk the night before, realize he had to be in Philadelphia that afternoon, snort a few long lines, pack up his bags, and board the plane. When he drove he would cruise upward of 90 MPH, snorting coke to stay awake and smoking dope to ease the boredom of the drive, steering up the road shoulders if the traffic in front of him was moving too slow. Larry knew Glen was reckless, but his old friend owed him more than a hundred thousand dollars and had no other way of paying the money back. Glen earned five thousand per week—which went toward the debt—and was paid one thousand per day in expenses when he was on the road, an amount Glen somehow managed to squander on whores (Glen liked to buy them two at a time), food, drugs, planes, cars, boats, you name it. Larry often said he didn't care and didn't even want to know about what happened in Florida or in airports. "I give you the money, you bring me the product," Larry would say. "That's all I need to know." Glen enjoyed the freedom that gave him and was willing to accept the risks. And when Larry would sit still for it, Glen could entertain him with stories that raised the small hairs on the back of the preppie dental student's neck.

Once a bag full of money had split open in the middle of a crowded concourse at the Philadelphia airport. He had swiftly stooped over, dropped the broken bag on top of the pile, and scooped up the pile between his arms. When he stood and looked down he saw he had gotten all but one fat bundle of hundreds—ten thousand dollars. So he kicked the bundle along in front of him until he made it to the men's room door and into a stall, where he patched things together as best he could.

He had gotten arrested in Fort Lauderdale for reckless driving with $576,000 in the trunk. The police impounded the car and held Glen overnight in the drunk tank, where he slept on the concrete floor and contracted a skin rash that took him more than a year to lose. But the next morning a friend posted bail and they recovered the car, trunk unopened, money safe and dry.

On a trip to Orlando, Glen picked up a blond named Marti and recruited her to help him move coke through the airport. He had twelve kilos on that trip. So they split it up in their bags and got in line to go through security. Marti went through the checkpoint with no problem, but just before Glen was to follow her, the X-ray machine broke down—which meant hand searches of luggage.

Glen just pivoted, grabbed his luggage off the counter, and said, "Oop! Forgot my ticket!"

He walked back up the concourse alone. Marti put her bag in a locker down the concourse and came back.

Meanwhile, Glen had ordered himself a scotch at a bar in the terminal and called Larry, who, as usual, was in a hurry. Glen wanted to forget this flight and leave the next day.

"I don't want to hear about it," Larry said. "That's your problem down there. We need that stuff up here tonight."

"Look, Larry, they're hand-searching everyone's bags."

"Go to a different terminal," Larry suggested. "Glen, have a couple of drinks and be brave."

"Fuck you," said Glen, and he hung up. Marti fetched her bag and they chartered a flight back to Philadelphia.

From time to time it would dawn on Glen that he was being used by Larry and his friends, that they didn't really consider him one of them. He was a wild man, a reckless lowlife they employed to take risks for them.

Willie Harcourt hooked up with Glen for one and only one deal in Florida. Unlike Glen, Willie was a quiet, cautious, introspective man who tried to stay constantly alert for subtle shifts in circumstance that might mean danger or the law. Willie's idea of a good run to Florida was to get in and get out as uneventfully as possible. He met Glen at a hotel in Fort Lauderdale in September of 1980, and almost immediately wished that he hadn't.

Instead of quickly making the deal for eight kilos, Glen wanted to take everyone out drinking and for dinner, then picked up two whores. On the way to the airport the next morning Glen drove over 90 MPH, passing slow-moving traffic by swerving over on the shoulder. Willie was terrified. Glen was enjoying himself.

When Willie got back to Philadelphia he called Larry and said, "I will never work with this guy again. He's going to get himself and the rest of us busted."

Larry explained that he had to keep using Glen. Glen owed him money. "If you won't work with him, you're cutting yourself out of thousands of extra dollars every month," Larry said.

"It's not worth it," said Willie. "Count me out."

Willie was not the only one who wanted nothing to do with Glen. Kenny and David and most of Larry's friends thought Fuller had some kind of death wish.

Oh, he was the life of the party when Larry and his friends all went out drinking or snorting together. Like when Larry threw a bachelor party for one of his friends at the Sheraton, the same room where Larry's bachelor party had been staged. Larry wanted Glen there, so Glen chartered a plane from Boston with Larry's brother Rusty. There was an especially attractive young blond hooker with green eyes and a rose tattoo over her left breast who stripped to her high heels and, loaded on bourbon and Quaaludes, orchestrated a group of the boys in a circle-jerk. Rusty kicked off the festivities by inserting cherries up the woman's vagina and eating them out, accompanied by cheers and laughter. Later on, she jumped up to dance on a glass coffee table, which shattered, depositing her naked rump on the heap of broken glass. She didn't feel a thing, just jumped up and kept on dancing. Larry and L.A. steered her, despite her protests, into the bathroom, and working with a first-aid kit they had summoned from the front desk, patched her up as best they could . . . Glen fit right in on those occasions.

But not always. One night after flying thirteen and a half kilos to Philadelphia in his carry-on luggage, Glen checked into the Bellevue Stratford Hotel and got dressed up for dinner. Larry and Marcia and Andy Mainardi and his wife were having dinner in one of the fine restaurants downstairs, so Glen assumed they had come to dine with him. He joined them at the table, and everyone was very pleasant until Andy asked Glen to speak with him privately. They walked away from the table and Andy whispered, "You're not invited. This is a private party."

Despite affronts like this, Glen had hopes of eventually taking over the business from Larry, or at least the New England branch. He knew that Marcia was pressuring Larry to get out, and that Larry had a lot of "legitimate" investments going. He had talked to Larry about taking over most of the business and just continuing to pay him a straight percentage for a few years. He knew he had competition. David Ackerman coveted Larry's longtime, big customers—Larry's did ten times the volume of anyone else, and he was the only one who had made millions. But Glen figured his year and a half of hard, risky work and his long friendship with Larry gave him an edge.

That was where things stood on Thursday, November 13, 1980, when Glen arrived in Philadelphia from Florida with ten kilos and checked into an apartment he had begun renting on the eighteenth floor of a building at Thirtieth and Chestnut streets. Glen got home early in the afternoon, after driving straight through twenty-four hours from Florida. Larry came over to help with the break.

They used two big aluminum bowls, first separating out the rocks from the shake, then blending inositol and lidocaine, spraying the mix with methanol and pressing that into rocks, then drying the rocks and packaging all the separate orders. It was hard work, lasting until well past midnight. By the time it was done Larry and Glen were coated with white powder from head to toe, numbing their eyes and lips and noses, dizzying them. A fine dust of cocaine lay over the walls and floor and furniture. While they worked that evening, Larry and Glen talked about going fifty-fifty on the business, and Glen said he was ready to start whenever Larry wanted. Larry had promised Marcia to stop by Christmas, he said, so they would talk about it again before then.

It was past two in the morning on Friday when they finished the break. Larry wanted Glen to get a good night's sleep and head up to Haverhill in the morning to deliver cocaine and cash to his customers there. But Glen was too wired to sleep. He and his friend Doug, who had come by to help, decided to leave right away. Glen filled a blue Samsonite suitcase that had belonged to Marcia with money. He preferred not to carry cocaine in anything unlocked because an open container could more easily be searched without a warrant, so he asked to use Larry's briefcase to carry the cocaine north. Larry needed the case to carry his cash.

"If you have to go now, just use a cardboard box," said Larry. "We'll tape it up real tight."

"No way," said Glen. "I'm not taking a box home."

But Larry was the boss, and he insisted. They packed two and a half kilos in the box and Glen carried it reluctantly down to the trunk of his car.

Glen was weary of driving. He took two Quaaludes and, stretching out on the backseat of the Cutlass Larry had recently bought for these long drives, told his friend to set the cruise control on 63 MPH. There had been a lot of busts along the New Jersey Turnpike lately. Once underway, Glen dozed.

He was awakened by the sound of a police siren. He opened his eyes and saw flashing red lights.

"Fuck!" he said.

Two New Jersey state troopers approached the car, asked to see the auto registration, and after looking it over asked Doug and Glen to step out of the car.

"I'm in my bare feet," said Glen. "Can I put my shoes on?"

They stood alongside the car as the troopers looked inside. One of the troopers found the remains of a joint on the floor under the front seat.

He approached Glen with a clipboard.

"We've got a consent form here for searching the trunk, but whether you sign it or not, we're going to search it."

He took the keys and opened the trunk. The other trooper stepped back to watch.

Glen saw his chance.

"Douggie, let's hit it!" The two jumped back in the car. Glen had a spare key in his hand. He jammed it into the ignition, but before he could start the motor, one of the troopers grabbed Doug and pulled him out the passenger door. Doug and the trooper tumbled together down the embankment. The other trooper lunged at Glen from the driver's side, pushing him over and poking a revolver in his ear.

"Don't you fuckin' move!" he screamed.

Larry got a call before dawn from his brother Rusty.

He said, "Glen got busted."

And Larry felt again the sinking feeling he had experienced on getting the news about L.A., about Andy, and about Dick Muldair. This was the worst yet. Rusty told him that Glen and his friend Doug had struggled with the state troopers, and that one of the troopers had broken his wrist. So there would be assault charges, resisting arrest . . . the works.

No one associated with Larry had gotten into such serious trouble. Andy had gotten off, L.A. and Muldair had gotten only ninety days. But this was bad. Larry knew the ten pounds of cocaine was enough to send Glen away to prison for years. That was a lot of pressure—what if Glen decided to cooperate?

No. Larry knew that of all his friends, Glen would be least likely to do that.

"I'll get him a lawyer," Larry said. "If you talk to him, tell him to hang on. I'll take care of him. We'll have him out as soon as we can."

Over the next two days, Larry put up $200,000 in bail for Glen and Doug. Then there was $50,000 to retain the services of one of the top drug lawyers in the country, a Washington, D.C., attorney allied with NORML (National Organization for the Repeal of Marijuana Laws). The ten pounds of cocaine Glen had been carrying represented a lost $224,000 in profits. The car, which had been seized, ran another $10,000. It pained Larry to see those figures lopped off his running profits column on his books. In his gut, it didn't matter that he was two million or more ahead of where he had started. Once a certain level was reached, Larry experienced any new setback as pure loss. Glen's bust was the largest single loss of Larry's dealing career.

Heat seemed to be coming from all sides. It had been a terrible year, one trauma after another—the robbery, Paula Van Horn, Ralph, the riot at the Arena, the police raid . . . now this!

Marcia was right. It was definitely time to cool it. But first he would have to recover that half million dollars.

In early 1980, Larry's childhood friend from Haverhill, his old drinking and doping buddy, Ricky Baratt, was back living at home in Plaistow, New Hampshire. Still nervous and chubby and insecure, Ricky had done a lot of drifting in the years since he and Larry had spent aimless summer evenings roaming the back roads of Haverhill getting high and drinking beer. He had gotten thrown out of Lawrenceville School for stealing a keg of beer from the back porch of The Rusty Scupper, a bar and restaurant in Princeton. He had tried to study music seriously, playing the saxophone at the Berklee College of Music in Boston, but instead of studying and going to class he got stoned or drunk every day and just sat around jamming with friends. Marijuana made Ricky lazy and apathetic, but he craved it.

After dropping out of Berklee and hanging around home awhile, he had made another big effort to straighten out, enrolling at the University of New Hampshire and signing up for a rigorous regimen of advanced math and science courses. Ricky felt that the sheer size of the challenge might force him to rise to the occasion. Instead, he fell behind so quickly that he spent months just sitting in class listening blankly, having done no reading, taking no notes, just going through the motions, listening to lectures he didn't understand. Finally he flunked out. He was an embarrassment to his successful family, although his father the doctor was ever-patient and encouraging.

To escape his failures and start fresh, Ricky loaded up his belongings in the old family Volvo his father had given him and, towing an old Volkswagen he meant to repair and sell, drove to New Orleans, where he worked fixing cars and playing his saxophone in a band. That lasted until the band broke up. Through a series of part-time jobs, Ricky drank so much he began to scare himself. Back to Plaistow he drove, still towing the Volkswagen, the black Volvo a few years more battered, and moved back in with his parents. His father found him work as a bookkeeper for his uncle, and Ricky applied for a job at the Western Electric plant in North Andover. A friend of his parents' helped find Ricky a job at the huge plant, which had just been taken over by AT&T. He ran a giant copy machine for six months, earning ten thousand dollars a year, and took an in-house electronics course. In the fall of 1980 he passed a test and qualified for an upgrade. By late spring, Ricky was a quality control inspector, testing electronic components and making eighteen thousand a year. He bought himself a Harley motorcycle and began, for the first time in years, to feel self-sufficient and whole.

That was when he ran into Larry again. His old friend was visiting his parents in Haverhill, and Larry stopped over to say hello, driving a brand-new black Volvo. It was the same kind of car Ricky drove, only five years and some sixty thousand miles newer. Ricky's parents had heard stories about Larry from the Lavins. Justin and Pauline were so proud of their youngest son. He was doing well in dental school and had somehow managed to make money playing the stock market. He had bought into a record company and a sports arena in Philadelphia . . . he was into so many different things, just exactly the way he had been as a boy! Only, who would have ever thought he would amount to so much, so fast!

It was the same old story for Ricky, only more severe. He was the weak, undisciplined, troubled one; Larry was the dynamic achiever, so outgoing, so pleasant, so successful. Only, just as he had as a teen, Ricky knew things about Larry that the adults didn't know.

On that trip, Larry sold Ricky three grams of cocaine for $225.

"I could have bought another new Volvo with what I made selling this just last night," Larry said.

They got to talking, and Ricky said he knew someone, a friend who owned a bar, who would probably be willing to buy up to an ounce at a time.

"No problem," said Larry.

Before Larry left for Philadelphia, he agreed to send Ricky an ounce of cocaine, to get him started.

A Federal Express truck pulled up in front of the house two days later. Inside the package were several cassette tape cases, each filled with tiny, one-gram vials of cocaine—twenty-eight of them. Ricky took the vials to a friend who he thought might be interested, but his friend did not know how to test the drug and distrusted the quality of coke from an unknown source packaged in such an unorthodox way. So Ricky was stuck with trying to sell the grams one by one, which made him nervous because that meant he had to deal with twenty-eight different people. Soon that number was reduced because Ricky had started snorting the supply, which meant there was even more pressure to make the sales. Now he owed Larry more than sixteen hundred dollars. He sold some of the grams, snorted most of them, and ended up sending Larry several hundred dollars from his own meager savings.

He confessed his loss to Larry, and told him it would have worked out better if the coke had arrived in one bag.

"No problem," said Larry.

The next day another Federal Express truck pulled up in front of the house. This time the delivery man brought a box to the door. Inside were not one, but *eight* one-ounce glass vials of cocaine! Ricky did some quick figuring. It was worth $16,800! Ricky was dumbfounded, and excited. Along with the shipment came instructions on how to demonstrate the product's quality.

He took one of the ounces over to his friend at the bar and immediately made a sale—earning back the several hundred he had lost. But over the next few weeks, Ricky snorted much of the re-maining shipment and had trouble collecting money from friends to whom he had fronted the stuff. No problem, Larry just shipped him more. Larry joked that he liked his people to be in debt; it forced them to keep coming back. Following Larry's lead, Ricky fronted more ounces to friends and kept a running record of what he was owed. Soon larger shipments were arriving via Larry's own couriers, first Glen Fuller, later a mutual local acquaintance named Brian Riley, who was working for Larry's sister—Larry was also sending regular shipments to his brother Rusty and to Jill. Ricky would arrange his schedule at AT&T to make sure he was home when a delivery was due. Within a matter of months, Ricky was carrying thousands of dollars in his pockets, great wads of tens and twenties that he would spend time exchanging at banks for neat stacks of hundreds. With that much money in his pocket, he couldn't resist buying drinks for his friends, eating out . . . pissing it away. He paid off his Harley and replaced the old Volvo with a sleek new Mazda Rx-7. He moved out of his parents' house into an expensive apartment in Boston where he had his own garage that opened when he inserted a plastic card in a slot out front.

But it was all an illusion. Right from the beginning, Ricky lacked whatever facility Larry possessed for coming out ahead. His debit column started larger than his assets column and just grew continually. Between bad debts and his own growing cocaine habit, he kept falling farther and farther behind, $5,000 . . . $10,000 . . . $15,000 . . . $20,000. . . . Ricky would lie awake nights worrying how he was ever going to recover all that he owed, imagining that Philadelphia hoods were going to show up at his door and break his legs. Unable to sleep, he would snort more cocaine, which would elevate his spirits temporarily but leave him still deeper in debt and even more frightened. He clung to his job at AT&T as the one real positive thing in his life. He just banked that paycheck every week. That was his money, which he kept separate from the cocaine dealings. He worried most that eventually Larry would want that.

These fears were all in Ricky's head, because Larry never even seemed concerned. The most he would do, over the phone, was get Ricky to run down his list of customers and check to make sure that the deliveries were being distributed and followed up on regularly. Larry seemed mostly concerned that Ricky wasn't making any money for himself, not that he was late in making payments. After talking to Larry, Ricky would feel better for a few days. He would follow up on Larry's suggestions; he would move the next shipment of cocaine, collect some money, and send it to Philly. But then a week would go by and the fears would sprout up again. The debt kept mounting . . . $25,000 . . . $30,000.

Larry would say, "No problem." He was just trying to do an old friend a favor, cut him in.

Ricky kept doing more and more cocaine. His debt kept mounting. His nightmares grew worse.

Back in Philadelphia, Ricky's plight was nothing more than a few petty entries on a long balance sheet. Business continued to grow unabated after Glen Fuller's bust in New Jersey.

No one was less surprised than big Willie Harcourt when Glen got busted. Willie felt vindicated. He had taken a substantial cut in earnings by refusing to have anything to do with Glen. Now Larry needed him again, adding more weight to the bags he was regularly delivering north for David and Ken. It had been nearly a year since he started making runs to Florida, and he knew what was going on down there better than Larry, Ken, David, or anyone else in Philadelphia.

So it bugged him to take orders from these dental students. Larry or Ken would get a long-distance call from someone like Miguel, who would say that he had a large quantity for sale if they could get someone down to Fort Lauderdale quickly. So they would call Willie and ask him to drop everything.

Once, earlier in the year, he had just come back from California after a week on the road. He had been at his girlfriend's apartment only a half hour when Larry called.

"I need you to head to Miami. Miguel's got something."

"Larry. It's nine-thirty at night in Miami. Can't it wait until morning? I'll fly down first thing."

"No. Miguel has to see you tonight or the kilos are going to be sold. And he says he's got one that's really spectacular."

"Larry, he's full of shit. He's lying to you."

Larry, in that maddeningly cheerful way of his, just said, "Willie, get on your traveling shoes."

So Willie had to say goodbye to his girlfriend and hustle out to Larry's house in Willings Alley. There wasn't enough time to pack the money, so they just stuffed bundles in Willie's jacket and cowboy boots and pants pockets. Larry had called and asked the airline to hold the plane, and Willie arrived on the concourse at a dead run. As he was getting off the plane in Miami, the bundles of money were evident in all his pockets. As he stood in the aisle, waiting for the passengers to file off the plane, a voice behind him said, "I don't know about all you, but I'm following the big guy!"

And there was laughter all the way to the last seat.

What made such matters worse was that Willie knew Miguel was a mess. The Cuban was wasted by Quaaludes and in over his head dealing. His phone calls to Philly were just desperate pleas for more cash. He would tell Larry he had something hot and Larry would jump. Willie would hustle down to Florida with mounds of money, only to discover that Miguel had no cocaine, or had stuff with too much cut to buy. There would be an ugly scene, with Miguel first threatening, then pleading. Willie would end up sitting on half a million dollars in cash in a hotel room for three days because he refused to turn over the cash until Miguel came up with quality cocaine. But no matter how many times this happened, he could never get the boys in Philly to listen to him. David had developed a "Little Napoleon" complex, barking his orders, insisting that Willie stay up all night on a break after having been on the road for nearly thirty hours with the delivery.

All through 1980, primarily through Willie's labors, the business had a constant supply of quality cocaine. His only break in the tiresome cycle of plane flights with money, long drives with cocaine, came when Larry's house was searched and everyone decided to let things cool off. They all agreed to just lie low for a few weeks.

But before two days went by, David was on the phone.

"I want you to go down and just get one," he said.

"No," Willie said, perturbed. "Things are hot right now. I've been in and out of that airport a million times, and if they know anything about Larry they know about us. Let's just stop for a week or two. What's the problem?"

"Larry's not going to be happy about this," said David.

They argued, and finally Ackerman made it an order. If Willie wanted to keep his job, he had to go.

"There's a million people who are dying to do what you're doing," David said.

Willie capitulated. His intuition told him that this was going to be it. He flew down and bought the kilo. Used to carrying up to six kilos at a time on airplanes, Willie had become a skilled packager. Working with a big satchel, he wrapped the kilo in baking soda and taped it, then wrapped a pair of jeans around it. He put towels on the bottom of the bag, put the jeans on top of the towels, and then laid a couple of layers of towels on top of that. He threw in more clothing on top of the towels, and then scattered items to distract the person monitoring the X-ray screen: cowboy boots, a hair dryer, a tennis racket, a big bottle of mouthwash, things that made a strong visible image so that the security guard spent the few seconds the bag was on the screen identifying very commonplace objects and ignoring the obscure mass in the middle. It was a tested technique.

What Willie hadn't noticed was a newspaper article in the *Miami Herald* about a rash of hijacking attempts by terrorists who filled mouthwash bottles with gasoline, then, on the plane, threw the fuel on a seat and threatened to ignite it. At the airport he put the bag on the X-ray machine, passed through the metal detector, and watched the woman monitor the screen as his bag passed through. A state trooper stood behind her.

"Put the bag through again," she said.

That had never happened before. Willie picked up the bag, walked around, and set it on the moving surface again. The woman watched it pass through again, and said, "Bring me the bag."

Willie felt like running. He picked up his bag and set it on a table beside the X-ray machine.

"I'm going to search your bag," she said. "Do you have any objections?" The trooper hovered over her shoulder.

"Of course not," said Willie. "Go ahead."

She unzipped the bag. The trooper leaned over to look, and she began removing items. Willie stood there with an odd numb feeling, registering no particular alarm. He was trying to look like an innocent passenger. It crossed his mind that in a minute he would either be walking toward the plane or heading in the other direction in handcuffs.

The woman pulled out the bottle of mouthwash, unscrewed the top, and smelled it. She turned to Willie and smiled.

"This is what we were looking for," she said, and proceeded to explain about the mouthwash problem.

Willie got on the plane and bought himself three bottles of vodka as a first round.

When he got to Philadelphia, he delivered the kilo and explained what had happened. Instead of offering sympathy, Ken criticized him.

"Why did you ever let them search your bag?" he said.

"Jesus, Ken. They wanted to search it. There's a cop standing right there. If I said no, do you think they weren't going to?"

From Willie's perspective, the smart boys in Philadelphia were spoiled brats. They had little understanding or appreciation of the risks he was taking to make their millions. Every time Willie had to walk into a strange hotel room and face small, dark men with guns he died a little inside. He spent the money he made liberally because there was no sense hoarding it. Sooner or later one of those transactions was going to go bad. It wasn't just paranoia, either. Every week the Florida papers had stories about people like Willie getting busted, or turning up in cheap motel rooms dead. He had a kind of sixth sense, or at least he thought he did. Anyway, he trusted it. It told Willie that he wasn't going to get killed doing this, but that eventually he and everyone else involved were going to pay. They weren't going to get away with it forever.

Still, by the end of 1980, Willie had earned about a hundred thousand dollars and had hopes of doing much, much better. After the raid on his house and Glen Fuller's bust, Larry was talking about getting out of the business for good. He had decided to sell out to Kenny and David in early 1981. That would make Willie top management. His dreams of earning enough money to open his own club were shouldered aside quite readily by the prospect of earning a million dollars.

Safety became Willie's primary concern. A million bucks would do him no good dead or in jail. After the mouthwash incident he tried to avoid flying, even though the thirty-hour drives seemed endless. In Florida, he had gradually been making progress toward a safer, more efficient way of doing business. The key was to remove the middlemen, to get off the street.

All along, Willie had been dealing with four to six sources, mostly Cuban. On each trip he would check out what each supplier had and pick the best, often ending up with two kilos from one, one kilo from another, three from another. There was Miguel, who was doing a slow, self-destructive free-fall on Quaaludes; Vivian, a tiny chain-smoking Cuban woman who dealt in her apartment right in front of her three children, who were old enough to know what was going on; Lester, the jeans merchant; and a group of sinister Colombians who scared him. In time, Willie found out that backing both Miguel and Vivian was a Cuban named Rene, a cheerful playboy who drove a boat of a '78 Monte Carlo, and always met Willie at the same bar in the Dadeland Mall near the University of Miami because he thought it was the best place in Miami to pick up women. He had long black hair and a thick beard and reminded Willie of the way Al Pacino looked in *Serpico*. Willie liked looking at the women but was always eager to get out and make the deal because he was nervous and felt conspicuous toting a satchel filled with cash for hour after hour in a crowded bar. Rene would rarely consider business until after he had taken a girl home from the bar and had sex—something he nearly always managed to do. It was through Rene that Willie met Pepe.

Pepe's Cuban friends had a different nickname for him. They called him Flaco, which meant Skinny. He was in his late thirties, with deep-set soulful eyes and such broad, prominent cheekbones that his face seemed swollen. Cocky and animated, clean-shaven with a thick black moustache, just three inches over five feet tall, Pepe always wore cowboy boots and a big cowboy belt with a Texas-sized buckle behind which he would thrust his thumbs when he strutted, looking for all the world like a cartoon mouse playing sheriff. Willie liked him immediately.

Willie first met Pepe at Rene's house. As the demand for cocaine continued to grow in Philadelphia, Willie had become like a member of Rene's family. After a night of partying they usually conducted business in Rene's home in a comfortable development off a canal in

Fort Lauderdale, where there were green lawns and tall palms and the squat stucco houses were all painted in pastels. On one such visit, when he was looking to buy four kilos, Pepe arrived at the door with the delivery. Rene introduced Willie, who over the past year had built on the Spanish he had studied in high school until he could hold his own in conversation. Willie could tell by the way Rene spoke to Pepe that the visitor was not just a runner, but Rene's boss. Willie guessed that Pepe had come by personally to check him out.

Willie was eager to impress. Ultimately, he thought, the safest way to do business in Florida was to deal with the top men directly. He withdrew a melt box from his satchel to test the cocaine, even though he knew the method was considered amateurish. After almost a year of this, Willie could tell by the look and feel of cocaine how pure it was, but Larry and Kenny and David always insisted on knowing at exactly what temperature it melted. But more important than his technique for testing the coke were his manners. In Willie's experience, there were two kinds of people involved in the cocaine trade, the flashy hustlers, who were dangerous (Glen Fuller was a perfect example), and the more businesslike, regular people, who could usually be trusted. He knew that the quiet, simple way he conducted business with Rene would make the best impression on his boss. He made no effort to deal directly with Pepe, but handled the transaction with Rene as he always did, handing over the cash after verifying the quality of the product. As always, he didn't take a drink or snort a line or smoke a joint until the business was complete. Then he relaxed and turned cordial. They all went out to dinner together.

On Willie's next two trips to Miami, Pepe was with Rene. He peppered Willie with questions: "Is this cocaine good? Is this the way you like to have it? Would you like to buy more? Would you like us to front you some?" Willie said no. They were buying just what they needed, although the demand was growing. The quality of the cocaine was consistently good. And, no, they absolutely would not take any cocaine on credit. Pepe told Willie that he was impressed with his courage, that few people dared to carry that much money or cash on planes. Willie told Pepe nothing about whom he worked for, just that he would be back in two weeks and he would want to buy roughly the same amount again. He emphasized that he preferred dealing with Rene and Pepe exclusively, and if they could maintain a steady supply of top-quality product he would buy from no one else.

Those three trips were the best Willie had taken. He was picked up at the airport by his suppliers, whom he knew and liked. They took him directly to Rene's house or an apartment he kept in Miami, exchanged six or seven kilos, then they went out to dinner and Willie headed home. For the first time Willie felt he could relax, that there was a simple, safe routine.

On the fourth trip, Rene and Pepe drove away from the Miami airport in a different direction than usual.

"We're going to my partner's house," said Pepe.

Willie knew that this was the big step. Pepe had mentioned that he had a partner, and Willie had gathered that the partner was his boss. Finally, after a year, he was going to get off the street completely.

The car pulled up to the gate of a beautiful home with a lush yard surrounded by a high gate. Parked in the driveway were two Mercedeses and an Italian sports car. The gate was opened by a young man who had been washing the sports car.

A beautiful dark-skinned woman answered the door and showed the men through a handsomely furnished foyer and living room into a wood-paneled den. One wall of the den was papered with a striking, bright poster depiction of an island sunset. Automatic weapons were displayed on another wall, alongside a tall bookshelf lined with volumes in Spanish and English. Outside the sliding glass doors on the other side of the room Willie could see a yacht tied up at a small dock off the backyard. A tall shirtless man in white shorts and sandals, with broad shoulders and a muscular build, stood up from behind the desk in the den as they entered. Pepe introduced him to Willie as Paco. He was younger than Rene or Pepe, only a few years older than Willie. After a year of dealing with Cubans who tended to be only half Willie's size, it was a pleasure to meet someone who looked him right in the eye. Paco had a slender, boyish, clean-shaven face, and his skin was much fairer than Rene's or Pepe's, though he was tan enough to look as if he had just stepped off a yacht. More than any other feature, it was his eyes that startled Willie; they shone with a dark intensity that made him seem especially formidable. Paco spoke no English to Willie. He directed all of his remarks to Rene in Spanish. After shaking Willie's hand he sat back down behind the desk and smiled and said nothing.

Willie had come down to buy six kilos, and for the first time, Pepe let him choose the six out of ten. No one had ever shown him a surplus and let him choose from them before. Willie painstakingly tested each of the ten kilos, melting a sample of rock and shake from each. It took almost two hours, with Pepe and Rene hovering around, offering to get Willie a beer or a drink. After all the strange encounters and close calls of the last eleven months, Willie was inwardly elated. He was finally in off the street!

After Willie picked out his six kilos, he handed over the cash and Pepe and Rene started counting.

Then something happened that hadn't occurred before. They came up seventy-five hundred short.

Willie felt a cold stab of panic. For the first time ever, as a sign of how much respect he was ready to show Paco, he had left the satchel of money behind when he went to the bathroom in another part of the house. He had always, *always*, carried the satchel with him at all times in previous dealings, even in Rene's house. It was so unusual for him to leave it behind that when he left the den, Rene had reminded him, "Don't you want to take your bag?"

"No. That's all right. I trust you," Willie had answered, looking not at Rene but at Paco.

And now the cash came up short. Willie knew that Paco had not taken the money. A man dealing this much cocaine, living in this house, with that wife, with that yacht, with those cars, *doesn't* pinch seventy-five hundred dollars when you turn your back on him.

So Willie asked to use the phone. He tried to call David, but there was no answer. So he called Kenny.

"Ken, something's wrong. The money's short seventy-five hundred. Look around your apartment."

"I gave it to David," said Ken.

"Look around your apartment," Willie demanded. He was starting to sweat. Paco was expressing irritation.

"What's going on here? Is this guy trying to pull something on us?" Paco asked Pepe in Spanish.

Ken left the phone for a few minutes and returned. "It's not here," he said. "Have David check his place."

"He's not home," said Willie. "Do you have a key?"

"Yeah."

"Go over there and look for it," said Willie.

Ken groused about it, but he could tell by Willie's tone of voice that it was a serious matter. "All right," he said.

Willie waited in silence with the Cubans for a half hour, and then phoned David's place. Ken answered.

"It's not here either," said Ken.

Willie felt sick.

Ken said, "Will, did you ever let the bag out of your sight?"

"Just for a second. I went to the bathroom."

"You mean you left it with them for a minute?"

"Yeah, but—"

"Well that's it! *They* took the money!" said Ken.

"No, Ken. They didn't take the money. Believe me. That's not what happened. It's our mistake."

"No way, Will. If you left it with them, those guys took the money. That's what happened and it's *your* fault. Take the cocaine you can pay for and get back up here."

Listening to one end of the conversation, Paco stood up when he heard that he was being accused. He was furious. While Willie was talking, Paco was screaming at Rene and Pepe, "Give this guy back his money! Get him the fuck out of my house! We're never doing business with him again!"

Willie, overhearing this, quickly got off the phone with Ken and turned to plead with Paco.

"Believe me, these people in Philadelphia, they don't know anything about the way things are done down here. They don't know you gentlemen like I know you. I know you didn't take the money."

Pepe, whose judgment in bringing Willie to meet his boss was on the line, argued in Willie's defense. But Paco was adamant.

"Give the man back his money and get him the fuck out of my house," he said.

Paco would not even shake Willie's hand as he left.

Willie flew back to Philadelphia that night crestfallen. All his hard work to make connections with the top man, all of it blown because somebody in Philadelphia couldn't count and because Ken, who had no idea what Willie had been going through, was stupid enough to casually insult the top man over the telephone. When he arrived at his apartment from the Philly airport, there was a message on his machine. David had come home and found the money. It had gotten thrown away with the brown bag that had originally contained the cash.

Willie phoned Rene.

"We found the money. As I said, it was our mistake. I'm coming back down tomorrow. I'd like to give it to Paco personally and apologize for the misunderstanding."

"I'll get back to you," said Rene.

Rene called back later that evening and told Willie to come ahead. The next day, Willie was back in Paco's den. Willie apologized, they shook hands, and Paco loosened up enough to begin speaking English. He opened a bottle of Taittinger champagne and they sealed their future arrangements. From then on, Willie would make arrangements through Rene, but would deal directly with Paco and Pepe.

And Larry Lavin's business, which had come a long way from a few big sacks of pot, was about to enter the big leagues.

S E V E N

Maybe You'll
See Smoke

Suzanne Norimatsu had fallen for David Ackerman the first time she saw him, four years ago, in the spring of 1976. She and her friend Christine Pietrucha were working as waitresses at La Crepe, one of the finer of Philadelphia's new, trendy Center City restaurants. Suzanne was tall and willowy, with straight brown hair and big brown eyes. She was twenty years old. Her father was Japanese and her mother was of European ancestry, and in Suzanne the mix had produced just a whisper of Asian influence, enough to give her features an exotic cast. Christine was pretty and blond and possessed of a cheerful wit and sweet naiveté.

This small, well-dressed, strikingly handsome young man came and sat at one of Suzanne's tables. After dinner, he left a tip and a note on a cocktail napkin.

"Suzanne: If you would like to do something with me next week, please call me at this number," the note said, and then David had written out his phone number. Beneath, in what appeared to be an afterthought, "If you are one who prefers to be called, please write and give me your phone number." Underneath that he had written his name and address.

Suzanne showed the note to her friend.

"He's cute," said Christine. "If you don't write to him, I will."

So Suzanne wrote. Within days, David called. They went out together to see the movie *All the President's Men.* By the end of June they were living together on Forty-first Street near Penn's campus. David was in his second year of premed. Originally he told Suzanne he was a math major. When she discovered, through one of David's friends, that he was in premed, she was more curious than angry.

"Why would you lie about a thing like that?" she asked.

He told her, "There are a lot of women at Penn who like to hit on premed students."

The first time David ever used cocaine—Suzanne would later have reason to remember it—was on the Fourth of July that year. Soon after Suzanne moved in with him they had a discussion about their drug histories. David said that he had smoked a lot of pot in high school but that he had quit. Suzanne said she occasionally liked to smoke a joint, but that she didn't think it was that great. "But I like cocaine," she said.

"I never had that," said David.

"You've never had cocaine?" said Suzanne, surprised.

"No. Never."

"I've had it at parties once or twice. It's fun."

On the Fourth of July, David showed up with some. It had cost him a hundred dollars for a gram. They snorted it.

"What am I supposed to feel?" asked David.

"Like a rush," said Suzanne. "A rush of energy."

"Do you feel something? Is it any good?"

"I feel it."

"I don't feel anything," David said, disappointed.

"I've heard that sometimes people don't feel anything the first time," said Suzanne.

David was skeptical. The next time was on Suzanne's birthday, January 21, 1977. David took her out to dinner and on the way home he produced a small vial.

"Look what I got for you!" he said.

That time they both liked it.

It was too expensive to be a regular thing. Cocaine was like a special treat between them over the next two years. They broke up in the summer of 1978, the summer after David's first year of dental school. David decided that he wanted to see other girls. It hit Suzanne hard. She lived at home for a few months and then went to Europe.

More than two years later, Suzanne was back working as a waitress, living in a house on Pine Street that Christine shared with her boyfriend. David called one day and said that he owed Suzanne three hundred dollars.

"If you owed me three hundred dollars, I'd remember," she said. "That's a lot of money."

"Don't you remember? We went to Paradise Island and I put it on my American Express card. And later, I couldn't pay it on time so I borrowed the money from you."

Suzanne remembered. "Well, it's been so long," she said. "I appreciate your calling, but don't worry about it."

"No," said David. "You don't understand. I've got the money."

"You do?"

"And I'd really like to pay you because I don't like to owe anybody."

David gave Suzanne his address on Fitzwater Street, and she stopped by. He was living with Gina, the girl he had met on the trip to Glen Fuller's house in Aspen in March of 1979. David asked Suzanne if she would befriend Gina, who was from Vermont and knew no one in Philadelphia. Suzanne felt awkward about it, but said that she would try. Then David told her that he was selling coke, and making a lot of money. He remembered that Suzanne had always liked cocaine and asked if she would consider working for him.

Suzanne said she would think about it. Over Christmastime at the end of 1980, Suzanne and Christine took Gina on shopping trips, and they all went out together for dinner with David. Then one night just before New Year's, David took Suzanne out to dinner alone. He told Suzanne about Larry, the guy who had started the business and made millions. Now Larry was hot, he said. The cops were watching him all the time and his phone was probably tapped. He wanted to turn the business over to David and his friend Ken Weidler, but the volume was ten times what David and Kenny were used to handling on their own.

"What do you want me to do?" Suzanne asked.

"Keep the books. Meet with people. I'll set you up in a nice apartment."

"Who will I be dealing with?"

"Mostly my friends. Everyone is very nice. You'll like them. If you don't like them, you won't have to deal with them. Just give it a chance."

Suzanne pondered this silently.

"We need someone we can trust," David said. He was ready to pay her fifteen hundred a week.

Suzanne almost fainted. She was earning, on a good week, less than two hundred dollars, and paying Christine sixty per month to rent a room. Besides that, she still had a yearning for David, who, if anything, had gotten better looking in the last two years, she thought. When they had broken up, it was because David was paying no attention to her. He seemed more interested in other women. Now the situation had reversed. David was living with Gina and lavishing attention on Suzanne! Right now it was ostensibly because he needed her to come to work for him, but Suzanne sensed that there was more to it than that. Throw into the bargain the attraction of making a lot of money and having access to a lot of cocaine, and it didn't take long for Suzanne to make up her mind.

David moved Suzanne into a beautiful loft apartment in Saint Charles Court, across the street from the old Hoop Skirt Factory at Third and Arch streets, in Old City, a newly fashionable neighborhood just blocks north of Philadelphia's historic shrines, where old warehouses and factories were being rehabbed into loft apartments and condos. It was early in January 1981.

For Suzanne, it was total immersion. Right away there was traffic in and out of her apartment at all hours of the day and night. David brought in a safe, and more money and cocaine than Suzanne had ever seen. Suzanne's place became the headquarters for the business, and it seemed that David was there twenty-four hours a day. When he wasn't there he was on the phone, calling to find out whether so-and-so had stopped by, whether the money was ready, whether a shipment had come in. . . . Suzanne was challenged and flattered by her job: to be trusted with more than a million dollars—and with so much cocaine! She had never finished college and was used to being considered pretty, but dumb. David made her feel smart and capable. She prided herself on keeping accurate books, and on making things work smoothly. It was the most interesting job she had ever had. Cocaine admitted her to a heady, exciting life. She used a lot of it, until her daily schedule stood on its head—she was up all night and slept every day until midafternoon. It was alternately exhilarating and exhausting. And, much to Suzanne's surprise, she *did* like everyone. The young men who stopped by to exchange money for cocaine were well dressed, educated, well mannered; they had interesting jobs; they were successful, *attractive* young men, the kind of young men she and Christine used to admire from a distance at La Crepe.

It didn't take long for Christine to realize what Suzanne was up to, and within weeks David had hired her to help out as well. He got Christine an apartment in the Hoop Skirt Factory Building across the street from Suzanne and installed a safe there. That way, the money and the cocaine were never stored in the same place. Christine's job was to run errands for David and Suzanne, to take out laundry, buy groceries, clean house, make sure the rents were paid on all the apartments (David rented three in the Hoop Skirt Factory Building and two in Saint Charles Court; the empty ones were for the breaks). Christine was paid five hundred dollars a week.

Suzanne was making almost four times that much. She was making so much money she felt guilty. David paid her a commission on every kilo that was sold. She had no living expenses apart from clothing; her rent and food were paid. She was too busy to do much of anything else. So her money just kept mounting on a running tab David kept in one column in the books alongside his own profit column. Because Suzanne was notoriously bad at handling her own money, David called the column "Suzanne's Enforced Savings Program." She told David she wanted to use some of it to start a free breakfast program for bums on the street. He laughed.

So Suzanne found impulsive ways to spend. She filled the apartment with fresh flowers every week. She bought herself expensive clothes. On a weekend in New York City in 1980, before she was contacted by David, she had passed on the street an art gallery that had an oversized, framed poster of Mick Jagger by Andy Warhol, one of a series of nine signed by both Warhol and Jagger. It was about three feet wide and four feet tall. Suzanne had this thing about the Rolling Stones. She had coveted that poster ever since. So when David sent her to New York to deliver some cocaine in late January, Suzanne made the delivery, collected thirty thousand in cash, and then steered across Manhattan in the big blue Cutlass with California plates that belonged to the business, heading straight for the gallery.

Making her way across town in heavy traffic, Suzanne was startled at one intersection by a big cop waving at her insistently. She trembled with panic as she rolled down the window.

"How's the surfing?" the cop asked cheerfully.

At first Suzanne blanked on the question. It was winter. What was he talking about?

"I said, how's the surfing?" asked the cop.

Then she remembered that the car had California plates. She grinned.

"Oh, fine, just fine! I love to surf!" she said.

At the gallery, Suzanne did not see the poster displayed, so she went inside and asked to see it. The salesman frowned, but led her to a room in the gallery where they had six of the series on display. She pointed to the one she had seen in the window.

"Can I have it?" Suzanne said.

"How are you going to pay for it?" asked the salesman, in a way that Suzanne interpreted as scorn, as if he were saying, "This isn't a poster shop, little girl."

"With cash," she said.

"Oh! I'll get the manager," he said.

It cost fifteen hundred dollars. They wrapped it and waited for her to bring the car around to the front of the gallery. Then they carried it out and angled it into the back seat.

When she got back to Philadelphia, she lugged the big brown package into the apartment house and up the steps. David was in the apartment with Mark Taplar and Danny Schneps, two young men David had recently recruited to help in different phases of the business.

"Come here, guys," Suzanne said excitedly. "Look what I got!"

They crowded around, and oohed appreciatively when she unwrapped it.

"I'm proud of you," said David. "You took your money and made a wise investment."

"You should lock it up someplace," suggested Taplar. "You'll be able to sell it for three times what you paid for it in a few years."

"But I didn't buy it to sell it again," she protested. "I bought it because I like it!"

It went up in her bedroom.

To Suzanne, Larry Lavin was a mysterious figure in the background, a voice on the phone, a person whom David obviously admired, respected, and even feared—in the sense that if he didn't please Larry he might lose control of the business. David wanted Larry to stay away for two good reasons. The first was that everyone considered Larry to be hot. After the raid on his house and Glen Fuller's bust in November (Glen was now free on bail and his lawyers were preparing such a blizzard of motions that he would not be convicted and sentenced in New Jersey until 1984), David and Kenny were certain that Larry was being watched. Second, David saw his opportunity to move in. After Glen Fuller's bust in November, Larry had agreed to turn over half of his business to David and Ken. They would be responsible for all of the actual details of running the business, while Larry would continue to collect half of the profits on sales to his own customers—who represented a far, far bigger monthly purchase than Ken and David's previous business.

After only a month of working with this arrangement, Ken had begun to back off. His classwork at dental school was suffering so badly that a concerned faculty member had pulled him aside to warn that if his work didn't dramatically improve, he wouldn't be graduating with the rest of the class in spring. He was having serious problems with his longtime girlfriend as a result of his habitual cocaine use and enjoyment of its sexual spoils—Ken and David were irresistibly attractive to the pretty girls of Philadelphia's nightworld who loved cocaine. For Ken, the deciding factor came in December. He had shipped two ounces of cocaine to a friend in California via Federal Express, and somewhere along the way the package got opened. As a joke, Ken had put on the package the return address of a dental school classmate who lived in his apartment building. About a week after the package was mailed, DEA agents kicked in his classmate's door. As it happened, the classmate was out of town, in Florida for Christmas vacation. So David and Kenny had to set up a vigil outside the apartment building, taking turns on the lookout in a car parked up the street, in hopes of intercepting their classmate before he returned to his apartment. They were certain that agents were waiting inside for the guy to come home, and they were afraid that the classmate, who knew about their dealing, would turn them in to the DEA if the agents got to him first.

They waited five or six nights, rotating, staying up all night. Finally they spotted him as he drove up at the end of the week. They intercepted him, explained what happened, and begged him to keep his mouth shut. The classmate agreed, but in coming weeks he began having terrifying nightmares about being implicated in Ken and David's drug dealing. He complained to Ken that he couldn't sleep without having visions of armed men breaking down his door in the middle of the night and opening fire. Partly to reassure the guy, and partly to reassure himself, Ken moved out. The incident sobered him. It brought him face-to-face with the risks he was taking, with how he was wasting his years in dental school, with the relationship he was throwing away. So he abruptly stepped back from the business, leaving David with all the work and, ultimately, with the lion's share of the profits.

On the other hand, David was like one possessed. When his lack of effort and interest in dental school began to affect his progress, he simply left school. All of his considerable charm, hard intellectual gifts, and inexhaustible energy were focused on one thing: making his million. The way David saw it, he could take his maximum risks and make his million in one year, then turn the business over to Willie Harcourt and become, like Larry, a rich, silent partner, removed enough from the business to be safe. That was the plan.

All Larry had to do was stay out of the way.

But Larry couldn't stay out of the way. He enjoyed being in charge, and he was smart enough to see that David, left alone, was rapidly making the cocaine business his own.

Larry's initial worries after Glen's bust had abated. After talking to Glen and to Glen's lawyers, he now knew that the New Jersey case, no matter how threatening to Glen, was unlikely to ever touch him. Larry regarded—(incorrectly)—the search of his home in Society Hill to have been an isolated event, stemming only from the arrest of the Vietnam veteran in New Jersey. And when nothing further came of it, he no longer felt particularly worried, especially now that David was building such an elaborate system to isolate him from cash and cocaine. Larry felt like chairman of the board. Marcia had stopped bugging him because, by all appearances, he *had* gotten out of the business. He no longer had to personally recruit runners, keep the books, count and launder cash, break down and package cocaine. In other words, by early 1981 Larry was comparatively free to devote himself to Marcia and to completing dental school, and he was still reaping huge profits from the sale of cocaine.

His two- to four-kilo-per-month operation of 1979 was now regularly shipping twenty kilos per month from Florida to Philly. The business was generating nearly four hundred thousand in profits *every month!* Since they were now dealing exclusively with Paco and Pepe in Miami, they were assured of a constant, safe supply of 95 to 98 percent pure Colombian cocaine.

Suzanne was not privy at first to all of these subtleties. All she could see was that Larry, whom she had never met, was the architect of this incredible moneymaking system, and that he held David in a kind of thrall. Larry was at once David's hero and someone whom he feared. David was forever worrying that Larry was going to object to the way things were being handled and just step in and take it all back.

Since Suzanne considered David to be the most brilliant, most commanding personality she had ever met, she could only assume that this fellow Larry Lavin was like David, only more so—if that was possible. She pictured Larry as a kind of superman, a fearless, dynamic, authoritative criminal genius.

One afternoon at Saint Charles Court, Suzanne was awakened by the bell. She pressed the intercom button.

"Who is it?"

"Suzanne, it's me."

She recognized the voice from talking to Larry on the phone. She buzzed the lock opening the door downstairs, and then hurriedly called David.

"Larry's at my door and he's on his way up," she told him.

"I'll be right over," said David.

Suzanne waited nervously to catch this first glimpse of the criminal mastermind. When she opened the door on this lanky, smiling dental student with the thick mop of black hair she was, well . . . she was disappointed. He seemed so ordinary. He was too much like everyone else. It was as if a myth had been shattered. She invited him in nervously, and Larry quickly put her at ease. David stopped by within minutes and they conducted their business, checking over the books. By the time they left, Suzanne found herself genuinely liking Larry. He seemed so sincere, so down-to-earth.

Still, it was hard to believe that he was the guy who had set this all in motion.

After a full year under Mark Stewart's control, Larry's money was spread all over town. There were regular boxing matches at the

Arena, and Mark had purchased a Continental Basketball Association team, renamed them the Kings, and recruited former Philadelphia Sixers star Hal Greer to be general manager and coach. He was trying to promote professional wrestling matches, and even hustled Larry out to the airport one night for a meeting with Bruno Sammartino. TEC records had bought out another small recording company, named WMOT, and was promoting a whole new list of soul music singles and albums, mostly for groups that had been popular a decade earlier. Mark had invested Larry's money heavily in an Atlantic City real estate deal. They were going to buy an old apartment building called the Barclay Building, extensively renovate it, and reopen it as the Atrium. And Mark had bought a limousine company that provided transportation for high rollers from Philadelphia to the big boardwalk casinos.

Despite the variety of these ventures, Larry realized by early 1981 that they all had something in common: They all soaked up his money without any appreciable return. With the exception of the limo company, which was relatively simple and seemed capable of thriving, the deeper Larry went into these amazingly complicated projects, the more questionable his investments became. To Larry, a pattern was emerging. Mark would come to Larry with a proposal that sounded exciting, a "can't-miss" opportunity. Money would be invested. Then problems would crop up. Mark would come up with feasible solutions. More money would be invested. Then more problems would appear.

The Barclay Building represented precisely the sort of investment Larry had had in mind when he first sought expert advice in early 1980. Atlantic City was bursting with promise now that the state had legalized gambling and the first few casinos were in full swing. Real estate values were bound to soar.

Mark had come up with the Barclay Building project last summer. It was a U-shaped, six-story structure just two blocks from the boardwalk near the Resorts Casino, with a restaurant on the first level. The owner was in serious financial trouble and about to lose the building to his creditors. If Larry agreed to loan the guy $160,000 at a 6 percent interest rate per month, Mark explained, it would shore up the guy's position. In addition to repaying the loan with interest, he would agree to pay a 20 percent loan fee. If he failed to repay the loan—and Larry and Mark never thought for a minute that he could—then Larmark, Inc., would get a second mortgage and the opportunity to apply for the legitimate financing they would need to purchase the property outright from the bank holding the original mortgage. The owner had a recent assessment that valued the building at far more than the $160,000 loan. Larry didn't see how he could lose money on a deal like that.

Papers were signed in the impressive offices of Larry's lawyer in a conference room where nearly a dozen attorneys worked on the deal around the long table. These trappings added, for Larry, a sense of surefire solidity to the project. Mark introduced Larry as his assistant and protégé, as someone who might eventually run his affairs. A few months passed, and, as expected, even with Larry's loan the Barclay owner ran out of money and his bank began foreclosure procedures. Nearly all the building's tenants were forced to vacate. Everything was proceeding as planned. Larmark succeeded in getting a letter of credit from an insurance company for an ambitious $3.5-million renovation project. An architect was hired to design the renovation, and he produced a handsome scale model. All of the open space in the center would be glassed over and the building would be renamed the Atrium. They worked out a deal with the first bank to assume the first mortgage and Larmark took over management of the building. All this cost Larry more money in fees and expenses, but it was exciting—he particularly liked the model. This was precisely the sort of thing he had in mind when he first met Mark Stewart. Then Resorts agreed to rent the top two floors. At last! They were getting somewhere!

But then, problems. The elevator wouldn't work and Resorts wanted to back out. It turned out there was a nice restaurant on the first floor that had just remodeled and could not be evicted without violating the lease. Meanwhile, the company that insured the original owner slapped a two-million-dollar lien on the building because it claimed to have been defrauded by the original owner. Mark and the lawyers assured Larry that the case would never hold up in court, but while the matter was being litigated, the trendy renovation was on hold. In the meantime, in addition to more legal fees (with no end in sight), Larry was paying the mortgage and footing maintenance and utility bills for the building, which were expensive and ongoing. . . .

Then there was WMOT-TEC Records. Right away Larry learned that the key to success in the record business is distribution. WMOT had a contract with CBS Records, which made it worth buying, so Larry signed the check when Mark first proposed the deal. Next they needed money to pay the recording artists and to fly them around the country to perform, then to pay the regional distribution men who could guarantee airtime on radio stations around the country, then to wine and dine the local disc jockeys at the soul music stations to keep WMOT-TEC's records playing at prime times, then to rent exorbitantly expensive time in modern recording studios to make the singles and albums. . . . Larry found himself shelling out money again and again. Mark then decided what they needed was to build their own sound studio in the basement of the Wellington Building. He had convincing reasons for wanting that, but when construction was done it turned out that the studio was not up to modern production standards and CBS refused to handle the records cut there. "It's good enough for practice," they said, "but not to record." When one of WMOT-TEC's singles, a punchy percussive rap number by Philadelphia artist Frankie Smith called "Double Dutch Bus," started gaining ground on *Billboard*'s soul charts, Mark decided the company needed a promotional presence in Los Angeles, which he could show to be absolutely vital, so a western office was opened, a staff was hired, and Mark started shuttling back and forth from coast to coast. Months later, Larry found out that Mark had incurred fabulous expenses in L.A., mostly in rental costs . . . not the least of which was leasing himself a new Ferrari.

The kicker was that CBS, which was reporting substantial nationwide sales for some of WMOT-TEC's soul music singles, was charging so much for pressings, promotion, and distribution that the net profit on sales, Larry's one source of return on all these investments, was close to zero.

To make matters worse, the ex-owner of WMOT filed a lawsuit claiming that Mark Stewart had reneged on his original deal. Larry knew how the man felt.

Lastly there was the Martin Luther King Arena, Larry's most conspicuous investment. After the riot in June, things had settled down. The Kings basketball team, which Larry had put up twenty-five thousand to help buy, was playing to crowds of a few hundred. The state boxing commission was probing charges that bouts at the Arena were strictly setups, opportunities for promising fighters to run up their KO totals by flooring palookas. Dick Muldair, Larry's old friend and runner, who after serving his ninety-day prison sentence took a job at the Arena, was calling Larry to tell him that Mark's employees at the Arena were stealing tools and, instead of working, were spending hours of unsupervised time each day getting stoned. There was only one truly promising fighter in their stable, Timmy Witherspoon, but nobody was willing to box him because Mark couldn't put together the kind of backing needed to attract fighters of Witherspoon's caliber. Mark brought in the Roller Derby, but nobody came to watch it because nobody in West Philly had ever even heard of Roller Derby. So he had taken to booking shyster preachers, including one who staged a show where he purported to raise a man from the dead. The resurrected soul stepped right out of a coffin on stage, and the gullible audience then filed past on stage enthusiastically to fill the empty coffin with cash.

By early 1981, Larry was catching on. Every time some new outrage would come to his attention he would rush to confront Mark, and every time the confident entrepreneur would manage to persuade the twenty-five-year-old dental student/cocaine magnate that the jackpot was just around the corner. Mark could be almost hypnotic he was so convincing. He knew so much more about business than Larry that he could, with a few charts and financial statements and a few deft sketches of what the future would hold, turn Larry's anger into positive delight. There were times Larry stormed down to the Wellington intent on withdrawing his support for a project, only to leave having agreed to make an even more substantial investment.

And, of course, there were other reasons for maintaining his relationship with Mark. In the year since they signed their agreement, Larry had gone from living in low-rent student housing to living in a modern home in the city's best neighborhood. He had gone from meeting with street hoods in his living room to conferring in boardrooms with some of the city's highest-paid legal talent. He had gone from reporting almost no income to Penn every year, to multiple salaries—each of these projects enabled Larry to convert more of his illegal money into holdings that were legal, even if they were also unprofitable. Larry knew of no other way to readily access his wealth without inviting legal problems.

In four months he would be done with dental school. Already Marcia was talking about moving out of the city and starting a family.

It was April of 1981 when they decided to move. Larry and Marcia had just returned from a week in Saint Thomas, Larry's last spring break before graduation. They had lived at 4 Willings Alley Mews for more than a year, but to Marcia the house would always be just the place where that Mark Stewart had put them up after the robbery. She hated it. Not one warm memory attached to it. During the huge parade celebrating the Phillies' World Series victory in October, a woman neighbor had been pulled off the sidewalk by a group of drunken men who tried to rape her. And earlier this year Marcia had been knocked down by a man who tried to grab her purse. A year of living there had just confirmed her desire for more space, for a lawn, trees, a garden, birds, for a house that was not entirely vertical, for a place that, in some way, reflected what she wanted.

So the next weekend they went driving out on the Main Line, looking for a house.

Larry had called a real estate agent, Ilene McHenry, and looked at the paper. The first place they stopped to see, on Waterloo Road in Devon, was a sixty-room mansion. Its owners had plans to divide the huge house, worth two million dollars, into four condominiums, so that the estate would be jointly owned. Larry pulled in one end of a U-shaped driveway and drove up to the front entrance. Marcia refused to even get out of the car.

"Are you crazy, Larry? Look at this place!" she said. She couldn't believe he was serious.

"I just want to look around," said Larry.

He stormed off by himself to walk around the grounds.

Marcia was alarmed by something McHenry had said trying to make conversation as they drove around that day.

"You never know about people," she said with a smile. "I sold a house to a nice young couple and it turns out they were running guns for the IRA."

Later, Marcia said to Larry, "Now, why would she say something like that?"

"She was just making conversation; trying to be nice. It was something that happened that was interesting," said Larry.

Marcia shook her head. "If you show a lot of wealth, Larry, people are going to be interested in where it came from. You're still in school!"

On reflection, Larry realized that something more modest would not only make Marcia happy, it would also be far wiser for one in his special financial circumstances. Marcia thought something in the $75,000-to-$100,000 range would be fine. Larry was thinking more on the order of $200,000. He figured they could sell the Society Hill house for at least $150,000 to $180,000, so a $200,000 home would be an appropriate step up. They went looking with McHenry the next weekend, telling her that they were prepared to spend only $150,000. In the time-honored real estate tradition, the first house she showed them was well over that ceiling, a two-story white brick Colonial with gray shutters on Timber Lane.

They would see a dozen other houses over the next two days, but nothing else compared. For a young man in a hurry to turn his criminal fortune into legitimate wealth and social position, the choice was perfect.

Timber Lane is in Devon, just a fifty-minute ride out the Paoli Line from Center City Philadelphia, but a journey that for most people can take generations. The Paoli Line is the old Pennsylvania Railroad's main line, from which the region takes its name. Its station stops— Overbrook, Merion, Narberth, Wynnewood, Ardmore, Haverford, Bryn Mawr . . . Paoli—are escalating rungs of Philadelphia's upper class, the oldest and most formal establishment in America. Devon comes seven stops after Bryn Mawr, out where city streets are just a memory. George Washington once rode up the wooded hills and down the green slopes of this gently rolling landscape, just south of Valley Forge. Most of the old estates of Philadelphia's homegrown aristocracy have been subdivided, but an equally rigid—if more pedestrian—hierarchy prevails. Next door to the white house with gray shutters lived the Eisenhowers, John and Barbara, parents of David Eisenhower and in-laws to Julie Nixon. On the other side lived a chemical company executive. Uphill, across the street, a retired admiral and head of the department of dental surgery at Temple University. Next to the admiral, a vice-president of the Mellon Bank.

Out here there was quiet: When a car moved down the gentle curve of Timber Lane, folks lean toward windows to watch. Out here there was order: landscaped lots on sylvan slopes, lawn services to keep the grass lush and trim, nurseries to sculpt the hickory, oaks, walnuts and white pines—and prep schools to prune the children. Timber Lane's residents had earned the money and power to have things their way. Their way was one of country clubs and stables, the annual Devon Horse Show and County Fair, Colonial-style inns for a quiet dinner out, and a Bloomingdale's in America's largest shopping mall at King of Prussia, just a short drive away. Their days were scenic, their nights serene.

"The only time we get a little excitement around here is when the Secret Service moves in," said owner Margy Conlin, who was out working in the front yard when Larry and Marcia stopped by with the real estate agent. "You see, Richard Nixon sometimes stops by to visit with the Eisenhowers next door, and before he arrives the Secret Service descends."

The house itself was set back about forty feet on a slight downward slope from a narrow, winding suburban lane in a neighborhood dominated by trees. There were six windows across the second floor and four on the first, two on either side of a broad door with a rising sun pattern set in the brick overhead. There were Colonial lanterns on either side of the door. A driveway curved down from the lane on the west side of the property, leading to an attached two-car garage. What appealed to Marcia most was the backyard. It ran from the back porch in a long gentle green sweep that was nearly as long as a football field. At the far end of the property ran a stream over which a previous owner had built a small Japanese-style bridge. A stand of maple and oak trees blocked the view of the next house, and on either side of the property there were bright yellow flowering forsythias, a white-blossomed little dogwood, and evergreens. Inside, the first floor was sectioned into four large, sunny rooms. To the left of the foyer was a living room, and behind that a dining room. Continuing clockwise was a kitchen and then, back at the front of the house on the right side of the foyer, a wood-paneled den. The staircase from the foyer led up to five bedrooms and two baths, one at either end. The basement needed work. A previous owner had intended to set up a medical office down there and had divided the space into a number of small rooms. Although it was not a new house, it had been especially well kept, and all of the plumbing and appliances were modern. For both Larry and Marcia, it was love at first sight.

The Conlins were asking $219,000.

"I love it, but it's too expensive," said Marcia.

"Don't worry. We'll be able to do it," said Larry.

Larry got his camera out of the car and walked the grounds snapping pictures so that they would have something to show their friends. When she got home, Marcia excitedly called her mother to tell her about the house.

But that evening, McHenry called. She had bad news. Just after he and Marcia left, the agent who had originally listed the house had come up with another offer. If Larry wanted the house, he would have to move fast.

Larry hung up and immediately phoned Mrs. Conlin. She said that they appeared to have a buyer already. Larry said he would like to make a better offer. Mrs. Conlin said he would have to speak to her husband, who was out of town.

"Where?" asked Larry.

"He's in New York," she said.

"Where's he staying?"

So Larry phoned the Yale Club in New York City and tracked down Dennis Conlin. After chatting amiably for a few minutes, Larry offered the full asking price for the house. Conlin was pleased. He said he had not expected to actually get the full asking price for the house. Larry hung up and told Marcia that Conlin had agreed; the house would be theirs. Larry then called his agent to tell her the good news, and she informed him that since her last call she learned that Mrs. Conlin had already signed an agreement with the other couple. Larry said she couldn't do that; he had already reached an agreement in New York with her husband. So Larry called Conlin back. He said he would check with his wife and try to work things out.

A short while later, Conlin called back to explain, apologetically, that his wife had, in his absence, made an agreement with another buyer. There was nothing he could do.

Larry was angry. He said he had called a lawyer, which wasn't true, but then Larry had learned a thing or two about playing real estate hardball from his involvement in the Barclay Building fiasco, and he told Conlin that he was prepared to go to court if necessary. It was nearly midnight.

"Look, we'll give you anything you want for the house," Larry said. "My wife is crying. She had just assumed that would be her house."

"There's nothing we can do," said Conlin.

"Do they have a mortgage contingency clause in their offer?" asked Larry.

They did.

"Then you can back out of it," Larry said. "Because I am making you an offer with no contingency."

When Conlin continued to hedge, Larry turned threatening.

"If you don't agree, then I'm going to put a lien on the house nine o'clock tomorrow morning," he said. "I believe I had an oral agreement with you. I'll tell my lawyer to prepare the papers right now."

Larry knew that the Conlins were planning to move soon.

"The lien will be there for at least ninety days," Larry said. "Even if my claim is turned down, it will drag on past your moving day. You won't have the money to buy your new home."

The next day the Conlins agreed to scuttle the earlier agreement and sell the house to Larry and Marcia for $219,000. Larry had them over a barrel.

At the settlement a few weeks later, Larry was warm and personable, as if nothing had happened. The sellers and their agent, who had lost half of the commission when the rival buyers' offer was turned down, despised him. Who was this twenty-five-year-old dental student, anyway? Larry had topped off their impression of him when, a week before settlement, he had offered to pay Conlin $40,000 in cash and write a check for the remainder. It was, in effect, an invitation to cheat the government out of almost 20 percent of the closing cost fees. And where in the hell does a dental student come up with $40,000 in cash?

Larry seemed more bewildered than disturbed when the older man responded with the look of someone who has just been served fresh shit on fine china.

In March, David chartered a jet and flew Suzanne and Christine and Gina with him to Saint Thomas. All three women were infatuated with him. Suzanne was his former lover. Gina was his live-in girlfriend. Christine had begun confiding a secret longing for David to her diary.

Soon after they got back, David began sleeping with Suzanne. He told her he wanted to keep their personal relationship secret, not just because of Gina, but because he didn't want everyone in the business to know that their relationship was more than professional. Of course, Suzanne told Christine about it right away.

* * *

By early summer, Larry owned a hit record. Frankie Smith's "Double Dutch Bus" was number one on *Billboard*'s soul charts. Larry thought it sounded dreadful, but first the record went gold, with one million sales, and started closing in on platinum. The magazine came to Philadelphia to do a big photo spread on Frankie Smith and Mark Stewart and WMOT, calling it the hottest small independent recording company in the country.

Of course, behind the scenes was a different story. At Mark's urgings, Larry had begun shelling out promotional fees to agents all over the country six months before. In Philadelphia, Mark acted as WMOT-TEC's agent, courting Butterball, the lead disc jockey for Philadelphia's leading soul station, WDAS, a bellwether for the industry. The stations had an A shift and a B shift. Tunes on the A shift got played every hour. For the right amount of money, the regional promoters would guarantee the A shift for your record, although no one ever discussed exactly how that was done. For Larry it was proof that one more supposedly legit industry was just a scam.

There was an art to pushing a record up the charts, provided you had plenty of money to spend. When a record jumped three spots on the chart, *Billboard* put a bullet next to it. It attracted more attention that way. That was how particular singles got a reputation for being hot. WMOT's promoters would strike deals with key stations to withhold airtime for the record for two weeks and then play it heavily in the third to boost sales for that week's surveys. The record would suddenly spurt up five notches or more, earning another bullet and building its own momentum. At one point Larry and Mark were able to orchestrate three records into the top fifteen. Larry was spending close to fifty thousand a month. CBS was reporting minimal net profits.

Nevertheless, WMOT-TEC looked like it was starting to fly. Mark wanted Frankie Smith to cut an album to cash in on the success of his single. That was another forty thousand. And Frankie and his band had to tour, which meant money for transportation, incredible hotel costs, clothes—a star has to look the part. The L.A. office was starting to run up bigger and bigger bills, and Mark had opened a West Coast branch of Celebrity Limousines. In all, there were now more than a dozen employees in California, some of whom, Larry learned, were making seventy-five-thousand-dollar annual salaries. By the end of the year, the total payroll for all of Mark's ventures topped seven hundred thousand. Larry found out indirectly that Mark had recently given his wife a Porsche. When he confronted his financial advisor with this, Mark said, "I've got money of my own, Larry."

But Larry had no idea how to get to the bottom of that.

Truth was, Larry was making so much money in 1981 that without Mark he wouldn't have known what to do with it. Mark knew a vice president at Bank Leumi who would take his periodic deliveries of sacks full of cash and spread it among almost a dozen separate accounts, so that no one deposit was greater than the ten thousand-dollar limit (beyond ten thousand the bank must report the deposit to Uncle Sam). There was a WMOT-TEC account, a Larmark account, an L's Inc. account, a Wellington account, a Mark Stewart escrow account, a King Arena account. . . .

"Double Dutch Bus" went platinum. Larry had twenty gold records printed and mounted on plaques, at about seventy bucks apiece. They served a useful purpose. Larry found that people were as ignorant about show biz as they were fascinated by it. All Larry had to do was show people the gold record, and immediately they thought they understood how he had made his money.

His friends were convinced that Larry was making a bundle. David and Kenny and even Willie Harcourt were eager to sink money into the record company. It looked like a sure thing.

But in all of the excitement and confusion, somebody at the Wellington Building neglected to pay Frankie Smith a large portion of his royalties. When the singer initially inquired, he was reassured that the difference would be forthcoming. He waited and waited.

But by late 1981, the singer's patience was wearing thin.

At the time Larry was buying his house in the suburbs, David was handling thirty kilos of cocaine per month. Larry and David were not only the primary sources of cocaine for metropolitan Philadelphia, the tentacles of their organization reached nationwide and even into Canada.

Billy Motto was doing a huge business in South Philly, selling to a diverse group of people far removed from the yuppie crowd familiar to Larry and David. Billy was by far the business's biggest customer, buying about fifty kilos total in 1981. He was just a month or two away from making his first million. As a "privileged customer," Billy was no longer paying the marked up price for cocaine. He was throwing his money in with Larry's and David's to buy wholesale. Larry had asked David not only to give Billy the first pick of each shipment, but to spend time teaching him all the ins and outs of testing coke, cutting it, making rocks, and packaging it. Billy took his lessons from David sitting by the stove in the kitchen of Suzanne's place. They met three or four times over about four weeks.

At one such tutorial, Billy remarked in his cheerful, matter-of-fact way, "You know, don't you, that at some point in the future we'll all be doing time for this activity?"

As a joke, it fell flat. Billy was the only one of them who seemed to regard that as a likely outcome.

Despite these sessions, perhaps because of them, David got on Billy's nerves. Billy had become a well-respected man in South Philly, and was used to being treated with deference. It was a different world from the one Larry and David knew. Billy, who also dabbled in loan-sharking, had men working for him who would attack people with baseball bats or knives if they crossed him. After Billy first met Suzanne, and learned that she was handling a lot of meetings with buyers at her apartment, he brought over a pistol and gave it to David.

"Suzanne doesn't want a gun," David said.

"Tell her just to leave it out somewhere around the apartment where people can see it," Billy said. "That way people will know that even though she's a girl, she's protected."

David treated Billy like a customer, like someone lower than him on the organizational scale. David would set up meetings with Billy and then not show up, something the South Philly dealer regarded as a slap in the face. Instead of laughing, as Larry always had, at how rumpled and disorganized was the paper money Billy brought along in brown grocery bags (it always added up to the exact amount promised), David bitched about it constantly and even tried issuing Billy ultimatums. Billy didn't like that, but for the time being he had no other reliable source for good cocaine.

In addition to Billy, David and Kenny and Willie Harcourt were all selling to their own circle of friends throughout Center City. David and Ken also had customers in New York City and in California. A buyer named Kevin had a steady business going in Bucks County, northeast of Philadelphia. A large portion of each Miami shipment was going to a woman in New England named Priscilla, who had customers throughout that region who were, on average, about ten years older then Larry. Brian Cassidy, a college student from Paoli, was selling to well-to-do younger residents on the Main Line, and also had a large customer in Pittsburgh. Paul Mikuta was selling to friends in Delaware, on the Main Line, in the Rochester area, and elsewhere. Steve Rasner, a dental school classmate who graduated a year before Larry, was selling to customers in the New Jersey suburbs of Philadelphia. There was a trio of Penn State students out in State College, in central Pennsylvania. Stu Thomas was selling to friends on the Jersey shore and another friend in Virginia. In New England, in addition to Priscilla, Ricky Baratt was still struggling to recover ground by selling in the Boston area, and Larry's brother Rusty and sister Jill were dealing substantial amounts. Reckless Glen Fuller, despite his pending charges in New Jersey, was still selling cocaine in Vermont and in Colorado. Larry had a customer in Tampa, Florida, who was selling two or three pounds at a time, and another promising customer in Phoenix, Arizona, named Wayne Heinauer, whom Larry had met through a friend at State College back in the days when he was selling pot. Heinauer had one customer in Canada. There was a grade school principal in central Pennsylvania whom Larry had met as an undergraduate. There were dozens of smaller customers scattered around Philadelphia and the region, friends of friends of friends. Their names filled pages in the neat ledger kept in the safe at Suzanne's. And each of these customers was a significant dealer on a smaller level, breaking their own purchases into dozens of smaller amounts for their own users, multiplying exponentially the total number of lives touched by Larry Lavin's enterprise. Virtually all of the customers were between the ages of twenty and thirty-five and all had enough money to spend upwards of seventy-five dollars for a gram of white powder to shovel up their nose. For many, the harmless drug they had tried for the first time at a party a year or two ago was now something they carried with them at all times, for a quick pop in the car before work, in an office lavatory several times a day, or in the corner of a bar after work. . . .

Managing this traffic in cash and white powder was a full-time job for nearly a dozen workers, most of them drawn from David's acquaintances at local bars and restaurants. David and Willie were much more cautious than Larry had ever been. They always kept the cocaine and the money in separate places, and met with customers away from both. Willie had recruited three other young men, Gary Levin, Daniel Schneps, and Roger Parsons, to help transport the kilos from Florida to Philadelphia, and they took turns making runs. Two would drive down, meet with Paco and Pepe, and purchase ten or more kilos right at Paco's house. It was a big change from the old seat-of-the-pants days. Willie would be met at the airport and driven out to Paco's neighborhood. He learned that Paco's relatives and associates owned all the houses on his block, so that there was no worry about neighbors growing suspicious. There were armed guards to provide escort, and lookouts posted at either end of the block with walkie-talkies to sound the alarm if anything unusual was happening outside. Willie got along famously with Paco and Pepe. His Spanish improved. Paco called Willie a "friend for life," confessing that selling drugs was not a desirable business for them but that it was the only opportunity life had given them. Paco said he had drifted through the Gulf of Mexico on a raft on his flight from Cuba to Texas. Paco looked forward to getting out of the business and retiring as a wealthy man. "Your children will come to my house and play with my children," he told Willie, "and we'll drink a toast to the old days when we had to do this to provide for our families' futures." Paco confessed that one of his dreams was to pay to have his father released from prison in Cuba and bring the rest of his family to the United States. Pepe wanted to build hotels in Mexico.

It got so that trips to Florida, once such a frightening chore, were a pleasure. On the drive home, the two runners would take turns behind the wheel. Willie bought two big cars so that there was enough room to stretch out and sleep on the backseat.

In Philadelphia, David would select the break house, or "factory," usually a vacant apartment rented by one of the workers using an assumed name. David moved the factory location constantly. In addition to staffing the whole organization with his own people, David shifted the operation from Larry's old West Philly neighborhood around Penn, to Old City. The money was stored in a safe at Christine's. The books were at Suzanne's, and coke was stored elsewhere—the location was kept vague. Customers met with Suzanne or David, and the cocaine would be delivered there once the money was counted. Larry still handled a lot of the negotiations by phone, taking orders from his friends and relaying the information to David or Suzanne, but he was spending at most only a few hours every day on the business. He was busy finishing dental school and preparing for the big move out to Devon, but he always had time for a friend with money to spend.

As business continued to grow, David decided it was time to negotiate a price break. He was curious to meet Paco and Pepe anyway. So he asked Willie to arrange a meeting in Miami.

"Let's get together for a bottle of Taittinger and blow a few grand and maybe I can get the price down," he said.

The trip was more like a vacation than business. David took Gina, and Willie took his girlfriend. They stayed at the Fontainebleau. Paco threw an extravagant party in the Presidential Suite of the luxury hotel, a huge two-story suite with a grand piano and bar, and filled it with friends. They spent four days, mostly just enjoying themselves, their money, their women, their success. But for several hours every day they would retreat back to Paco's house to talk business. Sitting around the wood-paneled study before the stylized island sunset scene, Willie and Paco, both big easygoing men, and David and Pepe, small and excitable, sipped scotch together and paused occasionally to snort a line of cocaine.

All along, ever since Larry had started buying kilos of cocaine in Florida more than two years earlier, they had been paying a fixed price of fifty-six grand per kilo. Paco and Pepe had been the main suppliers for almost everyone they had been buying from all that time. David's argument was that during that time their business had grown from only two kilos per month to more than thirty, and yet they had never been offered cocaine for a penny less. He emphasized that their business was cash only; they had never bought on credit and therefore had never been in debt. Implicit in David's pitch was that they were restless. They were good customers willing to pay up front. If Paco wouldn't offer a discount, they might be able to get a better deal elsewhere.

Paco was firm. He said his hands were tied by his brother, who ran his family's business. Besides, said Paco, to him, thirty kilos per month did not make Larry and David a big customer.

"A big customer buys a hundred kilos at a time," he said. He explained that the biggest customers put up one to two million at a time, investing and participating in the risky trips to Colombia to smuggle large quantities north. Unless they were ready for that, to become partners with him, then they were regular customers and the price would stay the same.

David wouldn't give up. When he realized he could not lower the price, he tried a different tack.

"If the price is fixed, what is it I can do to get some sort of a break?" David asked. "If thirty kilos isn't enough business for a month, then what is?"

"Fifty kilos," Paco said.

"If I can do fifty kilos in one month, what kind of break can you give me?"

It was evident to Willie that Paco didn't believe they could do it. It was a jump way out of proportion to the growth levels they had seen from Philadelphia. In 1980, for instance, thirty kilos represented an approximate total of *all* the cocaine Willie had transported. But, as if to humor David, whose eagerness amused Paco, the Cuban said, "Listen, if you do fifty kilos in one month, I'll give you a hundred grand in cash, or two free kilos."

That was the break David was looking for. He accepted the challenge excitedly. Before they returned home, Paco gave them three high-powered walkie-talkies, like the ones his men used to coordinate their escort and lookout assignments.

Back in Philadelphia, David geared up to meet the goal. For the last two weeks of April they artificially inflated demand, holding out on customers, making the rare claim that they were suffering a shortage. Then, during May, Willie and his runners made three trips to Florida. On the first two they brought back sixteen, then seventeen kilos. They pushed double orders of cocaine off on their customers, telling them that they anticipated another shortage in June. Pulling together cash from everywhere they could find it, Willie made the last run on the last day of the month, carrying close to one million dollars in cash down to pick up a final eighteen kilos—one more than the amount David had promised to buy.

The final break of the month was a marathon session over Memorial Day weekend, involving the largest single shipment of cocaine the business had ever brought north. It took place at Paul Mikuta's ranch-style house in Gladwyn, on the Main Line.

This was Christine's first break. She was excited when David asked her to help out, and not just because he offered her a hundred dollars per hour. Christine had been kept on the periphery of the business, which was like being kept on the outside of a tight-knit secret social circle that included her best friend, Suzanne, and the man she secretly admired, David. His invitation was a chance to become more fully a part of their group, which Christine considered glamorous and fun. She had heard about breaks, and now she was going to actually take part!

It had all the right elements of danger and suspense. As Willie's car approached Center City on I-95, he called in on one of the new walkie-talkies Paco had given them. David and Paul were in the lead car. Suzanne and Christine were in another. The idea was for David to guide Willie's car out to Paul's, but somewhere out near City Avenue, about fifteen minutes northwest on the Schuylkill Expressway, Willie lost contact with the lead car. He had never been to Paul's, so he turned around and drove back into Old City. When David and Mark realized things had gotten screwed up, they, too, doubled back.

To hell with the walkie-talkies. The three cars met outside Suzanne's place and just drove in a caravan out to Paul's.

Christine was shocked when Willie brought eighteen kilos into the house. That was nearly forty pounds of pure cocaine, worth 1.3 million dollars to the business. Cocaine users were used to seeing a small pinch of white powder in a glass vial or plastic bag. Here was enough cocaine to fill a barrel, three large suitcases full. She had known David and Suzanne were managing a big business, but it wasn't until she saw those stacks and stacks of white powder in kilo-sized plastic bags that she could picture just how big.

David was in heat over the enormous profits represented by the product in this room. He had all the formulas written out on a tablet for each customer, he had his calculator, and he paced the room like a little dictator, instructing the workers as they broke down the shipment into individual orders and weighed the packages on an expensive yellow electronic scale. Billy Motto and Paul Mikuta got uncut cocaine. Everyone else got a predetermined mixture of real rocks, "man-made" rocks, and shake, which had been mixed with a healthy portion of inositol, which David called "I," and lidocaine.

David and Willie had a loud argument before things got started.

Willie was seething. It had been a tough month, easily the most hectic since he had gotten involved more than a year earlier. He had been without sleep for nearly two days when he got back to Philadelphia. He had been snorting cocaine and drinking during a lot of that time, and he was exhausted. His plan had been to just drop off the cocaine and go to sleep for a day. But when he had phoned David on his way home, David had insisted that it was too dangerous to store that much cocaine in the city overnight. He proposed the walkie-talkie rendezvous instead.

"Okay," Willie had said. "I'll drop it off out there if you want."

When Willie arrived at Paul's, he had figured his night was over. But as he turned to leave, David said, "No, I want you to stay. We're going to break this up now."

"All of it?" asked Willie.

"Yes."

Willie knew it was an all-night task.

"Look, David," said Willie, peering down at his boss. "I just finished driving twenty-four hours from Miami. I was up the previous night buying all of this and putting it all together. Before that I had to drive down there. Forget it. I'm done."

They ended shouting at each other. Willie, who had a lot of money tied up in the business, and who had already invested close to $125,000 in WMOT-TEC, had much to lose by falling out of David's favor. David had hinted that at the end of the year, Willie would be in line to take over the business. Then it would be Willie's chance to make a million. But the big bartender was exhausted.

"You are the only one strong enough to press rocks," said David.

"I'm going home," said Willie.

"If you don't stay, you're fired," David said. "You lose your equity in the record company. You're out."

Willie knew David would do it. He bit his bottom lip, strode across the room and snorted about a gram of coke, and went to work.

Once they got started, there was cocaine over the entire room, over the rugs and walls, coating the drapes, the windows, the furniture. Everyone in the room was coated with the stuff. White powder choked the air, it stung and then numbed their eyes and ears, nose and mouth, and had the usual potent side effects. As if the contact high alone weren't enough, there were lines laid out on a dresser at one end of the room with a hundred-dollar bill rolled up alongside them. Christine's heart raced with excitement as she and the others, buoyed by bursts of exuberance, worked frantically. Someone had the Phillies game on in the corner, with the sound turned up loud. The men were sifting cocaine into big metal salad bowls using a series of strainers, each one smaller than the next. Rocks were separated from the powder and then broken down according to size. They ended with bowls filled with small, medium, and large rocks and a big pile of shake. The bowls were in a line on a big table in the middle of the room. Willie went to work spraying the shake and pressing it into rocks. He set the compressed material underneath a row of heat lamps set at another end of the room. David paced and calculated and gave orders. He was the only one in the room whose hands were not buried in white powder.

Suzanne got sick. She was upset about David's argument with Willie—she and Willie had become close friends. A few hours into the break she doubled over with severe stomach cramps. Christine took her into the next room and took her temperature, which was high. Every few minutes she would leave the break to sit with Suzanne, bathing her wrists with alcohol in an effort to keep her temperature down. Willie and Christine ended up doing most of the work themselves.

The break lasted for twelve hours. They started at ten o'clock Friday night and finished at ten o'clock Saturday morning. When they were done, Suzanne was still sick. Willie was so tired he felt delirious. Christine felt faint. Paul went home to get some sleep. He and Ken and Stu were invited to a Memorial Day golf outing with Larry and a picnic back at his place in Devon.

David collected his hundred-thousand-dollar rebate. In June, the business didn't buy one kilo of cocaine.

For the whole summer after moving in, there were work crews parked in the driveway of Larry and Marcia's house on Timber Lane. Construction of a swimming pool began in the yard. An attractive wooden fence was constructed around the pool area. Landscape crews dug holes and planted trees and bushes and flowers. On the sharply angled front roof were installed flat black solar panels that were supposed to reduce the house's gas bills sufficiently to eventually recover the $22,000-plus cost of installation. Monitoring and control equipment for the solar panels took up almost a fourth of Larry's basement. Marcia mentioned that she wanted to hang a lot of plants from rear windows, so Larry decided what she really needed was a greenhouse, and then decided what the greenhouse really needed was a Jacuzzi. He and Glen Fuller rented a front-end loader and excavated a big hole behind the southwest wall for a propane tank to supply energy to heat the tub. Contractors were hired for the more difficult task of excavating ground and knocking a hole in the south wall of the house so that there would be a direct entrance to the basement from the pool area. Larry had carpeting, snazzy diagonal wood paneling, and a bar installed to create the perfect setting for his heavy pool table, and rounded out the room with a TV screen and an Atari hookup with a boxful of games and extra joysticks and his big fish tank.

Neighbors watched from a distance with wonder. Marcia felt as if she were hiding in the house. She didn't want to meet the neighbors for fear of having to make up elaborate stories to explain how they could afford all the work going on.

But Larry, as usual, confronted the problem head-on. He strode across the lawn one day soon after moving in to introduce himself to the woman across the street. She was wheeling her garbage cans down her steep driveway to the street.

When she remarked that the previous owners had not stayed in the neighborhood for long, Larry responded, "I'll be here for a long time." She thought that was odd, but she liked Larry nevertheless.

Elicia Geisa and her husband owned the house down the hill and across the way from Larry and Marcia's back porch. They had the best view of all the construction work that began immediately after the Lavins moved in. Elicia's first glimpse of Larry was of this tall, skinny man, little older than a kid, pacing the backyard overseeing the work crews, always with a portable phone pressed to one ear. She walked over and invited Larry and Marcia to dinner.

Larry made a bad first impression on the Geisas. He and Marcia showed up on time, and after initial pleasantries, Larry basically took over. He talked and talked, mostly about himself. He began by stressing that he was not Jewish. People often assumed he was Jewish because of his name, he said, and maybe because his thick black hair made him look a little Jewish. Anyway, he was really Irish Catholic. The Geisas found it strange that he would start right in with that information, as if it were something important for them to know— which it was not. Right away Larry shattered one easy assumption about his obvious affluence. Without being asked, he said he had not inherited a penny. He talked about attending Phillips Exeter Academy and Penn on scholarship, and volunteered that he had made a lot of money investing in the stock market, first little amounts, then bigger. He told the Geisas that he was part owner of a record company, and that he owned some land at the shore, other things. Larry said he got a kick out of living next door to the Eisenhowers. He thought that was really neat. Marcia sat through the meal being pleasant. Inside, she was mortified. Why did Larry feel it necessary to go on like this around strangers?

When Larry and Marcia left late that evening, Elicia's husband remarked, "He's either into the Mafia, or drugs." And they laughed about it.

Directly across the street, uphill, lived Paul Farrell, a retired two-star admiral who had been head of the U.S. Navy Dental Corps. Farrell was head of the department of dental surgery at Temple University. Larry, again, strode directly across the street when he saw Farrell working in his yard. He introduced himself to the admiral and was delighted to learn that they were both dentists. Farrell had even attended Penn dental school almost four decades ago. The admiral later couldn't help but remark to himself that he had worked all of his career as a dentist, with great success, before he could afford to live on that block of Timber Lane. Here was this kid across the street, with an even bigger, nicer house, making rapid and expensive improvements, and he had yet to see even his first patient!

A few days after their initial meeting, Larry rang the bell and introduced Marcia and his mother-in-law. Mrs. Osborn, he said, had just sold her house in New Jersey and moved into the nearby Valley Forge Apartments. Farrell invited them in and he and his wife had a nice chat with their new neighbors. The Farrells liked the Lavins. They were a friendly, attractive young couple. In the military it is a custom to return such courtesy visits, so about a week later the Farrells rang Larry and Marcia's bell. Larry gave the admiral a tour, showing him the work going on in the basement and yard. The inside of the house was already completely furnished. Upstairs, Larry showed the admiral his gold record on the wall and explained that he had made a lot of money investing in the record company as a student. There were big, beautiful Persian rugs on the downstairs floors, and the furniture was mostly Colonial style. And everything was brand-new.

Graduation day was in late May. Larry's folks came down from Haverhill, and Marcia's mother and sister were there. Wearing his black gown with a purple sash, Larry took turns posing with his parents and with Marcia and then by himself in front of the dental school. His face had filled in since undergraduate days, giving him a stronger jaw and a more substantial, mature appearance. He was flush with pride. Larry considered the dental school diploma his finest accomplishment—and he had made nearly 3 million dollars along the way! His small fortune was already invested heavily in legitimate projects. He and Marcia had a beautiful home on the Main Line . . .

what was left for him but years of enjoying himself, having a family, maybe setting up a dental practice? It was ironic that dentistry, the profession he had wanted all of his life and worked so hard to achieve, was now purely a matter of personal preference. There was certainly no hurry about getting started.

Larry's passage through dental school had helped to shape the experience for the entire class of '81. More than a half dozen of its members, including two who had not made it to graduation day and several from the class that graduated in '80, were involved in the business. Larry's dealings were such common knowledge among his classmates that they poked fun at it in the yearbook. On page 47 there was a closeup photo of white powder on a small spoon poised under a nostril—"Sure don't smell like Temrex [a temporary filling material]!" read the caption. On page 64, Larry was pictured talking on a pay phone—a standard sight in the hallways of the dental school— and the caption beneath the photo read, "Resorts buy, Exxon buy, Healthco buy, Codesco sell." Codesco was the firm that had supplied dental equipment to Penn, and it was going out of business. Healthco was the firm taking over the contract. Exxon was just considered a blue chip investment, and Resorts, the casino, was a nod to Larry's growing interest in Atlantic City. Originally the yearbook staff had written a caption with Larry selling off dental supply companies and buying drug companies. The editor, Christopher Furlan, thought that was a bit too blatant, so, for Larry's sake, he changed it.

Larry's summer was spent acting as foreman for all the projects under way at his home. Marcia was concerned about how this looked, but she didn't complain too much. Just as she had hoped other watershed events over the past seven years would force Larry to make the final break from dealing drugs, she hoped that starting a dental practice, coupled with his enthusiasm for projects around the house, would leave little time for it. There had been, in Marcia's eyes, real progress. After their wedding a year ago, Larry's involvement in the business had fallen off dramatically. He was still on the phone a few hours every night, but it had been a long time since she had to deal with any of the sleazy characters Larry called friends. Then, after Glen's bust, Larry had stepped even further back, handing over the whole operation to David. She knew Larry was still making money. He was still poring over his assets every night with the same eagerness, and there were still hours of talking on the telephone, but Marcia still hoped it was just a matter of time.

Away during the day, still working at the VA hospital, Marcia would come home in the evening and all of the dirty dishes from the night before, and from breakfast and Larry's lunch, would be piled

in the kitchen sink. The house would be a mess. Larry would want
to go out to dinner with friends, and all Marcia would want to do
was take a bath, eat dinner, and relax. Sometimes Larry would just
leave. He bought himself a big silver BMW 703, thirty grand, top of
the line, and sometimes he would have fun just speeding along Waterloo Road, testing himself and the car against its dips and swerves
and its sudden flat-out rural straightaways.

With his business dealings with Mark Stewart and the cocaine
business mostly out of his hands, there was little for Larry to do. He
made some preliminary inquiries into opening a dental practice on
the Main Line, but found that there were elaborate politics involved.
There were seventeen dentists in Devon and sixteen in Wayne. The
region was oversaturated. To buy in you had to be willing to go to
work for one of the established practices, where you worked under
the thumb of a longtime practitioner. Most newly graduated dentists
have no choice. They have debts to repay and a career to get started.
But Larry, who at this point was making more than a hundred thousand per month selling cocaine, was in a position to pick and choose,
and he chose not to go the usual route. In fact, the politics of getting
started scared him. Who needed it? Maybe he wouldn't even pursue
dentistry.

He had other things to keep him busy. Just before graduation,
Larry bought the First National Game Room, a video arcade in a
shopping center way out in Chester County, west of Philadelphia.
Drawn to an interest in video games by Kenny, Larry had grown
addicted to Donkey Kong in his senior year. He used to slip across
busy Spruce Street from the dental school to play games at University
Pinball. After many odd hours hanging around the arcade, Larry
realized that it was an excellent cash business, just the thing he could
use to help legitimize his illicit dollars.

After shopping around, Larry purchased the arcade in Eagleville
shortly before graduation for fifty thousand dollars. He spent a lot of
time over the next few months playing video games, attacking each
of the newest games and playing until he was sick of it. When his
own interest waned, the investment didn't look so keen. Kids in Eagleville didn't have that much money to drop into video games. The
half-life of video games dropped off precipitously after the success of
Pac-Man. Pac-Man had been profitable at arcades for three years.
Donkey Kong, its biggest successor, lasted only six months. The next
generation of games was only hot for about three months. And the
practical details of running a small business got to Larry. When the
man he hired to run the place had a day off, Larry would have to go
and mind the store himself. No longer excited by the games, he got
bored. On weekends, he and Marcia had to drive out to the place and

count tokens for hours. Larry tried to make improvements. Using an Apple computer he had repossessed from a customer who owed him money, Larry used a standard business program to make printouts showing the productivity of each machine, so he could maximize the return on floor space by moving out games as soon as their play time began to fall off. But despite all his efforts, the arcade never made more than $125 per day and stayed on a stubborn downhill trend. Video games were a fad, and he had gotten into it after the fad had crested. He finally sold the place for fifty thousand and counted himself wiser for the experience.

Toward the end of summer his pool was complete, the greenhouse was done, the basement renovations were finished, and Larry was at a loss. He had invested in three expensive condos in a Mays Landing development called the Sandpiper, so Larry spent a week going down to look at them and attending settlements. But then that was over. He was disgusted with the Arena, which was losing more and more money. Every day Dick Muldair would phone to relate new outrages about Mark's management of the place. The Barclay Building project was still tied up in bankruptcy court, and in the hands of lawyers. And the record business continued to lurch along on its own, costing more and more money.

So Larry decided that since he spent so many hours a day worrying about his money, he might as well play with it full-time. He thought the best way to do that was to go to work at the Philadelphia Stock Exchange. His old pot-dealing partners L.A. and Andy Mainardi had gone to work for the exchange and were doing quite well. Larry had plenty of money to work with. So, with his friends coaching him, Larry went to the Securities and Exchange Commission office in Washington and applied and qualified for the exchange in one day. He bought himself a seat for sixty thousand dollars.

L.A. tried to warn him. No one succeeded at the stock exchange without putting in years of apprenticeship. One went to work for someone who owned a seat and gradually got a feel for the place, for its internal politics as well as the tricks of smart investing. When you owned a seat, you had certain responsibilities that required you to trade relatively large amounts. Without experience, you could lose your shirt—if not your whole fortune.

But Larry was nothing if not confident. He obtained the necessary recommendations, put up the money, and plunged in headfirst. As a "market maker," Larry was obliged to make markets in five stocks that he was assigned. He worked hard for a few months, but most of the time he was bewildered. People around him were making and losing millions, and Larry usually wasn't quite sure what was going on. Some days he lost big and some days he won. Most days he lost.

He spent hours viewing videotaped lessons on investing, poring over dry newsletters, trying to absorb in weeks the savvy his friends had developed over years. After the newness of the work wore off, and the losses began to mount, Larry was bored. Every morning he would drive his BMW in, arriving just before ten o'clock wearing his conservative business suit. All around him men would sit reading the *Wall Street Journal*. Larry would don the green jacket that signified the stocks he was trading in. When things heated up, there was a lot of shouting and pushing and people were rude. He learned that when someone was friendly toward him, they were usually just trying to find out something, or mislead him, or take advantage of him in ways he couldn't always decipher. So the work boiled down to a great big dry numbers game. Larry could see that the only ones really making a lot of money were the inside traders.

One day, as he was looking over that morning's *Philadelphia Inquirer*, Larry saw an ad for a dental practice. A dentist in northeast Philadelphia was looking to sell his practice for $175,000. Larry took off his green jacket and drove out to see the man immediately.

The practice charmed Larry. It was in a small, one-story stucco house on the busy corner of Frankford Avenue and Ashburner Street, at the end of a residential block of row homes in solidly working-class northeast Philadelphia. Directly across from the front door was a gas station that had been converted into a small muffler repair shop, and beyond that a small shopping center. Across the street to the west was Pennypack Park, and behind a block of residential homes to the south was Holmesburg State Prison. The offices were well furnished and the dental equipment was modern. The place was wired with stereo speakers and multiple telephone lines and an intercom system. The dentist was opening a new practice southwest of Philadelphia, a step up, so it wasn't that he was fleeing a losing operation. He told Larry that he had grossed more than two hundred thousand in the last year.

"Obviously, you're not going to be able to open the door and walk in here and do that," he said, "but you will be able to make a go of it."

He said he was surprised to see Larry because, as it turned out, the ad in the *Inquirer* had misprinted the selling price. The practice was being sold for only $75,000, not $175,000. The dentist certainly hadn't expected to attract many buyers for the latter price.

Larry bought the practice two weeks later, handing the dentist two cashier's checks for the entire amount.

To manage his seat on the stock exchange, Larry hired the young son of another "market maker" to stand for him. That lasted only a month or two. Larry's stand-in managed to lose another $55,000. He came to Larry with a plan to salvage his investment at the exchange. The price of a seat had gone way up since Larry had purchased his two months before, and the kid had located a buyer willing to spend $125,000. Larry quickly sold, recovering much of what he had lost during his ill-fated venture into the world of high finance.

With the house remodeling completed, Larry threw himself into setting up his new dental practice. He knocked on the admiral's door to tell him the good news, and the two dentists chatted about new techniques and the economics of setting up a practice. Larry knew the practice was too big for one dentist, so he offered a one-third interest to Ken, who already had half interest in a practice in South Philly. Within weeks, they were drilling teeth. Larry hired a secretary and an assistant and brought his Apple computer into the office to organize scheduling and billing. Right away he spent thousands of dollars to upgrade the equipment in the two operatories, buying modern devices and materials that few beginning dentists could afford.

By fall of 1981, Larry could honestly say that he had never felt happier in his life. He was still earning roughly a hundred thousand a month from the cocaine business, and doing little more than chatting on the telephone for an hour every evening and meeting twice a month with David to go over the books. The transition had gone smoothly in the dental practice. Larry got along well with his patients and found the work more exciting than he had imagined it would be. Hardly a day went by without some emergency disrupting the schedule. Because he wasn't in it for the money, Larry brought a special enthusiasm to his dentistry. He did a lot of work for free, and frequently undercharged patients when he knew the bills would hurt. He worked three days a week, putting in long hours, and spent one day a week on the golf course with Ken. On his commute to and from the practice, Larry would cruise down the Schuylkill Expressway and out Roosevelt Boulevard with the sunroof of his BMW open and the radio playing loud and feel like the luckiest man alive. His long drives back and forth to the dental office were welcome periods of solitude, times when he could mentally step back and survey the world he had created for himself. He was twenty-six years old, and he already had his fortune and his profession—everything was in place.

Only one thing was missing, and even that was on its way. Marcia learned in late August that she was pregnant.

Larry was finally wising up in his dealings with Mark Stewart. Over the last eighteen months there had been a lot of talk about "negative lending," whereby an investor, by pumping still more money into a losing venture, manages to turn the project around. It had taken

Larry a while to learn, but the traditional expression for "negative lending" was "throwing good money after bad."

"I want you to close the Arena," Larry announced at a meeting in Mark's office with David and Ken, who had both invested enormous amounts in the place.

Of all Larry's projects with Mark Stewart, he knew that the Arena was the closest to Mark's heart. The flashy wheeler-dealer had dreams of owning a major sports franchise, of being a well-known boxing promoter like Bob Arum and Don King. But the Arena was a joke. The Philadelphia Kings might as well have been playing in a high school auditorium for the audiences they were getting. The Roller Derby and the evangelists and the trumped-up boxing matches were an embarrassment. No one had been able to fix the place's heating and air-conditioning problems, so even when they were able to attract a crowd to the place, usually for a closed circuit fight, the smokey hot air turned the inside unbearable. Larry had heard from Dick Muldair, who had quit the place claiming that Mark had ripped off $250,000 he had invested shortly before going to prison. Muldair had horror stories to tell about the way Stewart's employees were stealing him blind. Larry had been the one most skeptical of the project from the beginning. After eighteen straight months of losses, he had no trouble turning a deaf ear to Mark's carefully reasoned protests.

"We're not going to fund any more money for payroll, we aren't going to give any more money for anything, period, unless you close the Arena," he said. "I don't care what you say, we're not giving any more money. It's stupid; we're just losing money. We're never going to recoup it. Let's just take the loss and try to sell it."

"Just give me two more weeks," Mark pleaded.

"What do you mean, two weeks?" said Larry. "What are you going to be able to do in two more weeks? There's not going to be one more event that's going to change anything, let's just get it over with."

Mark fell silent. Larry, Ken, and David knew that it was a blow to his ego. Here he was with the three students whose money he was supposed to be managing, and now they were confronting him with the conspicuous failure of his pet project.

As they would later recall, Mark repeated, "Give me two more weeks," and then quietly added, "I'm going to burn it."

Larry remembers receiving a call from Mark the next day. He said he had found some guys to torch the place. He was going to give them five grand up front and another ten after the insurance settlement. He asked Larry if he had a key to the place.

"No, I don't," said Larry. "Why do you need a key?"

"I have to give these guys one. I'll get it from Slim."

On Saturday, October 3, Larry remembered taking a call from Mark on his portable phone, out by the pool. It was one of the last warm nights of the year.

"Listen to your radio tomorrow," Mark said.

"Why?"

"There's going to be something on there interesting."

Larry didn't immediately understand, and didn't bother to ask for an explanation. After the meeting the week before at Mark's office, Larry knew he had taken the first step toward dissolving their relationship. He wanted nothing more to do with the man. So he just said, "Okay," and ended the conversation.

Later, listening to the Phillies game, it occurred to him. The Arena! Mark really was planning to have the place torched!

David Ackerman also remembered a call from Mark that night.

"Watch the sky to the west tomorrow morning," Mark said. "Maybe you'll see smoke."

E I G H T

It'll Just Be a Tax Case

Mark's handiwork was on the front page of the *Inquirer* metro page Sunday morning:

King Arena Damaged By Blaze
Homes evacuated near W. Phila. site

It gave Larry the creeps. Mark had blown even this. According to the newspaper account, there had been two alarms. The fire had started at about one in the morning and had burned for an hour and a half. Part of the roof had caved in and most of the Forty-fifth Street side had been destroyed. The damage would have been worse, but before an alarm was even sounded for it, the fire was noticed by a city fire fighter on a truck speeding to another blaze. Good luck or bad, depending on your point of view.

A few days later, Mark assured Larry that despite the city fire department's alert and valiant effort, the building was a total loss for insurance purposes. The insurance payoff, $1.25 million, would enable Mark to more than pay off Larry's investment.

So Mark immediately asked to borrow some of the settlement money in advance. He had this other project working, see, and with just the right push . . .

On New Year's Eve, December 31, 1981, there was a long line of black, white, and silver limos in front of La Truffe, a trendy French restaurant on Front Street, the first street west of Penn's Landing, the renovated waterfront area on the city's oldest, easternmost edge. Suzanne thought it wasn't a good idea to flaunt their youthful affluence with such display, but David was in an especially good mood.

They were engaged. David had invited more than twenty family members and friends to an extravagant banquet. His father and step-mother were there, and friends from the record company and the cocaine business. David wore a well-trimmed sparse brown beard and moustache, and dressed in a neat tailor-made black tux. Suzanne wore a strapless gown of black silk with flouncy billows of fabric across the chest and down one side. Her straight brown hair was cut in a shag, with straight bangs down to her eyebrows. There were three tall candles in between the floral arrangements that were spaced down the long table. In front of each plate were four crystal goblets, because tonight David's friends were not just going to drink wine, they were going to sample a tableful of rare vintages, some of them more than thirty years old. La Truffe's chefs had prepared an eight-course meal, each course a special gourmet creation. David wanted it to be, simply, the finest meal his friends and family had ever eaten. It was certainly the most expensive. The wines alone cost nearly ten thousand dollars.

An unspoken part of the celebration that New Year's Eve involved Willie Harcourt, who sat at the opposite end of the long table from David. Of course, not all of those present knew that David's largess came from cocaine dealing (although it was common knowledge among the restaurant staff). In the weeks of planning for this event, David and Willie had discussed a transfer of power. David was to continue collecting 25 percent of the profits, and Willie was going to earn the other 25 percent by taking over David's job. In honor of the transition, David presented Willie with a rare five-thousand-dollar bottle of cognac.

Ever since the confrontation over the final eighteen-kilo shipment last June, Willie had worked hard to disguise his contempt for David. He was almost twice David's size, and had at times been sorely tempted just to flatten him. Willie was better liked than David by the other workers. So the big bartender's feelings colored the whole organization's attitude toward David. Behind his back, Ackerman was called "that Little Napoleon" and worse. David's growing arrogance had even begun to alienate customers. Larry had heard complaints from Paul Mikuta and Stu Thomas, who had threatened to stop doing business with David.

Just that day, Billy Motto had decided to take his business else-where. Willie had returned to Philadelphia with a special order of five kilos for Paul Mikuta and Billy. It had been a hassle to arrange it, especially over the holidays. David had been planning for the party and meeting with Willie to effect the transition, and had decided to defer further shipments and sales until after the first of the year. But Paul and Billy had insisted, so David had geared up the machine for one more run in 1981. When the shipment arrived, just that morning, David called both dealers to let them know. Paul came by first. He tested all five kilos and took the two he liked best. When Billy showed up and learned that Paul had gotten first pick, he was livid. His deal with Larry assured *him* of first pickings. It was clearly a time for tact, a quality that was no longer part of David's makeup. Instead of smoothing things over, offering to make things up to Billy, David lost his temper. Here he had done Billy a favor by making a special run, and instead of gratitude he got shit! The two dealers raged at each other, and Billy stormed off without the two keys. That night, at the engagement party, David gave Willie a gold ring with rows of diamonds set in it that Billy had given him as a gift earlier in the year.

"I don't want it," David said. "You deal with him now."

Willie secretly felt sorry for David. The once-promising dental student had gone through a personality change. David had been a charmer when Willie first met him. His intelligence was just one of his winning qualities. But in the last two years he had lost his charm. His intelligence, while still crisp, was used like a whip to scourge and prod the people who worked for him. The same young man who had swept Suzanne off her feet and into the business just twelve months ago was now a tyrannical boyfriend who flew into rages at the slightest provocation. David was constantly accusing Suzanne of sleeping with other men. He would refuse to let her leave the apartment, and refuse to allow her to let anyone else in. That summer, for instance, after an authorized day trip to the beach with her sister, Kim had asked to stop upstairs after the drive back from Atlantic City to use Suzanne's bathroom. She had never been in her sister's new apartment. Suzanne said no.

"What, are you crazy?" said Kim. "I have to pee, all right?"

But Suzanne didn't dare. She had promised David to let no one in, under any circumstances.

There was growing tension between Larry and David because of David's erratic behavior. David, who lived in fear of Larry's just taking the business out of his hands, began to suspect everyone around him of conspiring with Larry. His paranoia reached comic proportions. One evening he flew into a rage after Suzanne used the expression "Okeydoke." David had asked her to make him a sandwich.

"That's a Larry expression!" he shouted. "Nobody else says that anymore! What have you been talking to Larry about?"

Willie knew the change had been caused by the cocaine. He had watched it happen. David had started "basing" in late summer. After formally breaking up with Gina and before he and Suzanne began living together again, David briefly took up with a woman who was addicted to this technique. Basing involved first mixing cocaine with ether and distilled water to turn it into a solution, and then drying it under a heat lamp or blow-dryer to, in effect, wash out the hydro-chloride that makes cocaine soluble and capable of being absorbed through mucous membranes. The resulting dry paste is cocaine in its purest form, far more potent than the powder most users suck up their nose. When smoked, the paste is taken up through the lungs with greater efficiency than snorted cocaine is absorbed through nasal passages. Basing is a highly addictive form of cocaine abuse, and a dangerous technique—comedian Richard Pryor would set himself on fire doing it. Once he got started, David would lock himself in his apartment for days at a time, calling out for more cocaine when his supply diminished. There were days when David would call Willie and ask him to bring food and leave it in the hall outside his door. This period lasted for several months. When the woman left, David stopped basing. But the experience seemed to have left him with an insatiable lust for cocaine.

But little of that was in evidence on New Year's Eve, when toast after toast of vintage wine was hoisted to the honor of the host and his lovely fiancée. David presented Suzanne with an heirloom, a val-uable diamond engagement ring that had been his grandmother's.

The total bill for the evening was thirty-five grand. Willie threw in five grand towards the tip.

Willie was grateful for the meal that night, for the fine bottle of cognac and the opportunity to earn his own million, but mostly he was glad because at last he would be rid of David Ackerman.

At least, that was the plan.

But if the first two months of 1982 were any indication, David was incapable of backing off. He continued to badger Willie con-stantly. On the night before Kenny Weidler's wedding, David sat through the night snorting cocaine and going over fine points of book-keeping and packaging formulas with Willie. Every time Willie would make a motion to leave, David would insist that he stay. It got to be 3:00 a.m.

"You're supposed to be in Kenny's wedding tomorrow, David. Don't you think you ought to get some sleep?" Willie said. The wed-ding was in upstate New Jersey.

"Don't worry," said David. "I've got a couple of 'ludes. I'll be okay."

Willie left at 5:00 a.m. He slept for about an hour, dressed, and drove to the wedding, getting lost along the way. He arrived at the end of the ceremony. David wasn't there. It had been a very traditional wedding, with six ushers and six bridesmaids. David was to have been an usher. His absence was glaring. When he arrived late for the reception, David stayed out in the car until Willie came out to coax him in. Ken was furious with David, and his wife, Barbara, wouldn't even speak to him.

Despite the festive New Year's meal, David's relationship with Suzanne was actually on its way downhill by the time of their engagement party, and it continued to worsen over the next few months. After the engagement, his jealous suspicions became psychotic. If Suzanne stayed out too long shopping with her sister, he accused her of having met with another man. If he found two coffee cups in the apartment, he accused her of having another man over while he was gone. And yet, on a trip to Atlantic City, when David decided he wanted to sleep with Kim, Suzanne's sister, he talked Suzanne into sleeping with one of the drivers. Kim refused to sleep with David, but Suzanne and the driver hit it off so well that their relationship continued—fulfilling David's worst fear. Living together in an apartment on Conshohocken State Road now, high on a hill in northwest Philadelphia, David and Suzanne would fight and fight until he would tell her to leave. She would throw some things together and head for the door, and then David would angrily refuse to let her leave.

On one of these nights, in anger David phoned Kim and told her to come and get her sister out of his apartment.

It was after midnight, but Kim was there in fifteen minutes. When she got to the door, David answered and told her to go away.

"Suzanne's not leaving," he said.

But on this night, Suzanne had decided that she really was going to go. She pushed David out of the way and started down the hall toward the elevator with Kim. As they waited for the elevator, David came running down the hall, pleading with Suzanne to return.

"I'm not coming back," said Suzanne.

"Leave her alone," said Kim.

David got angry and started shouting threats.

"Go away, David," said Kim.

"I'm leaving," said Suzanne. "And I'm not coming back."

David made a move to grab Suzanne, and Kim, who was smaller than her sister, pushed David back. David then turned and pushed Kim, and Suzanne lunged at David to protect her sister. There was more pushing and kicking and screaming.

Then from out of a side door next to the elevator stepped a security guard.

"Would you please keep it down?" he said.

"All I want to do is leave," said Suzanne. "And he won't let me leave."

"Look, I don't want to get involved, but just please keep it down," said the guard. And he left.

No sooner had the guard left than the fighting resumed. When the elevator doors finally opened, David started pushing his way in with the sisters, so Suzanne pulled the diamond engagement ring off her finger and flung it past David down the hall. Instinctively, David turned and went after the ring, and the elevator doors closed.

After hiding out from David at one place or another for a few weeks, Suzanne ended up at Willie's. When David learned she was there, he accused Willie of sleeping with her, which was not true. Eventually, Suzanne met with David and they reconciled. She moved back into the apartment, and, within weeks, the fighting resumed.

As David worsened, his relationship with Larry grew more and more strained. It bugged David that Larry was collecting twice as much in profits as he. After Larry split the business with David and Ken, his daily involvement had virtually ceased. David was the one working all hours of the day and night, managing a multimillion-dollar illicit business while Larry was golfing once a week, setting up his dental practice as a hobby, fixing up his beautiful home in the suburbs, whizzing around backcountry roads in his luxurious foreign car, finding ways of converting his hot cash into permanent wealth. David was willing to accept the arrangement because it gave him an opportunity to do likewise. But once he had made his million, it was his turn to step back from the business and begin enjoying the fruits. Only he couldn't. David didn't trust Willie to manage everything smoothly—he had no David Ackerman to take over for him. And, to make matters worse, David was collecting only about 35 percent of net profits—splitting new customers with Larry fifty-fifty, sharing his and Ken's old customers with Ken, and taking only 25 percent from Larry's old friends, the business's biggest customers. David had expected Larry to make him an equal partner, so that they would equally bear the cost of giving Willie his percentage. But Larry wouldn't go along with that.

On March 14, Larry's twenty-seventh birthday, Larry was at his parents' apartment in Haverhill. Most of his family had gathered to celebrate with a cake and presents. By this time, both Larry's older brother Rusty and his sister Jill had gotten heavily involved in dealing Larry's cocaine in Massachusetts and New Hampshire. Rusty was driving big expensive cars and embarking on large-scale development projects. Jill had been handling quite a few customers herself until, in 1981, her own abuse of the drug drove her to a nervous breakdown. Massachusetts state troopers found her raving in her car by the side of the turnpike in the fall of 1981 and took her to a hospital. Larry's parents and oldest brother, Justin, the physician, were ignorant of the source of the younger half of the family's sudden affluence—and of Jill's breakdown. They accepted Larry's stories about the stock market and the record company at face value, and why not? Hadn't Larry owned a seat on the Philadelphia Stock Exchange? Didn't he have a gold record to show for his investment in WMOT-TEC Records? Larry's brother Justin, who was earning good money teaching and practicing medicine, had begun calling his younger brother for financial advice. Larry had gotten in the habit of presenting his parents with thousands of dollars in cash, and was making plans to buy them a condominium in West Palm Beach, Florida, right on the golf course—both Justin and Pauline loved golf. So it was an especially happy gathering of an especially prosperous family honoring the youngest son, for whom every family member had reason for admiration and gratitude.

The family was around the table when the phone rang. It was David Ackerman, calling for Larry. He took the phone in a back room of the apartment.

Larry was irritated to be bothered at his parents' house, in the middle of his party. He thought none of his other friends would have been this rude.

David was slurring his words and speaking rapidly, obviously under the influence of cocaine or Quaaludes or both. He started off in a friendly way, but soon came to the point. He had an ultimatum.

"Larry, you have to give up five percent. Willie needs more to keep him going. We've got to give him more."

"David, I can't believe you're calling me here at home. There's no way I'm going to do that."

"You have to give this up. You're not doing any of the work now."

Larry just hung up the phone. He was too angry to discuss it further. The way he saw things, he had staked about a million dollars of his money to get David started; David had thrown in maybe five thousand at the start. Larry had given this smartass New York Jewish kid a chance to make a million dollars, and this was all the gratitude he had?

He stewed over the phone call for the rest of the evening. He felt David had ruined his birthday party. He and Marcia had planned on staying up in Haverhill for a day or two, but instead they got a flight back to Philadelphia that night.

For Larry, the phone call was the last straw. Billy South Philly, Paul Mikuta, and Stu Thomas had all stopped doing business with David already. And Larry was tired of David's finicky way of doing things. He was tired of having everything handled by David's people—Willie, Suzanne, Christine, Gary, Danny, Roger, Mark Taplar. . . . If it was a power struggle David wanted, then it was time to get it over with.

Larry drove home and dropped off Marcia, who was seven months pregnant, and then sped back down the Schuylkill Expressway to David and Suzanne's apartment. He entered shouting. David, who had had time to cool off, tried to be conciliatory, but Larry's mind was made up.

"I can't believe you called me at my parents' house to pull this," he said. He pushed David against the apartment wall.

David argued that the present arrangement was unfair to him.

"No, David. Your best customers are still my people. Who are they going to listen to? If I tell them to stop doing business with you, they'll stop."

"Be reasonable," said David.

"It's all over," Larry said. "You're out. This is it."

David quickly tried to back down, offering Larry a more attractive arrangement than his ultimatum on the phone.

"No, David. You're out. That's just it. I'm going to find a way to buy you out. I want you to sit down and figure out what you're worth right now, and I'm going to find a way to buy you out."

Together that night, with Suzanne trying to sleep in the back room, Larry tallied up $850,000 that David still had tied up in the business. He was going to get David that money, and from then on Larry was going to be back in charge.

Over the next few weeks, Larry had second thoughts. Maybe he should just let David have the business and settle for a smaller percentage. Ever since his meeting with Mark Stewart before the Arena was burned, Larry had been branching out on his own with legitimate investments. He and David had begun investing heavily in silver. Larry held certificates worth more than two hundred thousand, and checked the fluctuating rare metal's prices daily, sometimes buying more, sometimes selling off small amounts. Through his insurance agent, Larry had met Joe Powell, a silver dealer who bought scrap circuitry, silverware, or anything else that contained the precious metal and then recovered the silver from it for resale. Larry soon was loaning the dealer huge sums of money at an incredible 30 percent annual interest rate. Through Powell, Larry met a group interested in starting up a gold-mining operation in Nevada. He put up almost two hundred thousand for them to purchase a unique strip-mining machine that used centrifugal force to separate gold from sand and dirt. And he had thrown in with his old dental school classmate/appliance dealer Jonathon Lax on projects to renovate homes in South Philly and a housing project in Cherry Hill, New Jersey.

Despite his track record of poor investments, Mark Stewart had taught Larry a lot. Larry could put together an impressive financial statement with the best of them, and he had learned that bank presidents, as a group, had fools in exactly the same proportion as the population at large. So Larry felt that he was at last ready to begin acting as his own Mark Stewart. Those projects, along with the ones he was still mired in with Mark and his dental practice with Ken, took nearly all of his time. Now he would have to start supervising the cocaine business again. Marcia, if she found out, would be all over him—especially with the baby due in just two months. And Larry would be up to his neck again in risk.

But his pride was at stake. He couldn't let David Ackerman push him around. Already three of his best friends had taken their business elsewhere. David was falling apart. Just a few weeks earlier Suzanne had telephoned in a panic after David took several Quaaludes and passed out. Suzanne said he had no pulse. Larry had gotten a friend to rush over just to make sure David was alive, and then to sit with Suzanne until David came out of it. It was dangerous leaving the business in the hands of someone so out of control.

Besides, down deep, Larry missed the dealing. He had always enjoyed being the man in charge.

So over the next few weeks he laundered a few checks through his various enterprises to pay off his partner. Ackerman retained some control over the business for the next few months, but by June he was strictly a silent partner. Larry called Billy and Paul and Stu to let them know that Larry was back. And he began meeting with Willie Harcourt regularly, reacquainting himself with what the hell was going on.

Christopher Lavin was born on May 6, 1982. It was a doubly special event, because Stu Thomas's wife, Joanne, had her baby on the same day. Marcia and Joanne shared a room in the hospital, and Larry and Stu visited together, draped in blue gowns, taking turns cradling the pink newborns and posing for happy family snapshots.

That night, Larry and Stu celebrated in what had become Larry's standard way. Larry Uhr, the man Mark Stewart had hired to manage the limousine service in Atlantic City, delivered a couple of expensive casino hookers out to Timber Lane. Larry invited over Ken Weidler and a few other friends, and the happy new fathers snorted cocaine, drank, dropped Quaaludes, splashed in the Jacuzzi, and fornicated happily through the night.

Marcia, of course, knew nothing about Larry's acquired taste in whores. Ever since his bachelor party in 1980, Larry had been throw-

ing these bacchanals for all of his friends before they got married—
and nearly all of them did marry from 1980 through 1983. The events
were so notorious that Suzanne Norimatsu, one of the few women in
their circle who knew all about these parties (and felt privileged to be
let in on the boys' lusty secrets), once accused one of the boys of
getting married just so there would be an excuse for another one of
Larry's famous parties.

After the bash at the airport Marriott, the one when the hooker
had fallen through the glass table and left bloodstains on the bathroom
and the floors and walls, Larry was an unwelcome guest at the
hotel—even though he happily paid for all the damages. When he
had gone back to reserve the same suite for another party, the manager
had refused.

"My rooms can't take the wear and tear," he said.

So Larry just got someone else to reserve the suites, and had his
friends let him in through a back door. A highlight of that party was
a food fight and a woman who shaved off her pubic hair in the bathtub
to titillate the boys with naked genitalia.

The Atlantic City hookers were a more expensive, more attractive
lot than the girls Larry had hired in Philadelphia. It got so that on
his frequent trips to the New Jersey resort, Larry would routinely
ask Larry Uhr to fix him up with one. After attending to business,
Larry the millionaire dentist would deposit a large sum of money in
the cage and spend the afternoon gambling, retire to a comped room
upstairs for a romp with a whore, and eat a nice dinner before going
home. It was a side of his life Marcia never saw and had no reason
to suspect.

Larry's Atlantic City bachelor parties outdid the earlier ones at
the Marriott. Some went on simultaneously in two casino hotels.
Because he usually put so much money in the cage downstairs, the
hotels comped all the rooms and the limos and the food, including
expensive candies, open bars, flowers . . . whatever his heart desired.
Larry's friends would fly in from New England and arrive in stretch
limos, sometimes with a hooker on board to entertain them on the
drive over from Philadelphia. Larry and Paul and Stu and Billy,
veterans of these affairs, used to delight in inviting younger men who
had never seen parties like these before, then urge them to put on
shows with the hookers for everyone else. Glen Fuller, who was out
on bail awaiting trial in New Jersey, always threw himself into these
events with special gusto, as did stockbrokers Andy Mainardi and
L.A. The women would do anything for money, so they were open
to a far broader range of sexual play than most of the boys' wives—
everything from striptease to elaborate oral sex to props and lesbianism
and other odd practices.

Atlantic City became Larry's hedonistic playland. Larry would arrive with Paul at the casino, they would check into a room, and Paul would be on the phone immediately ordering up "two blonds with big tits" the way another hotel guest might call room service for a martini. In time, Larry developed a special relationship with a hooker named Janice, whom he would ask for regularly and sometimes put in charge of arranging to supply hookers for the next bash. For big parties there were a dozen or more girls and twenty or more of Larry's friends. The girls would accompany the boys down to expensive dinners and on the gambling floor, and sometimes, if enough money was offered, would spend the night. Glen Fuller once paid a woman eight hundred dollars to sleep with him through the night. One party threatened to turn ugly when there weren't enough hookers to go around. Larry had to set up a schedule, placing time limits on his friends' sex play. He had to walk up and down the hall knocking on doors to enforce it, and would encounter all sorts of decadent scenes. One of his friends, pants down to his ankles displaying a pitiful half erection, pleaded with Larry on his knees for ten more minutes with a woman—the combination of drugs and alcohol intensified the urge but sometimes dimmed the performance.

Larry felt he was giving his friends experiences that they would never otherwise have, moments they would remember for the rest of their lives.

In the case of the hot-tub romp on the night after Christopher was born, it turned out to be an occasion all involved soon regretted. About two weeks after the party, one of the men present suspected he was seeing symptoms of venereal disease. That meant everyone involved had to take precautions.

Larry wrote himself a prescription for a powerful antibiotic which called for one large, painful injection to the buttock. In the upstairs bathroom, while Marcia fed the baby down the hall, Larry unpacked a syringe and uncapped the bottle. Unused to the procedure, he jammed the needle in wrong the first time, bending it. He contorted himself, rapping his fist on the sink quietly, and fought back the scream.

Then he unpacked a new syringe, and took aim again.

Willie Harcourt was rapidly discovering that the great financial structure he was buying into was built on sand. He had a 25 percent interest in a lucrative cocaine business, and more than $250,000 invested in a supposedly successful record company. To legitimize his earnings, he was being paid a $200 weekly paycheck from Celebrity Limousines. A month into this new arrangement, the checks began to bounce. When he inquired, Willie learned that Mark Stewart had been taking money out of the limo company, which was in fact profitable, and was using it to make ends meet at WMOT-TEC Records, which, despite its hit records and surface prosperity, was in fact losing money. Willie, who was closer to Dick than were Larry, Ken, or David, felt he had to alert the investors to this travesty. But he was finding it impossible to get the two dentists together to confront Mark. Larry didn't seem to care that much anymore. He had evidently already written off the record company. When Willie asked Larry about his $250,000 investment, Larry gave only a vague answer that Willie knew meant the money was gone. To Larry, a quarter million loss in his dealings with Mark Stewart was routine.

In May, when Willie was in Florida on a buying trip, David got a friend to open up Willie's apartment and safe and inspected the books. When Willie came home, David was waiting in his apartment to accuse him of mismanagement. Then David sifted through the sixteen kilos Willie had just driven north, picked out a bagful of rocks, and left.

Willie sat there that night, outraged. It was obvious that he was not going to be given the autonomy that David had enjoyed with Larry.

He decided to quit. This and other things, added to Willie's constant fear of getting caught and going to jail, had finally opened his eyes. Suddenly, all Willie wanted to do was get as far away from the cocaine business as possible. He saw David as a hopeless cokehead, and he believed that Larry and Ken and David had ripped him off for $250,000. At 3:00 a.m., Willie loaded up the kilos, the scales, the sifters and bowls and lamps and the safe and every other piece of cocaine paraphernalia in his apartment, drove it all over to one of the empty Chestnut Street "factory" apartments, and unloaded it there. He tried to sleep when he got back to his place, but couldn't. So he filled a bucket with soapy water and, working with mops and a sponge, systematically scrubbed the floors, walls, and ceilings of every room in his five-story house in Center City.

Billy Motto stopped by at 11:00 a.m. looking for his four kilos.

"I've quit," said Willie. "They're not here. Get ahold of David."

Willie called David's apartment and left his announcement on the answering machine.

Then he drove to the Bellevue Stratford hotel, checked into a room, and called Larry.

"I've had enough," he told Larry. "I'm out. David's gone too far."

"Just relax, Willie," said Larry. "Just take a couple of days off. Order some champagne. I'll pay for it. Just cool out, let me talk to David. If you want I'll get you more money from David's percentage."

"No, Larry. I quit. This is it."

Willie then called Paco and Pepe in Florida to tell them that he was out.

When that was done, he slept. Two days later Willie took a cab to the airport with a hundred thousand dollars in personal cash, downed two vodka and tonics at an airport bar, and then boarded a plane for California.

Larry didn't fight hard to keep Willie. On reflection, he considered it a good thing. He was disappointed with Willie's bookkeeping, and besides, Willie had been one of David's people. Larry was in a mood to purge David's influence from the business entirely. Willie's departure made that job simpler.

The person Larry had in mind to run things was Brian Riley.

Brian was a twenty-nine-year-old native of Plaistow, New Hampshire, the northern neighbor of Haverhill. He was a big, gruff chain-smoking high school graduate with pale green eyes and thinning reddish brown hair and a red beard. His nickname was Bear. Brian had a muscular torso and a broad neck. His ruddy complexion and bad teeth and thick New England accent, combined with his size and his uneducated manner, made Brian more of a colorful character than most of the collegiate, suburban types in Larry's circle. Larry liked him for that. Brian had been in the seafood business at home, and he looked, talked, and thought like a tough New England waterman. Brian had known Larry from a distance growing up in Plaistow. He mostly remembered him as the kid who got busted with Glen Fuller for stealing two Ski-Doos from area dealers.

Brian had gotten married just out of high school in 1972, and had two children before he and his wife divorced. He remained, for all his hardened exterior, a devoted father who insisted on keeping regular visits in New England with his children even when he was in the thick of Larry's business in Philadelphia and Florida. He had gotten his start dealing through Larry's sister in 1980, flying down to Philadelphia to deliver money in a shoe box and returning with cocaine stuffed down the back of his shirt. Brian had taken over the New England operation after Jill's breakdown, and had turned it over to his largest customer, Priscilla, when Larry asked him to move to Philadelphia to become more centrally involved, in January 1982.

Larry explained that David Ackerman was letting himself get eaten up by cocaine, and that he had surrounded himself with all of his own people. Larry wanted Brian to learn the ropes and also act as his representative to the other workers.

"I want somebody on my side working in there," Larry told him.

Eventually, once David was out, he wanted Brian to run the business for him.

It was, of course, an extremely lucrative opportunity, and Brian leapt at it. He admired Larry's spirit, his cheerful, daredevil criminality. Brian didn't have the kind of education to hit it rich in the world by any conventional means, but that didn't mean he wasn't as ambitious as the next guy. He believed that cocaine, unless abused, was essentially harmless, like alcohol. The fact that it was illegal was a hassle, but then, that was what made dealing cocaine so enormously profitable. He understood that Larry wanted him to take tremendous risks, but that there were also tremendous rewards. And, in truth, Brian enjoyed the excitement.

Right away there was plenty of that. On one of his first breaks, working with David at Brian's house on South Street at 2:00 a.m., they ran out of inositol. Both Brian and David looked as if they had been working in a bakery. Brian's black jeans were white. He felt numb, and was strung tight as piano wire.

These two ghostly figures emerged from the back door of the South Street townhouse and walked across the alley to David's car. Before they had even started the car, a police cruiser zoomed up from behind and drew alongside. They shone a flashlight in at David and Brian. David flashed Brian a look of shock and despair.

"You guys see anybody come running up this alley within the last five minutes?" the cop asked.

They were looking for a burglar. Brian and David chatted with the police for a few minutes and then the cruiser pulled away.

In the months leading up to his confrontation with Larry, David's cocaine addiction worsened. He took to locking himself in his apartment again, for days at a time, with his cocaine. Suzanne and Christine would go by and bang on the door and plead with him to open up, to come out, sometimes without success. After Willie left in May, David's condition was a serious problem until Brian learned the necessary procedures and formulas for the breaks himself. David would insist upon everyone accommodating his own strange hours and work habits. He would rouse everyone at 2:00 a.m. and keep them working on through until late morning. To Brian, David and Larry during this period were like two old ladies arguing about their money.

Finally, in early June, Larry met with Brian and told him that he had accumulated enough to buy David out. Henceforward, Brian would be managing partner, earning six hundred per week and an additional thousand for every day he spent on the road. Larry told Brian to pull together a lump sum of cash from various safes and deliver it to David at the apartment on Conshohocken State Road in northwest Philadelphia.

Brian met David in the parking lot out in front of the apartment house, outside TGI Friday's restaurant. He handed David a suitcase filled with cash. At that point David was reconciled, and somewhat relieved to be putting the cocaine business behind him.

"Congratulations," said David. "You've made it to the top."

Then they went golfing. Brian could only play for nine holes. He had to catch a plane to Florida.

Paco and Pepe were very concerned about their lucrative Philadelphia connection with the departure of Willie Harcourt and then David Ackerman. They had never even met Larry Lavin.

They had reason to be worried. Brian Riley, unfamiliar with Willie's beaten track to Paco's house in Miami, had done some scouting around when he was in Florida. He discovered that the price of fifty-six thousand per kilo that Larry had been paying since early 1980 was way over the market in Florida. Brian found kilos of equal quality were selling for less than thirty-five! Checking with an old Penn State connection of Larry's, he learned that Billy Honeywell, whom Larry had met dealing pot as an undergraduate, had become a full-scale smuggler, flying his own shipments from Colombia to Jamaica, where officials could be bribed to mark the packages as fruit, and then on into the U.S., landing at clandestine Florida airstrips in the middle of the night down grassy runways marked by flares. The same group had boats shuttling from Florida to Jamaica, and a seaplane that they landed on isolated lakes and then quickly off-loaded onto speedboats and took off in again. Honeywell's price was only twenty-five thousand, and the purity level was the same!

Larry felt comfortable dealing with Honeywell because they had mutual friends in central Pennsylvania—Honeywell was engaged to the sister of Dan Dill, Larry's brother in his fraternity, now a successful broker with Kidder Peabody (and a sizable cocaine dealer) in Pittsburgh. Larry had always been impressed by how straightforward and honest his State College connections had been.

So soon after Willie and David left the picture, Paco and Pepe's Philadelphia business dried up. Since Paco had been behind all of the dealers Larry had done business with, dating all the way back to Miguel, Larry's first cocaine supplier, Larry had been a steadily growing, reliable customer for four years. It was a remarkable track record in such a volatile industry.

Pepe contacted Willie in California and begged him to arrange a meeting with Larry.

They met in Atlantic City in June, at Resorts Casino Hotel. Larry drove down with David, Suzanne, Paul Mikuta, and Brian. On the way down he joked about having contracted gonorrhea from the party at his house after Christopher was born.

"That's why I don't go to those parties," said David. "I knew that was going to happen."

Larry laughed. He was in a particularly cheerful mood. As far as Larry was concerned, it was a good excuse to throw one of his bashes. He had already made up his mind about dealing with Paco and Pepe. It was crazy to continue paying fifty-six thousand for kilos that he could buy for less than half that price. But in deference to Willie and to the years of dealing with Paco and Pepe, he was willing to hear Pepe out. Willie had flown up the night before from Miami with Pepe. Larry had arranged for the Cuban to have ten grand in the cage for gambling.

Pepe arrived wearing a green leisure suit, with a lot of gold displayed under the wide, open collar. Larry thought he looked like a caricature of a Florida dealer. Pepe began by asking Larry why the business had fallen off.

"It's simple," Larry said. "We can buy things a lot cheaper from someone else. Either you lower your price to be competitive, or we take the business elsewhere."

Pepe argued that they had a totally reliable supply of cocaine, that they were known to be trustworthy and capable because they had been doing business together smoothly for so long. He emphasized that the cocaine business in Miami was dangerous. If Larry went shopping around, he might be asking for trouble, either from the law or from unreliable dealers.

Larry acknowledged that. He said he was grateful for the business; they had made a lot of money together.

"But what about the price?" he said.

Pepe said that they were not just selling Larry cocaine, they were selling their elaborate security measures: the block of homes owned by family members, the walkie-talkies, the armed guards and escorts, the lookout systems. . . .

"But you can't lower your price?" Larry asked.

Pepe said they could not. The price was set by Paco's brother. They were powerless to change it.

"Okay, then we're done," said Larry. "It was good doing business with you. Thanks a lot."

Pepe was upset. He continued arguing, even pleading. Willie felt sorry for him. He knew that Paco would hold Pepe responsible for the loss of this account. It was not Paco's largest, but it was the largest Pepe had brought him. Pepe stressed that if Larry went somewhere else with his business in Miami, there would be a war in Miami. Paco's people could not just let someone take their business away. Larry had no concern about the consequences in Miami. As for risk, Larry said that came with the territory.

"This is a business, Pepe," said Larry. "I don't understand why you can't just see it. We've got to stay competitive. If we're still selling things for seventy-six bucks a gram, we're going to be out of business in a month."

They shook hands, and their lucrative business relationship ended.

Behind steel-framed glasses Chuck Reed's face is the face of a certified public accountant, round and bearded and sensitive, but everything else about him is big. He has sloping shoulders and long arms with thick forearms and big, strong hands. His straight brown hair is long and he has a close-cropped brown beard that covers a receding chin and broadens the wide oval of his face. Reed is a serious man, quiet and intense. He reveals little about himself in conversation, preferring to ask questions and listen dispassionately, leaving someone who has just talked to him with the feeling that they have just been turned inside out and politely discarded. He is used to knowing more than he is at liberty to reveal, and seems not just comfortable, but happy with that role. One rarely ends an encounter with Chuck Reed without wondering about what lay just beneath the surface of an answer or a question or about what caused the trace of amusement or anger in his eyes at something that was said . . . or wasn't.

Chuck was thirty-two years old and had been an FBI agent for only three years in June of 1982 when he was assigned to begin investigating the curious doings of one Mark Stewart. From the surface details Chuck was given, Stewart looked like a one-man Flying Karamazov Brothers of finance. He owned more than thirty companies on paper, but all of them were headquartered in the same tall stone apartment building at 1228 Spruce Street, the Wellington. It looked like he was into real estate, tax shelters, a record company, the Martin Luther King, Jr., Arena (now an ashen ruin), a failing Continental League basketball team, a limousine service . . . other things. The sheer dizzying complexity of these dealings was enough to make the federal government curious, but two things in particular had piqued the FBI's curiosity. Among Stewart's other activities, he held the title of sports and special events consultant for the Playboy Hotel and Casino in Atlantic City. On December 19, 1981, at a light-heavyweight championship boxing match between Matthew Saad Muhammad and Dwight Braxton, four coveted ringside seats had cradled the back ends of Nicodemo "Little Nicky" Scarfo, the reputed boss of the Philadelphia–Atlantic City mob, Philip "Crazy Phil" Leonetti, Lawrence "Yogi" Merlino, and Scarfo's nephew. The seats, directly behind Howard Cosell, had been comped to the notorious mafiosi by Stewart. And early in 1982, a Philadelphia rap artist named Frankie Smith had reported that he was not getting royalties from his 1981 gold and platinum recording "Double Dutch Bus." He had recorded the single with WMOT-TEC Records, which, curiously, had recently filed for bankruptcy. Why was a tiny recording studio with a big hit record broke?

Chuck Reed had worked as a certified public accountant in Vermont before joining the FBI. Bored by his job with a small auditing firm, he was intrigued by the stories told him by a retired FBI agent he met in 1979. When Chuck learned that the bureau was accepting applications from accountants, he applied and was accepted. After his training, he did general criminal investigation in Albany for a year, and was then assigned to a special white-collar crime unit in Philadelphia in 1980. One of the best things about the job was that there were no bureaucratic limits placed on his investigations. So a case that started out as an audit might lead off anywhere, and he was encouraged to continue following it. And if ever there was a case that might lead off anywhere, it was Mark Stewart's. Here was a guy flirting with tax fraud, owner of an aged sports palace in West Philly that had been torched nine months ago, who gave away valuable ringside seats to notorious mobsters.

Stewart's profile was so odorous that more than one federal agency had come sniffing. Alcohol Tobacco and Firearms agents were looking into the King Arena arson, and the IRS was intrigued by WMOT-TEC Records. Reed's role would be to look for the root of these suspicious leads.

Somebody's money was behind all this.

It was a happy family spring and summer on Timber Lane. The house and yard wore a profusion of blossoms, azalea and dogwood, roses and tulips. In the air was the balmy odor of new-cut lawns. Larry would awaken early to let out Rusty, the copper-colored Lab that was now full grown, and then open the window of his study on the second floor and throw tennis balls out into the backyard for the dog to chase. On one morning in late May there was a wild duck swimming in the new pool. Larry ran for his camera.

Christopher was baptized on June 27, which called for a family gathering around the new pool in the backyard. Marcia's brother and his wife were godparents. In July, Larry's sister was married in an outdoor ceremony in New Hampshire, which occasioned another gathering of the Lavins and gave Larry a chance to show off his new son.

There were long afternoons around the pool, with the dog plunging tirelessly into the water in pursuit of tennis balls. After a round on the golf course, Ken and Larry would sip beer and eat hamburgers. At night, Larry liked to sit on the back porch or by the pool talking on his portable phone, reading his dental journals, or going over his financial records while listening to the Phillies game on the radio. Marcia always went to bed hours before Larry did. He still had his old dental school habit of staying up until well after midnight. Before going to bed, Larry liked to prop his feet up in the den and watch the *Tonight* show or an old movie and eat a standard postmidnight fourth meal of three or four hot dogs.

Yet, much as Larry enjoyed the idea of being a family man, he chafed at the new homebound existence the baby demanded. Marcia was as happy with her new baby as she had ever been in her life. For the first six months she refused to leave Christopher with a babysitter, which irritated Larry, who had grown used to frequent outings for dinners with the Mikutas, the Thomases, or the Weidlers. Larry fought constantly against Marcia's fierce domesticity, and always lost. He had wanted to hire a professional to come decorate and furnish the house, but Marcia was indignant—she would do it herself, right down to sewing curtains for the windows. Larry urged her to buy new clothes, offering to take her on a spree, but Marcia always refused.

She loathed Larry's new style. She blamed it on Mark Stewart's influence. "Just like Mark Stewart," she would say with scorn, at each new sign of ostentatiousness. In school, Larry had lived as simply as—in fact, even more simply than—Marcia. He had seemed oblivious to meals, to what he wore or what he drove. Now Larry's shirts all had to be handmade and professionally cleaned. He carried a roll of cash in his pocket—"like a cheap hood," thought Marcia. When the kid down the street got finished cutting the lawn, Larry would pull out his wad and peel off a twenty-dollar bill when she thought five would have been more appropriate. Whenever Larry bought anything, it was always the most expensive and flashy version, whether it was a TV set or a new briefcase or his brand-new car. When she complained that Larry never helped with household chores, right away Larry wanted to hire a maid. "I don't want a maid!" said Marcia. She saw it as another step in the wrong direction. She was determined she would not let money change her the way it had changed Larry. If there was one type of woman Marcia had always despised it was the kind that wore heavy makeup, expensive clothes and jewelry, who had her hair and nails professionally tended, left her children with babysitters, who hired decorators to furnish her home and left home-making to the maid. Yet she often feared that this was the kind of woman Larry secretly wanted her to be. It just wasn't going to happen. Marcia wore no makeup. She preferred an old loose dress or worn jeans and a sweater. At night she still sat up doing cross-stitch and needlepoint.

Marcia was so wrapped up in her new role as mother that she

did not even notice that Larry had gone back to directly supervising the cocaine business. She was past arguing with him about it, anyway. All the years she had struggled to pull Larry away from his dealing and his persistent circle of male friends had failed. She was beyond trying to force him to change. It was enough that she had purged those things from her own life. She felt she had managed to create a normal family out of sheer force of will. There were four thick photo albums lined up in the shelf in the den, each filled with hundreds of snapshots portraying the happy, typical life Marcia wanted. There were pictures of her with Larry from all of their vacations and Christmases, a full album of traditional wedding pictures, snapshots of Rusty as a puppy, of Christmas parties and family gatherings at graduations. Now there were dozens of new snapshots portraying little Christopher's growth from month to month, newborn shots in the hospital, Marcia with Chris in the Snugli, Larry feeding the baby a bottle, the baby on his grandmother's lap, in the bathtub, in his carseat. . . . Larry was finally working as a dentist with what seemed like dozens of legitimate business interests to occupy him. To Marcia, the bad years on Osage Avenue and at Willings Alley Mews were a distant memory in the summer of 1982. She had succeeded in removing it from her life entirely. She never connected drug earnings with the beautiful home with its greenhouse and solar panels and Jacuzzi, Larry's BMW and her Volvo. These were all trapping of the world she had wanted for her family all along and that, with Larry's busy new dental practice, she and Larry could have expected to own eventually, even without any of the dealing Larry had done as a student. Now that Marcia was no longer working as a physical therapist, her pretty house in the quiet suburbs, her baby, and her busy husband the dentist were real enough to absorb all of her time and interests. It was all sweet hard-won victory.

It was not long before Brian Riley's connections in Florida were also calling him Bear. Since Larry had strict rules about using telephones, Brian had a regular sequence of pay phones and times worked out with his people for getting in touch. On Tuesday, November 16, 1982, Riley walked through bitter cold down to the end of his block—Larry had recently moved him to an apartment on Pennsylvania Avenue in a trendy neighborhood northwest of Center City called Fairmount, near Philadelphia's famous art museum—stepped into a bar and restaurant called Tavern on Green, squeezed into the tiny foyer between the outer entrance and the inner doorway to the restaurant, and placed a scheduled phone call to Miami.

"This is Bear," he said to his contact. "I'm coming down tomorrow afternoon. I'll need twenty."

"It might not be a good idea," his contact answered, a voice with a thick Hispanic accent. "Your grandfather is in town."

"My grandfather? What the hell are you guys talking about?"

"It's just not a good idea."

"I don't care," said Brian. "I got to come down anyway."

"All right."

So the next day Brian flew into Miami. He had prearranged to have more than a half million dollars driven down by Stan Nelson, a short, stocky Florida lawyer whom he had recruited to do the driving. Brian was met at the airport by two of his contacts and driven through a hard rain to the Omni Hotel. As Brian got out of the car under the hotel eave and started toward the front entrance, four men in suits surrounded the car parked at the curb behind him. The driver had just gotten out and opened the trunk. Brian didn't stop. He just went straight through into the lobby, where Stan Nelson was waiting, pale and shaking. Stan looked like a middle-aged businessman on holiday, wearing a pair of gray pants that belonged with a suit and a pastel yellow polo shirt stretched taut over a broad belly. His hair was black flecked with gray and he wore glasses.

"The president is staying here!" said Stan.

"The who?" said Brian.

"The president. Ronald Reagan. There's Secret Service all over the place! They're checking *everybody* out."

"Where's the car?" Brian asked.

Stan gestured out the front entrance and pointed to a car parked across the street.

"I don't want to go near it," he said.

"Well, we got to do something," said Brian. "Fuck it. Let's go get in the car and drive over to this guy's place."

Outside, the two men who had brought Brian were still shaken from being searched and questioned by the Secret Service. They had missed signs saying the front driveway was temporarily off limits, and were preparing to pull out after satisfying the agents that it was just an accident.

"We're parked across the street," Brian said.

"Follow us," the driver said.

They drove for a quarter mile and then pulled into the parking lot of a high-rise apartment building. Planning to exchange money and cocaine in a few moments, they wound up the spiral ramp through the multilevel parking garage to the roof. As they got out of the car, Brian and Stan each took a heavy suitcase full of cash from the trunk. As they walked away from the car two security guards and two men in suits ran across the empty parking area to stop them.

"You can't park here," one of the men said. "We're holding this as a possible landing area for the president's helicopter."

"I'll just take the bags in and you move the cars back down there," Brian said to the other men, gesturing back down to the ground-level lot. The guard said that would be okay. Stan handed one of the men his car keys.

Brian and Stan then took the bags inside and rode up the elevator. Once inside, Brian just looked at Stan and said, "Jesus Christ! What fucking timing I've got."

Stan looked faint.

They were let into the apartment by a third man, who poured them a drink and explained that Reagan was in town to commend the members of a south Florida antidrug force that had seized a record amount of drugs, guns, and cash that year.

"More than three billion dollars since January," the man said. "I heard it on the TV. He's going to be down there tomorrow morning." He pointed to a 110-foot Coast Guard cutter in the bay below. "That's the *Dauntless*. It chases down pot smugglers."

"Marijuana?" said Brian.

The men chuckled.

In the back room, Brian was shown twenty kilos of cocaine. Stan left, and Brian spent a few hours testing the merchandise. Afraid to leave the apartment again with so much cocaine, he sat through the night by himself, watching TV. He learned that Reagan would board the *Dauntless* the next morning and give a speech.

Brian snorted cocaine through the night and dozed for a few hours on the couch. He could imagine what a headline he would make if someone caught him in the middle of Ronald Reagan's antidrug party.

"They'd hang me from the bow of the boat," Brian told his host.

That morning Brian and his supplier watched from the apartment window as the presidential ceremony took place. On the television, they heard the president commend the Coast Guard crew.

"Without your efforts, these drugs would have been on the marketplace providing profits for organized crime, fueling the drug culture that has done so much damage to so many lives in our society," Reagan said.

"Fuckin' marijuana," scoffed Brian.

Fall more than lived up to its name on Timber Lane, blanketing Larry and Marcia's front lawn with a thick layer of red and orange leaves. Larry stopped before going to work one morning to pose in the front yard with Chris and Rusty. Larry wore a short-sleeve white shirt with a red-and-blue striped tie under a button-down collar. Chris was five months old, dressed in red corduroy overalls. Larry propped the baby on the dog's back and Marcia snapped the picture. They had never lived in a place that transformed so dramatically and beautifully with each turn of the season.

It was on a morning just a few days later, one of Larry's days with no office hours, that Marcia left Chris with Larry while she went shopping at the nearby Acme. When she returned, Larry was in the kitchen with Ken Weidler. Chris was in a little windup swing by the kitchen table.

Larry turned to Marcia as she came in through the door from the garage, her arms full of bags, and said, "We've got trouble."

"What?" said Marcia.

"The FBI is investigating Mark Stewart."

Marcia dropped the bags on the kitchen table.

"That's just great," she said. She was angry, angry at Larry. Marcia had always believed that Larry was headed for big trouble, and that Mark Stewart was its most likely source. Even the drug dealing never worried Marcia as much as Larry's association with Stewart. The dealing was all among friends. How could the police ever crack that? But ever since that first day she saw Mark, as she left for work that morning on Osage Avenue, Marcia had believed the man was trouble personified, a chilling presence in her world. She had grown to despise him more and more through the years, to despise his influence on Larry. She had complained and complained to Larry about associating with him. So hearing those words was like sudden confirmation of her worst fears.

"That is just *great!*" she repeated, shouting now. "Just what we need. What happened?"

"Mark didn't pay Frankie Smith the royalties he was owed by the record company."

Marcia wheeled around and stormed back out to the car to get more of the grocery bags. Ken gave Larry an awkward look. Marcia's angry reaction had taken them both by surprise.

"Well, I guess you can't go golfing today," said Ken sheepishly. He walked out through the garage toward his car.

Back in the kitchen, Marcia wanted more information.

"What's going to happen?" she said. "They're going to find out about your drug dealing!"

"Oh, no, they'll never find out about that," said Larry. "Mark would never say anything."

"Larry, wake up. If they start investigating him, they're going to see where the money is coming from and then they're going to come and see what you've been doing. They're going to see your name. The district attorney already has your name as a drug suspect."

Larry listened quietly. He hadn't thought about the drug raid in 1980.

"They probably won't put that together," he said.

Marcia started throwing groceries into cabinets and drawers.

"If anything, it'll just be a tax case. I'll be able to beat it," said Larry, half talking to Marcia, half to himself. "I have the practice now." Larry saw his dental practice as a shield of legitimacy.

"What about those checks for the house?" asked Marcia. The house, the pool, the greenhouse, the Jacuzzi, the BMW . . . all of these things had been purchased with checks through Mark Stewart's finagling.

"Don't worry," said Larry. "Mark will back me up."

"When?" asked Marcia.

"What?"

"When is this all going to happen?"

"Not for a long time. If anything happens it won't affect us for about two years."

Marcia finished putting all the groceries away. Then she took Chris and put him in the stroller and wheeled him out through the garage and up the driveway to the street. She went for a long walk with the baby up Timber Lane. It was a breezy autumn day, the sun dappling green lawns through a shifting lattice of autumn leaves. Marcia felt panicked. Larry's words, even his assurances, brought back terrifying memories of the year on Osage Avenue, the robbery, the move to the house she hated in Center City, the police barging in through the door at night. She had escaped all of that before bringing this baby into the world. She had carved out here, on this quiet suburban lane, the life she wanted for herself, for Chris, and for Larry. And now the old anxiety had tracked them down.

They would lose the house. They would lose it all.

Larry's receptionist, Cookie Yokum, interrupted his work on a patient to tell him he had an important call. So he excused himself for a moment and, in his office in back, punched the flashing light on his desk phone.

"Larry?"

"Yeah. Mark?"

"Can you get to a pay phone and call me back right away?"

Pay phones were now a routine with Larry and his workers. It was a strict rule. No business over anything but pay phones. But it was unusual for Mark to insist on the precaution.

So Larry ran out the front door without even putting on a jacket. There was a line of pay phones at the shopping center across the street. He called the number Mark had given him. As Larry later remembered it, the call went as follows:

"Larry, I just saw Larry Uhr in your lawyer's office," said Mark. Larry Uhr managed the limo company in Atlantic City. Mark said that Uhr had been in tears. The FBI was after him, he had said, and he was sorry, but he had decided to give testimony against Mark.

"What are you talking about? Why would he be giving testimony against you?" asked Larry. As far as Larry knew, there was nothing to hide concerning the limo company.

"Larry is the person I hired," said Mark.

"Hired for what?"

"The arson."

"Oh, my gosh." Larry just about dropped the phone.

Now the trouble was worse, much worse. Uhr was the person who arranged for some of Larry's Atlantic City parties and liaisons with whores. They had snorted coke together, and Uhr knew all about Larry's cocaine dealing. Larry had actually cultivated Uhr's friendship, letting him into his confidence in an effort to get a better handle on what Mark was doing with the limo company.

"I can't believe you would do that to me, Mark," said Larry. "Why didn't you tell me he was the one? If I had known that I never would have even talked to the guy."

Any hope that the FBI probe would miss the cocaine connection vanished. If Uhr talked, a tax case would be the least of Larry's worries. What was he going to tell Marcia?

N I N E

We'll Be Back

FBI Special Agent Chuck Reed was startled by his first look at Larry Lavin. Reed opened the door to Larry's dental office and there was his man, smiling warmly at him from behind the reception counter, saying hello . . . a lanky fellow who looked no older than a college kid.

Reed had known Larry was only twenty-seven, but confronting him now in his white dental smock—so boyish, so pleasant, so outwardly wholesome—gave the agent enough pause that he said nothing as Larry turned and walked back to his operatory, leaving Reed and IRS Agent Steve Gallon with a receptionist in the waiting room.

For nearly four months Reed had imagined this meeting. Ever since he had seized Mark Stewart's books at the Wellington in October, Reed had known that behind many of Stewart's fiscal acrobatics was a young dentist whom no one seemed to know anything about. And even though the case was progressing nicely against Mark Stewart, the FBI agent had found himself even more interested in the young, mysterious Lawrence W. Lavin, D.M.D.

It was Larry who had underwritten many of Stewart's multimillion-dollar investments. The young dentist obviously had a huge hidden income. He knew that Larry had gone to prep school and the University of Pennsylvania, that he lived with his wife and small son in a big house on the Main Line, and that he sped back and forth to this dental office in northeastern Philly three times a week in a sleek silver BMW 733. Reed had a hunch that there was only one likely way for a preppie dentist less than two years out of school to secretly make millions, and that was cocaine.

Reed knew Larry had been a hidden owner of the Martin Luther King, Jr., Arena with Stewart through an entity named Larmark, Inc. (Larry-Mark). Larry was not a suspect in the arson—Reed doubted he knew much about it—and the agent knew he couldn't prove his drug suspicions, but in his experience people were usually rattled when confronted face-to-face by the FBI. You never knew how they would react. Some people would just panic and talk.

So when an opportunity came to serve some of the tax case papers on Larry, Reed decided to accompany Gallon on the long drive out. It was a cold evening, February 19, 1983. It had snowed the day before, not hard enough to have closed things down, but the first significant snowfall of the year. The day had been sunny. Philadelphia in winter is a study in browns and grays. As darkness came and the slush under wheels turned icy, lights from street lamps and cars and traffic signals became a dazzling, dizzying confusion of reflections. It was a slow drive through rush hour traffic and it would be late before they got back, but Reed didn't mind. He wanted to personally enlighten Larry Lavin that the FBI had entered his life.

Cookie Yokum, the receptionist, didn't seem surprised when Reed and Gallon introduced themselves as federal agents. She told the men that Dr. Lavin was busy with a patient, that they needed to make an appointment.

"You tell Dr. Lavin that we want to see him *right now*," said Reed.

When Larry walked into his private office, Reed did not so much smile as grin. He and Gallon introduced themselves, and they all shook hands. Reed had positioned himself against the side of Larry's desk. Larry thought he could detect a trace of amusement on the FBI agent's face.

"Would you mind answering a few questions?" asked Gallon.

"Go ahead," Larry answered.

Leaning on his *Bah*ston vowels, Larry answered a question about himself by telling them he was from Haverhill, Massachusetts, and proudly running through his impressive credentials: Phillips Exeter Academy, University of Pennsylvania for B.S. and D.M.D.—the diplomas were in frames on his office wall. He said he knew nothing about the arson. He readily admitted his business tie to Mark Stewart, which surprised the agents. They had expected him to be more evasive. Larry forthrightly explained that he had met Stewart in 1980, and that he had gotten involved with him trying to promote boxing matches at the King Arena—although he mentioned nothing about being a part owner.

"Did you know that Mark Stewart was involved with the fire?" Reed asked.

"No."

"We know you're a key executive in a lot of his companies," said Reed. "We know you could furnish us with a lot of information."

"I knew Mark was having trouble with the IRS," Larry offered.

"In my eyes what Mark may have done wrong is transfer monies from one company to another, so funds were being spent in one place that were being generated from another. Whether that's illegal or not, I don't know. Also some of his depreciation techniques might be questionable, but I gotta tell you, I consider Mark a friend and I don't plan on testifying against him or hurting him in any way."

Larry hesitated, then added, "I think I better speak to a lawyer."

"Why don't we just go along for now," suggested Reed, "and any questions you don't want to answer, we'll just skip over."

Larry said that would be okay.

Both Reed and Gallon were taking notes on yellow legal pads. Reed was intrigued. Far from seeming rattled, Lavin seemed to be enjoying himself. He had the feeling that the conversation was like a chess game. To Reed, Larry seemed very confident of himself, very smart. He could see right away that he wasn't dealing with the kind of guy who was going to panic.

Reed asked Larry if he was financially involved in any corporations with Stewart.

"No," Larry said.

So the FBI agent started baiting. He asked Larry about Larmark.

The dentist hardly blinked.

"Oh yeah, that was when I was in school. I was thinking about leaving school to help run the Arena."

Reed asked him if he was aware of any connection between Stewart and cocaine dealing.

Larry said no.

"Are you a cocaine dealer?"

Again, Larry answered firmly, "No. Listen, I don't know whether I can help you or not. I think I have to get myself a lawyer and then get back to you."

Larry was a skillful liar. There are veteran agents who claim to be able to tell if someone is lying, but Reed thought to himself as he listened to the young dentist that if he hadn't known Larry was lying, he would have been completely taken in. It was a very convincing performance. To Reed, Larry's manner suggested that he felt he was smarter than the agents, that they would never get him. He was arrogant. That got under the agent's skin. All of which made Reed's next move especially satisfying.

He opened his briefcase, withdrew two thick documents, federal grand jury subpoenas that named Lavin Options, Inc., and L's, Inc., two other corporations in which the young dentist was involved with Stewart, and dropped them loudly on Larry's desk. Larry turned the papers silently. He seemed stunned. If they were aware of these corporations, then they knew he was making a lot more money than he was reporting for tax purposes. At the very least, Larry knew he was in tax trouble. He showed no alarm or surprise. He offered no explanations. But his smile was gone. He grew abrupt.

"Like I told you, I'm going to have to get a lawyer," Larry said, standing and gesturing for the agents to leave. Reed smiled. He and Gallon packed up their legal pads and pencils and walked toward the front door. As he reached the door, Reed turned.

He asked, "Where'd you get the money for the BMW parked out front, Larry?"

Larry stumbled. He began one explanation: The car was provided by Larmark, Inc.; but then he switched to another: He had mortgaged his house to buy it. Then he bailed out, defining exactly what his relationship with law enforcement agencies would be from then on.

"I'm not going to answer any more questions without my attorney," he said.

"Okay," said Reed. "We'll be back."

Before the agents left that night, Reed stopped to shine a flashlight in through the windshield of the BMW. Larry watched from behind the blinds of his office as the agent took out a notepad and wrote down the car's serial number.

Larry was in shock. He had anticipated this visit. A number of his friends had already been seen by federal investigators working on the Stewart case, and word had gotten back that they were asking questions about him. Fortunately, Larry Uhr had backed off his initial decision to testify against Mark, so Larry had less to fear. He had consulted with Donald Goldberg, a tall, dapper gray-haired lawyer considered one of the finest defense attorneys in Philadelphia. Larry had told Goldberg of his business relationship with Mark Stewart and turned over the original documents he had signed when he and Mark incorporated. He also told the lawyer that his resources came from cocaine dealing, but that he had stopped. Now he was trying to avoid getting dragged down by his partner. Goldberg, whose mellifluous voice and calm manner were as reassuring as his reputation, saw before him a decent, candid, likable young man who had made mistakes but was trying to put them behind him. He had advised Larry not to let on to the agents that he already had consulted with a lawyer—it would just further excite their suspicions about what he was hiding. Instead, the lawyer said, talk to them awhile. Answer their questions as far as possible without incriminating yourself. When the terrain gets dangerous, bail out, tell them you would like to consult with a lawyer before answering any further questions. Be polite.

Larry had done those things, but the session had been deeply disturbing. The subpoenas indicated that there would definitely be a tax case against him, which meant the possibility of going to jail. That was frightening enough. But, beyond that, there was the attitude of that bearded agent Reed. Larry felt as if Reed were sizing him up for the kill.

It all seemed so unfair. What had he done that was so bad? Had he killed someone? Had he stolen from someone? All he did was buy and sell harmless recreational drugs. How could they hold it against him for not reporting his income? It was illegal, for Chrissakes! If he reported it, he might as well just be turning himself in! Larry saw himself as a hardworking businessman. Down deep he believed his drug fortune had been earned through industry and intelligence. He had worked long and hard to make his money. The fact that his merchandise was outlawed seemed more like a legal technicality than a felony. Everyone knew that drug laws were a joke, that they were ignored by vast segments of society. What better proof of that than Larry's own success?

If trouble came, Larry always figured it would be from local police grabbing someone for possession or transportation. Those were the only kinds of busts he had ever dealt with. The punishment was usually probation or something insignificant.

Something in Reed's manner suggested this case was different. It was like something personal between them. Reed was going to try to nail him to the wall.

Larry couldn't understand.

"Why does the guy hate me?" he asked Marcia that night. "I can understand him doing his job, but why does he hate me?"

When Chuck Reed told Larry he would be back, he wasn't at all sure of it. He was fascinated by this young criminal's attitude. It was unlike any he had encountered before. Reed had confronted plenty of lawbreakers in his four years with the FBI, but he had never before felt *after* one in the way he felt he was after Larry Lavin.

It was like personal combat. Reed was used to his suspects' giving some small recognition that they were doing something wrong. Not Lavin. If he showed anything it was pique, as if to say, "By what right do you make trouble for me?"

Reed was enthused. This investigation was the richest, most challenging case he had been assigned. As the work progressed and the plot thickened, Reed and his newly assigned partner, Sid Perry, shared a mounting sense of eagerness. They saw Larry Lavin as an insufferably cocky criminal, someone who had grown rich thumbing his nose at the law, who felt he was smart enough to get away with it even after he knew they were on to him. This multimillionaire drug-dealing young dentist was like a walking insult to law-abiding society. Every day he was free gnawed at them. Reed and Perry knew the

FBI wasn't going to lose interest in the case, and they were confident that their patient efforts would eventually prevail, so in the most serious sense of the word, their work was fun. In Larry Lavin they had hooked a big fish. They were prepared to savor the long struggle of bringing him in.

Suzanne Norimatsu had moved back into her parents' house in Plymouth Meeting, an affluent suburb northwest of the city, after breaking up with David Ackerman in late 1982. She was reading a Stephen King novel in her bedroom when the doorbell rang downstairs.

Her father, Richard, a tall engineering company executive, called, "Suzie, there are some people here to see you." He did not sound pleased.

Suzanne knew immediately who it was. Her friends had been paid visits recently by Chuck Reed, and they said she was one of the people he had been asking about. She had met Chuck before, twice. She had been living with David back in December when the agent had stopped by the apartment to question him about the arson. A few days after that, Reed had stopped by the restaurant where Suzanne now worked. He had been kindly.

"You seem like such a nice girl," the agent had said. "Why are you hanging out with these gangsters?" Reed had asked her to just think about what he had to say. He would tell no one they had met, and she should tell no one. If she decided to help them build a case against Mark Stewart, David Ackerman, and Larry Lavin, it would just be between them. Suzanne had said no. She went home that night and told David what happened. She had not seen Chuck since.

But there he was, waiting in the living room with his badge out, standing beside Treasury Agent Tom Neff. Both men introduced themselves formally, showing their badges. Suzanne's father sat next to her on the couch across from the agents, who withdrew folders from their briefcases and opened them on their laps. They sat with pencils poised over yellow legal pads.

Suzanne had been coached for this moment by David Ackerman. He had told her to politely refuse to answer questions, and to ask the agents to phone her lawyer, who would arrange a meeting.

"We're investigating an arson of the King Arena," said Chuck. "What do you know about it?"

"I'm sorry. I can't talk to you. You'll have to talk to my lawyer," said Suzanne.

Chuck slapped shut the folder on his lap.

"You have a lawyer!" he said.

"Yes, I have a lawyer."

"Why do you need a lawyer?"

"Well, I just do," said Suzanne. "His name is Emmett Fitzpatrick."

"What's his number?"

"I don't know, but it's in the phone book."

"Don't be such a stupid girl," said Chuck. "Are you going to let these guys put words in your mouth?"

Then her father interceded.

He said, "You don't have to talk to her like that."

Several weeks later, when the weather was warm enough for Suzanne to be out in the driveway washing her car, Chuck Reed pulled up in front of the house again. The bearded agent strode purposefully across the front lawn. With him again was Agent Neff. Suzanne's heart leapt. She thought he might be coming to arrest her.

"Oh, no," she said, taking two steps back from the agent. "I can't talk to you. You have to talk to Emmett."

"He won't let us talk to you," said Chuck. "We're going to get that car you just washed. We know it was bought with cocaine money."

Suzanne just frowned at him.

"Just listen to us, Suzanne. You don't have to answer any questions. But I'll tell you right now, you better take that black hat off and put on a white hat. Mark Stewart, Larry Lavin, and David Ackerman are wearing the black hats, and you know it. If you think you're going to be loyal to them, and protect them, then you're going to go right down the drain with them. So you better wise up now."

Suzanne again said no, and the agents left.

But what Chuck had said stayed with her. Now that she was no longer living with David, and no longer involved with the cocaine business, she had mixed feelings about what was happening. Stepping back from the scene for a few months had given her a different perspective. She was no longer as certain as David and Larry that these earnest government men were doomed to fail. That business about "going down the drain" haunted her.

Later she wished she had asked, "Would it be all right if I just wear a gray hat?"

Brian Riley believed he had a sixth sense for trouble. When he got an uneasy feeling about what he was doing, and didn't stop, he invariably got hit over the head. But if he heeded this sixth sense and stopped in time, the hammer would fall in front of him or behind, but he would have just enough time to escape.

In March of 1983, Brian's sixth sense was ringing in his ears. Four months earlier, carrying two shopping bags full of money wrapped as Christmas presents, he had been stopped and searched by guards at Boston's Logan Airport. Almost a hundred thousand dollars was discovered in the packages. It was not against the law to carry that much money around, but it sure raised suspicions. Brian had to hire a lawyer and sign for the cash to get it back. After that he could feel the eyes of law enforcement on the small of his neck.

Then, for a few weeks, he had felt especially lucky. When his Datsun got stuck in the snow in southern Maryland on a drive back from Florida with more than fifteen kilos in the trunk, two state troopers had kindly stopped to help pull him out of the bank and send him on his way. When he and Paul Mikuta, on a different trip, got stuck in line at the Miami airport with several kilos hidden in their bags just as the X-ray machine broke down, there was nothing for it but to stand there whistling while the guards hand-searched everyone's luggage. Both Paul's bag and his own escaped with just an ineffectual, cursory grope.

But Brian could feel his luck running out. His anxiety was partly eased in late 1982 when Stan Nelson took over most of the running. By early 1983, the portly Florida lawyer was spending most of his waking hours in a car, either driving money down to Florida or bringing coke back to Philadelphia. Larry had met Nelson shopping for New Jersey real estate in 1981 and had loaned him sixty-three thousand to start a fruit-beverage distribution company in Florida. When the beverage company failed to generate sufficient profits to repay the loan, Larry suggested that Nelson earn the money to repay him by driving cocaine north. Stan started in the summer of 1982, and six months later he was handling most of the transportation for Larry's business. Larry liked turning over transportation to Stan because he was reliable, and because he did not fit the profile law enforcement agencies sought in airports and on highways—well-dressed young men with big suitcases or big cars. And Nelson was clever. He used the canning machine from the beverage company to seal kilos in odorless cans, and mixed the cocaine-bearing ones in with his regular truckloads of fruit-juice powder. It was the safest, most ingenious method Larry had seen.

So by January of 1983, Brian's responsibilities were reduced to keeping the books and breaking, cutting, packaging, and distributing the cocaine.

When the FBI and IRS stopped out to see Larry at the dental office, it further upset Brian. He told Larry right then that he should take his money and run, sell out to someone else and stay as far away from drug dealing as he could for the rest of his natural life. Larry just laughed.

"They can't prove anything connecting me with drugs," he said.

To help keep things that way, Larry drove up to New York City with Brian and went on a shopping spree at electronics stores, buying himself thirty-five thousand dollars' worth of equipment, including six scrambler phones in briefcases that would enable him to talk on the phone without fear of a wiretap and devices that could detect the presence of a bug. Larry had a ball talking shop with the store owners.

On the drive home, Brian said, "You really think you can fool the FBI?"

Larry said they would probably get him on tax charges because of his connection with Mark Stewart, but that he didn't think they knew the first thing about his drug dealing.

"I only sell to my friends, who won't help them," Larry said. "I never handle anything anymore, so they're not going to observe me dealing anything. That leaves the telephone."

Brian tried to explain that he sometimes got a feeling about these things, and the feeling was bad.

"Larry, things are too fucking hot. You're crazy. If it was the Philadelphia police or even the state police, maybe you would have a chance. But the FBI? Man, they go to college to learn how to bust people like you."

Still, Brian could understand how hard it was for Larry to stop. Brian himself found it hard to stop. He was making almost a thousand dollars a day, and had bought himself a condo in Florida and a boat and a house in New Hampshire up near where his kids lived with their mother. Larry, eager to avoid *any* suspicious activities himself, gave him almost complete autonomy. Brian liked the people he was working with. He played outfield for Billy Motto's softball team. At home or on the road he lived a partying life, with a big-breasted teenage girlfriend named Nancy at home and a loose and exciting social circle that included Kim and Suzanne Norimatsu. On the road he had money for expensive hookers, fine meals, and luxury restaurants. His work for Larry had accustomed him to a style he was reluctant to abandon.

But when Brian woke up one afternoon in his house on Pennsylvania Avenue and saw a SWAT team with rifles running across the front yards and police cars and vans up and down the block, he figured, "This is it." He pulled on his pants and waited for the door to crash in. He had too many kilos of cocaine in the closet to even think about flushing it down the toilet or hiding it.

But nothing happened.

Finally, Brian opened his front door and wandered out to see what was going on. He half expected to be grabbed and thrown to the ground. Instead, one of the cops explained that they had busted a cocaine dealer two houses down from Brian's.

That did it.

Brian's last ounce of luck was gone. He telephoned Larry and told him that he was clearing out.

"You're too hot," Brian said. "I got a bad feeling about it, Larry."

Larry didn't argue. Brian owed him fifty thousand dollars, but Larry agreed to settle for twenty-five. They met in the parking lot behind a restaurant near Larry's house in Devon. Brian handed over the money owed, and took off that night for New Hampshire.

In the months that Brian had been running the business for Larry, he brought down from Exeter, New Hampshire, a strange, rough-hewn motorcyclist with long brown hair and thick moustache named Bruce Taylor. Bruce had a coiled snake tattooed to his left forearm and rode a Harley-Davidson. Brian, who had known Bruce from high school days, asked him to come to Philadelphia with him in October of 1982 to act as his bodyguard. Bruce was reputed to be a martial arts expert and had a reputation in the small towns of northern Massachusetts and southern New Hampshire as a roughneck. He had been one of Brian's cocaine customers. So when Brian suggested bringing him down to Philadelphia, Larry went for it.

"He's a bikey type, but he'll do anything for us," Brian said.

For six months, Bruce was Brian Riley's shadow. At the first meeting where money and cocaine were exchanged and Bruce was left alone momentarily with $350,000 in a briefcase, he considered picking it up and running. But staying had its own advantages. By January of 1983, Bruce was injecting cocaine, two grams at a shot, three or four times a day. To explain the hypodermic needles and syringes in his apartment, he told Brian and Larry and others that he was a diabetic. He was making five hundred dollars a week and falling into debt, but there was no shortage of white powder.

Brian and Larry had taught Bruce the techniques of breaking down kilos, cutting them, making rocks, and packaging. He lived with Brian for his first months in Philly and moved to his own house around the corner on Twenty-ninth and Poplar in early 1983. But Brian quickly came to regret urging Bruce on Larry. His would-be bodyguard and assistant was clearly in over his head with cocaine. Bruce would fail to show up for meetings or deliveries, and Brian would have to bang on his door for up to a half hour to wake him up in the middle of the afternoon. Bruce was hopelessly inept at keeping the books. Larry would check weekly, and discover that deals that should have shown a tidy profit had somehow come out to be losses of fifty grand or more.

When Brian suddenly quit and left town, Larry had little choice but to hire Bruce to manage the business for him. Dropping the business altogether was something Larry never even considered, even with the FBI and IRS probes. Ever since he was a sophomore in college, now nine years ago, Larry had been tallying his net worth, recording its ups and downs in neat little columns of numbers. By the spring of 1983, Larry was worth nearly five million, but easily a third of that was tied up in the business, in debts, in product, or in cash being assembled for the next deal. Another third or more represented holdings of stocks, real estate, condos, silver certificates, and loans. By now this complex financial machinery had acquired a momentum of its own. Larry needed the cocaine business funds to keep the legitimate projects going—not one had proved significantly profitable. Only the limo company had promise, and Mark was raiding its budget to feed his many unhealthy projects.

Larry had what he considered three strong reasons not to just stop dealing. The first was greed. Owing to what Larry considered mismanagement during the year since he canned David Ackerman, he had sustained a lengthening series of losses. These were not actual losses, but the difference between what Larry felt he should have made on a given deal and what he actually made. Abandoning the business meant just accepting an amount considerably lower than the "Total" of his net-profits column, a setback of nearly a year. The second reason also had to do with greed. Larry had a total of $1.5 million tied up in the business, mostly in product and bad debts. He had been able to tolerate deadbeats in his business for so many years because the profits had continually grown so fast that each new deal more than recovered what was lost on the last one. To pull out suddenly was to lose the $1.5 million that Larry felt he had already earned. The third reason had to do with risk. Larry knew that all the people working for him and buying from him were not just going to stop buying and selling and using cocaine if he left the business. Larry believed that law enforcement had been kept at bay for nine years only because of his management ability. Larry trusted his business sense and his feel for the risks involved. If he let go of the controls, the machine was certain to break down, and the conspiracy would rapidly unravel. So when someone like Brian Riley or Ken Weidler cautioned him that he was "nuts" to keep on managing the business after he knew he was under investigation, Larry felt like screaming. Didn't they see? Now would be the worst time to walk away! It was a matter of self-preservation.

So it pained Larry to have to rely on someone like Bruce Taylor. He was a prime example of how bad things could get. When Bruce was high, which was most of the time, he was as reckless as Glen Fuller. When he came down, Bruce would just vanish for days at a time. Nearly every week Larry's phone would start ringing and his friends would complain that Bruce was supposed to do this or that and hadn't shown up. Larry would call Bruce's house and there would be no answer. Then he would go down and bang on the door for a half hour or more, just as Brian Riley had, until Bruce, looking wan and disheveled, would stagger out. Bruce had begun telling people he had leukemia, which was not true, but it helped explain his erratic behavior and frequent lapses. His plan was to someday just disappear with a lot of money and cocaine. If people believed he was suffering a fatal illness, he reasoned, they would be less likely to spend a long time looking for him.

Truth was, the way Bruce was living, a fatal illness was a fair approximation of his future prospects. One night, when he was briefly back in Philadelphia after leaving Larry's employ, Brian Riley was called by Kim Norimatsu, who was then living with Bruce (they had gotten engaged in April). Kim was distraught. Bruce was on the floor in the kitchen, flipping out. It was Bruce's birthday, and the accumulated doses of cocaine, alcohol, marijuana, Quaaludes, and whatever else he had taken had overwhelmed him. Brian rushed over to the house and sat through the night on the kitchen floor with Bruce, who was convinced that someone was trying to break into the place and get him. Bruce was earning a thousand dollars per week by late spring, but his cocaine use was so heavy he was actually accumulating a debt to Larry.

In an effort to keep a handle on things, Larry laid down strict rules for Bruce to follow. Breaks were to be done at constantly varying locations. Money, books, and product were to be kept separate. For communication (the expensive scrambler phones never worked right), Larry instituted the beeper system and laid down the pay phone law. No business was to be conducted on home phones whatsoever. No one was supposed to even know the home telephones or even names of one another. A message service had been contracted, and beepers were handed out to all key employees and major customers. When they called each other they just dialed the message center and indicated by a number (not a telephone number) whom they were trying to reach. The service then beeped the person being called, and the number of the pay phone being used by the caller would be displayed on their beeper. Then they called back. It was a good system. So long as everybody followed the rules and varied the pay phones used frequently, there was virtually no way the FBI could listen in. Larry, personally, was diligent. He carried around an orange Tupperware bowl filled with a hundred dollars' worth of quarters. If the feds ever tapped his phone, the most they were likely to hear would be Marcia calling the diaper service.

But none of Larry's precautions seemed sufficient to keep Bruce out of trouble. On July 12, Bruce was stopped by the Philadelphia police for going the wrong way down a one-way street. He had two kilos of cocaine in a black safe in the trunk, an ounce of cocaine in a plastic bag in the glove compartment, and he was smoking a joint. At police headquarters, Bruce later told Larry, one of the cops had come up to him with the baggie of cocaine.

"This is good stuff," the cop said.

"Why don't you keep it," said Bruce. "It's nothing."

"You're right," said the cop.

Another plainclothes officer asked Bruce to open the safe in his trunk. Bruce lied, saying he didn't know the combination. After that, he was locked in a holding cell. A few hours later he was released. There were no charges. The safe in the trunk was undisturbed.

Bruce called Larry that night from a pay phone.

"Okay, get your stuff together," said Larry. "You're moving."

Larry had been working on getting Bruce a house in Newtown Square, a suburb southwest of Devon. Bruce checked into a hotel with Kim that night, and several days later moved into his new house.

Bruce and Larry chalked up the mysterious lack of charges after the Philadelphia arrest to the ineptitude and corruption of the Philadelphia police. In fact, Bruce's arrest and release that night had been carefully orchestrated.

Ten days earlier, on July 2, Canadian customs officials at the border of Eastport, Idaho, and Kingsgate, Alberta Province, had stopped a thirty-year-old blond Canadian woman named Virginia Ann Dayton and searched her car. On the seat of her car they found a tan suitcase containing a kilo of 80 percent pure cocaine.

In Dayton's purse was a business card with the name Wayne Heinauer on it, and a number.

The Canadian border officials had been tipped off by U.S. Drug Enforcement Administration agents in Phoenix, Arizona. Eight weeks before, DEA Agent James White had received a tip that Wayne Heinauer, a young Phoenix construction contractor, was dealing cocaine. He was buying the drugs, the informant said, from a dentist in Philadelphia named Larry and receiving monthly deliveries from someone named Bruce.

During April, White and other DEA agents, along with Phoenix narcotics detectives, had staked out Sky Harbor International Airport and watched Heinauer, a solidly built man of thirty with brown hair and a moustache, meet with a succession of travelers, who typically flew in, met with him briefly, exchanging bags, and then flew on somewhere else. One of the travelers was Virginia Dayton. Another was a wiry, dark-haired, moustachioed man who had taken out a room at the Granada Royale Hotel under the name Bruce Taylor, and who gave his home address as Portsmouth, New Hampshire. Bruce was traveling with a woman (this was Kim Norimatsu). After the meeting with Heinauer, Bruce checked out of the Granada Royale and got a room with Kim at the Marriott Mountain Shadows Resort Hotel in Scottsdale. On Friday, April 22, agents watched Bruce and Kim as they bought tickets for Philadelphia at the airport under the name B. Winns. Agents in Philadelphia, contacted by the Phoenix office, watched at the airport as Bruce and Kim got off the plane. Philly agents reported that Bruce and the young woman had moved through the airport quickly, looking around and over their shoulders frequently, as if aware they were being followed. Agents attempted to follow them by car, but Bruce drove too fast and crazily for them to keep up, and they lost him.

Again on Thursday, June 9, Phoenix DEA agents were watching Heinauer's house when Bruce and Kim arrived, staying for ten minutes before leaving with Heinauer for the airport. This time they purchased tickets under the names Mr. and Mrs. B. Wayne and flew to Philadelphia.

At the airport, Bruce and Kim split up—to the DEA agents, it appeared as though they were trying to see if they were being followed. They got back together in a taxi, and the DEA agents, who had gone undetected, followed the cab back to Bruce's house on Poplar Street.

Through the weeks that James White in Phoenix had been exploring information about Wayne Heinauer and his connections, he had run requests for information about a dentist named Larry in Philadelphia through federal law enforcement computers. There was little to be had, except that an FBI agent in Philadelphia named Chuck Reed had been searching for information about a dentist named Lawrence W. Lavin.

The DEA agent and the FBI agent talked in June. Chuck had not known about Bruce Taylor. It was his first strong lead into Larry's cocaine dealing. Having the city police pick up Bruce had provided an opportunity for mug shots and fingerprints, without alerting Larry that the FBI was on to his courier. The idea was then to turn Taylor loose and keep watching him. Eventually he might lead them to Larry.

So the next morning, Reed and his partner, Sid Perry, staked out Bruce's house on Poplar Street. It would be a few hours before they realized he had vanished.

Marcia and Larry vacationed in Bermuda in May. Christopher was a fat-cheeked toddler with ringlets of fair brown hair. The little family stayed in a condo overlooking a palmy bay and aqua waters that darkened to ultramarine on the horizon.

Back home on Timber Lane, Larry snapped closeup shots of the explosion of springtime color in his backyard, which had been enhanced by two years of professional gardening. There were orchids and tulips and irises and violets and roses and lilies, a bonanza of reds and oranges and purples and whites. Beside the pool on a sunny afternoon weekend, with Chris bobbing in his inflated green froggie life preserver and Marcia paddling after him in the cool water, it was easy to forget the approaching threat of arrest and prison. Larry was confident that whatever happened, his lawyer could make the case drag on for years—Glen Fuller had yet to be convicted for his bust on the New Jersey Turnpike in 1980.

Larry was unaware of the new avenue agents had found into his dealing, but he was acutely aware that unless he retreated fast, Bruce Taylor was going to eventually be his undoing. Ever since Chuck Reed's visit to his dental office in February, and Brian Riley's departure a month later, Larry realized that the only safe thing to do would be to sell out. He could feel the federal investigation nipping away at the fringes of his illegal enterprise. Ken and David had been questioned about Mark Stewart. Andy Mainardi had been questioned. Suzanne and Kim Norimatsu had been approached by Chuck Reed. A former Arena employee named Rick Imondi had been questioned. Larry Uhr was apparently cooperating. One of Wayne Heinauer's customers had just been suspiciously busted on the Canadian border. All of these events had just confirmed Larry's belief that although the FBI suspected his cocaine dealing, they had no hard evidence. Still, it was wise to put as much distance between himself and the business as possible. Ideally, he would sell the business to someone who would manage it capably for him. That way he could retain a financial interest without having to be personally involved. He knew that he would have to accept even harder terms than those he had rejected when David Ackerman had tried to dictate a year earlier, but there was no alternative.

Larry's first choice to take over the business was Billy Motto. Billy South Philly had matured from a hustling street vendor with pot customers to a multimillionaire cocaine dealer. He had started off admiring and imitating Larry, but over the years Larry had come to admire and imitate Billy. Dressed in his pastel sweat suits, driving his black Volvo with retractable panels for hiding money and cocaine, surrounded by his retinue of respectful, silent thugs, Billy was a force to be reckoned with in South Philly. During years when the traditional Italian-dominated organized-crime families were killing each other off, Billy had managed to quietly carve his independent illegal niche. People tended to like Billy so long as they weren't on his bad side. He had an effusively friendly style, lavishing gifts on family and friends, always asking people if he could do anything for them, and seeming disappointed if they could think of nothing. Any promise was promptly kept. Billy was comically and unselfconsciously vain. He stopped out to Larry's dental office every couple of months to have his teeth cleaned—Billy was especially proud of his perfect teeth. After the cleaning, he would inspect the work carefully in the mirror and complain to the hygienist that they weren't quite white enough—and then laugh.

Billy was perfectly trustworthy and reliable in money matters, always paying up front, in total. Larry had gotten the idea for the beeper system from Billy. He admired the way Billy handled himself.

Larry had never gotten the kind of respect from his workers that Billy got from his. And Billy was an excellent businessman. Of all his customers, Larry was convinced that Billy had profited most. Billy had purchased a home in Boca Raton, Florida, with a swimming pool in the backyard, just like Larry's, and even bought himself a golden Lab, just like Larry's. He had a pretty girlfriend named Angela and was thinking about starting a family. Recently, Billy had obtained the contract to supply fresh produce to all the Super Fresh super-markets in the Philadelphia area, and he had purchased a flower shop in Center City, so in addition to his drug dealing and loan-sharking, Billy was managing profitable, legitimate businesses.

Larry and Billy met at a Steak 'n Brew on Route 202 in Devon.

"I know an indictment is coming," Larry explained. "I want to get out, but it's not that easy. There are lots of people, like Bruce, who would like to buy it, but they don't have the money. Besides, you know what a fuck-up Bruce is."

Billy said, "I'd like to help you, Larry. But the timing is bad."

Billy understood that Larry had a lot of money tied up in the business. And he knew better than most people could how difficult it was to just walk away. He explained that he had decided to get out of the business himself. He had gotten over the initial thrill of having money, and had learned that people who were once grateful for the loans and gifts he gave had come to expect them. The attention and respect that had been lavished on Billy in his South Philly neighbor-hood, and that he had enjoyed so much at first, had now become cloying and insistent. And there was another, more sinister problem. Some of the bigger organized-crime figures in Atlantic City and Phil-adelphia were paying more attention to Billy. He felt like a mouse caged with a lion. Billy wanted to get out while he could. He found himself spending more and more time in Florida, and his heart was more in the flower and produce business than in cocaine.

He explained these things to Larry.

"Even if I did want to get even more into it right now, I don't think it's worth the heat," he said. "You're hot, Larry. I think all of these people are going to be hot. It's all going to go down."

Larry was disappointed, but hardly surprised.

"I'm in the same boat you are," said Billy. "I'm looking for some-one who can take over things for me. But it's hard to find someone you can trust who can do the job."

On June 29, a group of FBI and IRS agents raided the Norristown offices of Joe Powell, Larry's silver connection. They seized Powell's business records and interviewed the somewhat shocked and intimi-dated Powell.

Powell told them that Larry had invested about $487,000 with him during the first six months of the year. Most of the money had been delivered in shopping bags full of cash. These investments, he said, were considered loans. Powell had agreed to repay Larry at a 30 percent per annum interest rate, and not to report the interest payments to the IRS.

Word got back to Larry right away. It was just one more piece of evidence for the building tax case, and a reminder that the investigation was not just going to go away.

Larry was desperate. He considered Bruce reckless and inept. If the feds didn't catch on to him, Bruce was going to drive away all his customers. It was no longer a question of finding someone he could trust; Larry needed someone with the resources to buy him out who was capable of carrying on the business without creating further legal problems for him and for his friends.

The one person Larry knew of who fit those two criteria was Frannie Burns.

Larry had finally met Frannie about six months earlier, after hearing about him for nearly a year. In late 1982, Larry lost Brian Cassidy, one of his best customers, to Frannie, who seemed to have a source for cocaine that was considerably cheaper than Larry's. Larry was angry. To get back at this new rival, Larry told Brian he might be interested in buying from Frannie himself. Soon after that, through someone who knew Paul Mikuta, Frannie delivered two sample kilos. Larry cut the kilos, Paul cut them again, and then they returned them to Frannie saying the quality wasn't up to their standards. It was Larry's way of thumbing his nose at the guy.

But word kept getting back to Larry about the incredibly low prices Frannie got in Florida, so eventually business instinct had won out over pride. He called Paul Mikuta, who knew someone who knew Frannie, and said he wanted to meet with his rival.

Their first meeting was in Frannie's beat-up blue Toyota, in the shopping center parking lot across the street from Larry's dental office. Frannie, who was Larry's age and married, was with his sixteen-year-old girlfriend, Sandy Freas. Larry was surprised by Frannie. He had expected someone more like himself, but Frannie was a short, chubby character with long straggly hair and a thick brown moustache. He talked with a pronounced lisp. Instead of being angry about the returned kilos, Frannie actually apologized to Larry.

"I know you didn't like the ones I sent," he said. "But I still think we can do business."

They had spent about a half hour talking, chatting about mutual friends in Florida and Philly, and about prices. Despite their obvious surface differences, Frannie and Larry had a lot in common. Frannie had built his business up on the Main Line, and owned a Dairy Queen outlet in a small shopping center off Route 202. They were both serious businessmen who were alternately amused and alarmed by the drug-abusing foibles of the people around them. There was an immediate rapport between serious dealers because they were the rare ones who treated the drugs strictly as merchandise. Larry knew how difficult and risky the business was, and he sensed that Frannie did too.

Frannie had an immediate problem. He normally employed his father-in-law, Harvey Perry, Sr., as his runner. But Perry was dying of cancer and was in the hospital for treatments. Frannie needed someone to make a run for him right away.

So Larry offered to let Frannie use Stan Nelson, and Fran accepted. It put things on a cooperative footing right away.

For most of 1983, Larry and Frannie had been loosely cooperating, playing Florida dealers off one another to lower the price per kilo down to just twenty-two thousand. After Billy turned down Larry's offer to buy the business, Larry met with Frannie at the McDonald's in Devon. Larry was familiar with the place because he and Marcia often took fourteen-month-old Christopher there.

Frannie immediately liked the idea of buying Larry's business. Larry wanted half a million dollars to just walk away. But Frannie proposed easing the transition. He wanted to gradually take over Larry's customers, paying off the half million in installments, and using Larry to help him establish a rapport with the customers. What Frannie actually had in mind, as Larry soon realized, was to take over the business and use its own profits to pay Larry off. They concluded the agreement in that one brief session.

"Frannie, you're the only person I've ever met whose greed exceeds my own," said Larry.

Larry urged Frannie to keep Bruce Taylor, who by then was the only one besides Larry who knew how to break, cut, and package the cocaine for Larry's customers. Frannie had never gone to such trouble. He just turned over to his customers the kilos as he got them from Florida.

"I don't need all that shit," Frannie said. "I'll just give it to them and they can do whatever they want to it."

"No, look, Fran. You can make more money my way." Larry scribbled some figures on a napkin, showing Frannie how much he could multiply his profits by cutting the coke and making rocks.

Frannie was amazed. "You make that much off a kilo?"

Larry basked in Frannie's admiration. It was rare to find someone who could understand and appreciate his formulas.

Frannie agreed to keep Bruce for a while, and Larry agreed to help smooth the transition by introducing Frannie to each of his customers and encouraging them to continue doing business with him.

Larry left the meeting that afternoon in late July feeling wistful but relieved. He knew almost nothing about Frannie, except that he had managed to create and build a cocaine business competitive with his own. Self-interest would dictate the rest. Frannie could make a lot of money selling to Billy Motto and to Priscilla in New England, even apart from the smaller customers. It was a propitious moment in the cocaine business. Wholesale prices in Florida had fallen in little more than a year from fifty-six thousand per kilo to twenty-two, yet customers in Philadelphia and elsewhere were still willing to pay the old prices. Wayne Heinauer in Phoenix was still buying kilos for seventy-six thousand! A person could get rich fast in a market like that.

A great weight had been lifted from Larry's shoulders, but, oh! the missed opportunity. To think he could have doubled his six million dollars by the end of the year!

Willowy Suzanne Norimatsu had gone to Europe in early 1983 after being approached by Chuck Reed and Tom Neff. While she was away her sister had gotten engaged to Bruce Taylor.

It was a strange twist. For years, Suzanne had been first girlfriend and then fiancée to the manager of the cocaine business, and Kim had been on the fringes of the organization, fascinated by it, by David, and by the cocaine. Now the situation had reversed. Kim was living with Bruce, who was running the business for Larry, and it was Suzanne on the fringes. She was still drawn to the cocaine and the excitement of the business, and she tasted a little of what her sister had felt during the last few years. She was attracted to Bruce.

Living at home with her parents, Suzanne spent much of her free time at the house in Newtown Square with Bruce and Kim. She and Bruce often sat up late playing poker and gin rummy. Bruce was attracted to both sisters, which began causing friction right away, and which came to a head in early August when, over one confused weekend, Kim and Bruce broke their engagement and Suzanne and Bruce wound up in bed—although not necessarily in that order. One week later, they impulsively chartered a plane to Las Vegas and got married.

When he lost track of Bruce Taylor in July, Chuck Reed was confident the would-be biker/cocaine dealer would turn up again soon. Phoenix DEA agents had been noting his comings and goings for several months.

Connecting with the Phoenix probe was a genuine breakthrough for the Philadelphia FBI man. Ever since Reed had become suspicious of Larry Lavin in late 1982, he had been painstakingly acquiring and compiling scraps of evidence to apply for permission to tap the telephones of Larry Lavin and his known associates. But it was time consuming, and the information was scarce. The best Chuck hoped to get was authorization, perhaps by late 1983, for a "pen register," a limited phone tap that does not permit agents to record conversations but that registers what numbers are calling to and are being called from a targeted phone. Employing this arm's-length surveillance was necessary to lay the groundwork for a real wiretap.

But the Phoenix agents were already way ahead of that procedure. They had enough solid evidence linking Heinauer to cocaine dealing that they were able to obtain a court order for a wiretap on his phone for one month, beginning August 12.

Suzanne and Bruce were married in Las Vegas on Saturday, August 13. By the following Sunday afternoon, Bruce was coming off the high that had sent him winging west. He hadn't taken along a sufficient supply of cocaine. So he called Wayne, and the DEA's tape recorders switched on.

Bruce told Wayne that he was in Las Vegas, and that he had just married Suzanne, Kim's sister.

"I was gonna give you a call this evening," said Wayne, laughing. "I wouldn't have caught you at home, would I?"

Wayne said he had met Suzanne once, a long time ago. Bruce asked Wayne if he had any "product" for a "wedding present." Wayne said that he did, so Bruce said he and his bride would be flying his way.

Bruce called again less than two hours later.

"You have a wedding present, right?" he asked Wayne.

"Yeah, oh yeah. I just went and got it to make sure that it was there," said Wayne.

"Oh, beautiful! I've been totally sleepish."

"What's that?"

"I've been totally sleepish," said Bruce. "A withdrawal symptom. And this is a hell of a time to fall asleep, on your honeymoon!"

Phoenix agents watched Bruce and Suzanne come and go on August 14.

Four days later, the tap on Wayne's phone began recording a series of calls between Wayne and Bruce as the Philadelphia dealer flew out to Phoenix with Harvey Perry, Sr., Frannie Burns's father-in-law—described by Bruce as "our new mule"—carrying two kilos. This was Wayne's first experience dealing with someone associated with Frannie. In one of their phone calls, Bruce referred to "the transition," which intrigued the listening agents. Evidently a significant change was under way in Larry Lavin's business.

They didn't have to wait long for an explanation.

* * *

On an unseasonably cool midday for late August, Tuesday the twenty-third, after the morning sun had burned the dew from the lawns in Devon and rush hour traffic had thinned on Route 202 and the Schuylkill Expressway, the boss pulled his big silver BMW up to a pay phone at the corner of Welsh Road and Roosevelt Boulevard in the Northeast. The booth was shattered and covered with graffiti, but by now Larry was suspicious of all the pay phones near his home and near his office. Since selling the business to Frannie, he had been playing things super safe. So he deliberately selected this booth for his call to Wayne Heinauer. He felt it was far enough away from both his home and the office to be safe.

Wayne had just gotten a two-kilo delivery from Bruce and Frannie's father-in-law, who had arrived in Phoenix the day before. Wayne had seemed a bit leery of dealing with Perry, so Frannie had called Larry the night before and asked him to call and explain things to Wayne.

Larry took from his briefcase on the car seat the hand-held computer in which he kept all his telephone numbers stored. He opened the trunk and fetched his heavy orange bowl of quarters. Then he punched the phone number on his computer, inserted several coins, and placed his call to Wayne . . . and the DEA.

"Hello?"

"Hi, Wayne?"

"Yeah?"

"This is Larry. How ya doin'?"

"Good, how are you doing?"

"Good," said Larry.

"Hey, what's been going on, dude?"

"I just thought I'd call up and shoot the breeze with you."

"Oh, very good. I've been wanting to give you a call and I thought I'd wait and see how things are going back there for everybody. So what have you been doing?"

"Well, I'm at a pay phone. I'm about to go to work. I'm just trying to see if I can get a bachelor party together for Bill Honeywell."

"Oh, really?"

"He's getting married next month."

Heinauer had grown up in the same western Pennsylvania town as Honeywell. He and Larry reminisced about mutual acquaintances from the days when Larry had dealt pot as an undergraduate. Then the phone clicked, demanding more quarters, and Larry got down to business.

"Anyway, I know Bruce explained to you what's going on, right?"

"Yes, uh-huh."

"So, that's good. It's a little hard on pay phones, but what I'm basically trying to do is have Frannie take over the job that I do, which isn't that much. But when there's a problem, you know, I'm always here so someone can be reached."

"Right, uh-huh."

"Bruce is an excellent guy and everything is working out well with him. But he can't always be reached, is one problem. Frannie can be reached really quick. He answers his beeper in like five minutes."

"Right."

"And he's going to put up money for buying things down there, which is nice," said Larry. "Can you believe Bruce got married?"

Wayne laughed. "Yeah, God! You're telling me! They came down, you know, after they went to Vegas. And I said, 'You gotta be kidding me. Man, I've only known you for a short while but, boy, you're hard to keep up with!' . . . I couldn't believe it. I said, 'Oh, you and Kim couldn't wait.' And he says, 'Uh-uh, it's not Kim.' "

Wayne asked about Marcia and Chris. They chatted for a moment about other mutual friends again, then Larry addressed the recent arrest at the Canadian border of Wayne's customer Virginia Dayton.

"I'm sorry to hear about that other thing that happened."

"Oh, yeah. Well, hopefully we're getting that straightened out," said Wayne. "It's just a stupid thing. People went against our plan, you know? And they went and got themselves popped."

"Yep."

"But we're working that out. I'm kind of in the hole right now. That's why, you know, I'd like to have everything sitting there waiting for you guys but I'm gonna be a little bit slow. I explained that all to Bruce."

Larry told Wayne not to worry. Then he reassured him about doing business with Perry, and with Frannie.

"It will take a while for everything to work out . . . eventually. I just wanted you to understand that you can call Frannie. Just tell him what you want, and boom, you know?"

"I do have a hard time getting ahold of Bruce sometimes," said Wayne.

"So, I tell you, Frannie is going to be real good," Larry said. "He can work with you. He'll do anything. If you need his father-in-law to deliver it anywhere . . . The neat thing is, that guy is dying of cancer, you know? He's only going to be around for another year or two. If anything ever happens to him, you know, he's not going to say anything, which is kind of neat."

Lavin asked about the quality of the coke that had just been delivered, and Heinauer said it looked "very nice." He said he might have some trouble selling it quickly. His competition was selling grams for sixty-five or sixty-six bucks.

"I just can't compete with them," Wayne complained. "I've lost like three or four customers."

"If you talk to Frannie," Larry said, "one thing is, you know, he does like about sixty or eighty [kilos] a month, between our business and his, and he gets it cheaper than I was getting it before. If you think it's going to be worthwhile to increase your business, you know, he'll give you a price break."

"Oh, okay," said Heinauer.

"So you should rap with him about that, you know. And he'll do anything. He'll send out every week. Whatever you want done, he'll do for you."

"Oh, that's good to know, very good to know."

"So I think it will be a little more organized now."

Heinauer explained apologetically that he was behind in his payments, and asked Larry to explain to Burns and Taylor that this was not usually the case.

"I told them you hate to owe money, but we like to get people to owe money. . . . We know you're good for it. You're good people, so everything will work out okay."

"So are your troubles working out?" Heinauer asked, referring to Larry's IRS troubles.

"Well, to tell you the truth, I think I'm going to end up going to jail."

"Yeah, that's what Bruce told me the other day."

"It looks like they've got this about seven-hundred-thousand-dollar tax case that, you know, there's no way of explaining it. They're gonna know, kind of, behind the scenes, what's going on, but I don't think they can prove that, but because of that I'll probably get a sentence on the tax thing. I'm just kind of waiting it out and trying to do the smartest thing possible. . . . That's one reason I made this move, you know. And I've just gotta sit back and wait and see what the hell develops. What I am telling everyone is to kind of learn from my mistakes. Always use pay phones. Never keep anything in your house."

"Right," said Wayne. "We try to do that program already."

"If you ever buy anything, you know, use cashier's checks. My biggest mistake was to put money through this record company, which was doing, like, five million dollars a year, so we didn't think putting through some checks for, like, fifty thousand or so would matter that much."

"But it caught up, huh?"

"But what happened was, one guy questioned his revenues. He didn't get paid enough, and that brought on the FBI doing a whole audit, and they just pulled every big check. And there were two hundred fifty thousand dollars' worth of checks to me, you know?"

"Oh, boy."

"So, like, when I bought my house or something. Eventually they started looking at everything else I owned, and one thing uncovered another. But, that's the way it goes. I'm still hoping. The one good thing is that I've never had any, I haven't been in any trouble whatsoever, and I gotta think that's gonna help somewhat."

"Oh, yeah, hopefully, yes."

"So we gotta see what happens. I'll give you a call maybe every month or so just to see what's going on."

"Very good. Very good."

"Obviously, if you ever hear of any problems with Frannie, I'm still here. All you've got to do is call me, and I'll know to go out and call you."

"Okay, good enough. Thanks a lot for calling. Good talking to you."

"Yeah, good talking to you."

"All right, bye."

"I'll see you."

Larry had no way of knowing it, and wouldn't find out for more than a year. But he had just handed his head to the FBI on a plate.

The DEA informed Chuck Reed the next day that his man had dropped unexpectedly into their web. What amazed the agents most was Larry's estimate that his business, combined with Frannie's, was doing sixty to eighty kilos of cocaine each month. A recent federal estimate of the total amount of cocaine being sold in the Philadelphia area each month was less than twelve kilos. They were doing more than that each *week*.

It upped the probe's priority. An organization that size was by far the biggest in Philadelphia history, and one of the biggest that law enforcement officials had ever uncovered in America.

T E N

Let's Get Out of Here

Christmas on Timber Lane was pretty as a greeting card. Marcia put one electric candle in each of the windows, which gave a twinkle of magic to the white house against the snow. She decorated the weeping fig tree in the dining room and the Christmas tree by the front window in the den. A full crèche was lovingly arranged on a shelf by the stereo. Wearing a handmade dress of red silk and a gold necklace, Marcia went to mass on Christmas Eve with her mother and the baby. On Christmas morning, Christopher plowed into mounds of brightly wrapped toys. Marcia preferred playthings for him that had educational value, little wooden puzzles or kiddie arts and crafts. For Larry there was a universal gym and a stationary bicycle.

Larry had heard almost nothing further about the FBI investigation in the more than ten months since Chuck Reed had stopped by his office. Maybe the FBI had given up. Larry figured that if they hadn't caught him in all the years when he was in the business up to his neck, they certainly weren't going to nail him now. His involvement with the cocaine business had virtually ceased. Other than occasional telephone calls to his old customers, smoothing over the transition to Frannie, and clandestine meetings with Frannie to pick up some of the money he was owed, Larry was doing nothing to incriminate himself further. As for the tax charges, just the passage of time seemed to ease his foreboding. What were they talking about anyway? With good legal protection he might get off with a big fine. At worst, Larry figured he might spend a year or so in a minimum-security prison for tax fraud. It was not an appealing prospect, but, when you weighed against it the more than five million dollars he had made, it wasn't a bad bargain.

Larry was cheerful enough about his prospects that he continued his annual tradition of mailing Christmas cards to all of his customers. He always chose cards with lots of snow falling on an urban setting, and personally inscribed them, "From Larry and the Gang!"

Marcia did not share Larry's optimism. She was done trying to argue with Larry about it, but she was convinced the government would discover his cocaine dealing and arrest him. It was only a matter of time. She believed their comfortable days together were numbered. Part of her felt sorry for Larry, and part of her was angry. Why wouldn't he listen to her? She had done nothing but warn him that this was coming since they were both sophomores in college. She was also angry with herself. How could she have stayed with him all this time? Now they had a baby. She had wanted this family and this life so badly that she had been willing to turn a blind eye to Larry's dealings, and to the approaching disaster. Marcia loved Larry. She could not have just given up on him even if she had wanted to. So she tried to hope. Maybe Larry was right. Maybe the FBI wouldn't be able to prove anything about his drug business. Maybe there would just be a fine and a short jail term. So, as she had for nearly ten years, Marcia played along.

They had prepared friends and family for the shock and embarrassment of his pending arrest and trial. Larry told everyone that he had gotten involved with some people who gave him bad advice. Now he was in tax trouble. He might have to go to jail, but he was going to defend himself as best he could. Poor Larry. Poor Marcia. Poor little Christopher. Everyone was sympathetic, and angry at the government for even threatening to disturb the picturesque harmony of this handsome, affluent young Main Line family.

How dare they!

One week before Christmas, the FBI placed a tap on Bruce Taylor's phone and on a whole raft of pay phones around Larry's home in Devon, his office, and even along the route back and forth. Chuck Reed had happened to spot Larry talking on a pay phone off of Route 202 one day as he drove past. So that one and the ones near it were also tapped. The conversation with Wayne Heinauer had provided more than enough just cause to authorize the taps.

From the first day the tap was placed the agents began recording evidence of Bruce Taylor's dealing. Bruce used his home phone in frequent, flagrant violation of Larry's beeper system/pay phone procedures. Larry had even encouraged Bruce never to use the same pay phone twice. But there weren't many pay phones at all out in Newtown Square. It was winter and cold outside. Larry was just paranoid, thought Bruce. So on January 7, when his beeper went off indicating that Larry was waiting for him, and displaying the number of the pay phone where he could be called back, Bruce waited for a few minutes to make it seem as if he had gone out to a pay phone, and then returned the call from his living room.

"How you doin'?" asked Bruce.

"Oh, I could be better," said Larry.

"Yeah, same here."

"I was fuckin' around with my hot tub, and you know those stupid stakes that people use to hold up tomatoes?"

"Yeah?"

"I turned the wrong way and caught one of those in my eyelid."

"Oh, baby!"

"So I sliced my eyelid open a couple of hours ago and I look like someone punched me, I got this big black and blue mark. . . . What's up?"

Bruce asked how long it had been since Larry talked to Brian Riley. Larry said that he called about every two weeks. Bruce still had some things that Brian had left behind when he skipped town. Larry punched up the numbers for Brian on his hand-held computer and read them to Bruce. They discussed a customer who was behind on payments, about whom Frannie had gone to Larry for help in collecting the debt.

"You'll have to work it out with him," said Larry, who was resisting pressure to get involved.

Larry said that he had hooked up Billy Honeywell, his source in Florida, with Frannie, but that Honeywell's prices weren't low enough to interest Burns.

"I think Frannie's getting them for around twenty-five now, just for your own knowledge," said Larry. Bruce was trying to go to work for himself with some of Larry's old customers, so he was partly in competition with Frannie, even though he was still buying from him. So Larry was imparting a little inside information to help his old manager. Bruce told Larry about his fancy new hot tub. Larry gave him detailed advice on how to keep the tub running properly.

"You use it a lot at first, then you get tired of it," said Larry. "Every once in a while I get back into it and use it for a while. It's hard with the baby. . . . So I got this gym set with all these weights and shit, kind of like a universal. Marcia gave it to me for Christmas, so I've been working out every couple of days."

"Oh, my God!"

"I'm trying to get in shape for when I go to jail."

"You gotta be," said Bruce, "otherwise you'll fuckin' be walking bowlegged. Just fuckin' nail the first person you see. The first person that gets close to you, fuckin' beat him."

"I was reading the other day in the paper this guy, for a hundred-eighty-thousand tax evasion, they gave him two years, and then another judge let him off on appeal, and it turned out that the judge had married the guy's lawyer, so the *Inquirer* did a whole page on it."

"Oh. Jesus!"

"The original judge said, 'I think people like this should go to jail; it's not right that they can just come out and go for a boating trip or something.' And these are Philadelphia judges. Just what I want to hear."

They talked on, Larry supplying Bruce with more phone numbers, complaining about people who still owed him money, chatting about Frannie. It was obvious that Larry missed being more involved. He had few opportunities to get together with his old friends. He was a person whose enormous expertise was lying fallow. Bruce's business was way down.

"With these prices you just got to try and make money by staying with the good people," Larry advised. "Don't take too much risk. . . . If you have a chance to make some money, make some money and put it away."

As the agents listened to the long, rambling conversation, they noted all the names of customers Larry and Bruce mentioned, and they realized that the tape had completed another important link in the case. They had Larry's conversation with Wayne Heinauer, and they had pictures of Bruce meeting with Wayne in Phoenix. Now they had directly established Larry's link to Bruce.

It was time to start reeling in the big fish.

It had been snowing hard through Monday, January 16. As was their habit, Suzanne Norimatsu-Taylor and her husband, Bruce, had gotten to bed in their downstairs bedroom at about 6:00 a.m. Tuesday morning. Suzanne slept the sound sleep of one spent by a long weekend of partying with cocaine. Normally she would have slept until early afternoon, but this morning the tall, dark-haired woman was awakened suddenly at about eleven by the sound of heavy footsteps on the outside stairs. Through partially opened blinds she could see men hurrying, carrying guns.

"Bruce, wake up! FBI! Shotguns!" she shouted.

Even with the blinds partly open it was dark in the bedroom. Sitting up in bed, Suzanne could see the pool table in the next room where lights were still on. At the far side of that room were the stairs up to the living room at ground level. Just as Bruce roused himself from sleep she saw legs descending the stairs.

"FBI! Who's in there!" shouted one of the lead men. "Get down on your hands and knees and crawl out here!"

Bruce rolled out of the bed on his hands and knees. He grabbed Suzanne by the hand.

"Get down on the floor!" he said.

Instead, Suzanne stood up, pulling on her robe, and defiantly walked into the next room. A female FBI agent stepped up and patted her down for weapons. There were about twenty agents moving around the house.

Suzanne and Bruce were escorted upstairs and told to sit together on the couch in the living room. As the agents methodically searched, Bruce and Suzanne dozed. One of the agents brought them a blanket. After about an hour, one of the agents escorted Suzanne downstairs to go to the bathroom and to let her get dressed. She pulled on a black jumpsuit in the bathroom. Bruce was then taken downstairs.

While he was gone, Chuck Reed approached Suzanne.

"See, Suzanne? If you had spoken to me six months ago, none of this would have happened," he said.

Suzanne pulled the blanket over her head and sank further down into the couch.

"I'm not fooling around, this is serious," said Chuck angrily. "Sit up! Are you sober?" Chuck turned to one of the other agents and repeated, "Is she sober?"

The agent nodded. Chuck turned back to Suzanne. "Do you understand that this is serious?"

"Yes, I know you're serious," said Suzanne.

"Well, now's your chance. You can help us get Larry."

Suzanne looked away, avoiding the bearded agent's steady gaze.

"Don't be so stupid, Suzanne. You know Larry is sitting over there in his hot tub, and he doesn't give a damn about you."

Chuck stood up silently and left the room just before Bruce came back.

For three hours Bruce and Suzanne were on the couch.

Sid Perry, Chuck's partner since the summer before, a smaller, easygoing agent with a soft Tennessee accent and a milder manner than his partner's, approached the couch and said, "We'd like to talk to Bruce."

Bruce followed Sid and Chuck into one of the back bedrooms. Suzanne waited, tucking the blanket more tightly around herself. A few minutes passed, and then Sid emerged from the back room.

"Bruce wants to talk to you," he said.

Suzanne joined her husband in the bedroom. They sat together on the edge of the bed. Bruce explained in a whisper that the agents had shown him pictures of him meeting with Wayne Heinauer at the Phoenix airport. Chuck had told Bruce he was going to be sent away to jail for a long time, perhaps as long as fifteen years, unless he was willing to help them now. He would still go to jail, but perhaps not for so long.

"What did you say?" asked Suzanne.

"I told them no. I said I wasn't going to make any deals."

He said the agents had asked what he was afraid of. One of the agents had said, "Frannie and Larry don't know where your family lives." Bruce said he had just laughed. Suzanne indicated to Bruce that she was behind him whatever he decided.

They were escorted back out to the couch.

At 3:00 p.m., Chuck came back in the living room and said, "Okay, stand up. We're going downtown."

Suzanne and Bruce stood up together. One agent clapped handcuffs on Bruce. Suzanne held out her hands, but the agent said, "No, Suzanne, you're not going."

"Good," said Bruce.

She was shocked. Bruce leaned over to kiss her goodbye, and whispered, "Call your uncle." Suzanne often referred to Larry as "Uncle Larry."

When the agents left with Bruce, Suzanne called her sister. Kim had stayed angry with her sister for about four months after Suzanne and Bruce ran off to Las Vegas and got married. But they had gotten together before Christmas and had a long talk and a cry. Now they were as close as they had ever been.

Before Suzanne said a word about the raid, Kim blurted, "Guess what just happened?"

"What?"

"The FBI was at Michael Schade's!" Schade was a Drexel student who had gotten involved with dealing through Kim.

"Oh, yeah?" said Suzanne. "Well, they were just here, too."

"What! Oh, God!"

"Yeah. That's right. I want you to call our uncle and see if we can see him later." Suzanne spoke cryptically because she assumed now that the phone was tapped.

"Okay," said Kim. "I'll be right over."

Suzanne asked Kim to first alert Larry.

Next, Suzanne called Emmett Fitzpatrick, a well-known Philadelphia defense attorney. Fitzpatrick had been retained initially by David Ackerman in late 1982 when the FBI approached him asking questions about Mark Stewart and the Arena arson. Suzanne had met the lawyer once or twice with David.

"They took Bruce away!" Suzanne said.

"Who took Bruce away?" said Fitzpatrick.

"The FBI!"

"Oh," said the lawyer. "Who's Bruce?"

"He's my husband!" said Suzanne. "I married Bruce. I'm not with David anymore."

"Oh, well, congratulations," said the bass-voiced attorney.

"Thanks," said Suzanne.

"Now, tell me why they took Bruce away."

"Well, you see, they had a search warrant, and they were looking for cocaine."

"But they didn't find any, did they?" he asked.

"Well, yeah, they found about a pound."

"Ahh, but it wasn't yours, was it?"

"Well, uh, no!"

"And it wasn't Bruce's either, was it?" he asked.

"No!" said Suzanne. She was cheering up.

"Where was it?" the lawyer asked.

"It was in this black box."

"Uh-huh. Is there a back door?"

"Yes," said Suzanne.

"What side of the bed was it on? The one closest to the door?"

"Yes."

"Mmm. That's very interesting. Do you know where they've taken him?"

"No."

"Well, you wait there. Try to find out where he is. If he calls you or you find out, let me know."

Suzanne hung up and waited. She walked through the house inspecting the damage. The house was a mess—had been a mess before the agents came, but now it was worse. She couldn't find her car keys. Late Christmas presents that Suzanne was planning to deliver to Bruce's nephews, about forty of them, had all been unwrapped. There was Christmas paper scattered around the floor in the basement, like the aftermath of a party. While the search was under way, Suzanne had felt excited about it all. It was at least *interesting*. But now she felt empty and sad. She wished they had taken her with Bruce. Suzanne assumed that the FBI was raiding everybody else that day, too, if they were at Wayne Heinauer's and Michael Schade's. She wanted to phone Larry and warn him and Frannie. Maybe there was still time for them to get away. But she was afraid to use the phone, and without her car keys she couldn't easily get to a pay phone. The agents had seized what cocaine they found, which was Bruce's personal stash. For some reason they had left behind a case of inositol on the dining room table. It was all tagged and marked for evidence, but they had left it behind.

Before Kim arrived, Fitzpatrick called to say that he had located

Bruce in a cell at the federal courthouse. There would be a hearing to set bail later in the day. That relaxed Suzanne. She was in the shower when Kim arrived in a cab.

"Can I have a line?" Kim asked, standing in the bathroom by the shower stall wearing tight jeans and a black leather jacket with Walkman earphones framing the wild curls of her hair. Kim was much smaller than Suzanne and had fair hair, but she had the same exotic blend of Japanese and European features.

"They took it!" said Suzanne.

"They took it all?"

"They scraped the top of the microwave," said Suzanne—that was where they sometimes drew out lines of cocaine for snorting. "They took it all."

Kim said she had phoned Larry at his office. He had wanted to know more. So she had promised to call when she got to Bruce and Suzanne's.

Suzanne told her sister that she didn't want to talk to Larry over the phone. She asked Kim to call him back and ask him to meet with her as soon as he could get away. Suzanne knew she would need money to post Bruce's bail.

So Kim placed the call. Larry's receptionist put her on hold, and then Larry came on with his usual cheerful hello.

"Why don't you just come over here when you're done?" asked Kim.

Larry groaned, as if to say he didn't think it was a good idea.

"No?"

"I'm dying," Larry said.

"He's dying," Kim said, speaking to Suzanne.

"You're torturing me."

"It's not good. You're not going to like it," said Kim.

"You should just tell me on the phone. I mean, what the heck, they've already been there."

"Well, uh, I don't know. Do you think?"

"Yeah, what difference does it make if they've already been there? She can tell me what happened, at least . . . what they said."

"All right. Hang on." Kim called to her sister. "Suzanne, pick up the phone! Larry wants to talk to you. He says since they've been here, it doesn't matter. He's dying to know what happened."

"Hello?" said Suzanne.

"How you doin' ?" said Larry sadly.

Suzanne listened as Larry explained why he felt it was safe at that point to talk.

"Just tell me what happened," he said.

"Well, uh," Suzanne fumbled for a way to begin. "We woke up

and there were about twenty of them running around here with shot-guns. And they had a search warrant. It was the same, it was Charles Reed, I don't, do you remember him?"

"Yep."

"Yeah, well, he came in later on. It was like his little—"

"Thing."

"Thing, yeah. He came in and, uh . . ."

"When was this? Early this morning?"

"They started at around ten o'clock this morning and they left around three, I think."

"Jeez."

"And I didn't know until the moment they were leaving that they weren't going to take me. I don't know why, because up until then they had said different. They had mentioned a couple of people's names, you know, that—"

"What did they find?"

"They found some cocaine and some money, and I called Mr. Fitzpatrick."

"Right. Did he call down there or anything?"

"Yes. He spoke to Bruce. . . . He called me back at four-thirty and said I needed, um, twenty-five hundred by—First they wanted a quarter of a million, then they reduced it to twenty-five thousand, I mean twenty-five hundred."

"That's a big move." Larry laughed.

"I know. Fitzpatrick was going, like, 'I did this for you.' By five o'clock, and I said, well, first of all, they took all my keys. I don't have any car keys or house keys, and they took all my money. So I said I didn't even have any money, I couldn't get down there by five o'clock. So he called back and said nine o'clock tomorrow morning I'll be able to post bail, down at Fifth and Market."

"Okay. So, how much of each thing do you think they got? A rough guess."

"Oh, about eighty-five."

"Eighty-five thousand?"

"Yeah."

"And the other thing?"

"About a pound, I think."

"And did they take all types of paraphernalia?"

"Yeah."

"I imagine what they would do is dump all that in, any cut or anything, and call it all one."

"Fitzpatrick did say to me that he can't represent Bruce because it's a conflict of interest with he and David."

"Yeah, well, you know. Someone can get someone else."

"Well, no, you see, they took all these—the evidence they took were pictures of me and David, anything that was written to me from David."

"And what? That's nothing, right?"

"No. It isn't anything, I mean, it's just strange that they want—"

"What did—can you figure any way that they knew to go there?"

"Oh, well, they said that they had photographs of Bruce and someone named Wayne from about a year ago."

"Someone named Wayne," said Larry, musing, unclear who that might be.

"Um-hmm," said Suzanne. "Who they were visiting today also at the same time."

There was silence on Larry's end. Then, softly, with real concern in his voice, "Ooh, my gosh!"

At first Larry thought, *Maybe it's a different Wayne, someone Bruce did things with on his own.*

"Did they mention a state or anything?" he asked.

"Yeah, it's out there."

"Yeah, they did?"

"Yeah."

"Ooh, my gosh."

"They said they had been looking at him for a while."

"Ooh, my gosh," Larry sighed. "A year ago!"

"Yeah. They showed him the pictures."

"So what did Bruce do this whole time?"

"Slept on the couch."

Larry laughed. "He slept there?"

"Yeah, me and him. We slept on the couch."

"They didn't really hassle you?"

"Well, no . . . well, they—That's why I don't—Every time he asked me questions about anyone, I wouldn't, I wouldn't look at him, so then they finally went away."

"They showed him a picture of him and Wayne a year ago?"

"Yeah. They did take him off into another room for a little bit. That's when they said they wanted to make a deal."

"And did anything happen?"

"No. He said that he didn't know any of these people to make a deal with, or anything about them."

"So they talked about me and David then, or do you think they were talking about other people?"

"Oh yeah, well, they talked to me about you guys."

"But, as far as making a deal, is that who they were talking to him about, or do you think they were talking about some other people, too?"

"Yeah, there were some other people, too, since they called me in, too, for that part."

"Well, did you recognize any of those other names besides David and I? Did you recognize anyone else they wanted to make a deal about?"

"Yeah."

"Who else was it?"

"Well, your other friend. I don't really know him," said Suzanne in a pleading voice. She had just told the FBI she didn't recognize the guy, so she was reluctant to name him now on a tapped phone.

"Right," said Larry. "Did they say a name, or . . . ?"

"Yeah. Uh-hmm."

"Begin with an *F?*"

"Yep."

"Any other names that you knew?" asked Larry.

"No, that was it. Just them."

"Unbelievable," said Larry. He was amazed at the tenacity of the agents. They had been following them all around the country for more than a year!

"Okay, so you're going to go down there at nine, right? I mean, there's nothing else we can do, right? Is there?

"You can lend me some money."

"Yeah, okay. Well, I will come and see you tonight."

"Okay."

"I don't know how great that is. Uuh," Larry groaned. Just how much deeper he was implicated was gradually sinking in. ". . . It's unbelievable that they would watch him for a year!"

"Well, you know what they said, they've been hanging around. I mean, they said that to me a year ago. That they would be around for another two years or something."

". . . I wonder what happened out there with . . . with Wayne," said Larry. "So, they tried to get real intimidating then and told him he was going to go away for a long time, that type of stuff?"

"Oh, yeah."

"Yeah? Great. Well, it will be interesting to see what Fitzpatrick says. Say the worst happens, what's the worst they can do? If they definitely have a good search warrant then they have that, and I'll be interested to see what— I'm just surprised that there weren't a lot more names if they had pictures of him and Wayne."

Larry knew that if they had been following Bruce for more than a year, they would have learned about a lot more people than Wayne. It didn't occur to him that the breakthrough in the investigation had *started* with Wayne, with the DEA in Phoenix. He assumed it had grown out of the local probe of his own dealings. There was a gap there that he found intriguing. He was worried about what more Bruce might say.

Larry agreed to drop money off for Suzanne. He said he wanted to talk to Bruce as soon as he was released.

Sweat was rolling from Larry's armpits when he hung up the phone. For the first time since the meeting with Chuck Reed and the IRS agent almost a year ago, Larry realized his predicament had significantly worsened. They were on to the coke business. His mind raced.

Drilling teeth was the last thing on his mind, but he had a patient in the chair all numbed up and a root canal in progress. There were other patients in the waiting room. . . .

Bruce won't talk, thought Larry. *We'll get him a good lawyer. He'll keep his mouth shut. He got into this business on his own. He wanted it. If you get in voluntarily it means you accept the risks. He's not going to pass it on to everyone else. Bruce wouldn't do that.* . . .

Larry took a couple of deep breaths, stood up, and put a smile on his face as he went to tend to his patient.

Bruce called Suzanne collect from the detention center that night. "Oh God, Suzanne!"

"Did Fitzpatrick say how it looked or anything?" Suzanne asked.

"He said it didn't look that bad, but he always says that."

"No, no, no. Now, he's pretty honest."

"Okay. The law says I'm gonna get at least ten years," Bruce said.

"Don't listen to them."

"I ain't. Fuckin' Chuck there, what an asshole."

"Isn't he?"

"Yeah. He says to me, 'Your wife set you up with us.' "

"Did he?"

". . . I told him to fuck off."

"Why didn't they take me?" asked Suzanne.

"They said they were going to arrest you later."

"Oh, really?"

"I think he's talking through his asshole. Because you could be running."

"Arrest me later, huh?"

"Yep. Oh God, I don't want to hang up. I'm gonna have to get off pretty quick."

"I love you," said Suzanne.

"I love you, baby. See you in the morning?"

"Nine o'clock."

"Come on down to this area."

"I will."

". . . Is there anything? Did they miss anything?" Bruce was feeling the hard effects of cocaine withdrawal.

Suzanne said they had gotten it all.

"Okay, down where I keep the tools? You know the shelf there, like, where you put the cans and stuff?"

"Downstairs there?"

"Yeah, and the Epsom salt?"

"Yeah."

"See if that little package is in there. That little silver thing that the cartridge came in."

"What cartridge?"

"Remember? The cartridge."

"Oh."

"In the storeroom that I was keeping the *D*s in?"

"Oh yeah, yeah."

"They get that?"

"I don't know," said Suzanne. "You want me to look? Hold on."

Kim chatted with Bruce for a minute while Suzanne checked the hiding place. Bruce said to her, "You got to get me something off somebody for when I get out of here!"

Suzanne then returned to the phone. "I can't find anything."

"It isn't there?"

"No."

"They found it, then," he said, disappointed.

Bruce asked Suzanne to check one other hiding place, and there was no cocaine there either.

"See if you can get me ahold of something tomorrow," he said. "Fix me a blast in the morning. A big one."

"Well, I don't—"

"If you can't, you can't," he said, dejected.

"I'll try," said Suzanne.

It was six o'clock. Bruce hung on the line a few minutes longer.

"Can you sleep there?" Suzanne asked. "What is it like?"

"It's horrible. It's, it's all niggers."

"Really?"

"Yep, same as last time. I got in a fight last time. Had to break the guy's arm."

"Uh-huh."

"I'm in the same place."

"Oh, no!"

"Naked," he said.

"Naked!"

"Yep, Suzanne."

"Why?"

"They took my clothes."

"I'm sorry."

"It's horrible."

"I love you," Suzanne said. She felt ready to cry.

"I love you," said Bruce.

Larry came over later. Kim and Suzanne sat on the pool table and Larry sat in an armchair alongside as Suzanne went back over in detail the events of the day.

He asked question after question, and tried to size up from Suzanne exactly what was Bruce's state of mind.

"Do you think that he might get scared?" Larry asked.

"Bruce is tough," said Suzanne.

Larry thought about that for a few minutes. "I guess Bruce has been around," he said.

He left them with twenty-five thousand dollars. When he was gone, Suzanne found her car keys. She wanted to make sure nothing would keep her from the courthouse in the morning, so Suzanne put on a mink coat and a mink hat. She and Kim drove into Philadelphia and checked into the Bellevue Stratford Hotel, got stoned, ordered room service, and watched TV through the night.

Bruce was released promptly after nine o'clock. He strode out of the marshal's office on the second floor with a happy grin and was embraced by the giggling sisters. They left in search of cocaine.

Several months after Bruce's bust, Chuck Reed stopped by the house on Timber Lane. Marcia's mother had just come over for dinner. She pulled her car in the driveway and entered the house through the garage into the kitchen.

"Who are those people sitting in the car outside?" she asked Marcia.

"What people?"

Marcia walked to the foyer and peeked out the window by the front door. There were two men in a car parked up on the lane. Marcia guessed right away that they were agents.

About fifteen minutes after that, the men got out of the car and came down the front walk to the door. Marcia was waiting for them. Chuck and the other agent showed their badges and introduced themselves.

"We would like to come in and ask you a few questions," Chuck said.

"Our lawyer has advised me not to answer any questions," Marcia said. "If you want to arrange a meeting, you can contact him. His name is Donald Goldberg." The other agent turned and started back. Chuck stood his ground.

"You know that your husband is in big trouble," he said.

"Good luck," said Marcia. "I'm going to close the door now. I don't mean to be impolite."

She shut the door as Chuck was saying, "Larry thinks he's got a hotshot lawyer and that he's gonna get off, but he's going away to jail for many years, if not life."

Chuck Reed had everyone in this case spooked. Nobody seemed to think that Sid Perry or Tom Neff or Steve Gallon or any of the other federal agents involved were anything other than decent guys doing their job. Larry had heard a lot of nice things about Sid Perry's quiet manners and friendliness. He often told people, when warning them what to expect before a visit by the FBI men, "From what I hear, Sid Perry is a nice guy. Chuck Reed is just an asshole." Everybody thought Sid was nice, but Chuck Reed stayed in their minds. Stories circulated about Chuck. People remembered exactly what the big, bearded agent had said, the look in his eyes, the set of his jaw. Reed-bashing became a favorite inside sport. Encounters with Chuck Reed became the grist for countless stories. Embellished and distorted, these minor incidents portrayed the lead FBI agent as an oaf on a frustrated vendetta, outsmarted at every turn.

So the visit to Larry's house ended with the image of a red-faced Chuck Reed bellowing threats through the front window after Marcia coolly closed the door. The visit to David Ackerman ended with David refusing to look up the name of his lawyer in the phone book while Chuck fussed and stormed around his apartment. Suzanne's story about "black hats" and "white hats" prompted gales of laughter. People claimed that Chuck Reed told them lies, made up stories about Larry owning clandestine airports in southern Florida and secret Caribbean estates, or about how Larry wouldn't hesitate to have anyone killed who got in his way.

To Larry, Chuck Reed was a CPA who had blundered into the biggest case of his career. He pictured the big FBI agent as having spent years huddled over ledgers in the dusty back halls of old courthouses, trying to catch the petty mistakes of corporate accountants. Now his probe of Mark Stewart's books had unexpectedly thrust him into the real world, complete with his comic-book vision of himself as the good guy, like "Nick Danger, Private Eye" from the old Firesign Theater albums, and Larry as some modern-day suburban version of Al Capone. With deep-seated memories of his father's old diatribes against government incompetence—what kind of person works for salaries like those anyway?—it was comforting and even easy for Larry to see the FBI as a group of clumsy but determined plodders, and none more representative than Chuck. These were years when cocaine was still considered a harmless, glamorous recreational drug, a status symbol. No one had yet heard of crack or of famous athletes keeling over dead from a few snorts. Laws against cocaine stemmed from the same bullet-headed ignorance evidenced by the old propaganda-film-turned-campus-classic *Reefer Madness*. Larry couldn't understand why the government would be so determinerd to catch him. He attributed the relentless nature of the now two-year-old investigation to Chuck Reed's private demons. He half expected that at some point a higher-up in the federal courthouse was going to find out how Reed had been spending his time and jerk him off the case.

And if they didn't, well, Larry was sure he would end up one step ahead of Chuck Reed in the end. Larry's attitude had shaped the theme of all the stories told about Chuck. His friends and associates looked for the traits in Chuck that supported this view. It was reassuring to see things Larry's way. They were all so much more together than Chuck Reed, so much more poised and intelligent, so much more *cool*. Surely guys like Chuck Reed never won in the end . . . but, then . . .

After the raid at Bruce and Suzanne's, Larry's old, optimistic scenario of paying a fine or going away on tax charges was shattered. If they had been watching Bruce for that long, and they had the tape of his conversation with Wayne, then they had a good chance of building a cocaine case against him.

It was time to develop a new option. If it all came down too hard, Larry realized, he would have to be ready to flee.

How exactly does a person disappear? In the back pages of *High Times* magazine there were sometimes ads for strange books published by an outfit called Loompanics Unlimited, based in Port Townsend, Washington. There were books and pamphlets on techniques of electronic surveillance, private-detective manuals, how-to books on everything from writing novels to lip reading to surviving nuclear war to exacting revenge on a former spouse to growing marijuana in your basement. An ad for a book entitled *New I.D. in America* caught Larry's eye in the spring of 1984—"With *New I.D. in America*, you can 'get lost' permanently," the ad promised. Larry sent away.

The little paperback was filled with step-by-step advice on how to obtain new birth certificates, drivers licenses, social security cards, credit cards, how to create bogus business entities, bank accounts, and how to use mail drops—sequential mailing organizations that forwarded letters from place to place for several weeks before sending them to their ultimate destination, obscuring the letter's origin. Along with the booklet came a catalog of other offerings that interested Larry. He investigated books dealing with wiretapping, and read up on how long it took the government to trace a phone call. He figured that if he and Marcia ran, he could occasionally call family and friends without fear of revealing his location.

As for where to run, Larry had not yet given it much thought. He had considered Ireland, being his ancestral home, but in talking it over with his friends he feared that the Irish Republican Army would find out about him and come after his money. Larry made telephone inquiries at embassies and found out that most countries would extradite him back to the United States for drug crimes. He knew from his conversations with Billy Honeywell that officials in Jamaica could be bought off fairly readily, and there were banks in the Caribbean that made a practice of asking no questions about large cash deposits. In March, Larry and Marcia and Christopher spent a week in Aruba. Lounging on the beach or at poolside in a luxury hotel, watching the gentle sway of palm branches in sweet tropical breezes, it was easy and inviting to imagine escaping the enclosing web of circumstance. How alluring it was to just *be someone else!* It would give Larry the last laugh on everyone—especially Chuck Reed. He would just pop out of the system—*poof!* Ever since his childhood on the lake in Haverhill, spending time with the Baratt family, Larry had fantasized about owning a boat. . . . Maybe it was time to pursue that dream.

At first casually, and then with increasing determination as the inevitable day of his arrest and indictment approached, Larry went to work.

One of the first things he needed was a printer. Larry called Billy Motto and asked if he knew someone, and the next day one of Billy's men phoned to set up the meeting.

Larry drove down to a health spa in South Philly that Billy secretly owned and where he often hung out. They met out front, and when they walked back to the manager's office in back, the people using it cleared out hurriedly. Billy sat behind the desk and Larry sat down across from him. The printer arrived right on time.

"This is Glen," said Billy. "Glen, this is John."

With that, Billy got up and left the room. Larry had to admire the way his longtime customer and friend did business.

Larry explained what he needed. He wanted copies made of his birth certificate from Massachusetts and of his own and Marcia's baptismal certificates with all the spaces left blank. Within a week he had a stack of blanks about a foot high. Next, Larry sent away to book collectors' clubs for personalized embossers that had an official-looking scales-of-justice design at the center. One embosser read, "From the

Personal Library of Larry Lavin." He ordered other embossers labeled "Library of the Sacred Heart Church" or "Le Haverhill Company" —he used the "Le" because the number of letters left "Haverhill" centered perfectly over the top. When he got the embossers, he altered them with his dental drills, filing away what he didn't want. Then, by combining the altered embossers, he could stamp his birth certificate with an official-looking seal that had "Haverhill" on top and the justice scales in the center. He performed similar effects with stamps on the baptismal certificates.

With these tools he was able to forge dozens of fake documents under names he picked from the phone book or made up or concocted by combining names of friends from his past. One of his false characters was named Sidoli, after his old friend from Exeter, whom Larry hadn't seen or spoken to in years. Another incorporated the name Rault, another Exeter friend. One of the names he made up, just because he liked the sound of it, was Brian O'Neil. Using techniques he picked up from *New I.D. in America*, Larry obtained social security cards for many of these identities.

He also began accumulating cash. He knew that the government was watching his bank accounts and investments, so he didn't dare withdraw large amounts from them, but Larry had many customers who owed him money. He made strenuous efforts to collect, with some success, and added to that growing sum occasional six-figure payments from Frannie Burns.

Larry had not made up his mind to flee, but he wanted to be prepared to move quickly if all hell broke loose. Down deep, Larry still hoped it wouldn't come to that. Running would mean giving up his dental practice and his beloved house on Timber Lane, and it would mean losing three-quarters of his hard-earned fortune. He figured the most cash he would be able to accumulate over the next few months was about two million. He would have to walk away from almost twice that much.

Despite the setbacks in early 1984, Larry still had reason to hope. Bruce hadn't told the government anything, as far as he could tell. Larry Uhr had not cooperated with the FBI as he originally said he would. Efforts to use Joe Powell and Mark Strong, a former Arena employee, against Larry had backfired—both had warned him privately. Everyone else contacted by Chuck Reed and Sid Perry and the Treasury agents had refused to talk. Larry knew they all had the best incentive in the world—protecting their own hides. And although he had learned, from Wayne Heinauer, that the FBI had recorded their August conversation, to his way of thinking, the whole thing had more to do with Frannie Burns than with him. It was consistent with the story he had given his lawyer, that he had been in the business but had gotten out.

So as spring approached, his biggest fear was that one of the minor players on the periphery, a small customer, say, or someone like Kim Norimatsu, for instance, might panic and offer to bare their soul (and his hide) in return for total immunity. So in addition to days that were already more than filled with dentistry, his multifarious investments, collecting money, and conferring with Frannie, Larry became more and more preoccupied with damage control.

One of the minor characters who worried Larry during this period was Michael Schade, a Drexel undergraduate who had met Bruce and gotten involved in the business during 1983. Larry had never met the kid. His apartment had been raided and he had been arrested on the same day Bruce had been taken in.

Early in April, soon after returning from the trip to Aruba, Larry made plans to meet with the red-haired, fair-skinned, nervous undergraduate. He just wanted to feel the kid out, find out how scared he was, reassure him and encourage him to hang tough.

Larry believed that the worst things they had on Schade were a few phone numbers and conversations he had had with Steve and June Rasner. Steve was a dentist in Cherry Hill who had graduated the year before Larry from Penn Dental School. He and his wife, June, had been dealing marijuana and cocaine and had used Michael for pickups and deliveries. Larry's idea was to get Michael together with the Rasners so that they could establish a consistent alibi to explain their relationship.

What Larry didn't know was that Michael Schade had already seen where his best interests lay. What Chuck Reed and Sid Perry had to say made a lot of sense. For a college sophomore, Michael was in a lot of trouble. It might not have been the kind of trouble Larry Lavin faced, but it was enough to daunt a nineteen-year-old kid. On the other hand, the FBI at that moment placed a very high premium on cooperation in the case they were preparing against the Lavin cocaine empire. They were offering him nothing less than what looked like a second chance on his whole life.

So there was a tap on Michael's phone April 12 when Larry called to arrange the meeting with the Rasners. Michael had never gotten a call from Larry before.

"Hello?" said Michael.

"How you doing?"

"Pretty good."

"What a web we weave," said Larry.

"Oh, man, I know."

"Anyways, obviously I want to put you and Steve together."

Michael was intimidated by Larry. He knew of him only as "the big boss." Bruce and Suzanne and others he had dealt with all liked Larry and held him almost in awe. Now to have Larry suddenly so interested in him was a little daunting. They discussed setting up a time for the meeting with the Rasners. Larry offered to come down and pick Michael up and drive him over to Cherry Hill.

". . . Steve wanted to get together in case they bring you people in," Larry explained. "If they ever give you immunity, you guys can say exactly the same story."

"Right."

"You know? Something about these numbers were mentioned."

"Right."

"And he wants to try and remember exactly what, what you both think was said."

"Right."

"And he can relate it all to, um, repayment of debt or something."

"Uh-huh."

"So what do you think?"

"Um, yeah, I guess so," said Michael. He was so nervous, knowing the conversation was being recorded, that he was trying to say as little as possible.

"My biggest worry is whether they had you on other tapes that same month," said Larry.

"Uh-huh."

"I'll talk to you more about that. But I think they had his phone tapped for the month of January."

Larry speculated about other conversations that might have been recorded between Michael and others. They agreed to meet the next morning.

Larry arrived promptly. Reed and Perry had considered putting a wire on Michael, but knowing of Larry's penchant for electronic gadgets, they feared he might have his car wired to detect it. They settled on a plan to just debrief Michael in detail after the meeting. They watched as Larry picked up the kid, and then followed from a discreet distance as they drove across Philadelphia to the Ben Franklin Bridge and into New Jersey.

In the car, Larry explained that they were going to meet the Rasners at a Cherry Hill restaurant named Olga's.

"I'm spending a lot of time lately driving around and meeting people, helping them to keep their stories straight," said Larry. He told Michael all about Glen Fuller, who was still out on bail awaiting disposition of the charges against him from 1980. Larry liked to use Glen as an example of what good legal talent could do for his friends in trouble. Here was a guy who got nabbed with multi-kilos in the trunk of his car, fought with the state cops at the arrest, and was still, more than three years later, a free man. The implication was that Michael had little to worry about.

"I can't believe Chuck Reed searched Bruce's house when he did," said Larry. "If they had been watching him for a year, why wouldn't he have gone in when he had just gotten a shipment? Bruce gets, like, ten to fourteen keys at a time, and Reed hits him when the place is empty. I don't get it." Larry laughed—one more anecdote for the growing legend of Chuck Reed.

Michael told Larry that he had enrolled in a drug clinic to kick his cocaine habit.

"I'm trying to get my head on straight," he said.

"My biggest worry is that Reed is going to get to Kim," said Larry. "She knows everything and everybody. . . . Did they ask you about Brian Riley?"

"Yeah."

"What did they say?"

"They knew about his getting stopped at the airport in Boston with all that money. They asked me if I knew anything about that."

"Jeez. Bruce didn't tell me that. When I talked to Brian I told him I thought they didn't know anything about him. I'll have to get ahold of him again. He calls his mother, like, every week. So I can get a message to him through her."

Then Larry entertained Michael with stories about how he had gotten involved in dealing drugs. Larry wanted Michael to like him, so he was trying to pour on the charm. His way of being charming was to talk someone's head off. He told him all about his old pot-dealing days at Penn, college man to college man, and trotted out all his favorite old stories. Just as Larry's father had a habit of telling and retelling his war stories, Larry had his well-polished anecdotes from college days. He had told the stories so often, always portraying himself as the reckless, fun-loving hero who got away in the end, that he frequently lapsed comically into the third person, as if he were talking about someone else. If you were in the right mood, Larry's storytelling was charming and funny. To Michael, who was just eager to get this all over with, Larry sounded like an awful braggart.

Then Larry told Michael about the arson of the King Arena. He explained that he had had nothing to do with it, that it had been Mark Stewart's idea.

"That's how this all started," he said. "I should have gotten out of all this then. But, hindsight is twenty-twenty! For some reason, I'm the one Chuck Reed really wants to get."

They talked about Bruce Taylor. Michael said that it was a shame that he was dying of leukemia, and was startled when Larry laughed.

"That's bullshit," Larry explained. "Did you fall for that? It's so stupid. Bruce tells people that because he figures if he ever splits with money from the business, nobody will come looking for him." Larry just shook his head.

Michael was shocked. He told Larry he felt foolish for believing Bruce all this time.

Larry told Michael all about the taped conversation between him and Wayne Heinauer.

"It's a very incriminating call," said Larry. "That's the worst thing they have on me."

He advised Michael not to cooperate with the FBI.

"Take the Fifth, because once a person starts talking, they have to keep on talking," he said. "If you take the Fifth, then they have to prove everything against you. In your case, they don't have very much. Make sure the lawyer your father is getting you is a criminal lawyer. If he's not, call me and I'll hook you up with Donald Goldberg. He's my lawyer. He could help you find somone who really knows what to do."

When they got to Olga's, Steve and June Rasner weren't there. Larry waited for a while, then called Steve's dental office and left a message for him to call back. He and Michael played video games while they waited for the call.

Rasner explained to Larry that he and his wife had seen someone with a zoom lens on a camera parked across the street when they got to Olga's, so they left.

Larry was irritated. "You're hallucinating now," he told Rasner. Steve said he didn't want to talk on the phone at Olga's, and asked Larry to go to a pay phone across the street. "You guys are paranoid," said Larry.

He hung up and they headed across the street to the pay phone. "Both of them are a bundle of nerves," Larry told Michael. "I hope they can keep their heads, or else we'll all be in a lot of trouble."

An FBI photographer captured the frown on Larry's face as he spoke that line.

Summer brought few new revelations. From what he could remember of the conversation with Wayne Heinauer, Larry had pretty much convinced himself that he didn't have that much to worry about. After all, he had mostly talked about Frannie! It just supported his claim to have gotten out of the business a long time ago. They certainly couldn't know anything about Frannie's recent payments to him. They had a lot of healthy (and correct) suspicions, but little proof. Everyone was being interviewed; no one was talking. That's how it looked from where Larry sat.

In spring, the U.S. attorney's office had offered a deal that had shocked Larry. Through Don Goldberg they explained that if Larry would assist their investigation of Frannie, then he might expect to get only a ten- to twelve-year sentence.

Ten to twelve years!

How stupid did they think he was? Larry had never known anyone to be sent away for more than ten years for selling marijuana or cocaine. And he had no prior offenses! His lawyer dismissed the government's offer as a sucker's deal. To Goldberg, who knew little of the magnitude of Larry's cocaine dealing and had been lied to about when it had ended, it sounded as if the feds were eager to enlist his client's aid, but they didn't seem willing to offer anything in return for it. Neither lawyer nor client had ever entertained the notion that Larry would be going away to jail for anything more than two years at most.

So Larry rejected the deal instantly. Whom were they trying to kid?

Larry went white-water rafting out in central Pennsylvania in May, and he and Marcia entertained at home around the pool several times over the summer. Marcia began noticing that fewer and fewer of Larry's friends were accepting their invitations to drop by the house and use the pool. Once, when his old undergraduate pot-dealing partner Andy Mainardi had visited, Andy came in someone else's car and insisted on getting out way down the block and walking up through backyards to the house. Marcia was insulted.

She sensed approaching doom, but she had grown used to that over the last two years. Christopher was a happy energetic two-year-old, absolutely smitten with his daddy, who seemed to have little time for him. Marcia dressed him in colorful outfits of matching shirts and overalls and snapped pictures of him at play with his porchful of toy trains and houses and blocks. Chris was especially fascinated with cars. He liked to sit on Larry's lap and pretend to steer. He paddled around the house in a little orange-and-yellow trolley car. Words came slowly to Chris. At two he was an unusually silent child. He understood a lot but seemed reluctant to speak. Marcia joked that he certainly didn't take after his father.

In late August, she learned she was pregnant again.

Larry awakened late on Tuesday, September 11. He had office hours that day, starting at 11:00 a.m., and he had several things to get done before then. The night before he had remembered some papers from his loans to Stan Nelson and Joe Powell that were tucked away in his desk. He knew he ought to throw them away. And there was one remaining embosser, one that he had altered to look like the official seal of the Church of the Sacred Heart, that should not just be lying around.

He was afraid to just throw these items in the garbage. For all he knew, the FBI might be going through his garbage. So Larry put the papers and the embosser in his briefcase.

Marcia had already left with Chris. Larry dressed in a white Lacoste sportshirt, yellow poplin slacks, and a pair of topsiders with no socks, ate a quick bowl of cereal with a glass of orange juice, and then took off in his big silver car for work. It was a gray, humid morning. Several times along the way Larry thought about pulling off into a shopping center or parking lot to throw away the papers and embosser in his briefcase, but the momentum of the car, the music on the radio—these were some of Larry's most enjoyable moments. Sometimes he just turned up the stereo and cruised. Other times he played games. On Roosevelt Boulevard the lights were synchronized, and Larry would race people, running red lights if he had to, always winning. He had been stopped about six times for speeding along this route—the sixty- to eighty-five-dollar fines were nothing. Larry considered these run-ins with traffic cops to be trifles. He made a point of donating generously to every law enforcement association he could find, plastering decals on the back window of his car and filling his wallet with cards from the Fraternal Order of Police, benevolent associations, sheriff cards, etc. When he lost his Pennsylvania license, he used one from Massachusetts. Larry considered himself to be a superior driver to most others on the road, owing to his summer employment as a cab driver in 1975, and he considered his car to be indestructible. So he felt entitled to drive as he pleased, and once he got going, he was loath to stop. He would use the dumpster in the parking lot of the shopping center across the street from his practice.

So instead of turning into the small driveway beside the dental office building, Larry proceeded on down Frankford Avenue another hundred yards, turned into the shopping center parking lot, and then doubled back across the lot in the direction of his office. He got out of the car and tossed the embosser and papers into the dumpster, then got back in to drive out of the lot and back down to the office.

But as Larry turned around in the lot and headed back toward the entrance he was suddenly surrounded by cars. Men began emptying from them, men with guns. They were pointing pistols at him! The man just outside his car window was leveling a handgun at him, shouting, "FBI! Put your hands up! Get out of the car!"

Larry jerked his hands up. But then he realized he couldn't just get out of the car because one foot was on the clutch and the other was on the brake. The car was in first gear. There were agents in front of the car who would be hit if he released the clutch. When he reached down with his right hand to put the gearshift in neutral, the man outside his window screamed, "Keep your hands up! Get out of the car!"

They were at an impasse. Larry just sat there looking harassed. One of the agents reached to open the passenger side door, but it was locked. When Larry started to reach down to release the automatic door lock, the agent outside his window screamed again. Finally, they caught on. Larry flipped the switch to unlock the door and the agent climbed in the passenger seat, shifted the car into neutral, and shut off the engine.

Larry climbed out, his hands over his head. He felt foolish. What was all this? The FBI had informed him he was under investigation more than a year and a half ago. He knew he was going to be indicted. Don Goldberg had told him it was customary in cases like his to just notify the person charged when the indictment came down. He had fully expected to be asked to come down to the courthouse and turn himself in. So why the big show? Larry was indignant, but what could he do?

One of the agents wheeled him against the side of the car and frisked him for weapons. Out of the corner of his eye he saw two other agents trot over to the dumpster. His heart sank. How could he have been so stupid? There had been at least six places along the way that morning where he could have stopped to safely dispose of those papers. The amounts involved in the loans to Stan Nelson and Joe Powell would just reveal more of his hidden assets. And the embosser! If they saw that, maybe they would catch on to his plans to flee! He wouldn't be able to get out on bail! A female agent put handcuffs on him.

"I would have turned myself in," protested Larry. No one responded.

Larry looked across at the front door of his dental office.

"Could you send somone over to the practice and tell them that I'm not going to be there?" he asked.

The agent answered, joking, "Yeah, I'll just go over and stand on that porch over there and yell you're the largest cocaine dealer in Philadelphia; they'll just love that."

"You have me, but I don't think you have to take it out on the patients," said Larry. "There's no reason why they have to sit there all day waiting for me, or for people to have to wonder what the heck's going on."

"We'll take care of it," said another agent.

They directed Larry into one of their cars. From the backseat he offered the driver directions back down to Center City and the courthouse. His hands began to feel numb.

"Could you loosen these handcuffs?" he asked the agent seated next to him.

"You aren't going to try any funny business?" the agent asked.

"What do you think I'm going to do?"

The agent took off the cuffs and loosened them, then put them back on Larry's wrists.

The car entered the great redbrick, boxlike federal courthouse on the western side, on Sixth Street. They drove down a sloping driveway, stopped as a wide steel garage door cranked open, and then entered an underground garage. Larry was led to an elevator and escorted into a basement room where he was to be fingerprinted and photographed. Larry had decided to keep his mouth shut.

"Are you Larry Lavin?" asked one of the arresting agents.

"I'm sorry, I'm not answering any questions until I speak to my lawyer," said Larry.

This angered the arresting agents, but Larry was just trying to play it as carefully as he could. He had gone down to the courthouse once before with his lawyer for fingerprinting and a mug shot. When Chuck Reed asked for Larry's social security number, Larry had answered, but then Goldberg had said:

"I hope you don't have many more of these questions because my client is not answering any more of them."

So even though the agents and clerks grew irritated, Larry remained silent.

An agent asked for his date of birth before snapping his photograph, and Larry answered, "Can I make a phone call?"

While the agents called upstairs to get Larry's birthdate for the placard he would hold for the mug shot, they allowed him to use the phone. He left word at Don Goldberg's office that he had been arrested. Then he phoned Marcia.

After spending the morning with Chris at a toddlers' center near home, Marcia had stopped off with him for an early lunch at McDonald's. They pulled in the curved driveway off Timber Lane just after noon. Marcia got out of her Volvo to open the garage door, and when she did she heard the phone ringing.

She ran in to answer it.

"How you doin'?" said Larry sadly.

"What's wrong?" asked Marcia.

"I was arrested today."

"Are you all right?"

"Yes. I'm all right."

"Where are you?"

"I'm downtown. The federal courthouse. I want you to stay home and wait for Don Goldberg to call and tell you what to do about bail."

"Okay."

"Go and find the deed to the house. We'll probably need every penny."

"Okay. I'll be ready," said Marcia. "Do you think they're going to let you out?"

"Yeah. I think so."

"Okay. I'll be here."

"I love you, Marcia."

"I love you, too, Larry."

Marcia hung up the phone and stood silently for a moment in the kitchen. It had finally happened. Then she realized she had left Chris in the car.

Marcia ran out through the garage. Chris was playing in the driveway. The car doors were locked. Marcia always drove with the car doors locked, and the driver's side door had locked when Chris closed it. Her keys were in the ignition.

She retrieved Chris and phoned her mother.

"Mom, Larry was arrested today," she said.

"What for?" asked Agnes.

"What do you think for?" said Marcia. She and Larry had long ago told her mother about his pending "tax troubles."

"I'm going to need you to stay here so I can go down and get him. I need you to watch Chris."

After she hung up the phone, Marcia scooped up Chris, changed his diaper, and put him down for a nap. Then she walked back out to the sun porch and sank into one of the folding chairs. Tonight everyone would know that Larry's problems weren't just "tax troubles." She ran her fingers over her womb, where their second child was just beginning to take form. This would be the last time she would sit out on the porch with her son like a normal person.

After calling Marcia, Larry was posed by the agents for his mug shots. He held a small placard with white plastic letters stuck in rows, reading:

FBI PHILADELPHIA

09 11 84

LAWRENCE W LAVIN

PH 87D-29408

DOB 3 14 55

SSAN

The look on Larry's face expressed it all. His lips were pressed together tightly and his eyes looked beleaguered. Overall Larry looked bored. His thick black hair covered the tops of his ears and swept down evenly across his forehead down to his eyebrows. With his open-collared sportshirt and wholesome collegiate appearance, Larry looked like someone who had opened the wrong door and wandered in somewhere he didn't belong.

After posing for the picture, Larry was allowed to phone his dental practice. Some of the patients had sat around for an hour waiting for him to arrive.

"Tell them I'm sorry," Larry told his receptionist. "Just tell the patients that I won't be in."

After that call Larry was taken down the elevator to the holding cells, where he was strip-searched, given a jumpsuit, and left in a small room with a table and chair.

He sat alone for a few minutes. Then the door opened and a casually dressed man of about medium height with short brown hair walked in.

"Hi, Larry. How are you doing?" he asked in a gentle Southern accent. "I'm Sid Perry. You know me, I'm the one you always say such nice things about."

Larry had never met Sid. He smiled and tried to be pleasant. Sid just asked a few questions about the Rolex watch they had seized along with Larry's wallet and briefcase. The watch had been a wedding present from Paul Mikuta and had an inscription on the back that Sid wanted Larry to explain. Larry did. Then Sid left. Larry was surprised Sid hadn't asked about the embosser.

Next, he was escorted into a room with, of all people, Frannie Burns! He tried not to act surprised. The room looked like a classroom. There were rows of chairs with writing surfaces attached to the arms. One wall had a blackboard and against the other wall was a long dark window. Larry guessed that people behind the window could look at him but that he couldn't see out the other way. Frannie was seated at one of the desks, looking straight ahead. They were left alone in the room together, each pretending that he didn't know the other. They assumed they were being taped or filmed. Every ten minutes or so agents came into the room to ask Frannie questions, then left again. Finally, both Larry and Frannie were taken down to share a holding cell in the basement.

On their way down to the cell, Frannie's lawyer, David Shapiro, met them in the hall.

"What's my bail going to be?" Frannie asked.

"Probably about half a million," said Shapiro.

"Dave, do you know what mine is going to be?" Larry asked.

"I'm pretty sure it's going to be two million or in excess of that," Shapiro said sharply. Not just the amount he cited, but the way the lawyer addressed him, startled Larry. It was as though he were suggesting that Larry was, by far, the principal figure. Larry had always considered Frannie to be doing the bigger business. Plus, Frannie had been arrested several times before, once for firebombing a Dairy Queen franchise. Larry was a dentist, for Chrissakes! He was amazed that his bail would be bigger than Frannie's.

Feeling somewhat more secure locked in the cell, Larry asked Frannie what he knew, whispering in his ear.

There was a third person in the cell, a stranger.

"He's a plant," advised Frannie.

So they quickly made plans for where and when to meet when they got out.

Within minutes after Larry was locked in the cell, Don Goldberg arrived.

"I've had a quick talk with the U.S. attorney," he said. "They're going to be asking a quarter of a million dollars."

Larry was immensely relieved. To gain release, he would only need Marcia to bring one-tenth of that to the courthouse.

"I think I can get it down," said Goldberg. "From you I need a quick list of liquid assets, what you can get your hands on right away."

Larry could have kissed the guy. Goldberg seemed determined to get Larry out as soon as possible. He drew up a list of money in local bank accounts, and the lawyer left.

Larry and Frannie waited in the cell for less than an hour before being escorted to the elevator and upstairs. They were seated in a room adjacent to a courtroom. Larry was surprised to see a crowd of reporters and sketch artists waiting. He sat down in the first of four rows of folding chairs. A court clerk came in and handed him a copy of his indictment and a thick stack of papers including the wiretap authorization and transcripts of taped telephone conversations— including the one last August with Wayne. Larry set the thick document down on the floor between his feet, leaned forward, and began paging through it with fascination and mounting alarm.

One by one, the other people arrested that day were led into the same waiting room. It was a mixed bag. Joining Larry and Frannie were Sandy Freas, Frannie's teenage girlfriend, two minor customers whom Larry had never met, and Kim Norimatsu. Also named in the indictment were Bruce and Suzanne, who were vacationing in New England, Steve and June Rasner, Mark Taplar, and three other small customers. Larry was confused. There was no logic to the indictments. How had the government hit upon this group of people, of whom only he, Frannie, Bruce, Suzanne, and Mark Taplar were central to the business—and each at separate times and places? Larry and Frannie were back to pretending they didn't know each other. No one in the room exchanged greetings as they entered, and each sat apart from the others. Larry exchanged a quick, silent look with Mark Taplar and then went back to his reading. His heart sank when Kim was led in, wearing blue jeans and sandals with her thick, curly hair pulled back into a long ponytail—why would they want Kim? If they were arresting her, they were arresting everybody.

"Hi, Larry," said Kim cheerfully.

"Not now, not now," Larry said softly, still looking down at the papers between his feet.

Kim took the chair behind Larry and kicked the leg of his chair.

"Larry, what are you doing?"

"Kimmie, not now," said Larry.

"Why are you pretending you don't know me?"

Larry looked up at her wearily. "We can't talk now."

"Do you know where Bruce and Suzanne are?"

"Not now," in a tone that finally shut Kim up.

Larry was increasingly mystified and alarmed by the document between his feet. He was no expert on legalese, but as he saw it, in addition to his indictment for conspiracy to distribute cocaine, and for using the telephone to further that conspiracy, he was being indicted under Title 21, U.S. Code Section 848, something referred to in the U.S. attorney's press release as the "kingpin statute." Larry saw that he was being named as the "kingpin" of the conspiracy, and that the punishment under that count of his indictment was not something on the order of ten to fifteen years, but a *minimum* of ten years and a maximum of *life!*

LIFE!

Larry had never even heard of the kingpin statute! As he read it over, he guessed that it was something tailored for a Mafia don, not for a kid three years out of dental school who dealt cocaine on the side!

LIFE!

Sweat formed down the furrow of his spine. Larry felt slightly sick to his stomach.

A marshal entered the waiting room and instructed the group to enter the courtroom. They filed in and took seats in the soft swivel chairs of the jury box. Larry sat next to Frannie.

"Have you ever heard of Section Eight Forty-eight?" he whispered.

Frannie just shook his head. When Larry turned toward the crowd in the benches at the rear of the courtroom, the sketch artists stared up at him dispassionately and started drawing. Frannie was trying to keep himself turned toward the wall. Larry felt peculiar, as if he were a character in a dream. Things seemed out of synch. The reporters and artists and federal courthouse workers who had gathered to observe this hearing—Larry was amazed by how many there were—were mostly his age, in their twenties or early thirties. They all seemed *just like him.* Yet Larry felt on display, as though he were something basically different from the crowd. It was an especially odd feeling for someone so used to being accepted, liked, admired, so much at the center of his youthful society. To be suddenly shunned, put on display and scrutinized so coldly, like a freak—it didn't seem quite right. It was as though the rest of the world were suddenly out of step . . . what was this? Didn't all these people smoke dope and snort coke at their parties? Larry could understand the way the cops treated him—heavy-handed, square-headed agents of the state, one of "Them"—but these people in the audience craning their necks, jotting notes, and frantically sketching, they didn't belong to "Them." They belonged to "Us." These were people *just like him.*

Everyone stood up when the man with the black robe entered the courtroom. The court crier introduced him as "the Honorable Tullio G. Leomporra"; he was not a judge but a U.S. magistrate. Sandy and Kim were let off with minimal bail and on their own recognizance. Larry found the mechanics of the hearing soothing and interesting. He alternately listened and continued reading through the indictment. Skimming over his conversation with Wayne Heinauer, Larry winced at how freely he had talked about Frannie. He could see that the recording was much more damaging than he had thought. Bruce Taylor was all over the summary of wiretap evidence. Didn't that son-of-a-bitch *ever* use a pay phone?

Chuck Reed took the stand to testify in favor of the prosecutor's request for a $500,000 bail for Frannie. Larry listened with surprise and wonder as the FBI agent did a number on Frannie. In the months since he had sold out to Frannie, Larry had learned that Burns was capable of violence—but could this be the same person? Chuck described Frannie as a vicious career criminal who was implicated in a firebombing, who had set aside two million dollars to bribe witnesses, and who had threatened to have anyone who testified against him killed.

When Shapiro got up to speak on Frannie's behalf, he began to roam the courtroom as he spoke. The magistrate abruptly told him to sit down.

Bail for Frannie was set at $250,000.

Then it was Larry's turn. He could hardly believe his ears when the prosecutor started in on him, describing his cocaine business as "the largest cocaine-distribution enterprise in the history of the Philadelphia area." They placed volume at sixty to eighty kilos per month—Larry recognized this estimate to be the volume he had quoted to Wayne Heinauer on the phone in August, when he was doing the sales job for Frannie. That volume represented Larry's guess of how much Frannie was doing combined with his own business, which he believed was the smaller of the two. His own business was closer to thirty kilos per month. The way the business was being described, it was made to sound as if Frannie worked for him, and that all the money from sales at the hypothetical volume of sixty to eighty kilos per month was being passed up to him. The prosecutor said the business generated five million per month. Larry's estimate of his net worth, after selling pot and cocaine for almost ten years, was just under six million.

Larry wanted to jump up several times to explain, but he knew he had to just sit there and take it. The prosecutor urged a bail of $250,000. At last Don Goldberg got up. Speaking with his authoritative, reassuring bass tones, Larry's lawyer argued simply and forcefully. His client was a professional. He had a wife and a child. He had never been arrested before and he had known he was under investigation for nearly two years. Larry Lavin hardly posed a threat to potential witnesses and had demonstrated his willingness to stay and face charges.

The magistrate set Larry's bail at $150,000. Larry grinned with relief.

Before going back to the holding cell, the U.S. marshals let Larry use a phone to call Marcia.

"If I'm going to get out today, you'll have to move fast," said Larry. "We need a cashier's check for fifteen thousand."

Larry instructed Marcia which account at the Provident Bank to withdraw the funds from, and begged her to hurry.

Marcia called her mother, and stood in the driveway outside until Agnes pulled in.

"Give me the keys," she said, as her mother stepped out of the car.

"Why can't you use your car?"

"Because Chris locked the keys inside."

Marcia sped to the Provident, arriving at 2:55 p.m., five minutes before closing time. She told the teller she wanted a check for fifteen thousand dollars. Marcia had never withdrawn that much money from a bank in her life. She expected the teller to ask her why. But instead the woman just smiled and asked for an account number.

Marcia drove home with the check. Her mother was still standing outside in the driveway when she got back.

"What's going to happen?" Agnes asked.

"Mom, I don't know," said Marcia. She explained that she had to go down into Philadelphia to get Larry. She didn't know how long it would take.

Marcia was shaking with fear and excitement. She stopped to get gas. All the way into the city her mind raced. Where exactly was Race Street and Fifth? What was the best way to get there? She had to be careful not to get in an accident, but she had to hurry . . . hurry.

She found the federal building easily and parked her mother's car two blocks away, at Fourth and Market streets. Walking briskly down the sidewalk, back toward the courthouse, the weirdness of the moment finally hit her. The gray morning sky had cleared into a bright blue late-summer afternoon. Across the street was the Liberty Bell pavilion and beyond that Independence Hall. A pretzel vendor on the corner offered her his wares. Marcia thought, *I'm on my way in to bail out my husband; should I buy a soft pretzel?* It was a strange adventure. Instead of feeling sad or angry, she felt almost amused, as though she were watching herself from outside.

Inside the enormous first-floor lobby, a cool, dark, echoing chamber, Marcia set her car keys in a little basket and strode through the metal detector.

"Could you tell me where the U.S. marshal's office is?" she asked.

She was directed up an escalator off to the side.

Inside the marshal's office, Marcia was directed to a clerk who took her check. Very quickly, Larry appeared behind a thick window. He was wearing handcuffs, which startled Marcia. A door opened and Larry was led out. He looked so sheepish and vulnerable. She had never seen him look like that.

"Thanks for getting here so fast," he said.

Larry and Marcia signed papers guaranteeing the full $150,000 bond against their house. The handcuffs were taken off, and the clerk said, "Okay, you can go now."

Larry didn't smile.

He said, "Let's just get the hell out of here."

E L E V E N

Time for a Vacation

"**W**here did you park the car?" asked Larry.

"A few blocks from here," said Marcia. She had a difficult time keeping up with his long strides as they exited the courthouse. "I've got my mother's car. Chris locked the keys in mine. Do you want me to drive?"

"No. I want to drive."

They walked down one long block in silence.

"You would think I was a murderer or something!" Larry exclaimed.

They drove directly over to Donald Goldberg's office across the street from City Hall. Larry was worried that the agents had found the embosser that he had thrown away that morning. He was so relieved to be out of that courthouse.

"I'm in deep, deep trouble," he told Marcia, but didn't bother to explain.

"Well, Larry, we knew this was coming for a long time," she said, trying to soothe him.

"But I didn't know," Larry said sharply. "It's much worse than I ever thought. You see, there's five counts to the indictment. One of the counts is under something called Section Eight Forty-eight. You can get life under that one! I want to know why the hell I was indicted under that and Frannie wasn't."

"Maybe it won't be that bad," said Marcia. Their roles were reversed; it was usually Larry telling Marcia things weren't going to be as bad as she feared.

"No," said Larry. "They've got me. You should read the tapes."

Marcia sat in the waiting room while Larry conferred with Goldberg.

Larry sat down opposite the lawyer's cluttered desk. The north wall of the office, to Larry's left, was one long window looking down on the ornate gray stone columns of City Hall.

Goldberg's first words after greeting Larry and expressing satisfaction at his release were, "I think Tom Bergstrom would be good for this case." He explained that his own specialty was in tax matters, and that Larry would need someone with recent experiences in cases like his own. Bergstrom was a former assistant U.S. attorney recently gone into private practice. He would have the kind of time and expertise Larry would need for preparing his defense.

It was unsettling. Larry was impressed with what Goldberg had done for him that day. He was grateful. Now to be told that Goldberg was not going to represent him further was alarming.

"I thought you were done dealing," the lawyer said pointedly.

Larry tried to explain that he really had stopped dealing, at least very soon after having consulted with Goldberg for the first time in late 1982. He had just been trying to collect money, to make back some of the millions he had lost in investments with Mark Stewart and Joe Powell.

"It was stupid," said Larry. "You're right. What can I say?"

"And I told you to stay off the phones," Goldberg said.

They got home shortly after five. The air had gotten suddenly cooler.

Marcia's mother asked, "Are you all right, son?"

"Yeah," said Larry, trying to smile.

"Do you want me to stay or go?" Agnes asked her daughter.

"I think you better go," said Marcia. "I'll call you."

Larry pulled down all the shades in the house, moving from room to room.

"I don't want people looking in," he said.

Marcia called the AAA to help her get the keys out of the car. While she was out in the driveway she saw the woman next door in her driveway. Neither woman said anything. When the keys were freed, she thanked the AAA man and walked back into the kitchen to start dinner.

Inside, Larry had on the Channel 6 news. The story of his arrest, complete with the mug shot taken earlier that day, was the lead news item.

"Larry, why in the world would you want to listen to that?" called Marcia from the kitchen.

He didn't answer. Marcia walked in to watch for a moment.

"That's the most important thing that happened in this city today?" asked Marcia.

Larry listened silently in his leather armchair, flipping channels to catch portions of the item on other stations. When the part dealing with his arrest was over, he turned off the TV and walked into the kitchen. He stood quietly for a moment, watching Marcia at work but with a distant look in his eyes.

"We may be leaving within six weeks," he said.

Bruce and Suzanne Taylor were in a cabin in New England the day of Larry's arrest. They learned of their indictment by phone. Bruce, who was out on bail, had left the cabin number with his lawyer's office.

They were advised to hustle home. If they were arrested in New Hampshire, it might take a while before extradition was completed. They would spend days, if not longer, being shuttled from prison to prison on their way back to Philadelphia for arraignment.

So they gathered up their things, half expecting swarms of armed agents to come storming over the quiet autumn hills, and drove straight home as fast as they could. They turned themselves in the next day, and both were again released on bail.

Tom Bergstrom looked like the kind of man you would want on your side of a goal-line stand. He stood well over six feet and had the shoulders and back of an immovable object. Bergstrom played basketball in college, served in the U.S. Marines, and filled his office with posters, drawings, busts, and statuettes of John Wayne. There was a hint of the Duke's manner in his muscular ease and lack of pretension. In his early forties, Bergstrom might have had flecks of gray in his hair, but it was cut too short to tell for sure.

Don Goldberg had called on the day of Larry's arrest and briefed him on the case. Larry had agreed to pay Tom a twenty-five-thousand-dollar fee up front. The big lawyer met Larry for the first time in Goldberg's office the next day.

What Bergstrom saw surprised him. While he had not expected to meet a bum—Larry had made a lot of money, after all—he had expected someone a little more gold-trimmed and high-gloss. Larry looked as if he had stepped off the cover of an advertising brochure for an Ivy League school. He was wearing a gray crewneck sweater over a white shirt with a button-down collar, brown corduroy pants, and a pair of topsider shoes. He looked and comported himself like everyone's idea of a perfect son: He was outgoing and friendly in a very pleasant way; he was candid, humorous, and self-deprecatory, obviously intelligent, clean-cut, and apparently genuine. Any reservations Tom had about defending the reputed cocaine king of Philadelphia eased. He liked Larry immediately. Tom's first impression coincided with Goldberg's assessment: This was a basically nice kid who had made some big mistakes—Big Mistakes. Larry was in big-league trouble. He was about to be martyred to his generation's lust for cocaine.

After chatting with Goldberg, who assured Larry and Tom that he would remain available for consultation, the lawyer and his new client strolled two blocks, past Claes Oldenburg's giant clothespin-shaped statue *The Kiss* and across busy Market Street, to Tom's office over Penn Center Plaza.

Tom went right to work. Larry answered questions seriously and candidly. He didn't seem distraught or angry, just concerned and determined to fight. Tom was able to tell him very little good news. At first glance, the evidence against him seemed overwhelming. With the 848 charge, the very best Larry could hope for would be the minimum ten-year sentence. Tom guessed that, realistically, the worst he might expect was thirty to forty years. If he got ten years, then with good time and an early parole, he would have to do seven years in prison.

"That's seven, period. You've got to do seven," said Tom.

The key to avoiding that, the lawyer explained, would be to get the U.S. attorney to drop the charge under Section 848. That would allow Larry to plead guilty to drug-trafficking charges and give the judge more flexibility at sentencing. It might be possible to whittle actual time served down to something like four years. But it would require cooperation. Larry would have to agree to testify against others in the case.

Larry said he couldn't imagine doing that. It would mean betraying virtually all of his friends and two members of his family. The only people close to Larry who *weren't* involved in drug dealing were his parents, the workers in his dental office, his older brother Justin, Marcia, and Agnes. He knew that once he started talking, he would have to keep on talking or he would lose whatever initial advantage he gained.

There was another reason not to talk. Even though he had listened with disbelief to Chuck Reed's description of Frannie, the more Larry thought about it, the more he realized elements of it might be true. Frannie was a reckless character. He had told Larry about pulling a gun on someone once, and had intimated that worse things than that had happened to people who crossed him, things that Larry would never have considered doing himself. And there was Billy Motto. Larry liked and respected Billy, but there was an aura of danger about his South Philly friend that was undeniable. Larry knew that Billy's supposed connection with the local mob was overblown; if anything was true it was the exact opposite—Billy lived in fear of arousing the attention of older, more powerful organized-crime figures. Philadelphia, after all, was in the midst of a wave of mob killings, sparked by the murder of longtime Mafia don Angelo Bruno. South Philly hoods were turning up dead nearly every week—*The Philadelphia Inquirer Sunday Magazine* had recently outlined a tour of South Philly restaurants where notorious mobsters had eaten their last meals. Billy had often told Larry that if these more murderous criminal types started to muscle in on his drug business, it would be time to get out of town and concentrate on peddling produce. Still, Larry knew other things about Billy. Once, for instance, when someone had stolen a large amount of cash from him, Billy had sought help from local mobsters and, for a fee, got his money back. Larry didn't know of anyone else who could have done that. Ever since he had known Billy, the South Philly dealer had been surrounded by armed, silent, loyal employees. On one occasion, one of Billy's men had attacked and seriously injured a man who had threatened Billy in a bar. Bruce Taylor told a story about the time Billy gave him a knife as a gift after he first started working for Larry. Billy had handed him the knife handle-first, said Bruce, and had said, ominously, "There are other ways I could give this to you." Maybe Billy had meant nothing by that, but Bruce had never forgotten it. Recently, one of Billy's closest friends and associates, Gregory Cavalieri, was found murdered in a park outside of the city. The police considered Billy a suspect. Larry knew how upset Billy was about his friend's murder—when Cavalieri was first missing, Billy had actually hired private detectives and taken out newspaper ads in an effort to find him. Larry was convinced Billy had nothing to do with it, but . . . it was just one more thing to consider.

No. Cooperating was out of the question.

The answer didn't surprise Tom. He knew few defendants turned state's witness readily, and he knew Larry's resolve would be more seriously tested in the months to come. So he outlined a few good ideas for pretrial motions dealing with suppression of evidence. There was a chance he could successfully defend against the Section 848 charge; after all, the relationship between Larry and Frannie was not as clear-cut as the government maintained. The amounts of cocaine being sold, at least so far as Larry Lavin was concerned, were in fact less than half the amount quoted in Larry's conversation with Wayne Heinauer. Evidence against Larry's involvement was overwhelming, but within the fine gradations of culpability and evidence defined by law, there was some hope, some room to maneuver.

Before Larry left that day, Tom spent some time talking to him about things in general. Larry told him how he had gotten started in the business, about what it had been like at Penn during the mid-seventies, when virtually everyone his age smoked pot, when the onus of criminality attached to dealing was little more than a joke. Larry talked about how the business had switched over to cocaine without missing a beat, and how fashionable the drug was, how popular its dealers, how profitable its sale. The one thing Tom couldn't understand was why Larry had not just stopped at some point. Why hadn't he stopped, say, after making a million dollars? Wasn't that enough to satisfy anyone? Why continue to take such risks?

Larry acknowledged how foolish it had been not to stop, in retrospect. But he tried to explain, talking about himself (as he often did to humorous effect) in the third person. He tried to define the worm in his gut that had kept him going all those years, even after making millions.

"I definitely was on the verge of quitting," he said. "If it wasn't for these losses. The hard thing to understand is how important it is for Larry all these years, he's got this sheet, and he always knows just exactly how much he's worth. I always tried to have a fair estimate of what's considered uncollectable debts and what's a realistic figure on what I'm worth. But once you reach a figure, you never want to be less than that. And then we find out, boom! we just lost five hundred thousand and I'd say to myself, 'If I can just make that back then I'll quit. Then I'll have enough.'"

"But where did this great need for money come from?" said Tom. "I don't get it."

"Tom, I saw my father work all of his life, work his ass off all of his life, and never have anything," said Larry. "I made up my mind that I was gonna have money. It's as simple as that."

Patients kept coming! Larry had almost expected his life to stop after the indictment and arrest, but on Thursday morning he drove to work in a new, leased BMW, and there were patients waiting for him when he got there.

In the year and a half he had been practicing dentistry with Ken Weidler, Larry had come to enjoy the work more than he ever imagined he would. The mechanics of dentistry, the drilling and filling, the probing of people's mouths, that didn't excite him, but the steady stream of people and problems was engrossing, even exciting. Larry found that his days at the office never went as they were scheduled. There were frequently emergencies, or unforeseen problems, so there was an art to keeping things flowing smoothly in the office. Larry was good at it. Because he had more money than most beginning dentists, he could afford the very best tools and materials for his work. He brought to his purchases of dental wares the same childlike enthusiasm he had always brought to buying pot, or coke or electronic gadgets.

At night he read up on the newest techniques, often conferring with his old classmates about what he was trying. Former classmate Chris Furlan, who had opened a practice in West Philadelphia, used Larry as a kind of *Consumer Reports*, waiting to see what materials Larry preferred after sampling a variety of, say, the latest mixtures for filling cavities that Chris could not afford to put to the test himself. Larry enjoyed running the office, dealing with "the girls," and, of course, keeping the books. He found pleasure in just doing something for people, easing their pain, fixing their bites, perfecting their smiles.

In the weeks after his indictment, Larry was grateful for the patients who kept coming, who still treated him with friendship and respect. His routine was a comfortable shelter from the storm that had engulfed his life.

Neighbors on Timber Lane kept their distance. Newspaper reporters had knocked on all the doors, even poor Mrs. Eisenhower's, the day after Larry's arrest. Most politely refused comment. Some spoke off the record, saying that they were not really surprised.

"When they moved in, they were so young," said one of the anonymous voices quoted in a story five days after Larry's arrest.

"People weren't appalled," said another.

Elicia Geisa stood in her backyard one day looking across as Marcia pushed little Christopher on the swing set in the Lavins' backyard. She felt little sympathy for Larry, but she did feel sorry for Marcia and the little boy. What was going to happen to them? She wanted to walk across her yard and talk to Marcia, to perhaps console her or befriend her, but she didn't know what to say. What did one say to the wife of the biggest drug dealer in the city on the occasion of her husband's arrest?

The man who lived next door, a chemical company executive, who was closer to Larry and Marcia than most of his neighbors, felt angry and betrayed. Like most of the homeowners on Timber Lane, he had children who were closer in age to Larry and Marcia than he was. He confronted Larry on the property line one weekend afternoon about two weeks after the arrest. They were both working in their yards.

"Larry, I don't know whether or not it's true, but if it is I want you to know that I take a very dim view of any drug-related activity whatsoever," he said. "It's terrible to get children involved in this kind of thing. I have children of my own."

Larry smiled sheepishly.

"That judge rounded me up by mistake," he said. "I got lumped in with some people who I loaned money to. I didn't know what they were doing with it. I just got some bad advice."

"Well, I hope you are innocent," the neighbor said. "But I take a very dim view of that sort of thing."

Marcia was miserable. She felt everyone was looking at her, whispering behind her back. She thought she saw something in the way a clerk at the supermarket smiled when she bought her groceries, or the way a neighbor just stood and stared and did not wave to her as she drove past on Timber Lane, or the way a teller at the bank pronounced her name when she withdrew her weekly household funds, or the way the people at the nursery treated Christopher . . . it was all out of step with the quiet normalcy she craved.

Marcia was beyond feeling angry or betrayed by Larry. She felt sorry for him. She worried about how she and Chris and the new baby, due in April, would live. Marcia was adamantly against going back to work before her children were old enough to be in school. She worried about what would happen to Larry, but along with worry and sadness Marcia could not help but feel vindicated by Larry's fall.

For years she had complained to Larry about the drug business, warned him that the risk wasn't worth it, made him promise to get out. Larry would always agree, apologize, promise, and then break his promises. Marcia had enjoyed their vacations, the house, picking out the furniture and the wallpaper, the expensive dinners out, but she never asked Larry for money and she never stopped wanting her husband to quit selling drugs and concentrate on earning a decent living with his profession. She knew their wholesome home life and growing family were due almost entirely to her. She had fought hard to pull Larry out of the orbit of his friends. Even though Marcia knew nothing of Larry's dalliances with whores, the business itself had caused serious strains in their relationship over the years. She had always stopped short of leaving him. Now he was to be taken away from her. Marcia had the spent feeling of someone who had done everything she could, and failed.

When Larry had started talking about fleeing that spring, Marcia hadn't paid much attention. She thought the idea was crazy, and, in fact, Larry himself wasn't yet serious about it. But right after his indictment and arrest, Larry started talking very seriously about running away. He mentioned places like Ireland or Paraguay or Colombia or Jamaica. What got Marcia was the way he just took it for granted that she and Chris would go with him.

So on a morning in early October, when Larry was getting ready to fly up to Massachusetts to obtain a driver's license for himself under the name of Richard Timmerman, one of his brother Rusty's friends, Marcia knew it was time to speak up.

"Maybe you should just go on your own," she said. "That way you would have less chance of getting caught."

Larry was amazed, and hurt.

"Why would I run then?" Larry asked. "What's the point? If I'm not going to be with you and Chris, there's no reason to go. That would be the worst thing about going to jail."

Marcia told Larry she had been giving it a lot of thought. She could live with her mother, who was a nurse, and they could make it. She told her husband that she would not leave the country. She would not raise her son in some foreign country. In fact, Larry had already begun to back away from fleeing America, which had been his first instinct. Down deep, the thing that Larry Lavin wanted most was an affluent, suburban American lifestyle. That was where his obsession with making more and more money led, not to some tropical backwater adventure. It was the life that had slipped away from him as a boy, and that he had played at during his years at Exeter. Besides, he would stand out more in a foreign land, and from the inquiries he made through his drug connections, Larry knew that no matter where he went he would have to pay off public officials for the rest of his life to stay free. He wanted to make a clean break, to leave criminality behind. So staying in the United States had begun to look more appealing to him anyway. It had a deliciously risky appeal, like hiding in plain view. Granting Marcia that much was easy.

But she was still unwilling.

"You have done this to yourself, Larry," she said. "It doesn't have anything to do with me or with Christopher or the new baby. They shouldn't have to suffer for what you've done. I am not going to do anything to risk my freedom. Do you realize what would happen if I ran away with you and they caught us, and I went to jail, too? Our children would be raised by strangers! I won't allow that to happen."

"What jury would convict you of a crime?" said Larry. "You're an innocent spouse. You would be doing what you're supposed to be doing as a wife. That's like a supernatural law that comes before any man-made law. If your husband tells you to do something, you do it, even though you know you're breaking the law."

"I'm not so sure it's like that, Larry," said Marcia. She told him to check with the lawyers. She would not go away with him unless she could be certain that if they ran, and got caught, she would not be culpable.

Larry sought legal advice on that question and obtained enough reassurance to satisfy his wife. What mattered most was that Marcia loved Larry. Questions posed by his legal problems were really no different from those she had faced in freshman year of college. She loved Larry in spite of his reckless ego, his obsession with making money, and his self-destructive ambition.

But Marcia never believed for a minute that all Larry's careful plans to vanish would work. She didn't argue with him about it, but deep down she saw all his running around, forging his false I.D.s, collecting cash, hatching schemes . . . all of it was pathetic. It was just a matter of time. They would drive off, move in someplace else, set up a life, and then, probably within months, there would be a knock on the door. She got a friend to put the question to several lawyers hypothetically: What would happen to the wife of a fugitive if she ran away with him and they got caught? All of the lawyers doubted that an innocent spouse would be prosecuted.

Marcia thought about little else through late October. She finally decided that she would go. She had stayed with Larry this long, she would stay with him until she could no longer. When she married Larry, that's what she had promised. So she felt comfortable. It was the right thing to do. They would eventually be caught, of that she was certain, but in the meantime the new baby and Chris, who was now two and a half years old and still years away from an age when he would have memories that would remain for the rest of his life, might get the chance to know their father. If he ran, so would she.

Larry gradually thinned possessions from the house, leaving enough furniture and odds and ends in each room so that the removals would not be obvious. Early each morning he would leave with the car trunk loaded with one or two blue footlockers, each about three feet long and two feet tall. Being careful to note whether or not he was being followed, Larry drove out to Valley Forge, to a storage lot where, using a false name, he had rented a garage. Over the next six weeks the garage filled with neat rows of footlockers.

Still, even with all this, Larry had not made up his mind to flee. Becoming a fugitive, severing ties with all his family, friends, and past, was a formidable step. He knew how difficult it would be to live happily with his family as a fugitive. The idea depressed him. He *liked* being Larry Lavin. He couldn't imagine spending the rest of his days as someone else.

"There are certain things I won't be able to do anymore," he told Ken Weidler on one of their last golf-course outings that October. "No more spending a lot of money, going to expensive French restaurants, and asking for the best wines. No more driving a hundred miles per hour. I'll have to figure out a good story to explain why I can afford things without going to work."

He told Ken that he was thinking about forging credentials and eventually practicing dentistry again.

"Larry, what do you want to do, put up a red flag?" said Ken. "It seems to me that would be the quickest way to get caught."

"You're probably right."

Ken didn't believe his friend and partner could pull it off. He joked that Larry was the only career criminal he knew: "Do you really think you can lead a normal, straight life?"

Larry took the question more seriously than Ken expected. "No, I don't think I can," said Larry. "I think I've got a little larceny in my soul. I have to do something, even if it's something little, like running a stop sign or something, just to know that I broke the law and nobody caught me. That will be the hardest thing to stop."

Later, Ken asked Marcia why she was willing to go with him.

"You may be successful for a year or so, but they're bound to catch you eventually," he said.

"Well, then we will have had that year or two," said Marcia.

Larry and Frannie got together frequently after their arrest, meeting in cars or in open spaces where they felt they could be certain they weren't being watched. Their lawyers managed to obtain on discovery stacks of FBI tape recordings, so they spent one long afternoon listening to the tapes on the cassette player in Frannie's Toyota.

They laughed about a lot of things on the tapes, especially about Bruce, who was the voice most often recorded.

"Did that guy *ever* use a pay phone?" Larry complained.

In the conversation between Larry and Suzanne, on the day the FBI had raided Bruce's house in Newtown Square, Frannie winced when he heard Larry press Suzanne to say whom she had refused to identify in the FBI photos. Larry had said, "Begin with an *F*?" Frannie just leaned forward in his seat and tapped his head against the top of the steering wheel.

"Larry, Larry, I can't believe you could be so stupid."

The FBI had been watching and listening a lot of times when Larry assumed they would not have been. There had been a meeting with Frannie in the parking lot behind the Casa Maria restaurant off Route 202 the previous fall. Frannie had needed to confer with Larry about some aspect of the transition, and Larry wanted to pick up a few pounds of cocaine for a friend. Frannie had pulled up next to Larry's car and said, "I think there's somebody watching us in that car up on the hill."

"Don't be so paranoid," Larry had scoffed.

There were pictures to show that Frannie had been right.

Likewise with the aborted meeting between Michael Schade and the Rasners. There was a picture of Larry exiting the restaurant that morning, snapped at the precise moment he was denouncing the Rasners for being "a bundle of nerves."

Larry and Frannie called each other so often over the next few weeks from pay phones that they got to know the numbers by heart. Larry would stop in a shopping center in Paoli, deposit his quarter, and beep Frannie. He would stand there conspicuously for ten minutes or more until the phone rang. Frannie would say, "You're at that row of phones in the shopping center in Paoli, aren't you?"

They met almost every night, varying their locations. At a meeting behind a local high school, where Frannie sometimes jogged his short fat frame around the cinder track, Frannie told Larry that the FBI had a diary written by his teenage girlfriend that was loaded with incriminating references to him and to Larry. At a meeting at an industrial center, Larry handed over some cash he had collected from a friend who owed Frannie. Larry had taken a substantial portion of it for himself. At a gas station they phoned Wayne Heinauer to find out more about what the feds had on him.

All the while Larry was planning to flee, Frannie was playing his own game. He saw himself as a double agent. He agreed to assist the FBI in catching his Colombian supplier in Florida and to give testimony against Larry, but then he would feed information back to Larry and other friends about what the government knew.

It was a dangerous time. Larry had two agendas: first, to learn as much as possible about the government case against him; second, to be ready to run before the door slammed shut.

Larry even threw himself a "going-away" party. He hadn't made up his mind to flee, but as his trial approached, it was becoming more and more likely. Bruce Taylor had agreed to cooperate with the government. Frannie Burns was cooperating—in a sense: No one was ever quite sure of what Frannie was doing, including the FBI.

So Larry invited Paul Mikuta and Ken, his old fraternity big brother Dan Dill, a longtime Allentown, PA. customer, his old pot-dealing partners from Penn days, stockbrokers Andy Mainardi and L.A., his good friend and customer, pilot Stu Thomas, and others to join him in Atlantic City for one last blast. He made plans to meet Billy Motto there, too. Larry had $125,000 in an account at a bank that he believed the government did not know about. He wanted to withdraw the money, then take a check down to one of the casinos and launder it. He had mastered this art over the years. The bank could not give him more than $10,000 in cash without reporting the transaction to the IRS, and the casino would not just cash the check without doing the same, so Larry had a system for getting around the requirement. He would leave a large check at the cage and collect chips. Then he would play games at the card tables, pretending to lose, all the while pocketing his chips and later passing them off to his friends, who would then cash them. At the end of the night it would appear as though he had lost the entire amount gambling, and he could walk out with most of his $125,000 converted to cash.

Larry drove down early that day and went swimming in the ocean. Afterward he sat on the beach with Billy Motto. Billy sent one of his men to get them hoagies and sat on a blanket with Larry talking about old times.

"You should stay and get it over with," said Billy. "How can you leave your mother and your father?"

Larry just laughed. Of all his friends, customers, and associates, he was convinced that the hustling street vendor from South Philly, the kid with a grade-school education whose up-from-the-streets palaver was so thick it made you laugh, the kid who hadn't wanted to sell cocaine because his people could barely afford to buy their ounces of pot, was the one who had not only made the most money but appeared to be the one most likely to escape jail for it.

Billy asked Larry how much money he had for running away.

"About a million-six," said Larry.

Billy was incredulous.

"After all those years?" he said.

"What can I say?"

They fell to talking about Frannie. Billy was furious with Frannie for cooperating with the government. No matter what kind of game Frannie claimed to be playing, to Billy's way of thinking it just wasn't done. He owed Frannie five hundred thousand, but he was refusing to pay until after seeing if his name came up at Frannie's trial. Larry had agreed to intercede about the debt on Frannie's behalf. For the last year, Larry had been in a ticklish position between Billy and Frannie. Billy was the biggest customer Frannie had inherited from Larry. So Frannie would ask Larry for advice on negotiating prices with Billy, and Billy would call asking for advice on how to deal with Frannie. Larry's main loyalties were with Billy, but the more money Frannie made, the faster Larry would collect the money he was owed. This conversation ended with Billy agreeing to turn over half the five hundred thousand to Larry for safekeeping.

For this trip Larry had called his favorite whore, Janice. She had arranged for women to join the other men in the casino, and she joined Larry and his friends for dinner. All ten dined together in the restaurant at Resorts, a final feast with their old irreplaceable friend. They took turns making toasts: To Larry . . . with whom they had

shared so much fun . . . from whom they had learned so much . . .
to whom they all owed so much . . . who was going away . . . forever.
It was an emotional night for Larry.

He was back in Atlantic City a few nights later, again with Janice,
to meet one last time with Billy and collect the money owed Burns.
He had arranged through a complex sequence of beeper relays and
phone calls to meet Billy in the lobby of a hotel, but Billy hadn't
showed up. In his hotel suite later, Janice was having a serious talk
with him. "I saw your picture in the paper and on TV," she said. "I
know who you are. If you want you can stay at my house for any
amount of time you need."

They were talking when someone knocked on the door to say
that Billy was on his way over. Billy and Janice had gotten in a fight
at a previous bachelor party. Janice had shoved Billy, and Billy, en-
raged to be insulted by a slut, had slapped her hard. She was afraid
of him. Larry knew this might be the last time he would ever see
Billy, and he didn't want the moment spoiled by having Janice in the
room. So he hid her in the closet.

Billy entered a few minutes later, carrying a duffel bag filled with
$250,000. He was nervous. Billy didn't like to be present when money
or drugs were exchanged, especially in the present climate of surveillance and arrests. He set down the bag on the floor.

"Goodbye, Billy," said Larry. He was choked up.

They embraced.

"Good luck," said Billy. He gave Larry a number to call if he
ever needed to get in touch.

Before leaving the room, Billy turned as he always had, dating
back to their first days of working together in the apartment on Osage
Avenue, and said, "Tell me it will be all right, Larry."

Larry said, "It will be all right, Billy."

When he left, Larry let Janice out of the closet, threw her on the
bed, and dumped the $250,000 all over her.

On Wednesday, October 24, Larry met with Ken Weidler's lawyer, Ron Kidd. Tom Bergstrom still had hopes that Larry would
come around when the reality of what faced him was at hand. He
felt he could negotiate something less than seven years. If not, he had
devised some cunning pretrial motions that just might suppress some
key evidence. So Larry had told Ken and others that there was a
chance he could get off with less than seven years. When Ken told
that to Kidd, the veteran criminal lawyer scoffed. So Ken had urged
Larry to get a second opinion.

Kidd was blunt. He told Larry that he should expect to be sentenced to anywhere from twenty to sixty years, most likely forty years.

"Everyone is going to cooperate; I know you don't believe it, but everyone including their brother is going to cooperate against each other and you," said Kidd. "In every drug case I've ever heard about, that's what happened. I know it's hard for you to believe that, but it will happen."

Kidd saw Larry's face turn ashen. On the notes Kidd was taking of their conversation he jotted, "Visibly shaken." By the time Larry left the meeting, his last lingering doubt was gone.

He met again with Frannie that night in Fairmount Park. Frannie explained that he was going to Florida the next day. The FBI was prepared to spring the trap on Diego Arbelaez, Frannie's supplier.

"You're not going to leave while I'm away, are you?" asked Fran.

"No, no, don't worry," said Larry, smiling.

"God damn it, you are!" he said, stomping off a few feet in mock anger. "I'm not going to see you again, am I?"

"Would I do that to you, Frannie?"

"You fucker! You're the only one who's going to get away with this whole thing, you know that? If you go, I hope I never see you again. I want to know that at least somebody got away with this."

On Friday, October 26, Larry was back in court. Wearing a gray pinstripe suit and a white shirt with a button down collar, with big Tom Bergstrom by his side, Larry faced Judge Louis C. Bechtle for scheduling of his trial on tax evasion charges. In addition to the five drug conspiracy charges, Larry had been indicted earlier in the month on five counts of tax fraud. The government estimated that he owed at least $545,000 in back taxes on his drug earnings. In addition to the possible life sentence for drug trafficking, he faced a potential twenty-five years of imprisonment on tax charges, five years for each violation. It was clear Larry would get little sympathy from Judge Bechtle, a judge known for his demanding courtroom standards and blunt demeanor.

"It's obvious Dr. Lavin didn't make this money doing root canals," the judge commented.

With Larry and Tom in court that day were Mark Stewart and his attorney. Ever since late 1981, when Larry had refused to pump any more money into the Arena, his relationship with Mark had gradually deteriorated. In all, Larry believed he had lost about two million dollars on his investments with Mark. The record company had gone bankrupt, the Barclay Building project in Atlantic City was still tied up in litigation, there was a continuing probe of the Arena arson that had held up the anticipated insurance settlement, the limo company was under investigation. Along the way there had been other, smaller ventures Larry had bankrolled for Mark. All of them had failed. Larry's estimate was that he had lost several million dollars in all through his association with Mark. And he blamed his legal troubles on his former mentor. If it hadn't been for the arson of the Arena, and forgetting to pay Frankie Smith's royalties, Larry was convinced he would never have gotten caught.

Last summer, he had even decided to gather taped evidence against Mark. If there was one person in the world he would consider giving evidence against, it was Stewart. His plan was to lure Mark into an incriminating telephone conversation and capture it on tape. From a pay phone near his dental office, Larry had clapped a suction-cup microphone over the speaker end of the phone, and started the tape as Mark came on the phone making a pitch for more money. As Larry remembered the conversation later, he began by baiting Mark.

"Don't you realize that you have caused this problem for everyone?" Larry said.

"Me!" said Mark.

"That's how everyone perceives it," said Larry. "Because of your not paying Frankie Smith a lousy thirty grand, all these people are going to go to jail."

"Well, if that's the way you see it," said Mark, as if to say, *"What horseshit."*

"What other way is there to see it, Mark?"

And Mark had launched into Larry, arguing that if it weren't for his continued drug dealing, there never would have been the kind of heat they were all experiencing. No one would have cared enough to look at things that hard.

Larry had become so agitated in this chicken-versus-egg dispute that he had knocked the suction cup loose from the phone. None of the conversation was recorded.

Now they were both in court together, facing the consequences of their combined mistakes, each feeling victimized by the other. They had not seen each other for many months. Larry knew that Mark had been financially ruined by the investigation and tax indictment. Still, as they rode down on the same elevator after the hearing, Mark was his usual optimistic self. He told Larry that none of what he had been charged with was illegal.

"I can beat this," he said.

Larry whispered to Mark, "I know what I have to do now."

"What?" Mark asked.

"You'll see."

Mark asked Larry if he had the original papers they had signed in 1980. Larry said he didn't.

Then Mark asked Larry for two hundred dollars.

Larry had about fifty dollars in his wallet, and his first instinct was to reach for it. Instead, he stopped himself.

"No," said Larry. "Sorry, I didn't bring my wallet."

Later he congratulated himself. At last he had learned to say no to Mark Stewart.

Tom was optimistic about the tax case. He explained that the dates on the IRS charges didn't coincide with the dates on the drug charges, and that since the tax case depended on the drug case, there was a good chance that the discrepancies would topple it. Larry said that it seemed so strange and somehow unfair to him that he could be sent away to prison for twenty-five years for failing to report illegal earnings: If he had reported the money, he would have just been advertising his crime! Wasn't it enough to catch and punish him for selling cocaine without throwing on additional charges for what amounted to not turning himself in? Tom asked Larry to set up a meeting with him on Wednesday so that he could more fully brief him on the purpose of his petitions and pretrial motions. There was much to be hopeful about. Larry said he would call.

Late in the following week, Chuck Reed got a tip that Larry Lavin was leaving. There was a moving truck out in front of his house on Timber Lane.

Swiftly, FBI agents descended on the neighborhood, parking cars at both ends of the block and staking out properties around Larry and Marcia's big white house. Agents phoned the people next door and asked if they would turn on the lights over their garage. Since the garage was on the side of their house closest to the Lavins' driveway, it would help the agents see what was going on.

The truck was in the driveway. Men were moving furniture out through the garage and loading it. Larry and Marcia were nowhere to be seen. Ken Weidler was supervising the loading.

So instead of closing in, the agents waited in the darkness as the work proceeded. When the truck was full, and Ken and another man got in and drove off, agents fell in behind. With any luck, the truck would lead them to Larry.

But instead, the truck led them straight to Ken Weidler's house.

Agents watched the truck through the night, hoping that Ken would get back in and lead them to Larry. But the next morning, Ken and his friends began unloading the contents into his own house. So Chuck and Sid moved in.

"Larry's gone," Ken told Chuck. He did not know exactly when he had left, and he had no idea where he had gone.

Ken said his friend and dental partner had called and invited him to help himself to anything left in the house. There was no crime in that, was there?

When Larry didn't show up for the appointment with his lawyer Wednesday, Tom called Larry's dental office. The receptionist said that Dr. Lavin was not in, and asked if he would like to speak to Dr. Weidler. Tom said, "No, thanks, I'll try him at home."

There was no answer on Larry's home phone.

So Tom called the dental office back and said he would like to speak to Dr. Weidler.

"Larry's gone, but I think he plans to get back in touch with you," said Ken. Larry had definitely moved out. Ken did not know where he and Marcia had gone.

Tom asked if Larry could be talked out of it.

Ken said he wasn't sure, but that he thought it was possible. But he didn't know how to reach Larry.

Tom urged Ken to have Larry contact him right away if he called again.

On Friday, Tom met with Assistant U.S. Attorneys Terry Batty and Dennis Wilson to discuss Larry's case. Tom said he hoped to convince his client to consider negotiating a plea. He outlined a "best-case scenario" where Larry would plead guilty to the lesser drug conspiracy charges and agree to cooperate fully with the government in return for dropping the charge under Section 848, the "kingpin statute." To his surprise, the government lawyers seemed interested. Tom was pleased. It meant Larry had a chance at the deal he had described as their best hope.

As the meeting ended, the prosecutors asked Tom if Larry had moved out of his house in Devon. Tom said that he had, but that he expected to be hearing from Larry soon, and he believed he would be able to deliver Larry to court for the next scheduled hearing. With news of the government's interest in the proposed plea bargain, Tom believed he had good reason to hope that Larry could be coaxed out of hiding.

When he returned to his office, there was a letter on his desk. It had a Philadelphia postmark and no return address.

"Dear Tom," the letter began, in a long sloping script in blue ballpoint on yellow lined paper. Tom recognized his client's handwriting.

"I'm sorry to have to write you this letter. I'm on vacation; an opportunity presented itself which I could not pass up. Please realize that I have every bit of confidence in you and in Don. The motions which you filed and the ideas you had were all creative and sure to have some merit. The problem being that even if the motions worked, the growing mound of testimony would have been overwhelming. I really felt that the best I could hope for without cooperating would be five to ten years in jail. If at all possible I would like you to continue handling my affairs. I will be in touch. I instructed my mother-in-law Agnes Osborn to call you if she has any problem. Please pass this on to Don. Again I *greatly appreciate* everything you and Don have done for me; unfortunately this is just a terrible predicament. The importance of being with my family compared to practicing dentistry heavily influenced my decision to take this vacation at this time.

"Again many thanks and until I see you again, Sincerely yours, Dr. Larry Lavin."

T W E L V E

An Idyll

It was the longest weekend of the year. Daylight saving time would end Saturday night, donating another hour to Larry and Marcia's escape. Larry would not have office hours again until Tuesday morning. He was not expected at Tom Bergstrom's office until Wednesday. With luck, it might be five days or more before Chuck Reed and the FBI learned he was gone.

They arose early Saturday morning, October 27, when it was still dark. It had been a cool, moonlit night. Marcia had been unable to sleep. After Larry's telephone conversation with Tom, he had spent the rest of the evening loading up the leased BMW and making runs back and forth to the storage garage. Marcia kept finding more and more things she wanted to take, and Larry, grateful for her decision to accompany him, was more willing than he might otherwise have been to oblige.

They loaded the car inside the closed garage that morning. Marcia had a few last things she wanted to take, a small end table, a lamp she particularly liked, a throw rug, and a few boxes of clothing. . . . Larry was impatient to get going. By the time they pulled out of the garage, the BMW was loaded down with boxes, furniture, odds and ends, Larry, Marcia, Christopher, Marcia's birds, Spooky (the black cat who had been with them since undergraduate days at Penn), and Rusty, the dog. Larry felt they might as well be pulling out of the driveway accompanied by neon signs and a brass band. Marcia shed no tears as she took one last look at the big white house. She had loved the house, but her last two months in it had been a nightmare. On this morning there was eagerness, fear, and excitement. They were getting away!

Larry had prearranged to meet his brother Rusty and Richard Timmerman in the parking lot of the Sheridan Hotel off Route 202.

They had rented a yellow U-Haul truck the day before in Timmerman's name, and Larry was carrying the Massachusetts driver's license he had obtained with his picture and Timmerman's I.D.

In the early-morning darkness, they quickly moved items from the BMW to the truck. Rusty and Timmerman followed in the car as Larry drove over to the storage garage in Valley Forge. Marcia eyed nervously the green hills on either side of the road. It was dawn. She expected SWAT teams to swoop down from the dewy shadows overhead. It took more than an hour to load the truck. Marcia entertained Christopher, trying to keep him out of the way.

When at last they got under way, Larry and Marcia embraced Rusty and said their tearful goodbyes. Larry had prearranged to call his brother on a regular basis at pay phone telephone numbers in Haverhill. Rusty and Timmerman then followed the yellow truck as Larry drove out to Route 202. They had gone no more than a mile when a lampshade Marcia had put up behind her in the cab, for fear it would get smashed in the back, blew out the window on the highway. Larry pulled over and Marcia ran out to retrieve it. Rusty had pulled over behind them. Just as Marcia prepared to dash out in the highway, a car ran over the shade.

She turned to Rusty. "Do you think it's a bad omen?"

He laughed.

"Take good care of him, okay?" he said.

"I will," said Marcia, and she ran back to the truck.

Larry steered back out on the road, leaving his brother, Philadelphia, his past, his identity, and his troubles behind.

On the day Larry was indicted, his parents had been vacationing in the Florida condominium Larry had helped them buy. The news was big in Philadelphia, and word of the arrest of a Haverhill boy found its way into the local Massachusetts newspapers with Larry's mug shot a few days later. But with his parents out of town, Larry had hopes that Justin and Pauline would never have to face the jarring headlines about his drug dealings. He had prepared them for his pending tax difficulties, even for the prospect of his having to spend some time in jail, but he had never mentioned drugs.

His hopes were dashed, though, when someone in Haverhill clipped the stories about him and mailed them to his mother. They arrived in Florida with a mean little note to the effect that she and her husband ought to know what sort of son they had raised.

To Larry's surprise and delight, his parents readily bought his explanation about making bad loans and getting bad advice when he talked to them on the phone. Justin and Pauline were nearly seventy years old, and both had been battling serious heart ailments. It was as though, after being so proud of Larry's accomplishments for so long, they were determined to cling to their pride in him and his little family.

On his trip north to get his fake Massachusetts driver's license he had stopped in Haverhill to tell them he was running away.

"I think I'm going to be leaving the country," he said. "So I guess this is goodbye."

His mother cried. His father reacted angrily, blaming the government for persecuting him.

"It can't be as bad as all that, can it, Larry?" he said.

Larry left them with fifteen thousand dollars and a promise that he would contact them again before long.

"Don't be surprised if you just see me walk up to you on a golf course down in Florida someday, or pull up beside you in a car and wave," he said.

Breaking the news to Marcia's mother had been even harder. In the years since Larry and Marcia had moved to Timber Lane, Agnes was by the house several times each week. She had a standing luncheon engagement with Marcia two days a week. She had moved to her condominium in Devon that summer to be close to her daughter and grandchild. In some way they were more like sisters than mother and daughter. Agnes was short and round, with gray hair and rose-tinted glasses. She shared Marcia's quiet outlook on life, preferring to keep her firmly held convictions about things to herself. She thought Larry was a fine son-in-law, even though they had never been close. He was certainly a wonderful provider. When that Chuck Reed had come to her apartment to ask if she knew Larry was mixed up in drugs, she was shocked.

"My son-in-law? No way!" she had said, and meant it. "Larry doesn't use drugs. I'm a nurse. If he were on drugs all these years I would have been able to detect it."

The agent had walked around her nicely furnished condominium and said, "Did Larry buy this for you?"

"No he did not," she said indignantly. "I sold a house in New Jersey my husband and I lived in for thirty years, and I bought this!"

After that she was ready to believe the FBI was persecuting Larry. She could see how ready they were to jump to false conclusions. So even after the indictment and all the bad publicity, Agnes had rallied to Larry's support.

Now they would have to tell her that they were leaving her life, most likely for good. Marcia was her baby, and Christopher was so precious to her. She had helped Marcia raise him far more than Larry had. Leaving Agnes alone in her condominium in Devon was like pulling her entire life out from under her. Marcia was painfully aware of how hard it would hit her mother. She and Larry had even briefly considered taking Agnes with them. But when they realized it would mean she could have no further contact with her son and her other daughter, nor with her other grandchildren, they knew it would be asking too much.

Marcia put off telling her mother until the last possible moment. She broke the news over dinner at Bennigan's, a restaurant in the King of Prussia Mall, the night before they left. Agnes was furious and bewildered, but Marcia had made up her mind.

"I'm going with him because I love him," said Marcia. "I can't picture myself living here without knowing what's happening to my husband. Larry is convinced he can do this and not get caught. I have to give him this chance."

"Doesn't he realize that the people who made these rules and regulations, that set up this justice system of ours, are just as smart as he is?" said Agnes.

Yet she was powerless to stop it. If she couldn't talk Marcia out of it, she could never dissuade Larry. Agnes felt as if she had just been told a perfectly healthy loved one had less than twenty-four hours to live.

Larry had stopped at her condo later that night to pick up Marcia's sewing machine. His mother-in-law said nothing to him. He knew she was hurt and angry.

"You shouldn't feel too bad," said Larry. "You've got your son and you've got your other daughter and two other grandchildren."

"That doesn't change the situation any, Larry," she said. "I am still losing a grandson and I am losing my daughter."

Larry had no answer.

"What you are doing is taking my daughter and my grandchild away from me," said Agnes.

They had parted on that note. Larry felt bad about it, but what could he do? He comforted himself with the knowledge that, however hard leaving was on him, it was harder on Marcia, and she had decided to go.

Saturday morning dawned sunny and hot on the highway. The cramped cab of the truck had no air-conditioning. Marcia had Chris on her lap, the cat over her shoulder, and the dog on the floor beneath her feet.

They were driving south. Larry aimed straight down Route 202 to Route 13, an interstate that pointed down through Delaware and bisected the Eastern Shore of Maryland. They were headed for Virginia Beach.

Deciding to go to Virginia Beach was just a coincidence, which is one of the reasons Larry liked the idea. There was no logic to it. If there was any logic to their destination it would be possible for someone to figure it out. He had gone to a travel agency shortly after his indictment to get some papers notarized, just because there was a seal on the window outside that advertised a notary public. In the agency he had picked up a brochure on summer rentals, and it had occurred to him that if he and Marcia ran, the safest thing to do first would be to find a staging area—a place where they could run to immediately and spend a few weeks or months making arrangements before moving on to a more permanent destination.

It hit him as he stood there that the best place to do that in early winter would be a beach community. There would be ample short-term rentals available. In late October it would be relatively deserted. And rental agents were used to handling short-term leases, so they were not likely to ask too many questions. Among the communities with rentals listed in the brochure was Virginia Beach. He and Marcia had spent a day there years ago on a trip to Williamsburg with Stu Thomas. They had loved the area, with its Colonial flavor and gentle Southern style.

So Larry had called a rental agent several weeks earlier, using the name Brian O'Neil, and said that he had accepted a teaching position at the University of Pennsylvania for one semester after having been overseas for several years. He and his wife and son planned to spend a few months touring the East Coast before settling into Philadelphia, he said, and they wanted a nice apartment for just a few weeks to a month. The agent asked for references, and Larry explained that they had been traveling overseas for several years, never staying in one place for too long, and that he hadn't kept addresses or phone numbers. He called back several days later and the agent had found him an apartment. So Larry had mailed a cashier's check to pay for the first month's rent, and told the agent to expect him sometime within the next six weeks.

They stopped for lunch at a McDonald's somewhere in Maryland. It was late afternoon when they crossed the long, scenic Chesapeake Bay Bridge-Tunnel from Kiptopeke, Maryland, to Virginia Beach. As they came off the bridge, Larry pulled over. He had planned to take the little silver Beretta, the pistol he had purchased four years ago after the robbery on Osage Avenue, the one that had been pushed into Paula Van Horn's ribs, and throw it off the bridge. Larry knew that the gun was one more positive link to his criminal past. It was also a symbol of the criminal path he had pursued so ambitiously the last ten years. He got out of the truck and started to walk back toward the bridge, but there were too many people around. So he returned with the gun still in his pocket.

* * *

Marcia was supposed to be Susan O'Neil, but she refused to go by that first name. Larry argued that it was best to change both names; why do it halfway? But Marcia said she would not become a Susan, period. So they compromised. She took Marcia as her middle name, and though her official name would be Susan M. O'Neil, she would continue to go by Marcia.

After picking up the key to their apartment, which was just one block from the beach, they spent the rest of the day until dark hauling lockers. The apartment was small, just two bedrooms, a kitchen, living room, and bath. Twice on that late afternoon there were knocks on the door. Both times Marcia felt her heart leap. She expected to see men with guns encircling the house at any moment. The first knock was neighbors, a young navy man and his wife, who lived next door, stopping by to say hello. The second knock was the cable TV man. On the drive down, Marcia had said she wanted to get a cable hookup in as soon as possible because Chris enjoyed certain programs in the afternoon. She thought such an abrupt transition for him might be eased if he still had his cartoons.

Larry had said, "We don't need to call anybody and pay a fee. I know how to tap right into the cable myself."

Marcia was dumbfounded.

"Why in the world would you run a risk like that? We can afford to pay the fee."

"Okay, okay," said Larry, laughing. "Old habits are hard to break."

So the cable TV man arrived before dinnertime to make the connection.

On the day after they arrived, Larry rented a storage garage and removed the last of the footlockers. He and Marcia only needed a few of the lockers to tide them over in the furnished beach apartment. It was hard work. Marcia was three months pregnant and unable to help, so Larry spent hours lugging the heavy lockers himself. Then he found a used-car lot and bought himself a small white Plymouth 6000, using the license and registration of Richard Timmerman. This was just an interim purchase. Larry intended to fully adopt the names Brian and Susan O'Neil as soon as they could obtain Virginia driver's licenses under those names. Buying the car gave Larry pause. He had to give Timmerman's Social Security number and other information. It occurred to Larry that if anything got back to Richard, then one person would have a clue where he and Marcia had gone. Larry had been scrupulous about the secret. *No one* knew. His brother Rusty had even acted a bit offended when Larry refused to entrust him with the location. But Rusty and Richard knew that he was using Timmerman's I.D., at least initially, so any stray mailing from Social Security reflecting this purchase would be a tip-off. But they had to have a car, and there was no other way to get it. Larry planned to dump it and get something nicer as soon as he and Marcia decided where to settle. So the car would just serve their purposes for a few weeks. Just to be safe, Larry rented a private postal box to use as Timmerman's official address.

Two days later, Larry drove the truck to Washington, D.C., and in a downtown hotel met Timmerman, who had agreed to drive it back to Philadelphia. Larry parked and walked a few blocks to the hotel. He gave the registration clerk the name Richard Timmerman.

"What is this, a joke?" the clerk asked.

"What are you talking about?"

"You're already checked in," he said, and pulled the card to show Larry the name.

"Oh . . . that's my brother," said Larry. "I was just going to use his name so if he got here after me he would see that he already had a room."

Larry met Timmerman upstairs and turned over the key. Richard had thirty thousand dollars with him, part payment of an outstanding drug debt in New England—the last of the money owed Larry that he had any hope of collecting. They ordered drinks from room service and sat around chatting for a while. He told Timmerman that he had been driving straight for more than a day—he didn't want them to know that he was actually staying just a few hours away. Timmerman explained how he and Rusty had agreed not even to see each other for about six months, just in case the FBI was watching Rusty. They said goodbye again, and Larry took a taxi to the airport. He flew back to Norfolk that night and Marcia picked him up at the airport.

Those early-winter weeks on the beach were perfect therapy for all the excitement of the last year. One of the first things Marcia noticed, happily, was that the telephone *never rang!* Larry went for daily jogs along the beach with the dog, and took long walks with Marcia and Chris. They had never been to a resort community in the off-season and were delighted by the way it reverted to a small town, with friendly neighbors who would stop and say hello and introduce themselves, and merchants who got to know you by name. After a few days of the solitude and quiet, they began going to area malls just to get out of the house. They bought a new color TV to replace the older one in the apartment, a video tape recorder, a new camera, put a deposit on a tape club. Marcia bought a microwave oven. One weekend they drove to Williamsburg, where they had visited as college students, and spent the day taking in the sights. Larry and Marcia loved the Colonial flavor of the area. Without ever really sitting down to a formal decision, over the first few weeks they both decided that this was where they wanted to stay.

Their flight had gone as smoothly as they could have hoped. So far, Larry's juggling of identities and Social Security cards and post office boxes was going well. No one knew where they were, so it was no more likely that somebody would be looking for them in Virginia Beach than anywhere else in America. The more Larry felt comfortable in the little beach apartment, the more he liked the idea of staying. It was so close to Philadelphia, and to FBI headquarters in Washington, that it might, in fact, be the best of all places to hide.

Besides, on his long walks and morning outings with the dog, he had begun to eye the fishing boats lined up along the piers and in dry storage racks at Lynnhaven and other marinas up and down the inlets and bays. Ever since he was a boy vacationing at the Baratts' house on the lake outside Haverhill, he had fancied having his own boat.

So in early December, he started visiting realtors in the Williamsburg and Hampton Roads areas. After looking at a few locations, Larry found a house he wanted. It was set in a remote, wooded location outside Williamsburg, near the confluence of two rivers where the water was deep enough to float a big boat. The house was an old mansion, big enough to have a separate upper-floor living area with its own bedrooms, kitchen, and bath for live-in servants. Larry thought it was perfect. To Marcia, it was reminiscent of the mansion Larry had fancied when they first went shopping for a house on the Main Line.

Instead, they settled on a new suburban development called Middle Plantation, one of many affluent subdivisions going up on wooded marshlands in the rapidly growing area between Norfolk and Virginia Beach. They bought a new house set on a corner acre at the end of a block called Royal Oaks Close. It was a two-story redbrick house with a red front door, with a front and back yard almost identical in configuration to the house they had abandoned on Timber Lane. The backyard formed a long, gradually sloping rectangle back to a wooded lot. On the back, southern side of the house, the steeply sloping gray-tiled roof was broken by seven separate skylights, so nearly every room of the house was flooded with sunlight. It was a neighborhood identical to Timber Lane in almost every respect, big family dwellings set well back from a quiet street, with driveways that curved up along the side of the property to attached garages. Housed in these neo-Colonial homes were the families of bankers, businessmen, stockbrokers, and professionals, the youngest of them with teenage children.

Larry, as Brian O'Neil, offered the full asking price of $235,000 for the house in order to top a competing bid, and signed a contract with the builder, Les Williams, in the second week of December.

Before closing on the deal, Larry took Les aside and offered him $35,000 of the sale price in cash. He told the builder that he had been a stockbroker in Philadelphia, and that he had suffered a mild heart attack that he had never told his wife about. His doctors had instructed him to take it easy for a few years, so, Larry explained, he had sold off his assets quickly and moved south. So he was stuck with a lot of money in cash and was looking for ways of investing it. Williams gladly agreed to take the $35,000 in cash. They recorded the sale price of the house at $200,000.

Converting that $200,000 from cash into cashier's checks took a long time. Larry had to visit more than twenty banks, because any check in an amount greater than $10,000 required a report to the government. He had a list of all the banks in his vicinity and checked them off one by one to make sure he didn't accidently put two iden-tities in the same bank. To avoid suspicion, before obtaining a cashier's check in a large amount, Larry opened accounts at each bank, de-positing a seed amount of money, then gradually, over two or three trips, built up the account to almost $10,000. Then he would make a trip in to withdraw the cashier's check. He tried to vary his ap-pearance, sometimes going in wearing blue jeans and a sportshirt, other times dressing in a three-piece suit with an expensive topcoat.

Keeping track of all these accounts, post office boxes, and iden-tities was a dizzying, full-time occupation. In all, Larry invested $920,000 in stocks under a total of twenty-two separate identities, each with its own private mailing address (usually a box that he rented at various U-Haul centers), bank accounts, Social Security numbers, etc. Larry bought himself a small Epson home computer and used it to help keep track of his twenty-two separate identities and addresses. Since the only way to obtain Social Security registration without answering a lot of questions was to apply before age eighteen, all of Larry's false identities were for people under eighteen years old. By spring he started to get notification from Selective Service at many of his post office boxes, so he had to stop in the local draft office and register, pretending to be only eighteen years old. It was necessary to file tax forms for all of his identities. Larry kept looking for ways to simplify these dealings, but as time went by they seemed to just grow more and more complex.

They moved into the new house before Christmas, keeping the beach apartment for a few weeks until they had time to purchase rugs and furniture. Larry bought a black Plymouth Voyager with imitation wood paneling on the side for himself, and a maroon Nissan Maxima station wagon for Marcia. The house was still mostly barren, but Marcia was able to piece together enough furnishings and trappings to make Christmas cozy. The tree went in the bay window area of the living room, set on a bare wooden floor. Around it she placed potted poinsettias, and she hung cloth angels from the window latches. Across the room, before the fireplace, was a blue throw rug, a big red leather chair and foot rest, and a handsome mahogany coffee table Larry's father had made and that they had carted in the U-Haul. There was a big Sony stereo TV in the corner on a footlocker and a new sofa against one wall. Marcia lined the mantelpiece with Christmas candles and hung the holiday stockings that she had knitted herself. On Christmas Eve, Marcia left out a rabbit cup half-filled with milk and pieces of butter cookie on a plate, with a note that read, "Dear Chris, Thank you for the milk and cookies. Rudolph liked his carrots. Have fun with your new toys. Merry Christmas, Santa."

As spring approached, Larry went right to work re-creating his beloved backyard layout. He added a spacious back porch with a built-in Jacuzzi. He hired a swimming pool company to build a small backyard pool in the shape of a Mickey Mouse head. Larry helped design little cleaners for the pool bottom that popped up when switched on and then sank back down flush with the bottom when switched off. He selected a special kind of seashell finish to decorate the concrete edging and the pool deck. Alongside the pool Larry had a play area constructed with a slide, a fort, jungle gym, and swings. Landscape crews filled in low-lying areas of the property and planted beds of azaleas and tulips. A big wooden fence went up around the long perimeter of the backyard. It soon looked even nicer than the house they had left behind.

For Marcia, despite her fear that every knock on the door or strange car cruising up the block was the FBI, these were some of the happiest months in her marriage to Larry. They were together with Chris, and a second child was on the way. Larry was busy handling his money, opening bank accounts, and making investments in stocks and bonds, but he was home most of the time. The phone almost never rang. Larry committed himself, for the first time since his son was born, to spending an hour of time with Chris after dinner every day, playing games, going for walks, wrestling on the floor, or just watching TV. It was odd the way things worked out, but it had been Larry's arrest and indictment that had finally forced Marcia's dream into reality. They were at last a normal family, eating dinners together, working on their own house, going shopping together, being parents. Larry spent hours over the holidays sitting in the big red chair reading a Robert Ludlum novel with one of Marcia's yellow-and-orange handmade afghans thrown over his long legs. Marcia could gaze out of the kitchen on a scene that perfectly matched the ideal she had sought for so long. Larry's downfall had humbled him. The threat of prison, and of losing Marcia and Chris, seemed to have finally awakened him to what was lasting and valuable in his life. He had new respect for Marcia, and showed new vulnerability in his dealings with her. They still argued over things and still occasionally got on each other's nerves, but they made decisions mutually. They were in this together.

Meeting neighbors was a trauma. On one of their first days in the new house, a man who lived across the street rang the doorbell to invite the new family to a Christmas party. The neighbor introduced himself and talked for a moment about the party, and then said, "What's your name again?"

"Larry," said Larry, startling himself with the slip. "Er, it's actually Brian," he said, "but my wife calls me Larry. Larry is my middle name, and her brother's name is Brian, so she never called me by her brother's name."

"Well, Larry is a perfectly good name because that's my name!" the man said.

At the party Larry and Marcia introduced themselves to the neighborhood as Brian and Susan, but explained that they really called each other by their middle names, Larry and Marcia. People tended to call Marcia Marcia, but Larry easily became Brian. Their best friends quickly became Jess and Babette Miller, who lived directly across the street. The Millers had teenage children, but also a little boy about Christopher's age.

Brian was a big hit on the block. He was frequently the only man in the neighborhood who was home during the day. So when a woman's water pipe burst down the block, she came running for Brian. Larry crawled down through the flooded basement to turn off the water main, then spent the rest of the day hauling out furniture and rugs and mopping up. At one of the first meetings of the community association, the O'Neils won first place for having the prettiest yard in the neighborhood. The prize was a year's worth of professional lawn care. "How ironic," said one of the neighbors. "Brian and Marcia are the ones who need it least! Their house looks like they've lived there for twenty years already!" Most of the homeowners were growing lawns from seed. Larry had taken the quicker, more expensive route. He had covered his with a thick blanket of healthy sod early in spring.

Larry explained his affluence and ease by telling his neighbors that he was a computer whiz. He had founded his own small computer company in Philadelphia just after graduating from college, and had built it into a successful enterprise. Then he had sold out to a larger computer firm for a big price tag, and, as part of the deal, he had promised not to go back into the field for three years. Thus his early, youthful retirement.

Marcia worried as Larry became a more and more popular figure
in the neighborhood. She figured the fewer people who knew them,
the fewer questions they would have to answer, the fewer lies they
would have to invent. But Larry seemed to *enjoy* being put on the
spot and having to invent stories to explain himself. After a while, it
was hard to keep track of all the stories Larry had told. Marcia felt
like crawling under a rock with every false detail of her husband's
clever conversational concoctions. But it was like a game to him. He
was incapable of turning down a party invitation, or of sitting in the
house while people were out and about in the neighborhood, or of
letting other people manage the new community association. It wasn't
as though he didn't have a good reason to back off. Why couldn't he
just become a little bit more reclusive? Why couldn't he keep his
mouth shut?

Shortly after buying the house, Larry bought himself a twenty-
six-foot boat, a Sea Ray Weekender. In January, Larry signed up to
take scuba diving lessons at the Lynnhaven Dive Center, near the
marina. After the lessons on their honeymoon in Hawaii he had longed
to do it again. So he took a few weeks of lessons in the swimming
pool at the dive center, and formed close friendships with the society
of divers—many of them local policemen or fire fighters. He bought
the most expensive diving gear, which endeared him to the store
owner, and by March, when conditions were right for ocean diving,
he was spending two or three hours every day at the shop. Within
months, Larry and his companions were making deep dives thirty to
fifty miles offshore, searching for old wrecks a hundred feet down.

Once he started diving, Larry had again established a separate
life away from home, a life that satisfied his pleasure in taking risks
and for being in the company of men. He frequently left early in the
morning and came home late at night. His promise to spend just one
hour each day after dinner with his son was forgotten just as swiftly
as so many other promises before it had been.

During the first months of 1985 there were few reasons for Larry
and Marcia to fear detection. Larry had even made a few calls home
from pay phones, to Ken Weidler and to his brother Rusty. Through
them he got word back to his family and to Marcia's mother that they
were settled and doing well. Larry wanted news about the drug case,
but the group that had been indicted with him had not yet gone to
trial. He learned that his wild old friend and former runner, Glen
Fuller, had at last been sentenced to four years in prison by a New
Jersey judge for his 1980 arrest driving cocaine north on the turnpike.
But Glen had been released immediately, pending the outcome of his
appeal, and was living in Aspen. Larry had to laugh about that. He
learned that he and Mark Stewart had been sued, along with officials

of Bank Leumi Le-Israel, for conspiring to loot WMOT-TEC Records of two million dollars, and then in January, his old mentor Mark Stewart's problems worsened further when he was indicted on seventy-four counts of filing phony tax statements for clients of his tax shelter schemes, and indicted separately for laundering a half-million dollars of Larry's drug money through his various enterprises. Larry wished the courts luck in getting to the bottom of that mess—he considered a half million a generous understatement. Frannie Burns had helped the FBI nail Diego Arbelaez, his Colombian supplier, with 170 pounds of uncut cocaine in his Hollywood, Florida, garage. Larry's other friends and former associates had all retained lawyers and were waiting in fear for the other shoe to drop. His former cocaine-dealing partner David Ackerman had kicked his cocaine habit and gone back to dental school.

Whenever Larry hung up the phone and walked back to his car under sunny Virginia skies, braced with the musky smell of salt air, it was like returning through some warp in time and space. What was happening in Philadelphia was like some fast-receding nightmare. Larry was grateful to have escaped it all, and proud of himself for having had the presence of mind and cunning to give himself a second chance. Often he would resolve not to call again for a few years, just to play it perfectly safe. Marcia thought he was crazy to make these occasional calls. But then, a few weeks or a month later, as the appointed time for his next prearranged call approached, he would find himself pulling into a shopping center lot and hunting up a phone as if drawn by some force out of his control. Some part of Larry missed being at the center of the storm.

He had still not gotten driver's licenses for Brian and Susan O'Neil. Larry was afraid to have his picture taken by the Virginia State Police. What if they checked photos against a list of fugitives?

So he put it off and put it off until one morning, pulling out of Middle Plantation on his way over to the dive center, his Maxima was flagged down by the local police. Larry was in a cold sweat. He had been going 35 MPH in a 25-MPH zone. As he handed over his Richard Timmerman Massachusetts license, the one that listed him as thirty-nine years old and twenty pounds heavier than he was, Larry could see all his carefully laid plans wash away in a moment. Even if the cop didn't question the license, wouldn't the ticket go on the record of Richard Timmerman in Massachusetts?

The cop didn't notice anything unusual about the license. He gave Larry a speeding ticket and drove off. That afternoon, Larry called the sheriff's office and explained that a friend of his from out of state had been driving his car on a visit, and had gotten a speeding ticket. If the ticket was promptly paid, would it still go into the computer and go on his record in Massachusetts? The clerk at the sheriff's office said yes, the ticket would go into the Virginia computer, but that no, it wouldn't show up on his friend's record in Massachusetts automatically. The information could be accessed in Massachusetts, but they would have to inquire about it first.

Larry was relieved, but the incident prompted him to see about getting new driver's licenses for himself and Marcia. Posing as novelist Robert Ludlum, Larry called the state police and explained that he was looking for some general information as background research for his next book. The state police spokesman was eager to oblige.

"I'm a big fan of yours," he said.

Larry asked if it was common practice to search through driver's license photos for fugitives. The spokesman said no, it would just take too many man-hours for too few results, and it would be too difficult to do. It just wasn't practical.

The next day, Larry and Marcia took driving tests, and within weeks they were both carrying new Virginia driver's licenses under their new names and address. It was a big breakthrough. Larry felt the last hurdle had been cleared.

But then there was the baby. Larry was worried because he knew Chuck Reed had a good idea of when the baby was due. He knew the new obstetrician/gynecologist would want Marcia's history, and the hospital would want forms filled out, addresses, phone numbers, immediate family, etc. Larry did not want the doctor or hospital to even know their address or phone number.

But the preliminaries went smoothly. They found a doctor who did not ask too many questions. On the hospital forms they left many questions unanswered. Larry found that since he was willing to pay for services in advance, very few questions were asked.

He and Marcia attended birthing classes together, and on April 5, as they finished eating dinner at Pizza Hut, Marcia said, "I think we had better go straight to the hospital from here." Larry dropped Chris off at the Millers' and drove to the emergency room.

Less than an hour later she gave birth to a dark-haired baby girl. Larry was amazed. For Christopher, Marcia's labor had gone on for more than ten hours, and in the end the doctor used forceps to help with the delivery. This birth was over so quickly there had hardly been time to generate the kind of excitement of the first. Larry drove home to pick up Chris, and tied pink balloons to one of the trees in the front yard. Marcia and Larry named their daughter Tara Erin O'Neil.

Larry didn't care that much, but Marcia wanted the baby baptized. She had enrolled in the local Catholic church, and within weeks of bringing baby Tara home, Marcia and Larry were attending group discussions with other new parents preliminary to having their babies baptized.

But baptism presented another problem. They had no friends as close as Jess and Babette Miller, their next-door neighbors, so they were the obvious choice for Tara's godparents. But wouldn't they think it was odd to be asked to play such an important role after having known Brian and Marcia O'Neil for only several months?

Larry invited the Millers over. He told them that he and Marcia wanted them to be Tara's godparents, "but I think I owe you an explanation," he said. "You may have noticed that we are never visited by our families, or by old friends. There's a reason for that."

Larry swore the Millers to secrecy. Then he told Jess and Babette that he and Marcia were really not Brian and Susan O'Neil.

No. Those were false identities. Jess and Babette were spell-bound. There had always been something vaguely mysterious about their young, moneyed neighbors.

"Marcia and I are living in the federal Witness Protection Program," said Larry.

He explained that he had turned state's evidence to convict some of his partners in the computer company in Philadelphia, so, for his own and his family's protection, the government had given them new identities.

The Millers promised to keep their secret, and gladly agreed to stand as godparents for Tara. Marcia felt deep chagrin. It was the most calculated lie she had ever been party to in her life, and it made her skin crawl to see how easily it had come to Larry. He was delighted when the evening was through. They had pulled it off! Marcia felt sick to her stomach.

With all the confusion and household disruption of bringing home the new baby, Larry and Marcia wanted a special treat for Christopher on his third birthday. They invited the Millers' little boy and threw a birthday party for Chris at Showbiz Pizza Place, a fun kiddie restaurant with a giant mechanized puppet show and lots of games and rides. They all sang when the Shobiz mascot, Billy-Bob the Bear, a cuddly costumed bear with oversized orange-and-yellow striped overalls, waddled out carrying a cake with white icing and three candles on top.

Marcia had been better than Larry about calling or writing home. She had written two letters to her mother, which were sent through the mail drop to the address of one of her mother's friends. Larry had scanned the letters carefully to make sure they contained no clue to their whereabouts. After Tara was born, which occasioned the second letter, he had insisted they dress her in blue for the picture and tell

Agnes that their new child was a boy. In that letter, Marcia had strongly urged her mother to keep silent about anything having to do with her or Larry. Marcia knew that the FBI was putting pressure on, and she knew her mother resented their leaving and wanted them back. She worried that, even though Agnes did not know where they were, she might cooperate with the FBI in trying to find them. So she wrote fervently to her mother, trying to emphasize the importance of her silence and patience.

Marcia wrote her mother for a third time in early June. She had snapshots of the baby to send. So with her rounded feminine script on stationery decorated in the upper left-hand corner with a rose, she composed a brief note to her mother.

> Dear Mom,
> Hi! I finally got my pictures back. Isn't the baby *cute?* He's doing OK now but at 2 wks he had a cold, then got a virus that lasted over a week. I had him in for all sorts of tests & then they finally decided it was a virus. The poor baby screamed for a week—everything's fine now. Chris had a great birthday. We took him & his best friend to one of those pizza places like I used to go to at home with video games & rides & the bear brought out his birthday cake & sang him a song— he was thrilled! He loves this little boy from across the street who's 4-and-a-half. They have so much fun together. They are out in the sandbox right now. I enrolled Chris in a nursery school for 2 mornings a wk starting in September. The place is so neat with lots of toys, puzzles, playdough, jungle gyms—I want to go too! . . . I am well. I still have 10 pounds to lose—but it's coming off slowly & I'm still nursing the baby. Larry is doing great. We are very happy. We went to a barbeque at the neighbors on Memorial Day. They have four kids and the people next door came with their 3—so we all had fun. Chris is so happy here & he's talking up a storm. . . . I'll send you more pictures when I can. I hope you are happy & are taking care of yourself—we love you & are always thinking of you.

She signed off, "Love, Marcia."

But before sending the letter, she and Larry learned more about what was happening back in Philadelphia.

At first, Ken Weidler was the only person besides Rusty Lavin whom Larry had trusted enough to telephone regularly since running away. But in spring Larry began to grow a little more bold. He placed a collect call to the New Jersey workplace of Marcia's brother, Richard, who told Larry that Agnes and Ken Weidler seemed to be getting the most pressure from the FBI. Both were bitter about their predicament: Larry and Marcia hadn't trusted them enough to confide where they were going, and the FBI refused to believe they didn't know. Chuck

Reed had been stopping by Agnes's townhouse once or twice a week. He had gotten her to open up Larry's house in Timber Lane so they could go through it without a search warrant. Marcia, who also spoke with her brother on the phone, was angry when she heard what her mother had done. She passed some harsh words to her mother through Richard, urging him to tell her how important it was to give the FBI no help at all.

In another call, this one to an old colleague at the Penn Dental School, Larry learned that his old partner had been in the school library checking over "demographics," statistical studies indicating where there was a surplus or shortage of dentists. If Ken was looking at the charts, it most likely meant he was thinking about opening a new practice. Larry had left him with a thriving one, so why would he be shopping around?

After hearing what had been said about her mother, Marcia added a postscript as long as the original note. Her tone had shifted from the happy daughter reflecting on all's well to a stern, urgent voice filled with the fear Larry's occasional calls let into their idyllic family life:

Hi, again. Larry just spoke to our friend & I'm glad I didn't mail this letter. I'm so sorry if I made you feel as though I didn't trust you. The only information I get about you is secondhand & the way it sounded was the FBI was really pushing you & that you were having a hard time dealing with it. So I felt I must keep saying to be careful what you say to the jerks & with what you have (letters, pictures) since you think they broke in once. I may have made my point too often & too strongly in my letters to you but please remember that our lives & the happiness of our kids is at stake & I cannot take chances. So please overlook any harsh words I may have used. Larry also felt that we can finally say that we have a daughter—I'm glad for you to know the truth so I can send you pictures of her as a girl—as usual, if you are ever asked the sex *refuse to answer!* I'm also sorry that Ken and Barb were offended by Larry not trusting Ken—again I wish everyone would realize that we have to protect ourselves first & worry about others' feelings last. Our lawyer told us not to contact him so we didn't. I'm glad you're seeing them. I think of them often & hope that everything works out for them. Well, I hope I made you feel a little better—please still be careful. I know Ken was able to get a phone # to us so Larry could call him—please try to do the same through the same channel. I would really love to talk to you—it has been so long. Larry should call our friend two weeks from the last time—so see what you can do. Chris wants me to write a note to you—'Dear Grammy Mommy, Me got robots, toys, new house, me love you.'

He misses you & I do too.

Love,

Marcia

The questions raised about his best friend and former dental partner's conduct haunted Larry enough that he skipped his next two scheduled monthly calls to Ken. In a previous call, months before, Larry had been warned by Tom Bergstrom not to phone Ken Weidler and David Ackerman. He told Tom that he didn't believe Ken would ever betray him. There was something between him and Kenny that ran too deep for the government to penetrate. In fact, after skipping the two prearranged calls, Larry had second thoughts. If he couldn't trust Ken, whom could he trust? Besides, curiosity was eating at him. Larry believed only he would be able to tell what was really going on with Kenny. And the only way to do that was to talk with him.

So Larry sent word through Richard of a time and place to contact Ken. Marcia was dead set against it. It was foolish to call in the first place, she argued, and even more foolish to call after they had been given cause to suspect that Ken was cooperating. For all they knew, the indirect information they were getting about Kenny might have been his way of warning them to keep away.

But Larry had made up his mind. He drove out to a nearby shopping mall. Marcia stayed in the van with Christopher and the baby. Larry promised to keep the call down to two minutes, which he felt would ensure that it could not be traced, and told Marcia to watch the digital clock on the dashboard and signal him when time was about up. It was a sunny, hot Saturday, June 8, 1985. In a hallway just inside the doors to the mall, where he could still see Marcia in the parking lot, Larry fed quarters into the pay phone and punched in the Philadelphia area code and number. The line was busy. Larry tried again. Again it was busy. So Larry walked back out to the car, waited another five minutes, and then tried again. Again, the phone was busy. Larry debated with himself, then tried one last time.

"Yo!" said Ken.

"Kenny," said Larry.

"Oh, oh, Larry," said Ken, pronouncing his friend's name as a baby would, "Way-wee," the way he always did when they were joking around. "I couldn't believe it. This fuckin' guy would not get off the phone."

"I was just about to give up, man. Maybe you had somebody to see or you weren't there or something. You fucked up—"

"Kenny here! Kenny was gonna go to the shore but Kenny didn't go to the shore 'cause—"

"Sorry," said Larry. "I didn't know whether you would be working today or not."

"Come on!" groaned Ken. Larry had always teased his friend about his lackadaisical work habits. "This is *Saturday*. What's wrong with you?"

"Well, first of all, I want to tell you I'm sorry. You know, I heard that you told Marcia's mom you thought I didn't trust you and all that stuff."

"Yeah?"

"So . . ."

"Well, she said the same thing."

"Well, I *don't* trust her," said Larry, laughing. "I do now, but, you know, she's not as smart. You know, she took him to my house."

"You want to hear what the story was behind that? At least what she told me?"

"Yeah."

"She said that Reed came to her door and said that he wanted her to take him up to the house. And she said, 'Well, I can't do that,' and that she would have to call Bergstrom. So she called Bergstrom and Bergstrom apparently said they'd either do it today or they would come back with an order, a court order for her to do it tomorrow."

"Oh, really?"

"Yeah."

"Okay," said Larry.

"So she wanted me to press upon you that she didn't just, you know, go open the house up to him. She called the lawyer first and that's what he told her to do."

"Yeah. I see. That's too bad. You know, Richard should have told me that."

"Yeah," said Ken.

"He should have told me that. He made it sound like . . . but, aw, I don't want to waste too much time on the past. I'd like to hear what's going on with you. But I'll just tell you, the only reason I didn't call you is I called Bergstrom one time, before this happened, you know"—Larry was referring to his flight—"and he had just talked to your guy. And he said, 'Just don't talk to Weidler or Ackerman.' He said, 'They're under extreme pressure right now. . . . I'm telling you. Don't talk to them.' So I hear that, and then I call Joe. . . . He's telling me that you're, you're in there looking at demographics. I'm there . . . well, why would he do that? And I said, 'I guess he's looking for a new practice.' And then he says, 'Well, I don't really know.' But then I'm thinking about it, well, jeez, it sounds like, you know, you're under all this pressure, that you're going to be moving practice, and, ah, so I just didn't want to add any more temptation. That was my bottom line."

"Yeah?" said Ken.

"I took this one little course and I found out they can tap a phone in two minutes. They can find out. You know how I found out? These numbers where people call for suicides. You know? If they hang up, they just drop the phone, that's how long it takes them to find the place."

"Oh, Jesus!"

"But, anyway, tell me what's going on," said Larry.

They discussed the dental practice. Ken had been having a hard time making a go of it without Larry. He had never been the one to keep books or deal with the women who worked as receptionists and hygienists. Larry had always taken care of that. And the "girls," as they called them, had always liked Larry more than Ken. So it had been difficult, and Ken had been looking for a buyer to take over Larry's patients and his own.

Then the conversation wandered. Larry told Ken about the new baby, about how she had been sick with a virus and how the doctors scared him and Marcia by ordering up a whole battery of tests that had all proved negative. He had recently taken Chris to his first visit with a dentist.

"It killed me," said Larry. "He's telling me he's got some type of overbite. I'm there, 'Oh?' I felt like saying, 'Is it a Class Two?' You know?"

They talked about sports. Ken teased Larry about his facility for picking losers. Larry had picked the Miami Dolphins to beat the San Francisco 49ers in the Super Bowl, and the 49ers had won. And Larry had picked the Celtics to beat the Lakers in the NBA championship, and Boston had lost a game the night before.

Out in the car Marcia was signaling Larry that time was up, but he felt comfortable talking to Ken now, and had decided to take the risk. He waved back to Marcia, indicating that he was going to stay on the line. She scowled and just shook her head sadly.

Larry asked Ken how his legal situation was developing. Ken said he was definitely going to be charged for tax fraud, but he still might escape drug charges. He told Larry that Mark Stewart had just been sentenced to four years.

"Oh," said Larry.

Ken laughed. "I thought—"

Then Larry erupted in laughter.

"I thought you'd be interested in that," said Ken.

Larry suggested that Ken give them everything he knew about Mark Stewart, but then realized most of what Ken knew was hearsay.

"Well, I can remember meeting him before the fire," said Ken.

Larry reminded him of the meeting where Mark had said, "Just give me two more weeks."

"Yeah . . . but that can't be corroborated, right?" said Ken. "I mean, what if the boy [meaning David Ackerman] decided to say that, the same thing, too? . . . It looks like the boy's got a problem. The boy doesn't think he has a problem."

"The bad thing about that is you, if you really push that [the meeting with Stewart], they can probably charge you with that, too."

"Yeah."

"At least, that's my thought. . . . Even though it was vague . . . it looks like everyone conspired to do it then, and actually we had very little—"

"Input," said Ken.

"Control," said Larry. "It was just, we were listening to what he was going to do. We didn't have much choice anyway."

"Well, wasn't one motive . . . to get you . . . the insurance settlement?"

"Right. Right. . . . You know, I just can't believe the stupidity of it all. You know? Every month you get older you just think how you handled different things in your life and you just can't believe them, you know?" Larry laughed wistfully.

"Yeah," said Ken.

"So I gotta just think back like to fraternity days, how I would have handled things now, you know? It's just, it's just so different . . . but, so anyway."

"So I don't know what my exposure is," said Ken.

"But they haven't done any more, huh?"

"Not yet."

"Do they project any dates or anything?"

"No."

"So you're in that same limbo as when I left?"

"I'm in limbo and the reason, that's one of the reasons I'm liquidating," said Ken. He said he wanted to convert his assets into cash, anticipating the cost of defending himself from the pending indictment, and he also didn't want to just leave the girls in the office jobless and the patients without a dentist. Conversation drifted back to children. Ken's little girl had just started to walk. Larry said Christopher, who had been slow learning to talk, "won't shut up . . . sometimes I just have to put my hands over my ears, I just can't handle it anymore, you know?" He said Chris was adjusting well to the baby.

"It is a girl," said Larry.

Ken told Larry that the FBI had been questioning everyone in their office, all their friends.

"Kenny out on the limb here," he said. ". . . All friends left Kenny. No Boy. No Way-wee."

"Boy in New York now?"

"Boy in New York. Boy's setting up with Dad. Doesn't think he has a problem, and, ah, thinks you're in the Witness Protection Program."

They both laughed hard.

"No, I'm in a much better situation than that," said Larry.

"Yeah?"

"I like my situation, Ken, I think."

"Huh?"

"Yeah, I like my situation. If everything could clear up and change, I don't think I'd go back anymore. I'm just having too much fun."

"That's good."

"I don't think I'm really into playing dentist anymore, you know?" said Larry, laughing.

"To playing dentist?"

"No, I said I don't think I'm really into that anymore. I like talking to people but I don't really like drilling, I guess. . . . I never really liked doing the work, you know? I realize that now, now after having not done it. You know, at first it really bothered me, now it doesn't. . . . You really see how people think about doctors when you, when they don't know you're a doctor, you know?"

"Yeah?"

"When you hear comments like, 'This guy had this piece of land because he's a doctor,' and, you know, they wink at you or something. You know what I mean?"

"Yeah. . . . So, your picture's in the post office. Do you know that?"

"No!" Larry laughed with surprise.

"You're 'Wanted,' Way-wee."

"It's really in the post office?"

"Sure is," said Ken.

"I looked in the post office here and I didn't see it."

". . . They said it wasn't posted on the wall. Like, there's this thing of 'Wanted' people and it was in it."

"I'll have to check that out," said Larry.

"Yes, Way-wee, you could have a nice picture."

"That sucks . . . it just kills me 'cause every time I read those they're for real *severe* people."

Larry asked about his house. Ken said it was still empty, the grass was overgrown. It painted a sad picture for Larry. They talked more about the sale of the dental practice. Then Ken asked about Rusty. Larry said he was amazed, but the FBI didn't seem to be giving his family much trouble. They had not even spoken to his parents.

"It's very weird," said Ken.

"They don't even make the minimal—"

"That's what your mother-in-law says. She goes, you know, 'They've been here, why don't they go see Larry's parents?' "

Larry laughed.

Ken ran down the list of their friends and associates, giving Larry the latest news. The Rasners had gotten off—no jail time. Suzanne Norimatsu-Taylor had been sentenced to two years. Her husband, Bruce, had gotten ten.

"Taylor got ten?" said Larry.

"Yeah."

"He got the Eight Forty-eight conviction."

They discussed money that was owed Larry by various people. Larry asked Ken to steer any payments to Rusty, so that he could use it to help support his parents.

"Well, I'm glad to hear that you're not going to jail or anything yet," said Larry.

"Not yet. Way-wee, that bring up another point. If Kenny go to jail, will you help wife and family?"

"Yes, yes, yes. I make sure your wife get constant amount of it," said Larry, laughing lecherously. "That's not going to happen, right? Do you think?"

"I don't know. All I can say is, if something happens to me, I'd like you to somehow maintain an open communication with, somehow with me, and if I feel that there's a problem, like if I, if, if they want me to do something, if we have a prearranged time, I was thinking that if I answer the phone and say 'Hello'--instead of 'Yo!' or 'Way-wee!'—just hang up and don't, don't ever call me again."

"Uh-huh."

"Okay? I don't think, I don't know if that is going to happen, but . . . So if I ever say 'Hello,' then just—"

"Good," said Larry. "See, I don't mind calling you today because I'm several states away from where I live anyway, you know? So it doesn't really bother me. They can fuckin' do all they want, but it would be pretty hard for them to. 'Cause I had to be out of town anyways."

"Yeah."

"See, I'm in the real world again, Ken. You know, I got a job and—"

"You do?"

"Yeah."

"You got a job, Way-wee?"

"Yeah, a little bit. Once in a while I do some work."

"Yeah?"

"Most of the time I work out and just take it easy and read books. Run Marcia around."

"You play any golf?"

"No, I really haven't. I just haven't got around to that yet."

". . . So, you losing weight?"

"I'm swimming and all that," said Larry. "No. I'm about the same weight. I have to run Marcia around all the time and, you know, it's the same old life. Going to malls, going to stores, buying this, buying that. Fix up the house . . . all that type of stuff takes up so much time."

"Yeah."

"My lawn. I'm heavily into, you know, gardens and all that stuff."

Larry announced that he had won the local award for having the prettiest yard.

"I can't believe it. And I guess you did it, huh? You didn't hire somebody?"

"No, no. Well, I hired, but they were under my supervision, you know," said Larry, laughing.

"Well, you're such a dork."

"No, I couldn't do it myself, but I'm *into* it, you know? Like, this lawn I have sprinkler systems in and all that type of stuff. I put paper underneath my beds so no weeds will grow up through—"

"Underneath your flower bed?"

"Yeah. Things that you'll never dream about."

"I, I never even heard of doing that!"

Larry gave Ken gardening advice, advice on how to keep his Jacuzzi clean, advice on how to make it look like he was losing money in Atlantic City while converting checks to cash, advice about books— Larry was reading Elmore Leonard's *Glitz*.

"So what Kenny gonna do if he get indicted? You don't have any suggestion on how to leave, do you?"

"Well, you can't leave," said Larry.

"No?"

"You don't have the personality for it. And I don't think you're gonna have to. I think . . . if they really come down and convict you of everything you were guilty of, I mean, you're still pretty innocent. You know what I mean?"

"Yeah."

"I mean, I just can't see, unless Rasner really strengthened their position or something, I mean . . . everything else will make you look like you were just on the sidelines. I think it will be very hard to prove. That's my gut feeling. I mean, it could have been just my nicety that I gave you money, you know."

"You're one nice guy, Way-wee."

As Larry was talking on, checking up on old classmates, regretting that he was going to be missing his five-year dental school reunion in 1986, talking about how easily Marcia had given birth the second time, a security guard with a walkie-talkie walked toward him down the hall. On Ken's end, the phone suddenly went quiet. Larry could feel his body just quake momentarily as the guard approached him . . . could he possibly? . . . he had talked for a long time . . . is this it? . . . and walked straight past.

"There's no one hanging around there, is there?" Larry asked, breaking the silence.

"No, why?"

"Oh, a security guy just walked by."

Larry wanted to get off the phone now. He took down another number to call Ken in a few months. He told Ken that Marcia had just recently written a letter to her mother, and that it should be arriving sometime soon. Ken said that Marcia's mother had been in tears the last time he talked to her, upset that Larry and Marcia believed she would betray them.

"There hasn't been one thing I've done so far that's traceable," said Larry. "Even if I was on the other side working on it. That's the way I try to look at it. . . . So hopefully I can maintain that. . . ."

They agreed to talk again on the first Wednesday in August, at 9:00 a.m.

"Later on."

"Talk to you."

"Bye."

"Bye."

Larry hung up the phone and walked back to the car, still feeling slightly dazed as he always did after a long talk with someone from the past . . . from all that.

At the pay phone in suburban Philadelphia, Ken Weidler stepped aside as the hand of the FBI agent reached to turn off the tape recorder and tracing equipment.

Chuck Reed and Sid Perry had responded differently to Larry Lavin's sudden disappearance in November. Chuck was angry. To him it was just another example of Larry's arrogance. And it was embarrassing. Chuck had grown up in a generation that was cynical about law enforcement because it seemed like the little guys, the addicts and the street hustlers, were the only ones who ever got busted. Myth had it that the top men were too rich and powerful and smart to get caught. Here they had nailed the top man—arguably the most successful drug dealer in the city's history—and he had gotten away.

To Sid, with the sudden disappearance of Larry Lavin the case had taken a disappointing but intriguing turn. Just when they were about to reel in the big fish he jumped the line and swam away. It made for embarrassing publicity, but law enforcement experts understood that it was just impractical to keep suspects under twenty-four-hour surveillance when they were out on bail awaiting trial. Running away was, in fact, a very rare occurrence—statistics showed that only the smallest fraction of serious criminals, even those facing possible life sentences, skipped bail and disappeared. Most fugitives were caught within days or weeks. It was clear from the first day that Larry Lavin wasn't typical. Suddenly the altered embosser they had found on the day of his arrest in September made sense. They hadn't known what to make of it at first. Now it showed how carefully Larry had planned his flight. How interesting.

Both young agents were in agreement on their response to his flight, however. They knew it was a detective's once-in-a-lifetime challenge: to track down a truly intelligent, educated criminal with the daring, the motive, and the resources to remain a fugitive for good. Most career detectives accumulate a couple of cases like it over the years—the ones they can't abandon. Chuck and Sid were going to measure themselves against this one. They were going to catch Larry Lavin if it took them well into their retirement, some twenty-five to thirty years down the road.

At first the trail was cold. Larry had told no one where he was going. No one.

Chuck was convinced of that after putting the pressure on Agnes Osborn for a few months. From interviews with Larry's friends and associates, they knew Marcia was much, much closer to her mother than Larry was to his parents. And Marcia was going to have a baby in just a few months. If there was no contact with Agnes, either direct or indirect, then Larry and Marcia had made a completely clean break with the past. It was conventional wisdom in the FBI that nobody, ever, makes a completely clean break.

So Chuck stopped by to visit Agnes regularly. He knew she didn't like him. That was okay.

On one visit to her apartment, he watched from a distance as Agnes unloaded groceries from the trunk of her car and took them in the house. On her second trip out to the car, she took a child's red wagon from the trunk, filled it with groceries, and wheeled it in the front door.

Chuck bounded from the car to the front door and rapped on it loudly.

Agnes's quizzical face appeared behind the storm door. She scowled when she saw it was the FBI agent again.

"They're here, aren't they?" said Chuck.

"Who?"

"Larry and Marcia. Let me in."

"They are not here," she said.

"Then who is the little red wagon for?"

"It's my grandson Andrew's Christmas present," she said.

When he had gotten nowhere with Agnes after the first two months, Chuck paid a visit to her ceramics teacher. To help cope with boredom and loneliness after Larry and Marcia left, Agnes had begun attending ceramics classes three or four times a week. Chuck introduced himself to her teacher, explained what he was doing, and asked if the older woman had ever mentioned anything about her daughter or son-in-law.

When Agnes learned that Reed had talked to her teacher, first she was embarrassed about going to class again, then she was angry. She called Tom Bergstrom and complained about "that Chuck Reed fellow," and Bergstrom had spoken to the U.S. attorney's office about harassment of innocent citizens.

Chuck had backed off after that.

There had been no leads on through spring until Chuck and Sid were able to make Ken Weidler see his fate clearly. Either he could expect to go to jail for ten years or more and stay loyal to his best friend, or he could help the FBI find Larry and spend maybe two years, maybe less, in a minimum security prison. For Ken, who had bailed out of the cocaine business years before for fear of courting arrest and punishment, the alternative became clear as the day of his indictment loomed. He was doing it to protect himself, his wife, and his daughter. He didn't feel good about it, but when his back touched the wall, his priorities were clear.

At first, when Larry skipped his prearranged phone calls, it had seemed as if the son-of-a-bitch was psychic. How did he know that it was no longer safe to call Ken? The agents suspected that their cooperating witness had somehow passed a warning to his friend. Ken had to be reminded that his deal depended on results.

Larry's rambling talk with Ken was more than enough for the FBI to trace his location. He had phoned from a pay phone in a mall in northern Virginia, area code 804. With all his talk about being out of town and being several states away from home, they could only assume that he was living somewhere in the Delaware, Maryland, or Virginia area. Larry's old friends remembered that he had always talked fondly about owning a boat.

Also of interest in the conversation was Larry's mention of a letter with snapshots of the baby that Marcia had recently mailed her mother. Although Chuck had gotten heat for approaching Agnes's ceramics teacher, it had paid off. He knew that Marcia's previous letters had been first sent to the ceramics teacher, and then passed on to Agnes.

So they began intercepting the ceramics teacher's mail, and sure enough, within the week the letter from Marcia arrived.

It was carefully worded, and there were no obvious clues. But Chuck and Sid were intrigued by the lines about Chris's birthday party. They both had kids. They both recognized the kind of place Marcia described as a Chuck E. Cheese Pizza Time Theatre, a cute party place, a combination pizza parlor/arcade/amusement park. Children loved it. Both agents had taken their kids to Chuck E. Cheese outlets, and it was just as Marcia described it . . . except . . . what was this business about a bear bringing little Chris his cake?

They checked with the Chuck E. Cheese folks, and, sure enough, they didn't have a bear. But there was a chain just like theirs that operated primarily in Southern states. Its name was Showbiz Pizza Place, Inc. There were two Showbiz Pizza outlets in the 804 area code region. One was in Richmond, where the agents doubted Larry would have settled, and the other was in Virginia Beach. And, yes, it featured this short, cuddly mascot with a country accent who wore big red-and-yellow overalls.

His name was Billy-Bob the Bear.

THIRTEEN

Does This Have Something to Do With Larry?

Round, timid Ricky Baratt never earned a penny in the four years he had been dealing Larry's cocaine. From day one he was in debt. His life was dictated by the demands of dealing. He would be up all night drinking beer, smoking pot, and snorting cocaine, then he would go to work in the morning at Western Electric and snort more cocaine to stave off a hangover and stay awake.

When he first started using cocaine, after Larry shipped him his first supply via Federal Express, it had given Ricky a great rush of good feeling. Playing his saxophone or his piano, he felt an effortless virtuosity. He could stay up all night drinking, then snort a couple more lines and stay up all day feeling supercharged. As time went by, he found that no matter how many white lines he snorted, he never attained the same euphoria he had felt at first. And after several years of steady use, all joy had gone out of the experience. He needed the drug just to keep a kind of equilibrium that approximated normalcy—Ricky could hardly remember what truly normal felt like at all. And even that rough "normalcy" had a price. Cocaine aggravated his already tender nerves. There were times his heart beat so hard he felt certain that people around him could hear it inside his chest like a hammer. He associated with no one except those involved in the business. He was always lonely and depressed and afraid. Living in his Boston apartment, driving a sleek Mazda Rx-7, carrying a wad of twenties in his pocket, Ricky had all the outward manifestations of success, but life seemed to have trapped him on the down escalator—no matter how hard he tried to climb out of debt to Larry he just lost ground. By late 1983, Ricky's debt totaled well over

$150,000. But Larry didn't mind. He kept shipping kilos north. Ricky was just a small customer, an old friend.

Larry was doing him a favor.

Somehow, despite his growing drug dependence, Ricky managed to hang on to his job at Western Electric. In 1984, Ricky used the money he had been banking from his job to make a down payment and obtain a mortgage for a house on Sunset Lake in Haverhill, near the place where he and Larry had long ago spent summers with his parents.

Ricky made sure his father and mother saw only the surface of his life. They were pleased with his steady progress after years of drifting. His parents had nothing but stunned admiration for their son's old friend Larry. Whenever they saw the Lavins they heard more about their phenomenal youngest son's success. Once, Ricky's father asked Justin, "So, I hear Larry's working on his first million!" When Ricky relayed the comment to his friend, Larry said, "Tell Ted I've hit it."

His parents never got the word when Larry was arrested in Philadelphia, or that he had jumped bond and was living in hiding. Ricky never told them.

Friday, June 14, 1985, was a regular workday at Western Electric for Ricky Baratt. He was looking forward to spending time over the weekend with his family. Sunday was Father's Day. In the ten months since Larry's bust in Philadelphia, Ricky's life had come together. His source of cocaine had dried up, and Larry's flight had relieved him of the crushing burden of debt. At work he had been selected for a training program to work on secret military contracts. That morning he had taken advantage of his half-hour morning break in his usual way, by smoking a joint in his car on the lot outside the Andover plant, so he was feeling relaxed as he walked back in the front door. But instead of just waving him in as usual, the guard at the front door told Ricky that he was wanted in the security office.

Ricky assumed he was going to get word on his application for security clearance for the training program.

When he entered the security office, a Western Electric guard told him that the FBI wanted to see him.

"What about?" asked Ricky.

"I guess it's about your security clearance," he said.

Two men wearing suits stood when Ricky entered the office. A company security executive was seated behind the desk.

"Mr. Baratt?" asked one of the standing men.

"Yes?"

"We're with the FBI. You're under arrest for drug trafficking."

At first Ricky thought it was a joke.

"Okay, now what do you really want?" he said.

"No, no," said one of the agents. "This *is* what we want. We're here from the Eastern District of Pennsylvania."

Ricky could hear his heart start to pump loudly and felt a sudden rush of panic, but then he took a deep breath and urged himself to stay calm. Larry had always told him to say nothing if he was arrested.

The agents showed Ricky a document and asked him to sign it. He read over it quickly.

"No, this says I'm willing to waive my rights," he said. "I don't want to do that."

"Okay," said one of the agents. "Stand up."

Ricky stood. The agents began searching his pockets, taking his money, his wallet, and his watch. They put his hands together behind his back and handcuffed him. Then they led him out the door, walking him out through the crowded offices. His friends and co-workers watched with looks of astonishment.

Oddly, Ricky felt calm, even detached. It might have been the effects of the joint he had just smoked out in his car. He worried about his dog. If he was going to be in jail overnight, or over the whole weekend, who was going to feed and walk the dog?

In the ten months since Larry's arrest, Ricky had been living in a kind of fantasy, deluding himself with the hope that his crime was too small to warrant prosecution. He had not realized until then how much he had feared and dreaded this moment.

And yet, he felt oddly peaceful and resigned. A great weight of worry lifted. On the long ride to the courthouse in Boston he tried to imagine what evidence they had against him. Rusty Lavin had said his name had been in one of the crude ledgers seized at Bruce Taylor's house, but that had happened almost a year and a half ago. How much could they make of that?

At the courthouse he was left in a concrete holding cell with a group of Hispanic men.

"What's going to happen?" he asked the agent who led him into the cell.

"Well, you're going to be arraigned, and if you make bail, you'll go home," he said.

After about an hour they led him out of the cell and took him for fingerprinting and a mug shot. One of the supervising agents told Ricky that he was allowed to make a phone call.

"Who should I call?" Ricky asked. "I don't have an attorney. I don't even know one."

"Think of someone to call," the agent said. "You've only got one."

So he called his mother. There was a long silence on the phone as he explained.

"Does this have something to do with Larry?" his mother asked.

"Possibly," said Ricky. He was nervous about talking on the phone in the marshal's office. "Just find me a lawyer. Call somebody."

By late afternoon a lawyer arrived at the courthouse and obtained Ricky's release on fifty thousand dollars' bail—the judge accepted the lawyer's word that the five-thousand-dollar bail deposit would be paid on Monday. Ricky borrowed five dollars from the attorney and took a train and a cab back to the plant. It was early evening. His car was the only one left on the lot.

He drove to his parents' house. Over dinner he told them for the first time of his experiences with Larry over the last four years. His father and mother, who had been patient with him for so long, again listened sympathetically. They said they had known something was wrong, but never exactly what.

"Now that we know," said Dr. Baratt, "we can do something about it."

Ricky felt a great sense of relief, and an enormous sense of gratitude for his parents' loving response, and even a certain sense of pleasure at finally being able to expose Larry Lavin, the superstudent, the dentist, the financial whiz kid his parents had always admired, for what he was.

"Gee," said Dr. Baratt. "I guess Larry wasn't as smart as we all thought."

On Monday, the FBI pulled in its nets. Thirty more of Larry's friends and associates were arrested and charged with conspiracy to distribute cocaine.

Among the catch: Paul Mikuta, Billy Motto, Ken Weidler, David Ackerman, Willie Harcourt, Brian Riley, Stu Thomas, Danny Schneps, Gary Levin, and Stan Nelson. Also arrested were Jeff Giancola, Larry's old friend from Phillips Exeter, now an attorney with the U.S. Small Business Administration in Washington, D.C., and Gordon Acker, the fifth former Penn Dental School student charged in the conspiracy. Soon the FBI would add to the list Dan Dill, the fraternity brother who introduced Larry to dealing at Penn and who had gone on to become a vice-president with the investment firm Kidder Peabody, and Christine Pietrucha, Suzanne Taylor's faithful friend.

In a statement issued to the press, an FBI spokesman named the missing Larry Lavin as architect of the drug conspiracy, and said, "This case typified the insidious greed that now permeates all walks of the American way of life, which has resulted from the large profits obtained from the sale of narcotics. Those involved came from all walks of life. Prior arrests and records are the exception rather than the rule. . . . Most of those involved have been considered affluent and productive members of their community."

At the courthouse, big Willie Harcourt sat next to Ken Weidler on the same row of seats Larry and Frannie Burns had occupied ten months earlier. Willie could remember the night four years ago when Ken had offered him a chance to get involved in the business. Ken had been so successful then. It was as though he glowed with affluence and style.

Now Ken's head was down. He didn't want to look Willie in the eye.

"I'm sorry about this," said Ken.

Summer was long and hot in Virginia Beach. Larry spent every available day on the ocean. He took turns inviting his neighbors out on the boat, pulling them on water skis and fishing with them. His scuba diving grew more and more adventurous and frequent.

At home, Larry continued to sink roots into the community. He loaned money to a friend on a home construction project, and spent forty thousand for an expensive cement pump to help expand the business of the contractor who had built his backyard pool. Working with the owner of the diving shop, Larry discovered that scuba gear imported from Taiwan cost a fraction of what the dive shop was paying American manufacturers. In pursuing that he learned that the Port of Hampton Roads, in order to encourage business, offered generous assistance to businessmen interested in having merchandise imported. Larry was convinced that if he hit upon the right product to import, he could build a thriving legitimate business for himself.

These nascent ideas were all in Larry's head the day he told Ken that, even if all the legal troubles somehow went away, he might not want to come back.

Larry bought himself a bigger boat that summer, replacing his twenty-six-foot Sea Ray with a thirty-two-foot Wellcraft. He liked to take out parties of three or more on his excursions, and the smaller craft was just too cramped. The larger vessel was better equipped to handle ocean waters miles offshore, where Larry liked to dive. He loaded down the cabin of his new vessel with sophisticated electronic navigation equipment, a depth finder, and other devices. Fishermen who docked their boats at Lynnhaven liked to take Brian O'Neil along on their outings because he would dive and tell them where the fish were swimming. Larry preferred diving to fishing anyway.

It was on one such outing that he had met Pat O'Donnell, a retired FBI agent who was working for the state police's white-collar crime unit. When Larry came home and told Marcia that he had been out all day with someone from the FBI, she panicked. She thought they should just pack up and move out. But Larry felt so comfortable with Pat that he began going out regularly on the boat with him and his friends, some of them state policemen and FBI agents. He and Marcia, who thought the idea was insane, even attended a Christmas party at Pat's house.

Brian O'Neil was a remarkable friend and neighbor to the Virginia Beach community. He loaned money to his friends liberally, and took pleasure in cultivating his growing reputation for warmth and generosity. He talked Jess Miller's teenage son out of a chewing-tobacco habit by giving the boy an amazingly detailed technical description of the progress and consequence of mouth and gum cancer. He lectured at the local high school class of another neighbor, Andrew Payne, about investing in the stock market. When one of his scuba-diving buddies, Walter Heller, confessed that he had a lifelong ambition of tracking down and meeting his real mother (he had been put up for adoption as a baby), Brian coached the diver on methods of tracking down missing persons, leading him to private detective agencies that eventually found the woman living in California. Then Brian threw a party and took up a collection—donating a liberal sum himself—to send the diver on a trip to California to meet his mother. When one of his friends broke up with his longtime girlfriend, Brian had hours to spend fishing, drinking beer, or just sitting around the pool, lending a sympathetic ear, helping to ease the heartache. Brian inspired loyalty and deep affection in those he befriended, everyone from neighborhood teenagers to the retirees with whom he fished and dove off Lynnhaven's piers.

In January, Brian took a trip to the Florida Keys with a group of his diving buddies. He had read all of Ernest Hemingway's novels, so he spent the better part of one day looking through the author's house and favorite haunts.

Marcia watched with little surprise as Larry's friendships, his diving and fishing, and his new business interests gradually pulled him back out of the narrow family orbit they had enjoyed so briefly after fleeing Philadelphia. She looked back fondly on the weeks that they had spent in the beach apartment, when the phone never rang and Larry had nothing to do but spend time with her and with Chris. Their shared sense of danger had for a time brought them closer than they had ever been. By early 1986, Larry was every bit as busy and preoccupied as he had ever been dealing drugs and practicing dentistry. It was as if they lived separate lives, Marcia at home with the children, Larry out and around, looking on his family role as more of an obligation than a joy.

News from their past life was frightening and sad. Larry's friends and associates were all going to jail. One morning Larry read in *USA Today* where twelve of his coconspirators were sentenced, but it didn't include what the sentences were. He got the numbers from his brother: David Ackerman, 15 years; Ricky Baratt, 5 years; Frannie Burns, 16 years; Dan Dill, 5 years; Willie Harcourt, 8 years; Paul Mikuta, 12 years; Brian Riley, 12 years; Stu Thomas, 7 years; Billy Motto, *20 years!*

Larry could guess why Billy had gotten hammered. Of all those involved, of all the Ivy Leaguers and young professionals, grade-school-educated Billy Motto had known better than anyone what the risks were. It was Billy who had insisted all along that eventually they would all go to jail. Larry knew that the feds would consider Billy an "organized-crime figure." From life in South Philly, growing up as a teenage drug addict, fighting his way out of real poverty, Billy knew more about consequences in the real world than any of Larry's other friends. He was the one who tolerated violence in the collection of his debts. So, in that sense, he was the most seriously criminal of them all. But Billy was also the only one who would never squeal. Everybody else had mouthed the ideal: "If you can't do the time, don't do the crime." But Billy had really meant it. He would never flip. And the government wouldn't forgive him for that.

It was interesting to note that Ken Weidler had only received two and a half years. Larry, who had never called Ken back after their conversation in June, wondered how Kenny had managed to pull it off. *Two and a half years!* What could Kenny have given them that was worth so much?

In his happy isolation, Larry could view with detachment the collapse of his business and the downfall of his friends. He could congratulate himself for being the only one smart enough to have gotten away. It alternately made him feel like a genius and like a schmuck. In the late-night hours after Marcia had gone to bed, he would sit watching TV, eating his standard plate of hot dogs, and sometimes his freedom and satisfaction turned to feelings of guilt and betrayal. After all, *he* was responsible for destroying all those promising young lives. But the feeling would pass. Larry could think of no instance when he lured someone into the business, or forced them to stay when they wanted out. It was like some accident of history. It had landed him on his feet, and everyone else on his ass. And there was no way *that* was just luck.

Larry learned in late winter that the FBI planned to indict both his brother Rusty and his sister, Jill. He talked to Rusty on the phone almost every week. In desperation, Larry called Tom Bergstrom to see what he could do. Tom told him that the FBI might be prepared to leave Rusty and Jill alone if he would turn himself in.

"How much time would you be willing to do?" Tom asked.

"To tell the truth, Tom, right now I can't see myself doing any time in jail at all," he said.

Although it weighed heavily on his conscience, Larry knew that he would not turn himself in to save his brother and sister. There was a simple, ugly truth behind the decision. He loved his brother and sister, but he loved his freedom more. His year as a millionaire fugitive had been the happiest year of his life. How could he voluntarily give that up? At worst, Rusty and Jill would have to be away for a few years. Judging by the sentences his associates had received—*Billy had gotten twenty years!*—Larry knew he could expect to spend a decade or more behind bars.

He told Tom that he wanted to wait and see whether they really did arrest Rusty and Jill before making up his mind.

"Then it will be too late," said Tom.

But Larry had already decided.

In early April of 1986, "Brian" piloted a fishing and diving expedition forty-five miles offshore.

Loaded down with beer, crabs, bait, air tanks, and diving equipment, he eased through the Lynnhaven outlet with his friends Lee, Wally, and Barry before sunrise. Only the glow of all the electronic equipment in the cabin illuminated the blackness of the ocean. The water was still and flat. As dawn approached, the sky and ocean glowed a deep reddish orange that slowly faded until the first blinding flash of sun edged over the rim.

Their destination was the sunken remains of the *Morgan*, a U.S. Liberty cargo ship from World War II that had carried tanks, tank parts, Harley-Davidson motorcycles, and 70-mm shells. The *Morgan* had crashed into a commercial freighter on its maiden voyage out of Norfolk harbor. Larry's electronic gadgetry located the sunken wreckage easily, and buoys were thrown overboard to mark its location. It took about forty minutes to maneuver the vessel directly over the wreck. Larry and Lee took turns with Wally and Barry diving down 120 feet, exploring the remains of the cargo vessel. That afternoon, Larry located the sunken remains of the *Cayahoga*, a 125-foot Coast Guard cutter that had taken seventeen trainees to their deaths when it sank. Larry anchored over the wreck and took a nap while his friends fished.

When he woke two hours later, a thick fog had rolled over the boat. He had planned to dive down to the wreckage, but the fog would make it impossible to see the buoys for an anchoring run. They decided to head back. Negotiating the fog with the boat's electronic equipment was easy.

As the vessel got under way, Larry climbed back down into the cabin to warm soup for himself and his friends. He had installed a small microwave oven in the cabin, and found occasion to use it on every outing. As he worked in the cramped space below, Larry shouted up to his friend Barry, asking how far they were from land.

"The monitor says six miles," Barry shouted.

But before the last words were spoken, there was a crash and Larry was thrown against a cabin wall.

In an instant, he and his friend Lee exchanged a terrified glance, expecting to hit water. But nothing happened. The vessel was oddly stationary, as if it had suddenly been lifted out of the water.

Larry dashed up from the cabin and climbed directly out to the bow.

Not more than six feet away, an amazed jogger stood staring up at Larry from the beach!

"Well, we're here!" shouted Larry.

Few surprises compare with hitting the beach when you're supposed to be six miles at sea. Larry realized immediately what had happened. It was his own stupid fault. The electronic navigator had originally been programmed to guide them out of Lynnhaven, through the channels and out to sea. It followed a sequence of coordinates from Point A, Lynnhaven, to Point F, the longitude and latitude of the sunken cargo ship. When they had turned around, Larry had neglected to reverse the instructions. So instead of automatically proceeding from point F back through the coordinates to Point A, the Wellcraft had steered directly to Point A. The shortest distance to Point A, Lynnhaven pier, was a straight line that traversed, unfortunately, a decidedly solid stretch of Virginia Beach.

Larry swam out and anchored the vessel, then unloaded all of the valuable gear from the boat, and accepted a ride home. There he changed into dry clothes, told Marcia what had happened, and then drove back out to spend the night sleeping in the cabin.

He awakened to the voice of a small boy yelling, "Hey, Mom! There's someone inside!"

Larry climbed back out on deck into the morning light. A crowd of about thirty people had gathered on the Seventy-eighth Street beach to inspect the accident. The tide was out, so there was a good five feet of beach between the rear of the boat and the water. A photographer from the Virginia Beach newspaper was taking pictures. Larry thought, *Just what I need.*

A reporter approached him and began asking questions. What could Larry do? He answered the questions, and then he begged the guy not to take his picture or use his name.

"Look, I was playing hooky from work yesterday. I'll lose my job," he said. And the reporter obliged.

The story, with a picture of his boat under the headline "High and Dry," ran on the front page of the next morning's newspaper. It took most of the next day to free his boat and have it towed back to Lynnhaven pier. His picture went up at the Lynnhaven boat house, and for the next few weeks he was ribbed everywhere he went about running aground.

The boat was badly damaged—the props, the rudder, the engine mount. It was the beginning of the good season for fishing and diving, so it pained Larry to be spending the first weeks of May trying to get his vessel seaworthy. After weeks of work, it was due to be shipshape by May 16.

Through it all, Larry had laughed. His friends were impressed.

"Brian, you're too much," said his friend Lee. "Anybody else would have been furious."

Larry said, "Lee, this is nothing. I've fucked up a lot worse than this in my life."

When an investigation is successfully resolved, the steps to that happy end seem obvious. But no answer is the obvious one until the hunt is done.

So there were many months of work left for Chuck Reed and Sid Perry after they intercepted Larry's phone call to Ken and Marcia's letter to her mother. In addition to preparing and giving testimony at the trials of all those charged in the expanding cocaine investigation, and to continuing to build evidence against others, the agents gradually took steps to further narrow their search for the ringleader. By summer of 1986, they were convinced that Larry and Marcia were living under assumed names somewhere along the Maryland-Virginia coast, most likely in Virginia Beach or Norfolk. There were hundreds of active and retired FBI agents living in that region. So one of the steps they took was to have color photographs of Larry and Marcia enlarged and mailed to everyone on the FBI's mailing list.

And so it was that one morning, just weeks after Pat O'Donnell had helped "Brian O'Neil" rock his beached thirty-two-foot Wellcraft into the water, and then helped him down a few beers to celebrate, two photographs dropped out of an envelope from the FBI regional office in eastern Pennsylvania.

There was no need to even look twice. The long neck and green eyes and thick mop of black hair were unmistakable.

Dr. Lawrence W. Lavin, fugitive cocaine dealer. That certainly explained his wealth and leisure. What a shame. What a damn shame.

Marcia had a bad dream when they were in Virginia Beach. In the dream, she was being led away from her house by men in suits, and Chris and Tara were being taken off in a different direction. Brown-haired Tara was a year old and not yet walking, wearing the pretty blue plaid dress she had worn Easter Sunday when Marcia had insisted on getting everyone dressed up and going into Norfolk for the afternoon. Chris had just turned four. He was wearing his shorts with his suit coat and tie. In the dream, Marcia knew as her children were led away, Tara cradled happily on the stranger's arm and Chris holding his hand, both with their back to her, that the separation was going to be permanent, that her babies would be raised by strangers.

She had learned in late April that she was pregnant again.

On the morning of May 15, a bright blue-sky Thursday, Larry and Marcia made love before the children awakened. As they lay in bed afterward, Larry explained that he was going to spend the day getting rid of an accumulation of documents he had been keeping in a briefcase in the crawl space over the ceiling in the garage. When he prepared tax returns for his various identities, he had assembled records of all his identities and accounts. It wasn't a good idea to have them all there in the house. If he got caught, then the feds would know how to track down all of his resources. Not that Larry ever expected to get caught. But there was no harm in playing it safe. He told Marcia that his boat would finally be shipshape the next day, so he wanted to get the papers squirreled away safely before then. He said it would take him most of the day to drive around to his various postal boxes and safe-deposit boxes. Marcia often came along on these trips.

Then the children were up. There were diapers to be changed and outfits to be pulled on. Marcia went straight to work and Larry went down to the kitchen to get himself breakfast.

As Marcia prepared breakfast for the children, the phone rang. It was Roy Mason, one of Larry's fishing friends. She heard Larry agree right away to go out fishing with him that morning. So much for the earlier plan.

"Is it all right with you?" Larry asked.

"Yeah. Just stay here with Tara while I run Chris to nursery school," she said.

Marcia finished feeding the children and then walked Chris out to her station wagon and drove him the few blocks to the nursery school. When she got back, Larry had Tara outside watching as he loaded up his van with a cooler and his fishing gear.

It was a typical quiet morning. Marcia took Tara for a swim out in the pool, and did household chores as the baby napped. She picked Chris up at the nursery school at noon, and then fed both children lunch. Chris went over to play in the backyard of a neighbor's house, and Marcia drove up to the Giant supermarket to get a Smithfield ham for supper. When she got home she put Tara down for her afternoon nap and put away the groceries. She had never fixed a big ham, so she went over her recipe and started preparing it. At about three-thirty, after Tara woke up, she walked across the street to bring Chris home.

She was in the kitchen preparing dinner, Chris was lying on his stomach on the couch in the den watching his cartoons, and Tara was rolling around the kitchen and foyer in her wheeled walker, when the doorbell rang. Marcia thought it must be Girl Scouts selling cookies. She had seen girls out in the neighborhood earlier that day. But from the kitchen she could see, through the long narrow windows on either side of the front door, that there were a man and a woman waiting.

She knew immediately who it was.

Should I open the door now or should I try to get out the back? she thought, but realized immediately that the idea was ridiculous. She crossed the foyer and opened the door.

"Yes?"

"What's your name?" said the man.

"Marcia O'Neil."

"What's your husband's name?"

"Brian O'Neil. What do you want to know this for?" she asked.

"We're with the FBI," he said. "We've arrested your husband as he came off a fishing boat out at the Lynnhaven pier."

Marcia just stood there frowning.

"I think you better let us in," the woman said. "Or the neighbors are going to see what's going on."

"Do I have any choice?"

"No," said the woman quietly.

So Marcia opened the door and let them in. Tara came wheeling down the foyer to the man, who stooped to pick her up. Marcia quickly gathered up her daughter.

"Larry gave us the name of a neighbor who can take the kids," the male agent said. "You are under arrest. Let's get your kids out of here so they're not exposed to this."

Marcia could see there were agents on the back porch. Out the front window she could see more in the yard and driveway. She walked back toward the kitchen with Tara and, without even thinking about what she was doing, inspected the ham, set Tara down, took a big knife from a drawer, and started slicing it.

"I'm sorry," said the female agent. "You can't move around the house freely anymore."

"Well, who's going to feed my kids?" asked Marcia, turning with the knife in her hand.

In the other room an agent switched off the TV and Chris started to cry. Marcia set down the knife and turned off burners on the stove. Then, with permission from the agents, she let the dog, who was barking loudly in the basement, out into the backyard. Chris was still crying.

"Who are these people?" he asked.

The house was filled with agents, who had begun searching every surface and drawer upstairs and down. The lead agent, whom she had met at the door, started reading Marcia her rights. She felt she was in shock.

Nancy Payne, her next-door neighbor, entered through the front door with another agent. Nancy was crying.

"I'm sorry," she said, not knowing what else to say.

"Please take care of the kids," said Marcia. "How long am I going to be held?" she asked the agents.

"Maybe three or four days, maybe more," the agent answered.

Nancy took Tara, and her daughter Beth, a teenager, came in behind her to take Chris. Beth was escorted upstairs to get some diapers and clothes for the children. Then Marcia was alone in the house with the agents.

They finished reading Marcia her rights, and she said she understood. She signed the statement, pausing to say, "Well, I guess I can use my real name now, huh?" She signed, for the first time in eighteen months, "Marcia Lavin." Then they showed her another document, this one turning over the house and all its contents to them.

"I'm not going to sign this until I talk to a lawyer," she said.

"Okay," the agent said. "You don't have to sign anything right now. We'll get you to do it tomorrow."

"Where is the false wall?" asked one of the agents.

"What wall?"

"We had reports that there might be guns and drugs," he said.

"There's nothing like that here," said Marcia.

Marcia asked if she could change clothes if she was going to be taken out. She was escorted upstairs, and in the bathroom, with an agent waiting outside the door, she pulled off her shorts and top and put on blue jeans and an Oxford shirt. She collected her real I.D. from her jewelry box, her Pennsylvania driver's license, her old Penn I.D., and her Social Security card. She was asked to remove her diamond earrings and wedding ring, and they gave her papers to sign turning her possessions over to them.

Again, Marcia demurred.

"I'd like to talk to a lawyer before I sign this," she said.

Marcia thought it peculiar that she felt so strangely emotionless.

"I'm sorry," said the female agent, "but I have to put handcuffs on you."

Marcia gave her a look of disbelief. "Do you really think that's necessary?" she asked.

"Yes. It's policy," the agent said.

So Marcia held out her hands.

"You can drape your sweater over your hands if you don't want people to see," the woman said. Marcia nodded. The agent draped the sweater over her hands and led her out of the bedroom. Down the hall Marcia could see a crowd of agents huddled over the computer in Larry's office.

As they moved across the front yard toward the car, Marcia felt the urge to check her mailbox. She had been busy in the house all day and had been meaning to get to it. Right away she realized what a ridiculous thought it was. It was strange, she thought. Like with the ham in the kitchen. Her mind clung stubbornly to household routine, as though she were determined not to acknowledge to herself at some level that this was actually happening. She looked down the handsome block of Royal Oaks Close and recalled that just an hour or so ago she had walked up with Tara in the stroller and Chris alongside, without a care in the world. And, just like that, it was gone. Marcia was confident that she would be released after at most a few days or so, but she knew her life would never be the same again.

Inside the car, the agent reached around Marcia for the seat belt, then hesitated.

"You're pregnant, aren't you?" she asked.

"Yes," said Marcia. "Just two months."

"Is it okay to put on the seat belt?"

"Yes. It's okay."

On the drive into Norfolk, Marcia thought about the children. The Millers were out of town that week. Marcia thought how lucky she was that Nancy Payne had been home. If not for Nancy, she would have had no place to send Chris and Tara. It would be a trauma for Tara to spend the night away from home, away from her mother, but at least it was with familiar people in a familiar place.

In Norfolk they drove past Waterside, the waterfront shops and restaurants where Marcia had dragged Larry on Easter. She was glad they had done that. It would probably be the last time they would go anywhere together again as a family.

The courthouse was nearby. They drove into a parking garage and then led Marcia upstairs. It was past dinnertime. Pregnancy always made Marcia voracious.

"Can I have something to eat?" she asked.

"We don't have anything here," the agent said.

"How about something to drink?"

One of the courthouse workers overheard Marcia's requests and offered her his tray full of food.

"No, thanks," she said.

One of the agents emerged from a room with a diet Coke.

Further down the long tile hallway, she heard Larry's voice.

"Is he here?" she said.

"Yes," said the agent alongside her. "He's in the next room down."

"Can I see him?"

"After you're finished," the agent said. "We have to get your picture and your fingerprints."

They had trouble getting the camera to work when they took her mug shot. Marcia perched on a stool holding up a placard with her name and birthdate on it. They took her fingerprints.

After that they led her to an upstairs office. Larry was waiting alone for her there. It was sunset outside, a beautiful urban panorama under a glowing red orange sky.

Larry grimaced when he saw her. He looked disheveled and worn-out. Then there were tears in his eyes, and he was shaking, crying. He couldn't get any words out. She took his hand as they sat down together on a couch under the window.

"I'm sorry" was all Larry could say. It came out as a gasp.

"Don't worry about it," said Marcia, trying to soothe him. "You gave me the best years of my life. I don't regret a single day. I don't blame you. I still love you."

Larry just sobbed. Tears rolled down his face. He told Marcia he had signed over everything to get her released.

"Are you all right?" Marcia asked. She was always worried that he would get beaten up by arresting agents, even though the ones who had brought her in had been kind.

"I'm all right," said Larry.

Then an agent came back in the office and led Larry out. Marcia asked if she could use a phone. From the phone on the office desk she called Nancy. The children were fine. They had eaten dinner and were watching TV.

"I don't know when I'm going to get out," said Marcia.

"As long as you need me to keep them for you, I will," said Nancy.

"Thanks," Marcia said. "Just don't let them go to anybody! Don't let them out of your sight."

"I won't," said Nancy. "They're mine."

When she got off the phone, Marcia gave the agent escorting her the phone number for her mother and for her brother.

"Ask them to contact our lawyer, would you?" she said.

After waiting for another hour or so, Marcia was led down to a car in the garage and set in the backseat alongside Larry. They were driven back to a Virginia Beach jail. Larry's hands were cuffed behind his back, so he couldn't sit comfortably. Marcia's hands were cuffed in her lap.

"Just like Bonnie and Clyde," said Larry, who had regained his composure completely. They both laughed.

It was a long ride and both Larry and Marcia felt goofy. Larry told her about how he had been arrested on the pier at Lynnhaven. Marcia listened to him and watched the stars against a night sky that darkened, as they drove, from deep violet to black. Marcia had a wistful feeling. These would be their last moments together for a long time, she thought. She rested her head on his shoulder for part of the ride.

At the jailhouse, Larry was led away by three guards.

"I love you," he said.

"I love you, too, Larry," said Marcia. Women guards escorted her off in a different direction.

As she walked up the sidewalk to the front door of the jail, Marcia couldn't see Larry, but she could still hear his voice.

Epilogue

Federal Courthouse, Philadelphia

Larry Lavin's earthly day of reckoning took place September 4, 1986, in two sterile modern courtrooms, long, narrow, carpeted chambers without windows, noise, or odor, beneath ceilings that reach thirty to forty feet above the judicial dais.

Presiding over the first hearing, Larry's sentencing on drug charges, was the Honorable Louis H. Pollak, a slight, pale man with bald head and wire-rimmed glasses. Beneath the outward calm of the courtroom that morning was real drama. Judge Pollak had the power to lock Larry Lavin away for the rest of his life.

Larry sat behind one table with his lawyer, Tom Bergstrom. Seated at a table alongside were assistant U.S. Attorneys Ron Noble and Tina Williams Gabbrielli, who had prosecuted cases related to the "Yuppie Cocaine Conspiracy." Seated with them were Chuck Reed and Sid Perry.

In Larry's defense, Tom Bergstrom presented expert testimony that attempted to explain the psychological roots of his client's greed. Then, one by one, he elicited warm tributes from Larry's Virginia Beach friends, who had traveled north to do what they could for the fun-loving, generous man they knew as Brian O'Neil. Tom concluded with a stirring, emotional plea for lenience.

But these were fragile impediments to the onrushing momentum of justice. In the year and a half since Larry had first been arrested, public attitudes toward cocaine use had gone through a dramatic transformation. The harmless party drug, the glamorous aphrodisiac and success symbol was now perceived as the new killer on city streets. With the advent of crack, with the recent shocking death of University of Maryland basketball star Len Bias, cocaine had shifted in public perception from the category of illegal but culturally approved drugs like marijuana to the dark category of addictive killer drugs like heroin.

This was no merely technical distinction. In 1969, in the enormously popular movie *Easy Rider*, the soundtrack sang of the difference between a dealer and a pusher:

> *The dealer, the dealer is the man with the*
> *love grass in his hand.*
> *For a nickle or a dime he'll sell you lots of*
> *sweet dreams,*
> *But the pusher is a monster, Good God!*
> *He's not a natural man.*
> *God damn the pusherman!*

Larry had always seen himself as a "dealer." Now, at the height of a national mania over crack (a word Larry had learned only months before) and a new recognition of how addictive and insidious were the long-term effects of cocaine, Larry was being portrayed as a "pusher." And not just any pusher, but "Dr. Snow," as *Philadelphia* magazine had dubbed him, the biggest pusher in the city's history.

Speaking for the government was Gabbrielli, a sober young woman with glasses and long light brown hair:

"Dr. Lavin headed up the largest, the most sophisticated cocaine enterprise ever prosecuted in the Eastern District of Pennsylvania. So far in this morning's proceedings not much has been said to remind us of the extent of his criminal involvement. . . . I think it's important to dwell for a moment on how much cocaine we're talking about. We've seized, through the assistance of a cooperating witness, David Ackerman, records of the Lavin organization for 1981 and part of 1982. In 1981, it shows that the organization purchased approximately two hundred fifty kilograms of pure, uncut cocaine. This cocaine was then processed, cut, and resold throughout the United States. Based on available information, the government believes it could easily show the organization distributed approximately a thousand kilograms of cocaine. *A thousand kilograms of cocaine.* That's a million grams. Once the cocaine is sold, it's usually cut at least one more time before it's redistributed on the streets. Even if it was cut only once to a fifty percent purity level, which is still very high quality, that's two million grams of cocaine. An eighth of a gram is considered an individual's dosage amount. That would be sixteen million individual dosage amounts. That's enough cocaine to turn on every man, woman, and child in . . . Philadelphia, Pennsylvania; Wilmington, Delaware; New York City; Boston, Massachusetts; Baltimore, Maryland; Washington, D.C.; Pittsburgh, Pennsylvania; Chicago, Illinois; Denver, Colorado; Phoenix, Arizona; and San Francisco, California. The government submits we have not caught a small fish, . . . but rather a kingfish.

". . . Lavin is thirty-one years old. He's led an exceptional life, one full of excitement, power, thrills. He's been a multimillionaire. He estimates, himself, he made five million. Perhaps it was more. He had money to throw extravagant parties, live in the best neighborhoods. He had money to be generous with, to loan to friends. He was able to help others in Virginia Beach. After all, it was easy. The money came easy. Now, however, it's time for Lavin to pay that price."

Gabbrielli concluded that Larry ought to be sentenced to "at least" thirty years.

Judge Pollak listened as Larry stood to defend himself, arguing that his business had been based on "friendship," not violence, and that he had never been fully aware of the harm caused by cocaine.

When Larry sat down there was a long silence in the courtroom. All eyes fell on the slight, black-robed figure on the dais. The silence lasted a full minute before Judge Pollak looked up from the papers before him and began to speak.

"Why do we have such a full courtroom today?" the judge asked, scanning the crowded benches and standing spectators in the far corners of the chamber. Among the crowd were the press, Marcia Lavin and friends, observers from the courthouse, assistants on the U.S. attorney's staff, and even the judge's daughter, who knew how long and hard her father had considered the matter.

"People are sentenced in the United States in courtrooms like this . . . every day," said the judge. "By the weekly hundreds we send people off, sometimes to incarceration, sometimes to probation. Mostly the process does not demand this much attentive interest. Is Dr. Lavin's case different from most?

". . . Our psychologist witness characterized Dr. Lavin's case as an American tragedy. He saw close analogies to the terrifying Dreiser story. . . . I think we have a tragedy here, and perhaps it's an American one, . . . but I don't think that it's quite the one that Dreiser had in mind.

"We saw Dreiser's hero come up, and then we saw him go down. He didn't join us. Why do I say 'us'? Because this courtroom, which is so well attended today, . . . is a middle-, upper-middle-class, upwardly mobile, largely professional courtroom, mostly white, making it, and we are, are we not, concerned and even fascinated by Dr. Lavin because he is what? Very close to being one of us? . . . I'm suggesting that we focus on Dr. Lavin's case because we identify with him and are frightened by what he did, and by what others might easily have done. We are worried and we are terrified about what is about to happen to him when he is cast out of our society. That's part of what is so frightening.

" . . . The distribution of masses of cocaine throughout our society is the distribution of a terrible poison. It seems reasonable to suppose, even though we cannot document each of the sad, sad cases, that people by the hundreds or by the thousands, by the tens of thousands, have been victimized by Dr. Lavin's and his colleagues' conspiracy. . . . And the victimization does not necessarily end with the breakup of this conspiracy. It seems reasonable to suppose that people by the hundreds, by the thousands, by the tens of thousands, were introduced into a self-destructive way of life from which they may take years and years to extricate themselves, or may never, and are likely to do their time in prisons or die sick and alone. These are dreadful crimes.

"Do I agree with the government that Dr. Lavin should be sent away for thirty years, at least? I do not. Do I agree with Dr. Lavin's lawyer, Mr. Bergstrom, that the minimum called for . . . is an adequate disposition? I do not."

Judge Pollak sentenced Larry to fifteen years under count five, the Section 848 "continuing-criminal-enterprise" charge, and fined him a hundred thousand dollars. On the other counts, he imposed a total sentence of seven additional years in prison. *Twenty-two years.* The courtroom received the news with silence. Larry sat motionless in his chair, his back to the crowd.

"I repeat," said the judge, "that we do have here today a form of American tragedy: the fall, from extraordinary grace, of someone who on the record is clearly capable of doing very good things, has done very good things, for friends and family. It is not at all surprising that many are deeply devoted to this person, and that must be borne in mind at the same time that we bear in mind that Dr. Lavin, witting or unwitting, has done terrible things to our society. . . . They deserve no sentimental glossing over. They deserve punishment."

That afternoon there was a second hearing before Judge Louis C. Bechtle, whose task it was to sentence Larry on five counts of failing to pay income taxes on his illicit earnings. Each of the five convictions—Larry had pleaded guilty—carried a possible five-year prison term and ten-thousand-dollar fine. There was hope that after the morning session, Judge Bechtle would not make his punishment "consecutive" to the drug term—add more prison time to the twenty-two years imposed by Judge Pollak. Since the tax crimes could be seen as a mere corollary to the central crime of drug dealing, Judge Bechtle had the defensible option of making his punishment "concurrent"—allowing Larry to serve time for his tax crimes at the same time that he served time for the drug charges.

It was immediately apparent, however, that Judge Bechtle, a

jurist of short temper and few words, was not disposed to treat the case before him as a shadow of the drug conspiracy case.

Judge Bechtle gave no speech. He noted with distaste, "Our nation is awash in these drugs." Then he sentenced Larry to the full five years' imprisonment on each of the first four tax charges, and five years' probation on the fifth. He imposed a ten-thousand-dollar fine on four of the charges, and a hundred thousand dollars on the fifth.

Summing up, the judge announced that the twenty years' imprisonment and five years of probation he was imposing would be served *consecutive* to the twenty-two years Larry had received that morning.

Marcia sobbed. Larry looked as if someone had just slapped him in the face.

Afterword

I was originally drawn to Larry Lavin's story by the suspicion that, had I made a few decisions differently in my life, I might have gone down the same road. Larry started his drug business by peddling small bags of marijuana from his frat house at the University of Pennsylvania. He made money and friends . . . and one thing led to another.

Just a few years before he got started, I was a student on a college campus in Baltimore. A friend from Penn (as it happens) delivered to me one afternoon, unsolicited, the largest bag of pot I had ever seen. He dropped it on the floor of my bedroom and suggested that I break it down into small bags, mark up the price slightly, and sell it off. We could split the profits. I could see myself becoming the most popular man on campus overnight. I remember sitting and staring at the bag for a few minutes, and then deciding I wasn't going to do it. My friend left disappointed and bewildered by my lack of ambition. I had figured it was one thing to be an occasional user, quite another to be a dealer. It wasn't exactly a moral decision, because one who buys and uses dope occupies no significantly higher ground than the seller. For me it was a question of risk, of how serious I was willing to be about breaking the law. To stray across the line from time to time to get high was different than seeking profit in illegality.

When stories about Larry first broke in Philadelphia in the mid-1980s, I was a reporter at *The Philadelphia Inquirer,* and I remembered back to that moment in college. What if I had decided to sell? Might I have gotten tempted by the ballooning profits, too? And when the market shifted so smoothly from pot to cocaine, with its exponentially higher profit margins and larger earnings, would I have been able to resist the opportunity to make millions?

Larry and I were contemporaries. I knew the world he had come from, and, like him, I was now married and embarked on a career with small children at home. Attitudes toward illicit drug use had changed dramatically in a few short years. My own generation had experimented liberally and then moved on. For many, the brief cocaine craze of the late 1970s and early 1980s had been a kind of last fling before settling fully into the responsibilities of adulthood, career, and parenting. Cocaine, for that brief period, was seen in the same light as marijuana, a harmless recreational drug banned by ill-informed, uncool, and uptight elders. Then, seemingly overnight, cocaine the party drug became cocaine the killer. Len Bias's death, the rising toll of addiction, and the violent rise of the Andean cocaine cartels exposed a dark underside to all the fun. By the mid-eighties, the crack epidemic was beginning. Addicts combed my neighborhood in Philadelphia nightly, stealing anything they could carry off. Dealers like Larry Lavin became major public enemies. I could easily imagine myself as him, onetime life of the party, dentist, husband, father, sitting in a courtroom charged as an organized crime kingpin, facing a potential life sentence, wondering what the hell had happened. When Larry and Marcia and the kids vanished . . . well, I understood that, too.

I didn't work on the story initially for the newspaper, but when *Esquire* magazine approached me about it in 1985, I welcomed the assignment. Larry was still a fugitive. This audacious yuppie cocaine kingpin who had seemingly gotten away with millions, while everyone else in his nationwide organization had been busted and sent to jail, had intrigued then-editor Lee Eisenberg. With the help of FBI agents Sid Perry and Chuck Reed, I researched and wrote the story, but Larry got caught before it ran. With the daring fugitive in custody, *Esquire* dropped the piece. But in the process of researching the story about him, I had grown even more intrigued. I wanted to meet this man I had spent months trying to understand.

It turned out that Larry wanted to meet me, too. He had stayed in touch with his family and old friends—which had been his undoing— and they had told him that a writer was poking around for information about him for a piece in *Esquire*. He had been dreading its publication, knowing that photographs of him in a national magazine might blow his cover in Virginia Beach (which is why Perry and Reed were being so helpful). But, knowing Larry as I do now, he was also curious and even a little eager to see what the magazine would say. At that point he still took a little pride in the illicit enterprise he had built, and his infamy. So one afternoon not long after he was arrested and returned to Pennsylvania, I got a collect phone call from the Chester County

Prison. I drove down and met him for the first of what would be many long interviews.

I found him to be a charming, intelligent, and candid to a fault. Indeed, in time I think Larry began to realize that in his efforts to explain himself to me, he was painting an unflattering portrait of himself. His wife, Marcia, had been against his talking to me at the beginning, but as time went by and as Larry's misgivings grew, Marcia warmed to the project. It hit home in particular with stories (related cheerfully to me by Larry) of romps with whores in Atlantic City. Marcia had not known about these things when she ran away with him. Marcia might not have known about all of Larry's activities, but she was not blind to his failings. She told me, "Maybe this is exactly what he needs. Maybe this book will finally force Larry to see himself as he really is."

Larry didn't react strongly one way or the other to the book, at least not to me. There were parts of it he didn't like. He hadn't anticipated my telling all the lurid details of his philandering (*But, Larry, why did you think I spent all those hours sitting with you in prison asking questions and taking notes?*), and his memory differed from others I had interviewed about certain incidents—for instance, the scene with Paula Van Horn, Glen Fuller, and the gun in chapter five (Larry denied that Paula had ever been threatened with a gun). By the time it came out in 1987, Larry's primary response was chagrin. The twenty-five years tacked on to his prison sentence by Judge Louis C. Bechtle had taught him a harsh lesson about the price of notoriety. Larry had lost all interest in being a legend.

He has been in jail now for fifteen years. His thick black hair has turned gray. Marcia divorced him, but they remain friendly, and he still visits with his children and talks to them on the phone. His oldest, Chris, is in college. His girls are in high school. He works out a lot, practicing yoga and running long distances around the exercise yard at the federal penitentiary in Rochester, Minnesota.

Everyone who was convicted of selling cocaine with Larry has long been out of jail. Most served fewer than five years. In 1999, Larry filed a legal challenge to his prison sentence, arguing that his lawyer, Tom Bergstrom, had improperly advised him about a potential plea bargain. Bergstrom did one final favor to his old client by testifying, in effect, against himself. The judge has yet to rule on the question, and neither Larry nor his current lawyer, Peter Scuderi, hold out much hope to prevail. Sid Perry, who now works in the FBI's Baltimore office and is nearing retirement, and former assistant U.S. attorney Ron Noble, who now lives in Paris and heads Interpol, were among those who came back to Philadelphia to testify in the case. They were startled when they saw Larry in court. All that running in prison had turned his tall, slender frame gaunt. That, along with the gray hair, had drastically aged the former yuppie kingpin.

"He looked so frail," said Perry. "I could hardly believe my eyes. The minute Ron and I saw him, we looked at each other and said, 'Let him out.'"

Perry said that he had been shocked on Larry's sentencing day when Judge Bechtle more than doubled the carefully rendered twenty-two-year sentence imposed by Larry's trial judge, Louis H. Pollak.

Chuck Reed—Perry's partner and Larry's old nemesis—was not there to testify. He had been killed in 1995. Working undercover on another drug case in Philadelphia, he was negotiating a buy with a suspect when the conversation took a bad turn. The target of the probe shot him. Reed shot and killed the man before expiring himself.

"It was a tragedy," Perry said. Reed had been wearing a wire, but his old partner has never been able to bring himself to listen to the recording. "Chuck was a talent, a true talent. Apart from the Lavin case, he did some things as an agent that were just unbelievable."

Today, freedom for Larry Lavin is still most likely eight years away. Knowing how eager his customers and accomplices were during his heyday as a drug dealer, Larry still doesn't see himself as someone who preyed on society, or who overtly harmed anyone. He once insisted to me that no one he knew or sold to was addicted to cocaine. Judging just by the characters I got to know researching this book, he was wrong. Nearly all of the people around Larry were struggling with addiction to some degree. But unlike most crimes, all of Larry's "victims" were eager ones, and would likely have sought out the drug elsewhere if he wasn't in business. His crime was in part generational. Larry was less a predator than an enabler. While millions partied with cocaine, he profited. To my way of thinking, there is only a small moral difference, and more than twenty years in prison seems an excessive price to pay for it.

But Larry is a survivor. He remains resolutely cheerful, and does not seem bitter or angry about anyone. He has carved himself a life inside prison and talks about it as animatedly as he used to tell me about his exploits as a dealer. I get a Christmas card from him every year with a long letter updating his life and that of his children, and it's no different than those I get from old friends living in suburbs and cities all over America. He participates in a book club and helps manage a small electronic cable–manufacturing operation at the prison that employs disabled inmates. Over the years he has taught computer skills and worked as an aide at a prison hospice. He runs a bridge group one night a week. "You would think that someone in prison has all this free time," he says. "I am surprisingly busy."

He had a parole hearing earlier this year, and the hearing officer recommended a slight reduction in the time he has left to serve. That recommendation must still be approved in Washington. Larry has become expert in the arcane bureaucratic algebra that determines time served, and he isn't optimistic. Like most prisoners who have been locked up for a long time, he is inured to the casual unfairness of the system. He has seen violent criminals get out of prison. He has seen drug dealers who dealt in far larger amounts than he ever did come and go with lesser terms. He doesn't complain. It is just the way it is.

Mark Bowden
March 2001